ENCYCLOPEDIA
of
SOCIAL ISSUES

ENCYCLOPEDIA
of
SOCIAL ISSUES

Volume 5

Poll tax – Supply-side economics

Editor

JOHN K. ROTH

Marshall Cavendish
New York • London • Toronto

Project Editor: Robert McClenaghan
Research Supervisor: Jeffry Jensen
Acquisitions Editor: Mark Rehn
Photograph Editor: Valerie Krein
Production Editor: Cynthia Breslin Beres
Proofreading Supervisor: Yasmine A. Cordoba
Layout: James Hutson

Published By
Marshall Cavendish Corporation
99 White Plains Road
Tarrytown, New York 10591-9001
United States of America

∞ The paper in these volumes conforms to the American National Standard for Permanence of
Paper for Printed Library Materials, Z39.48-1984.

Library of Congress Cataloging-in-Publication Data

Encyclopedia of social issues / editor, John K. Roth
    p. cm.
  Includes bibliographical references and index.
   1. United States—Social conditions—Encyclopedias. 2. United States—Economic conditions—Encyclopedias. 3. United States—Politics and government—Encyclopedias. 4. Canada—Social conditions—Encyclopedias. 5. Canada—Economic conditions—Encyclopedias.—6. Canada—Politics and government—Encyclopedias.—I. Roth, John K.
HN57.E59 1997
306′.0973—dc20   96-38361
ISBN 0-7614-0568-2 (set)   CIP
ISBN 0-7614-0573-9 (volume 5)

First Printing

PRINTED IN THE UNITED STATES OF AMERICA

Contents

CONTENTS

ENCYCLOPEDIA
of
SOCIAL ISSUES

Poll tax: Required fee paid to the government by a citizen wishing to exercise the right to vote. Several Southern state legislatures enacted poll taxes in the late nineteenth century as one way of preventing African Americans from VOTING. One rationale for the taxes was that elections cost money and the voters should pay for them. In reality, however, poll taxes kept many poorer people away from the voting booths. Typically, wealthy Southerners would pay the fees for poor whites but not for African Americans. The

This Alabama resident saved poll tax receipts that allowed her mother to vote in local elections between 1920 and 1931. (AP/Wide World Photos)

Twenty-fourth Amendment to the U.S. Constitution outlawed poll taxes in 1964.

Pollution Probe's Clean Air Commute: Annual campaign against smog. Pollution Probe, an independent Canadian agency established in Toronto in 1969, challenges governments, businesses, and citizens to reduce vehicle and industrial emissions that create health and ENVIRONMENTAL problems. On Clean Air Commute Day, thousands in Toronto and Vancouver leave their cars at home or cut their pollution through vehicle-emissions testing. The campaign seeks lifestyle changes, mandatory emission and fuel-efficiency standards for new cars, mandatory vehicle testing and maintenance, and regulation for cleaner gas blends.

Polygamy: Marriage system that allows an individual to have more than one marriage partner simultaneously. Technically, "polygyny" occurs when a man has several wives, and "polyandry" occurs when a woman has several husbands. Since almost all the world's polygamous marriage systems are polygynous, the term "polygamy" generally refers to "polygyny." Polygamy is practiced in many cultures and is often part of the exercise of religious beliefs; it is, however, illegal in the United States and Canada, both of which outlaw bigamy, or the having of two spouses.

Population Council: Organization founded in 1952 to promote the investigation of population problems. Since its formation, the Population Council has sought to stimulate and sponsor research and education about world population and to help developing countries establish programs to control population growth.

In the early 1950's, economists, public health professionals, and popular authors warned that the world's population was increasing more rapidly than its supply of food and natural resources. Trips to Asia convinced John D. Rockefeller III, grandson of the founder of Standard Oil Company, that if the explosive growth of population in underdeveloped nations continued, it would damage the world's environment, deplete its material resources, and hinder efforts to help the poor. In 1952, after failing to persuade two philanthropic organizations—the Rockefeller Foundation and the Rockefeller Brothers—to make population issues a central focus of their work, Rockefeller created the Population Council to promote the investigation of population problems.

During the next ten years, as the American people became increasingly concerned about the world's growing population, the council sought to achieve two controversial goals: to provide technical assistance to aid developing nations in curbing their population growth and to persuade the United States to undertake a study of its population. The council's work, during its first decade of existence, helped to make the study of population issues (demography) a new discipline in colleges and population problems an important aspect of American foreign policy.

During the 1960's and 1970's, the council became more international in composition and mission. It financed scholarly research on population trends in less developed nations and assisted some of them in establishing national population policies. At the same time, council publications and the testimony of its staff at congressional hearings strongly influenced U.S. policy on population issues.

Staffed by men and women from more than sixty nations, the council by the mid-1990's sponsored programs in more than fifty countries in Latin America, Africa, and Asia. Headquartered in New York City, with regional offices in Bangkok, Cairo, Dakar, Mexico City, and Nairobi, it had an annual operating budget of about $50 million supplied by national governments, U.N. agencies, foundations, and individuals.

To improve the life and reproductive health of current and future generations and to achieve a "humane, equitable, and sustainable balance between people and resources," the council conducted programs in the biomedical, health, and social fields. Scientists working for the council created two reversible birth-control methods—Norplant implants and a type of IUD. In developing countries, the council played a leading role in improving the quality and availability of family-planning services. It labored to make abortions safer, prevent the spread of sexually transmitted diseases, and develop a variety of programs to care for women after they gave birth. The council also provided fellowships to assist scholars in developing nations studying in the social and health sciences and worked to educate policymakers around the world by holding conferences and publishing two scholarly journals. Through these methods, the Population Council has done much to raise global awareness about population issues, so that by the 1990's hundreds of national policies and dozens of international organizations sought to monitor and direct the course of population trends.

Population explosion: Exponential growth of humanity that has led to a doubling of world population since the 1950's, to almost 6 billion people by 1995. The impact of this growth on economic development and the natural environment is complex and not completely understood. Population size, economy, and the use of resources are clearly linked, and most debate centers on the nature of this interaction and what to do about it.

History. The terms "population bomb" and "population explosion" were first used in a pamphlet issued by the Hugh Moore Fund in 1954, but recognition of the phenomenon preceded this date. Thomas Malthus, an English cleric and economist, proposed in 1798 in his *Essay on the Principle of Population* that population growth tends to outstrip food supply and that the way to prevent suffering was to reduce fertility. The Malthusian view dominated demographic thinking through the first half of the 1900's, but contemporary concerns can be traced to improved predictions about population sizes. One of the most influential was made by demographer Frank Notestein, who in 1945 projected that world population would reach 3 billion by the year 2000; that level was actually reached before 1960.

Fertility decreased as mortality declined in Europe and North America, but in economically disadvantaged regions of Africa, Asia, and Latin America, large families continued to be the norm even after mortality had declined. This resulted in precipitous growth between 1950 and 1970, from 1.8 percent during the period 1950 to 1955 to 2.1 percent during the period 1965 to 1970. From 1970 to 1980, world growth rates declined to a rate under 2 percent, largely the result of decreases in fertility and slower decreases in mortality. Government-led fertility declines were responsible for most of this decrease in three large countries representing two-fifths of the world's population: India, Indonesia, and China. There were also unexpectedly sharp declines in the birth rates of industrialized countries. The world growth rate since 1980 has been about 1.7 percent and is not expected to decline further; it may even increase as a result of a relatively greater proportion of people in their reproductive years.

The growth rate of Canada has been greater than the rate for the United States during the period 1950 to 1990, because of relatively higher immigration into the country, but North American growth rates during 1990 to 1995 have averaged 0.71 percent, with fertility below replacement levels.

Debates. Efforts to reduce family size in the 1950's and 1960's were fueled by the belief that rapid growth impeded socioeconomic development: More people had to make do with less. In the United States, support for family planning began before World War II in the South, although most of the clients were African Americans, a situation that comic and commentator Dick Gregory and others considered racist.

Demographic research in other economically disadvantaged regions of the world indicated that most women would have fewer children if they could. The Rockefeller and Ford foundations funneled money into research and education through the POPULATION COUNCIL and the International Planned Parenthood Federation (IPPF). Starting in 1965, the U.S. government provided funds for population programs through the Agency for International Development (AID). The United Nations, led by Western and Asian countries, particularly India, Sweden, and the United States, also tried to encourage governments to institute family-planning programs; the U.N. Fund for Population Activities (UNFPA) was established in 1967.

These efforts to limit family size were criticized after a shift to conservative leadership in the 1970's. The Federal Office of Population Affairs was created in 1970 and legitimized the use of federal money for family-planning services for poor Americans, although no monies could be used to fund abortions. In March, 1972, the Commission on Population Growth and the American Future published a report advocating planning for population stability, improvement of family-planning services, including ABORTION, and prevention of illegal immigration. President Richard Nixon refused to approve the report because of its abortion position, and the controversy intensified when the U.S. Supreme Court in the 1973 case *ROE V. WADE* prohibited interference with a woman's right to an abortion during the first three months of pregnancy. There was also debate on whether to provide contraception to minors without parental consent.

President Jimmy Carter commissioned the Global 2000 Report (1980), which predicted a more overcrowded, polluted, and less politically stable world. President Ronald Reagan did not support the report, claiming that it did not allow for future scientific discoveries. By 1985, the United States had eliminated funding to the IPPF and UNFPA, a position reversed

A 1972 U.S. Census Bureau display on rising population. (UPI/Corbis Bettmann)

only after President Bill Clinton took office in 1993.

By contrast, Canadians favored growth in the 1950's and 1960's, although in 1973 the Conservation Council of Ontario and the Family Planning Federation of Canada determined that Canada was overpopulated. The Green Paper on immigration in 1974 and the Science Council of Canada in 1976 also stated goals of slowed growth. After the recession of the 1980's, however, growth was supported by allowing moderate levels of immigration.

Arguments Against Population Increases. Increasing crowding, pollution, soil erosion, DEFORESTATION, water shortages, species extinctions, climatic changes, and periodic famines are well-documented and are at least partly the result of rapid population growth in some parts of the world. A number of scholars expressed concern about these effects, including Paul EHRLICH in his book *The Population Bomb* (1968) and Garrett Hardin in his classic paper entitled "The Tragedy of the Commons" (*Science*, December 13, 1968). Both argued that having large families with no consideration for the destructive impact on environment was immoral, and both suggested reducing population growth to replacement levels, or "zero population growth." Ehrlich points out that although developed nations may be contributing less to population growth, they have a disproportionate impact on global environment, consuming 75 percent of all raw materials and producing a similar percentage of the waste. Barry Commoner, a plant physiologist, wrote in *The Closing Circle* (1971) that ecological damage was more the result of the types of technologies employed rather than population growth per se. Donella H. Meadows and her colleagues also predicted future problems based on the exhaustion of nonrenewable resources in *The Limits to Growth* (1972).

The alarm expressed moved demographers and policymakers in most countries to advocate a reduction in population growth, which is believed to depend on better family-planning programs and investments in human development, particularly education, health and hygiene, and improvements in the status of women.

Arguments for Population Growth. Some economists do not believe that rapid growth means that the same resources have to be shared by more people. Julian Simon argues that population growth is valuable in *The Ultimate Resource* (1981). Simon agrees that there are often short-term negative impacts of increases in population size, but he believes that science can reveal only the effects of different sizes of population and associated policies. Whether a population is growing too fast or not depends on one's value system. Simon argues that supplies of natural resources and energy are not finite in an economic sense; that per capita food production has been increasing and the lands needed for agriculture decreasing; that life expectancy (an indirect indicator of pollution levels) is increasing; that immigration is economically beneficial; and that per capita income grows when population grows.

Politicians also contend that there are no powerful nations that are numerically small, and many are concerned that the decreasing proportion of the world's peoples in the industrial regions (from 22 percent in 1950 to a projected 9 percent in 2025) will result in a further reduction in their influence.

Ongoing Controversy. The relationship between population growth and economic growth is complicated. Whether people invest and save, the kinds of markets, the availability of natural resources, the level of technology, and the number and quality of the labor force all play a role in the growth of an economy and may ameliorate some of the negative impacts of population growth.

The impact on the ecosystem is more problematic, and level of consumption is an important predictor of ecological deterioration. Social and environmental considerations, however, can be integrated with discussions about economy and technology, an approach endorsed by the United Nations and called "sustainable development," or development that addresses present requirements without reducing opportunities for future generations. The difficulty is that not all agree on what is being sustained, for example, level of economic activity or growth of that activity. Saving and sharing on a global scale, coupled with increased use of renewable resources and reduced levels of waste, will be necessary to implement this kind of development.
                                    —*Joan C. Stevenson*

SUGGESTED READINGS: Excellent reviews of the negative effects of population growth and what can be done to combat such growth are given in Paul Harrison's *The Third Revolution* (New York: I.B. Tauris, 1992) and in Lindsey Grant's edited collection *Elephants in the Volkswagen* (New York: W. H. Freeman, 1992). A more positive view is again expressed by Julian Simon in *Population Matters* (New Brunswick, N.J.: Transaction Publishers, 1990). Population policy and change in Canada are described in Roderic Beaujot's *Population Change in Canada* (Toronto: McClelland and Stewart, 1991). For up-to-date reviews of population trends, see the inexpensive and accessible publications of the Population Reference Bureau: *Population Today: News, Numbers, and Analysis* and *Population Bulletin*. A more scholarly but still accessible journal, *Population and Development Review*, is published by the Population Council and covers contemporary population issues.

Pork: Term applied to government payments, projects, rewards, or other perks given to individuals or groups to ensure their loyalty to a politician or party. Derived from the larger expression "pork barrel," a satirical allusion to a barrel of tasty pieces of meat (representing wasteful and unnecessary expenditures), "pork" can also refer to any portion of a legislative bill, or an entire bill, perceived to be wasteful and politically self-serving. Completely irrelevant components of a bill intended to entice other legislators to support it or to please a select group of constituents is also said to be "pork."

Pornography: Depiction of erotic behavior intended to cause sexual excitement. Pornography has received considerable public attention because it is often causally associated with various social ills, particularly sexual violence against women.

Pornography has long existed in the United States in limited form and through legal and illegal channels. It began to appear more openly in the late 1950's and has since steadily grown in volume. The legal side of the pornography market is estimated to generate approximately $10 billion in annual sales, which would put it in the company of many Fortune 500 companies. Approximately 20 million adult magazines are purchased every month, and sexually explicit films account for between 10 and 15 percent of the videocassette market. Despite this apparent popularity, national polls have indicated that 72 percent of the American people want a crackdown by the government on pornography, a number that swells to 92 percent when the subject is child pornography.

Changing Legal Climate. Displays of pornography in the public arena were practically nonexistent in American society before the late 1950's. The legal climate that set the tone for much of American law in the first half of the twentieth century was based on an English legal precedent established in *Regina v. Hicklin* (1868). In this case, an English court ruled that a work

was obscene if it tended to corrupt and deprave minds that were open to such immoral influence and into whose hands the material might fall. The *Hicklin* decision also recognized the need to protect individuals who may be particularly susceptible to the corrupting influence of the material.

Hicklin guided American law until it was challenged before the U.S. Supreme Court in *ROTH V. UNITED STATES* (1957). *Roth* effectively overturned the *Hicklin* precedent by taking an absolutist view of the First Amendment: The government should not prohibit speech or publication even if a judge or jury thinks such speech or publication will have an undesirable impact on thought. The concept underlying *Roth*, and the majority of legal opinions since, is that unfettered speech is essential to social growth, even if it should offend the sensibilities of some people. The *Roth* decision was affirmed and strengthened in *MILLER V. CALIFORNIA* (1973) and again in *Pope v. Illinois* (1987). A number of separate but related First Amendment legal decisions have been handed down in *Young v. American Mini Theatres* (1976) and *Renton v. Playtime Theatres* (1986); these cases circumscribed a city's ability to regulate sexually explicit material through zoning ordinances.

Impact of Technological Changes. Only a handful of organizations dominated the mass-media industry in the first half of the twentieth century, and the advent of television in the 1940's and 1950's did not greatly change this domination. The early years of television were confined to the major networks, and their broadcast technology was relatively crude, with many households getting limited and often poor reception. In the second half of the twentieth century, mass-media technology became more sophisticated and less costly, allowing smaller companies entry into the market with alternative programs. Such programming, by the end of the twentieth century, included the widespread availability in major markets of hard-core, triple-X-rated television shows; smaller metropolitan markets gained access to late-night, soft-core pornographic movies via satellite or on cable stations. The widespread diffusion of pornography was further accelerated by the introduction of videocassette recorders (VCRs), which were owned by more than 80 percent of all households by the early 1990's. The increasing popularity of VCRs paralleled the decline of triple-X-rated movie houses, since hard-core movies could be rented at independent video outlets in neighborhoods across the country.

Other technological developments toward the end of the twentieth century vastly extended mass-media forms of communication and entertainment. Dial-a-porn telephone businesses developed, and INTERNET computer sex talk and provocative E-MAIL messages became common. VIRTUAL REALITY was developed, suggesting to some that virtual sex may one day replace physical sex for some people.

The Case Against Pornography. Many Americans feel that pornography has become not only ubiquitous in American society but also increasingly explicit in its depiction of the sexual act, which has led to intensified opposition to the various forms of por-nography. The most intense secular criticism comes from FEMINISTS who argue that pornography denigrates women.

Though some of the more radical feminists argue against the depiction of any form of sexual activity, many feminist critics make a distinction between erotica and pornography. At issue is not the sexual act but how the sexual act is depicted. In erotica, there exists a loving sexual relationship; people are shown sharing an emotional as well as a physical bond. Pornography, on the other hand, not only is more prevalent but also often portrays an abusive relationship. Thus, critics of pornography feel that women are treated as faceless sexual objects with no rights who are physically abused and are often portrayed as being sexually stimulated by this abuse.

Pornography that depicts women being raped and enjoying the experience occurs in approximately one-fourth of all pornographic materials and has often been directly linked with influencing a RAPE mentality among men. Less blatant forms of violence found in pornography are seen as attributable to a sexually calloused attitude. Nonviolent pornographic fare also sends a message about how women should be treated, portraying women strictly as sexual objects. Additionally, women are portrayed as being unaware that they want sex; it becomes the man's responsibility to force

A 1989 antipornography rally outside a Florida striptease lounge. (AP/Wide World Photos)

Pornography

himself on the woman to release her dormant carnality. This theme is fairly prevalent in pornography and has been directly linked by some researchers to date rape and acquaintance rape.

Pornography has also been alleged to influence three other social values. First, nonviolent pornography promotes marriage as undesirable among men and women viewers; it also substantially decreases the desire to have children among women who have been extensively exposed to pornography, and, to a lesser degree, a decreased desire among men for offspring. Second, viewers of nonviolent pornography are physically less satisfied with their mates. Finally, viewers of nonviolent pornography tend to overestimate what is sexually acceptable behavior in society. This affects their moral judgments of right and wrong, a situation that is clearly established in repeated mock trials in which both men and women who have viewed pornography are more willing to absolve a rapist and less likely to see a rape victim as suffering any serious or lasting harm compared with individuals who had not been exposed to pornography.

Prosocial Aspects of Pornography. Exposure to pornography does not necessarily lead to mimicking the behavior depicted; indeed, the principle of catharsis suggests that society actually benefits because pornography keeps those who watch it from acting out their sexual urges. Aristotle believed that audiences' emo-

Critics argue that pornography has become ubiquitous. (Wide World Photos)

Antipornography activists in New York City, 1987. (Impact Visuals, Ansell Horn)

tions were aroused by the actors and that this arousal purged audience members of the emotion. Sigmund Freud modified Aristotle's original idea somewhat by suggesting that the most effective method of purging an emotion is to release it directly, though Freud did believe, like Aristotle, that indirect expression also reduces the strength of the feeling. In either case, the implication of catharsis is that negative impulses can be channeled into harmless areas through the vicarious act of watching others.

Though adherents of pornography as cathartic cannot prove their thesis, neither can it be disproven. Advocates of this prosocial position suggest that while some individuals might act sexually aggressively to-ward another after viewing pornography, the majority of viewers do not mimic what they view. This point is supported by research indicating that sexually experienced individuals do not change their sexual range of behavior after viewing pornography. As for those who do act antisocially, it is held that they were already antisocial in their behavior. Supporting this contention is data that 70 percent of rapists and at least 60 percent of nonfamilial child molesters reported that deviant fantasies were readily evoked simply by the sight of women or children.   *—John Markert*

SUGGESTED READINGS: The feminist evaluation is detailed in a collection edited by Daina E. H. Russel's *Making Violence Sexy: Feminist Views on Pornogra-*

phy (New York: Teachers College Press, 1993). Readings assembled by Donald Alexander Downs provide the basic points of the counterargument in *The New Politics of Pornography* (Chicago: University of Chicago Press, 1989). A detailed examination of the wealth of research, both pro and con, on pornography is assembled by Dolf Zillman and Jennings Bryant in their book *Pornography: Research Advances and Policy Considerations* (Hillsdale, N.J.: Lawrence Erlbraum Associates, 1989).

Postpartum depression: Affective disorder afflicting some women after childbirth. Symptoms include depression, disinterest in activities, loss of weight or appetite, sleeplessness, agitation, fatigue, feelings of worthlessness, inability to concentrate, and thoughts of suicide. Postpartum depression is relatively common, being seen in as many as one out of four women in the year following delivery; untreated, it may become severe and permanent. Treatment includes early recognition, support, counseling, and the use of drugs. In contrast, postpartum "blues" are mild, transient episodes characterized by episodes of crying. This less serious condition occurs in most women within a few days after delivery and usually resolves spontaneously with reassurance and support.

Post-traumatic stress disorder (PTSD): Anxiety disorder resulting from exposure to an extreme stress outside the range of normal human experience (for example, acts of war, terrorism, or natural disasters).

PTSD is characterized by a specific set of causes and symptoms. The primary cause is exposure to a traumatic event. A person may experience the event directly (for example, an earthquake or rape), witness it occurring to someone else (armed robber or murder), experience a threat of death or serious injury, or learn that a loved one was involved in or threatened by a similar event. In all cases, terror, intense fear, helplessness, and agitated or disorganized behavior are primary responses. Following these initial reactions, the individual experiences a variety of symptoms for at least one month, either immediately or at a later time. First, the trauma is reexperienced in a number of ways: Intrusive recollections, recurrent dreams, feelings of reliving the event, and distress or physiological reactivity upon exposure to similar situations or stimuli are common. Relatedly, there is avoidance of situations or stimuli associated with the trauma. Deadened reactions and detachment are also common. Finally, increased arousal is notable and may be displayed as sleep difficulties, irritability, concentration difficulties, a heightened startle response, or a hyperalert state of scanning one's surroundings, known as hypervigilance.

The disorder does not automatically result when someone is exposed to severe stress. Many people have time-limited reactions and do not go on to develop PTSD. Some experts argue that PTSD would be experienced by anyone following exposure to sufficiently extreme stress. Others argue that PTSD only occurs in vulnerable individuals with personality or physical compositions that predispose them toward anxiety disorders. Overall, estimates in the United States suggest that between 1 and 14 percent of individuals may report experiencing PTSD in their lifetime. For groups such as soldiers, people living in violent environments, or those living where natural disasters are common, prevalence rates reach as high as 58 percent over a lifetime.

PTSD came into increased public awareness following World War II, the Holocaust, and the Vietnam War. Traumas such as childhood physical and sexual abuse and domestic violence also have been linked to PTSD. Treatment advances point to the importance of debriefing individuals following trauma and helping them talk about their experiences in an attempt to become deconditioned to the traumatic event. Treatment, however, remains complex. PTSD is often complicated by personality difficulties, substance abuse, and family problems; no single treatment works for everyone.

Two controversies have emerged with regard to PTSD. The validity and legal admissibility of repressed memories of a trauma surfacing years after the traumatic event are being debated. Also, the occurrence of violent behavior by individuals with PTSD against the perpetrators of their trauma has been spotlighted. In this case, the behavior of the PTSD sufferer has been framed as self-protection and, therefore, not legally open for prosecution. The scientific and legal issues in both of these cases are likely to remain the subjects of debate for years to come.

Poverty: Poverty is defined as the lack of sufficient funds to purchase adequate food, housing, clothing, medical care, and other goods and services to maintain an acceptable standard of living. Opinions differ regarding poverty's more precise definition, causes, and

A Vietnam veteran receives counseling for post-traumatic stress disorder. (UPI/Corbis-Bettmann)

Poverty

remedies; nevertheless, there is broad political and societal consensus that poverty is a major problem around the world, even in developed countries such as the United States and Canada.

Poverty Rates. Each year, the U.S. federal government establishes family income amounts (known as "thresholds"), based on family size and composition, that define poverty. In the United States, the number of persons below the official poverty level was 39.3 million in 1993. The overall poverty rate, or the percentage of persons living in poverty, was 15.1 percent; the poverty rate for families was 13.6 percent.

Children are more likely to live in poverty than are persons in any other age group. Among U.S. citizens under the age of eighteen, 22.7 percent lived in poverty in 1993. The poverty rate generally decreases with age, reaching a low for all groups (9.9 percent) for individuals aged fifty-five to fifty-nine years. For persons age sixty years and above, poverty rates are slightly higher: Persons age sixty to sixty-four had a poverty rate of 11.3 percent in 1993; the rate was 12.2 percent for persons sixty-five years and older.

Trends. In 1993, more people lived in poverty in the United States than at any time during the previous thirty years. The poverty rate, however, was only slightly higher than the 1992 rate of 14.8 percent and was slightly lower than the 1983 rate of 15.2 percent. In general, poverty rates in the early 1990's were about the same as or slightly higher than the rates of the 1980's, higher than those of the 1970's, and lower than those of the 1960's. Because of population increases, however, more people lived in poverty despite generally declining poverty rates.

Relationships to Race, Ethnicity, Gender, and Family Structure. Members of certain population subgroups are more likely than others to live in poverty. In 1993, 15.1 percent of the total U.S. population lived in poverty. The poverty rates were 12.2 percent for whites (9.9 percent for whites who were not of Hispanic origin), 33.1 percent for African Americans, and 18.8 percent for members of other races. The poverty rate for individuals of Hispanic origin of any race was 30.6 percent.

The pattern was similar for the poverty rates of families. White families had the lowest poverty rate; families that were neither white nor black were next, followed by Hispanic families of any race and by black families.

The relationship between gender and poverty is more a relationship among gender, family structure, and poverty. For example, 6.5 percent of the married-couple families in the United States lived in poverty in 1993; this compares with 35.6 percent of families in which a female was the household head without a husband present. Single-parent families headed by black and Hispanic women had poverty rates of approximately 50 percent.

Geographic Factors. U.S. poverty rates vary by geographic location. For example, in 1991, the highest poverty rates by geographic region were in the South (16.0 percent), followed by the West (14.3 percent), the Midwest (13.2 percent), and the Northeast (12.2 percent). Although the South had the highest overall poverty rate, the highest rate for whites was found in the West (13.5 percent), the highest rate for blacks was found in the Midwest (37.7 percent), and the highest rates for Hispanics was found in the Northeast (36.3 percent).

In general, poverty rates for rural areas exceed those for urban areas. In 1991, rural poverty was 16.1 percent, while urban poverty was 13.7 percent. Central-city poverty, however, was higher than either, at 20.2 percent. During the late 1980's, poverty rates declined in rural areas while they increased in metropolitan areas. The decline in rural poverty was related to a decline in poverty among farm residents during the period. Rural poverty rates were higher for African Americans and Hispanics (38.9 percent and 33.9 percent, respectively) than were urban poverty rates for these groups (31.6 percent and 28.3 percent, respectively) and central-city poverty rates for the same groups (35.3 percent and 32.9 percent, respectively). Central-city poverty rates were higher for whites (15.4 percent) than were rural (13.6 percent) or urban (10.6 percent) rates.

Poverty in Canada. During the 1980's, both the United States and Canada saw increases in unemployment rates and wage inequality. While the poverty rate in the United States increased during the decade, Canada's poverty rate fell.

Canada usually has a lower rate of poverty than does the United States. The reason is not that the poorest people earn more in Canada: Poverty rates in the two countries are approximately the same before public assistance benefits are included in income. Canada's social support system, however, is more generous (and perhaps more effective) than that of the United States, as well as offering universal coverage for all citizens under many programs.

Causes. The causes of poverty are numerous and complex; to cite one reason or cause as more important

Although rural poverty rates exceed those for urban areas in general, central cities have the highest poverty rates, as seen in the decaying landscape of North Camden, New Jersey. (AP/Wide World Photos)

than another is often more a matter of opinion or personal belief than of fact. This point should not be taken lightly, as beliefs about the causes of poverty powerfully affect proposed remedies. In general, however, the causes of poverty can be grouped into three related categories: labor supply, labor demand, and demographics.

Labor Supply. As stated above, the poverty status of a family is a function of the family's income or earnings and the number of persons in the family. Earnings are related to the amount of work that is done by family members and the amount received for each hour worked. For example, a person working for minimum wage ($4.65 per hour in 1995) who worked 40 hours per week for 52 weeks, or 2080 hours, would earn $9,672 that year. That level of income was below the poverty level defined for a family of three by the federal government.

The Congressional Research Service found that in 1990, 63.2 percent of all poor families with children included someone who worked during the year. Nearly all (98.8 percent) of the nonpoor families with children had someone who worked that year. The government defines a "full-time worker equivalent" as between 1,750 and 2,080 hours of work performed over the course of a year, whether by one person or several. In 1990, 27.1 percent of all poor families with children were found to have had one or more full-time worker equivalents. Nearly all (93.4 percent) of the nonpoor families with children had one or more full-time worker equivalents. A strong correlation exists between the number of hours that the members of a family work and the likelihood that they live out of poverty. This is not to say, however, that those in poverty do not work.

The total number of hours worked by a family is

related, as would be expected, to the number of adults in the household. More than half (53.8 percent) of married-couple families with children had a combined work effort of one or more full-time equivalent workers, whereas the combined hours worked exceeded one full-time equivalent worker for only 12.7 percent of female-headed families with children.

Labor Demand. Income from working is determined jointly by the number of hours worked and the amount paid for each hour. The wage commanded by an individual in the labor market is related to the demand for the skills possessed by that individual. People in poverty tend to have skills for which there is relatively little demand or for which there is a large supply.

Wage rates and earnings increase, on average, with the amount of education an individual has obtained. The U.S. Bureau of the Census reports that in 1990, the mean earnings of year-round, full-time workers with only an elementary school education was $18,726 for men and $12,988 for women. Male high school graduates earned $26,568 on average, and female high school graduates earned $18,346. The pattern of increased earnings continues for college graduates. Male college graduates working full-time had mean earnings in 1990 of $43,808, whereas women with the same amount of education had mean earnings of $28,316.

Although mean earnings for both men and women increase with educational attainment, the returns to education for women are lower than for men. The difference in earnings between men and women with elementary school educations was 44.2 percent of those women's earnings in 1990. Stated differently, the mean earnings for these women was only 69.4 percent of that for men. Among people with a high school education, women earned 69.1 percent of men's average earnings. Finally, for college graduates, women's average earnings were only 64.6 percent of men's. The gap between women's and men's earnings thus increases for those who are more educated.

As might be expected, poverty rates are higher for families with household heads with lower levels of education. The U.S. Bureau of the Census reports that the poverty rate for all families with a household head twenty-five years of age or older was 9.7 percent in 1990. If the head had less than a high school education, the rate was more than double the overall rate, at 21.8 percent. Families headed by persons with a high school diploma were slightly less likely to be in poverty relative to the full group. This group had a poverty rate of 9.3 percent. Of families with a head with one or more years of college, the poverty rate was even lower, at 3.8 percent.

Demographics. A leading demographic factor related to living in poverty is the number of adults living in the household. Households with two or more adult members are more likely to generate income exceeding the poverty level than are households with only one adult; they have more hours available to them to work, and family responsibilities can be shared. The federal government reports that single persons composing their own households had a poverty rate of 22.1 percent in 1993. This rate was higher than that for all persons (15.1 percent) and that for all families (12.3 percent). Women who lived in a single-person household had a higher poverty rate than men in the same situation, with rates of 25.7 percent and 18.1 percent, respectively.

A second demographic factor related to being the only adult in the household is being a single parent. The government defines a custodial parent as someone living with a minor child of their own from an absent parent. There were 11.5 million custodial parents in 1991. Approximately 3.4 million custodial parents were married in 1991. In other words, there were 8.1 million single parents in the United States that year; 7.2 million single parents were women, and 0.9 million were men. The poverty rate for currently married custodial parents was 12.5 percent. Of the 8.1 million single-parent families, 3.3 million (40.7 percent) lived in poverty. More specifically, 3.2 million (44.4 percent) of the mother-headed families were in poverty, and 0.1 million (11.1 percent) of the father-headed families were poor. Looking at individuals rather than persons, about half (50.1 percent) of the persons living in female-headed families with children lived in poverty.

A closer examination of the single-parent families headed by mothers reveals that the likelihood of living in poverty varies considerably by the current marital status of the mother. In 1991, divorced single mothers were the least likely to be in poverty, at 28.7 percent. More than half of the never-married (56.5 percent) and separated (55.2 percent) mothers were poor.

A cause of poverty related specifically to single-parent families is a lack of child support from the absent parent. Only 4.0 million custodial parents received any money in child support in 1991. Divorced custodial parents (46.5 percent) were the most likely to receive child support payments, followed by those who were currently married (41.7 percent), separated (25.9 percent), and never married (16.6 percent). Of those custodial parents living in poverty, only 0.9 million out of 3.7 million (23.1 percent) received child support.

Receiving child support can make the difference between living in and living out of poverty. In 1991, for custodial parents with a child support award or agreement (with a legal entitlement to child support payments), the mean total money income was $19,217 (of which $2,961 was child support income), whereas the mean total money income was $15,919 for those who did not receive any child support payments. For those custodial parents without an award or agreement, mean total money income was $13,283. Note that the poverty threshold for a family of four in 1991 was $13,924.

Social Costs. The social costs of poverty take many forms. Some of them are direct, in the form of money spent on social services for the poor, such as provision of food, medical care, and rent subsidies. For every dollar spent on the poor, as little as fifty cents may end up as a net increase in the income of poor people. The inefficiencies in helping the poor take the form of reduced labor supply, reduced savings, and other "distorted" choices, as well as administrative costs of running social service programs.

Homeless people line up to receive food at a shelter in New York City. (AP/Wide World Photos)

Poverty

Poor people report more health problems than the nonpoor. Various studies have showed, however, that the poor have limited access to health care as a result of a lack of health insurance, the indirect costs of health care utilization, the limited hours of service of health care providers, and the limited number of private providers in low-income areas.

Research on the intergenerational transmission of poverty offers mixed findings. On one hand, individuals who grow up in poor families are substantially more likely to experience poverty as adults than are those who do not grow up in poor families. On the other hand, more than half of the people who grow up in the bottom fifth of the income distribution will not be there as adults. Some factors associated with poverty, such as growing up in a single-parent family, are associated with events such as dropping out of high school and premarital pregnancy, which in turn are associated with poverty and welfare use later as adults.

Social costs of poverty take other forms as well. Children who are poor often are undernourished and therefore have difficulty maintaining concentration in school. They may not, therefore, develop to their full potential and achieve higher levels of education, which are associated with income. They therefore lose individual earning power, and society loses their productive potential. In addition, adolescents may be forced to work to help support their poor families, again limiting educational opportunities. Some poor people resort to crime, resulting in societal losses because of the need for increased police protection and antitheft measures.

Remedies and Political Controversies. Remedies for poverty often are tied to beliefs concerning the causes of poverty. Some remedies involve more government involvement; other remedies have less. Some rely on individual initiative; others focus on providing goods and services to the needy.

Some suggested remedies are long-term. One such proposal is a "healthy kid" program that would ensure that children receive adequate medical care, through a system of community health centers. This program would not reduce poverty in the short run but would improve children's health and their chances of moving out of poverty as adults. Other long-term programs include training programs for adults to improve their job skills and other types of educational reform. More immediate remedies include restructuring the federal tax code to allow for a refundable tax credit for children, as a replacement for the current child exemption (which offers little or no benefit to people with low amounts of taxable income), a system to ensure a minimum child support benefit to custodial parents, and continued use and expansion of the Earned Income Tax Credit.

Others see reducing the disincentives to work found in the current welfare system as the key to reducing poverty. Political debate centers on reforms to Aid to Families with Dependent Children, the primary public assistance program available to poor families in the United States. Congress periodically has moved toward making significant reductions in program eligibility and benefits, and the 1990's saw several such proposals. Consideration was given to turning a majority of the responsibility for this program over to the states, with funding being provided through block grants. Additionally, eligibility restrictions are being considered, in the form of limiting the amount of time during which a parent can receive benefits. After that time, the parent would be required to find employment. As part of most of such proposals to cut or limit benefits, public assistance recipients would be aided in their quest for self-sufficiency by enhanced training and support services and expanded child-care benefits.

Prospects for Elimination. In 1964, President Lyndon B. Johnson declared unconditional War on Poverty and committed resources to a campaign against economic deprivation. In the decade following Johnson's declaration, new social-welfare programs were introduced, and old ones were expanded. Optimists believed that government actions could solve the poverty problem. By the late 1970's, after the United States had experienced oil shocks, slow economic growth, and high inflation rates, a pessimistic view emerged. By the 1990's, many tended to regard Johnson's War on Poverty as a failure, because poverty continued to pose a national problem.

Some analysts believe that the government was too optimistic at the outset of the War on Poverty and too pessimistic at the outset of attempts to scale back the social safety net during the Ronald Reagan Administration. Others perceive a major shift in thinking about antipoverty policy. Their view can be characterized as reflecting realism, rather than optimism or pessimism. They postulate proposals that, if undertaken, would reduce poverty but not eliminate it. They are more confident in some proposals than in others and understand that some proposals will require more research, experimentation, and trials before they can be implemented.

—*Steven Garasky*

SUGGESTED READINGS: Doug A. Timmer, D. Stanley Eitzen, and Kathryn D. Talley report on the homelessness experiences of nine individuals and families in a series of ethnographic studies in *Paths to Homelessness: Extreme Poverty and the Urban Housing Crisis* (Boulder, Colo.: Westview Press, 1994). Steven Pressman's *Poverty in America: An Annotated Bibliography* (Metuchen, N.J.: Scarecrow Press, 1994) annotates research and analyses by economists, sociologists, and other social scientists on the causes, consequences, and cures of poverty in the United States. William A. Kelso, in *Poverty and the Underclass: Changing Perceptions of the Poor in America* (New York: New York University Press, 1994), provides broad explanations of poverty that focus on both individuals and the economic environment in which they live.

Constance F. Citro and Robert T. Michael edited *Measuring Poverty: A New Approach* (Washington, D.C.: National Academy Press, 1995), which thoroughly examines issues surrounding the measurement of poverty, including defining thresholds and resources, and the use of poverty measures in government assistance programs. Diana M. DiNitto provides a look at the politics of poverty through the development of social welfare policy in *Social Welfare: Politics and Public Policy*, 4th ed. (Boston: Allyn and Bacon, 1995). Bradley R. Schiller, in *The Economics of Poverty and Discrimination*, 6th ed. (Englewood Cliffs, N.J.: Prentice-Hall, 1995), offers a conceptual discussion of poverty combined with an empirical description of contemporary poverty and its major causes.

Irwin Garfinkel examines child support enforcement in the United States and proposes a new system to ensure child support payments based on program reforms implemented in the state of Wisconsin in *Assuring Child Support: An Extension of Social Security* (New York: Russell Sage Foundation, 1992). The *1994 Green Book: Overview of Entitlement Programs* (Washington, D.C.: U.S. Government Printing Office, 1994), put out by the U.S. House of Representatives Committee on Ways and Means, is an annual publication that provides background material and data for each program within the jurisdiction of the committee, including Aid to Families with Dependent Children.

Michael Sherraden, in *Assets and the Poor* (Armonk, N.Y.: M. E. Sharpe, 1991), examines the role that savings, investment, and asset accumulation can play in permanently moving families out of poverty. Robert Haveman and Barbara Wolfe's *Succeeding Generations* (New York: Russell Sage Foundation, 1994) traces a representative group of America's children from their early years through young adulthood, identifying significant influences on and causes of children's later success.

Poverty, rural: POVERTY can be defined as an inability to provide sufficiently for basic needs, such as food and housing. According to the 1990 Census, more than 14 percent of the population of the United States fell below the POVERTY LINE as established by the U.S. Department of Agriculture. Although citizens of industrialized nations usually associate poverty with conditions visible in inner-city areas, poverty also exists in the rural regions of all countries. Victims of rural poverty may, in fact, live under far more horrendous conditions than poor people in cities; the rural poor do not have access to basic city sanitation services and social safety nets that the urban poor can utilize.

Rural poverty may be far more difficult to eliminate than urban poverty. Job opportunities in rural areas are often limited in number or seasonal in duration. Farmworkers may be able to find work for only a few months out of the year. Thus, migrant farmworkers make up a significant portion of the rural poor in the Southern and Western United States. While state and federal governments have attempted to stimulate economic development in rural areas, such efforts frequently have mixed results. Tourism, for example, is often touted as a good choice for sustainable development, both in the United States and in developing nations that have a problem with rural poverty. Studies of areas that have strongly promoted tourism, however, have revealed that the majority of jobs generated are seasonal, low-paying, and part-time, while at the same time increased tourism drives up the local cost of living. If an area becomes sufficiently popular as a tourist destination, land values and rental rates may climb so high that low-income local residents are forced to leave the area. Rather than benefiting from increased tourism, many of the rural poor are often left worse off.

Similarly, while efforts to attract industry to rural areas may bring in new business, that business may not actually help the local rural poor. Industries locating in rural areas may instead look upon the poor as a source of cheap labor ripe for exploitation. This is especially true of industries that process agricultural products, such as meatpacking plants and poultry-processing facilities. Wages in the meatpacking indus-

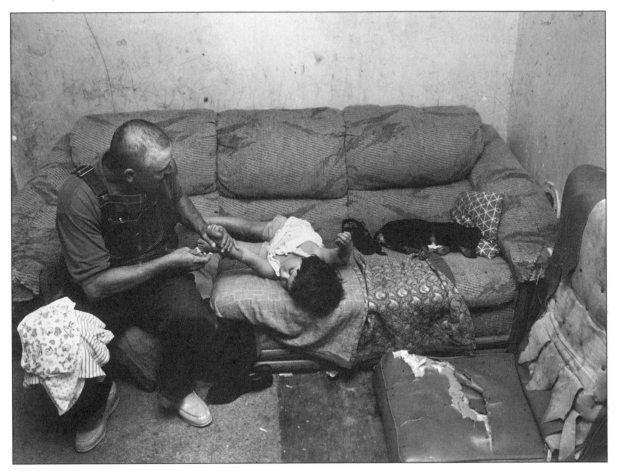

Farm laborers and other rural residents often find it difficult to earn enough to lift their families out of poverty. (Impact Visuals, Thor Swift)

try fell by 50 percent during the 1980's. In addition, where choices for employment may be limited to working for one employer or not working at all, workers often tolerate unsafe working conditions rather than risk losing their jobs.

Finally, the obvious solution for the problem of rural poverty, that the poor relocate to a prosperous area where jobs are more plentiful, may be unthinkable to individual poor persons. Many of the rural poor are persons who left school early and have no specialized training. Surviving from week to week on little money, these poor lack both the funds and the skills necessary to make a fresh start.

Poverty, women and: Income insufficiency is the most commonly used criterion for determining POVERTY in the United States. According to a 1988 study by Laurie Bassie, women and children represent 64 percent of the U.S. population and 77 percent of the nation's poor. Households headed by females have grown tremendously since about 1960.

A person is considered poor if he or she does not have enough money to acquire the basic necessities of life, primarily food and shelter. The U.S. Department of Agriculture determines the amount of money necessary to survive for a year by multiplying by three an estimate of the food budget required to meet minimal nutrition requirements. The resulting sum is termed the "poverty line"; the amount for a family of four in 1991 was $18,293. In that year, approximately thirty million persons (about 12 percent of the population) in the United States lived at or below the poverty line.

In a capitalist economic system, the inequality of income is one form that poverty takes. The amount of money one has is a primary determinant of one's life circumstances. It has been shown that those with lower incomes experience higher rates of a number

This woman from rural Kentucky managed to earn her high-school equivalency degree but has been unable to seek full-time employment because she cares for her grandchildren. (Impact Visuals, Barbara Beirne)

of social problems, including physical illness, mental health difficulties, housing problems, and lower levels of education.

Two causes account for women being at or below the poverty line. First, women who head their families often bear most or all of the economic burden of raising the children. Secondly, because of sex discrimination, occupational segregation, and sexual harassment, women who seek to support themselves and their families through paid work are disadvantaged in the labor market. Seldom prepared to be the primary breadwinner, women are more inclined to have "jobs" rather than careers. They make job choices that emphasize flexibility and adaptability, rather than income potential.

These handicaps are reinforced by a highly discriminatory labor market. High levels of occupational segregation of women continue. Women are trained most often for traditionally female occupations, such as clerical work or food service, which rarely pay enough to support themselves, let alone a child.

Many people believe that a profound change in society's economic system and the value orientation would be necessary for a more equitable distribution of income. There is a gap between the wages males earn compared with females. Considering all the jobs in the U.S., full-time, year-round working women average only 69 percent of the wages men are paid. Until the 1980's, women's earnings hovered between 58 percent and 60 percent of men's. Education does not correct this gap in wages. Women with college educations earn less than men who have only high-school diplomas, according to a 1988 study by Margaret Andersen.

Others feel that women must be able to compete with men in equal jobs if they expect equal pay, completely disregarding the possibility of discrimination in the workplace. American women must decide between a family and a career or learn how to combine the two.

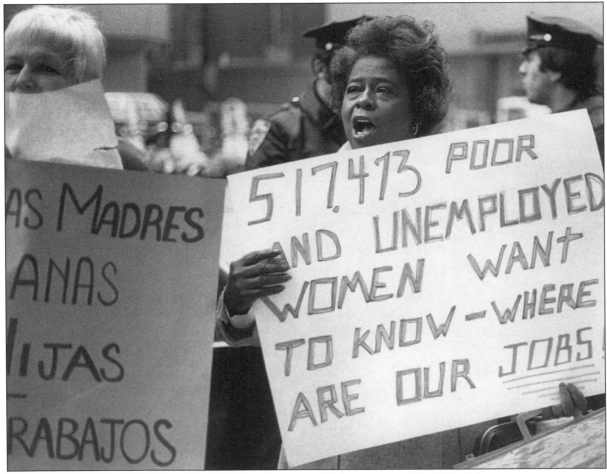

Women protest 1980's cuts in federal job programs. (Hazel Hankin)

Unless women are willing to educate themselves and seek careers, they can expect to remain among the economically disadvantaged classes in American society.

Poverty line: Economics term. The poverty line represents the amount of money needed to purchase what has been defined as the minimum acceptable level of goods and services. Those people who fall below the poverty line are "poor." Because resources and expectations change over time and differ among societies, the poverty line differs among societies and is continually adjusted. In the United States, the poverty line was first established officially by the Social Security Administration in 1960. Food, housing, and health-care costs remain primary considerations in defining poverty. There is continuing debate as to whether government transfers such as Medicare and Medicaid should be considered as income.

Powell, Colin (b. Apr. 5, 1937, New York, N.Y.): U.S. Army general. In 1989, Powell became the first African American to serve as chairman of the Joint Chiefs of Staff, the highest U.S. military advisory group. Powell served twice in Vietnam during the Vietnam War; later, he commanded ground forces in South Korea, West Germany, and the United States. In 1986, he was appointed commanding general of the Fifth Corps in Frankfurt, Germany. President Ronald Reagan named Powell assistant to the president for national security affairs in 1987, and he received the Spingarn Medal in 1991. After his retirement from the military, he became the subject of much media attention when it was rumored that he might seek the 1996 Republican presidential nomination. Despite polls showing that his candidacy would have broad appeal, Powell announced that he would not run, but he remained an influential figure whose support was eagerly sought by Democrats and Republicans alike.

Pregnancy Discrimination Act (1978): Federal legislation amending Title VII of the CIVIL RIGHTS ACT OF 1964. The Pregnancy Discrimination Act extended application of the earlier legislation's terms "because of sex" and "on the basis of sex" to include discrimination based on "pregnancy, childbirth or related medical conditions." The 1978 act specifically covers receipt of employment benefits, effectively re-versing Supreme Court decisions in *Gilbert v. General Electric Co.* (1976) and *Geduldig v. Aiello* (1974). The act established pregnancy as comparable to other conditions that have similar effects on employment decisions; because of it, pregnancy cannot affect employment decisions unless a pregnant employee differs from others in her ability to work.

Prejudice: Judgment based on incomplete, insufficient, or irrelevant information. There are three important aspects, or dimensions, to prejudice: cognitive (beliefs), affective (feelings), and conative (behavioral tendency). Prejudice, therefore, is multidimensional.

Dimensions of Prejudice. The cognitive dimension entails knowledge or information regarding the object of prejudice. This knowledge or information is frequently derived from stereotypes, which are overgeneralized images portraying all members of a group as carbon copies of one another. All members of a particular group are believed to share the same characteristics, whether positive or negative. In each case, there is a failure to recognize individual differences. Since not all people are the same, the knowledge derived from stereotypes is often incorrect.

The affective dimension entails the feelings and attitudes elicited by the object of prejudice. These feelings can be positive, such as trust, admiration, or attraction, or negative, such as hate, fear, or envy. While the feelings may be related to the beliefs, they are not dependent upon them; thus, we may believe someone is a kind, intelligent person, but still not like him. In the same way, we may like someone whom we believe to be a bad person.

The conative dimension is concerned with a tendency or inclination to act in a certain way toward the object of prejudice. Such an inclination can be to act in a positive or negative manner, and is to be distinguished from the actual behavior, which may be different, since inclinations are not always acted upon. We may be inclined to help those we like and hurt those we dislike, yet treat everyone the same.

As can be seen from the aforementioned dimensions, prejudice can be either positive or negative. A person may be prejudiced in favor of someone or something or be prejudiced against someone or something. It is in this negative sense that the term is most often used. Prejudice often results in DISCRIMINATION, which is an action or behavior that is unwarranted and, therefore, unjust. Discrimination is treating someone or something differently based on irrelevant criteria. A common example of this is using sex or race to determine employment, pay, and promotions. In virtually all cases, a person's sex and race are irrelevant to the requirements of the job. Like prejudice, discrimination can be either for or against someone or something.

Relationship of Prejudice to Discrimination. Prejudice and discrimination are sometimes confused with each other. This may be due to the failure to distinguish between an inclination to act, which is a characteristic of prejudice, and the action itself, which is discrimination. Furthermore, it is often believed that prejudice is the cause of discrimination and that they necessarily go together; thus, it is believed that a prejudiced person will discriminate and an unprejudiced person will not. Discrimination is, therefore, accepted to be a sure sign of prejudice.

The American sociologist Robert Merton, however, has explained that this is an oversimplification and is not necessarily true. In fact, there are two types of prejudiced people, referred to as bigots, and two types of unprejudiced people, referred to as liberals. An "all-weather" bigot is a person who is prejudiced and always discriminates. A "timid" bigot is a person who is prejudiced but may or may not discriminate. Such a person's behavior depends on the probable consequences of his or her behavior; such a person will not discriminate if it would be disadvantageous to do so. The situation, rather than the prejudice, dictates behavior. An "all-weather" liberal is a person who is not prejudiced and never discriminates; a person such as this probably exists only in theory. A "fair-weather" liberal is a person who is not prejudiced but who may discriminate if the circumstances favor such behavior. Like the timid bigot, such a person is influenced by the situation. Both the fair-weather liberal and the timid bigot are influenced by legal, social, and economic considerations. Antidiscrimination laws, social criticism, and possible loss of jobs or customers are effective deterrents to discriminatory behavior. On the other hand, lack of legal sanctions for unequal treatment, together with social acceptance or encouragement of bias, and economic advantage from discriminatory practices all promote such behavior.

Distance is sometimes seen as a measure of prejudice: The greater the distance a person wishes to maintain from a member of a group, the greater the prejudice that person has toward the group. There are two kinds of distance, physical and social. Physical distance refers to the amount of space between two ob-

jects. When a person does not want to be in the proximity of a member of a group, such as sit at the same table or live in the same neighborhood, it is believed to indicate the presence of prejudice. While physical distance is measured in terms of space, social distance is measured in terms of the degree of intimacy that a person is prepared to establish in his or her relations with others.

A well-known measure of social distance, developed by the sociologist Emory Bogardus in 1925, is based on the willingness of a respondent to interact with a member of a given group in the following six situations: as persons to be excluded as visitors to the country, as citizens of the country, as coworkers, as neighbors, as fellow club members, and as close kin by marriage. Each succeeding situation entails a greater degree of social acceptance and a corresponding decrease in social distance. In a series of five studies, which began in 1926 and ended in 1977, Bogardus discovered that in the United States, prejudice toward thirty different ethnic groups has remained relatively constant, with the greatest negative prejudice directed against nonwhite non-Europeans and the greatest positive prejudice favoring white Western Europeans and their descendants.

Prejudice is not innate. Like other knowledge, attitudes and behavior that support prejudice are learned. Research has found that it is learned through interaction not with the objects or victims of prejudice but rather from interaction with prejudiced people; thus, many individuals have prejudices against members of groups that they have never met.

Theories of Prejudice. There are many theories that attempt to explain why people become prejudiced. These theories can be grouped into the following general categories: psychological, economic, and sociocultural.

Among the more popular psychological theories are scapegoat, authoritarian personality, and symbolic theories. Scapegoat theories generally explain that people have certain biological, social, or psychological needs that they are not always able to satisfy. When they are blocked from satisfying their needs, they become frustrated and angry. If the source of the blockage is beyond their control, such as fate or a more powerful person, anger is displaced and directed against an available but seemingly weaker victim. Through rationalization, reasons are formed to justify the selection of the alternate object of anger. Thus, frustrations result in aggression against certain socially acceptable victims. Other types of psychological explanations are

During World War II, some Americans allowed their anger against Japan to prejudice their attitude toward Americans of Japanese descent. (UPI/Corbis-Bettmann)

personality theories that state that certain types of personalities are more prone to prejudice. One type of personality that is identified is the authoritarian personality. Characteristics of this personality include conventionalism, authoritarian submission, authoritarian aggression, superstition and stereotyping, power and toughness, destructiveness and cynicism, projectivity, and an exaggerated concern with sex. Symbolic theories explain how certain groups are seen to symbolize something that is hated, feared, or envied. For example, people are prejudiced against blacks because black is often used to represent death and evil.

There are several economic theories. Economic competition theories state that when people are in competition with a recognizable group for scarce or limited economic resources, such as jobs, hostile feelings may result toward members of that group. Research has indicated that lowerclass whites exhibit more hostility toward blacks, while upperclass whites exhibit more hostility toward Jews. Economic exploration theories hold that negative feelings and beliefs develop toward a group that can be exploited; thus, racist dogma evolved as a means to justify the economic exploitation of slaves. This type of theory is espoused by Marxism.

Sociocultural theories include such explanations as cultural transmission, which states that prejudice is learned along with other aspects of culture, and status gains theories, which hold that prejudice helps some people feel superior or attain higher status. These latter theories point out that such status is available to all members of the supposedly superior group and is, therefore, much easier to attain than status that is based on individual merit. Prejudice may also result when the status of a dominant group is challenged and called into question by a subordinate group.

—*Philip E. Lampe*

SUGGESTED READINGS: The relationship between prejudice and discrimination and the implication for social policy is discussed in Robert Merton's "Discrimination and the American Creed" in editor R. H. MacIver's *Discrimination and National Welfare* (New York: Harper & Row, 1949). Explanation of theories and relevant research is presented in Gordon Allport's *The Nature of Prejudice* (Boston: Beacon Press, 1954). Theories of prejudice, the history of discrimination in the United States, and efforts to eliminate it are discussed in Thomas Pettigrew, George Frederickson, Dale Knobel, Nathan Glazer, and Reed Ueda's *Prejudice* (Cambridge, Mass.: The Belknap Press of Harvard University Press, 1982).

Premarital sex: Acts of sexual gratification or reproduction occurring before marriage. As individuals' bodies mature physically and become capable of sexual reproduction, sexual interest and experimentation increase. Because there is approximately a ten-year gap between sexual maturation and the average age of marriage, the practice of a variety of sexual activities before marriage is commonplace.

Premarital sexual activities can be categorized into three main types. Petting, which is defined as sexually touching or caressing another person, can be further subdivided into three kinds of activities. Light petting is touching of a sexual nature with clothes on, avoiding the genitals (for example, hugging). Medium petting is touching the genitals with clothes on. Heavy petting is touching the genitals with clothes off, including mouth to genital contact. Masturbation is self-stimulation for the purpose of sexual pleasure. Sexual intercourse is the insertion of the penis into the vagina.

Studies of premarital sexuality from the 1970's to the 1990's have revealed two American trends. First, people are engaging in heavy petting and sexual intercourse at earlier ages. Second, the number of people engaging in those premarital activities has been increasing. Analyses of these sexual trends demonstrate that the greatest behavioral changes are among white adolescent females.

Standards in regard to premarital sexual intercourse can be classified into four categories. Chastity requires both males and females to abstain from sexual intercourse outside of marriage, whereas the "double standard" makes that requirement only of females. "Permissiveness with caring" says that sexual intercourse before marriage is acceptable as long as one cares for one's partner, whereas "permissiveness without caring" does not require any kind of caring or commitment as a prerequisite for sexual intercourse. For the past thirty years, permissiveness with caring has been the standard that most people have followed. It is interesting, however, that research in the 1990's has demonstrated increases in people choosing either chastity or permissiveness without caring.

Numerous factors affect whether or not people will engage in various forms of premarital sexual activities. Lower socioeconomic status, lower intelligence, and the breakdown of the family system have all been linked with a greater likelihood of engaging in premarital sexual intercourse. Many studies have demonstrated that PEER PRESSURE is usually the dominant factor in whether or not people will engage in sex before marriage. Those whose friends are virgins have a greater probability of remaining virgins than those who choose sexually experienced friends. The possibility of SEXUALLY TRANSMITTED DISEASES is another factor that many consider before choosing to participate in premarital sexual activities. Protected sex cannot prevent all sexually transmitted diseases (for example, genital warts), and females are much more likely to contract a sexually transmitted disease from an infected partner than are males. Finally, deciding to have sex with another person is a moral choice, and people's beliefs can play a crucial role in making that choice. The more devout people are, the less likely they are to engage in premarital sexual intercourse.

SUGGESTED READING: Ed Wheat and Gaye Wheat provide a comprehensive discussion of sexuality in *Intended for Pleasure*, rev. ed. (Old Tappan, N.J.: Revell, 1981).

Prenatal care: Education and actions that are designed to promote the well-being of an unborn child. Molecules of many substances pass through the placenta and have an impact on the unborn child. Thus, it is crucial that pregnant mothers understand and practice proper prenatal care.

Prenatal care involves an awareness and avoidance of teratogens, factors that can cause birth defects. Teratogens are usually most dangerous during the embryonic developmental stage (three to eight weeks after conception) when all organs of the child develop. Different organs have different periods of greatest vulnerability. For example, the brain is the most vulnerable fifteen to twenty-five days after conception; the heart, twenty to forty days. The impact of teratogens is also affected by the amount and type of teratogen. Thus, the higher the amount of alcohol consumed by the mother, the greater the likelihood of severe brain damage; similarly, increasing levels of cigarette smoking increase the probability of premature birth and respiratory problems.

Teratogens can be categorized into four groups: drugs, diseases, pollutants, and maternal health. Most drugs, legal or illegal, prescription or nonprescription, can cause birth defects. The three most frequently used drugs—caffeine, nicotine, and alcohol—all can cause severe behavioral and physical abnormalities in the developing child. Many diseases, including viruses, bacterial infections, and sexually transmitted diseases, pose significant hazards to the well-being of an unborn child. Among the pollutants, lead, mercury, and radiation exposure are highly teratogenic. Finally, lack of maternal health, both psychological and physical, can lead to greater harm to an unborn child than either maternal age or number of previous births.

Prenatal care also involves three protective factors: adequate nutrition, proper medical care, and social support. Nutritionally, a 2,600-calorie diet, sufficient in calcium, protein, and vitamin intake and low in sugar and salt, is advocated. Malnutrition is linked with miscarriage, stillbirth, and improper brain development. Early and frequent medical care throughout the pregnancy is associated with lower rates of birth defects and pregnancy-related complications. A higher degree of social support, particularly how helpful a mother feels her family, relatives, and friends are, is positively correlated with a pregnant woman's psychological and physical health.

It is important to realize that it is impossible to eliminate every potential hazard to an unborn child's health. Pregnant women should take steps to promote the well-being of their unborn children. Striving excessively for the perfect pregnancy, however, is more likely to lead to worry and steal away the joy to be found in the human life inside the womb. A sensible approach involving proper rest, exercise, and diet and an avoidance of drugs, infections, and pollutants will go a long way toward ensuring a safe and healthy pregnancy.

SUGGESTED READINGS: Richard Abrams provides sound advice about medicine use during pregnancy in *Will It Hurt the Baby?* (Reading, Mass.: Addison-Wesley, 1990). The effects of alcohol on unborn children are discussed by Michael Dorris in *The Broken Cord: A Family's Ongoing Struggle with Fetal Alcohol Syndrome* (New York: Harper & Row, 1989).

Preservation: Environmental and resource-use doctrine. "Preservation" connotes the complete protection of natural resources or environments. The term is often used as one end of a doctrinal continuum extending through "CONSERVATION," which seeks to manage the use of resources, and "exploitation," which advocates unrestricted use. Arguments between adherents of the various positions constitute much of the debate over ENVIRONMENTAL ISSUES.

Presidency, U.S.: Executive branch of the U.S. government. Created by Article 2 of the Constitution, the office of the president wields political and military power. Designed as one of three coequal branches of the federal government, only the presidency holds the power to execute the laws passed by Congress.

The presidency may be traced back to the "critical period" of American history (1781-1787), when the United States faced numerous problems, including a lack of strong executive leadership. In 1787, the founding fathers issued a call for a convention in Philadelphia that produced the Constitution.

Delegates to the Constitutional Convention agreed with a proposal calling for a powerful executive who could command military forces, direct foreign policy, and veto unwise laws. Although some conventioneers, having just rid themselves of the tyranny of King George III, worried about the evolution of another monarchy, they nevertheless trusted their instincts that the first president, George Washington, would not abuse his powers.

Washington did not disappoint them. Twice elected unanimously, he faithfully executed laws and wisely employed his powers as commander-in-chief of the armed forces. When Washington quashed the "Whisky Rebellion" by leading thirteen thousand troops into Pennsylvania (the only time a president has led an army into battle), he accomplished two important goals: He ensured the payment of taxes necessary to guarantee the country's survival, and he proved that a chief executive could wield power without becoming a dictator.

Washington basically established the American presidency. In his farewell address (September, 1796), Washington issued invaluable advice to his successors. Presidents, Washington said, should serve only two terms, should avoid partisan politics, and should avoid permanent alliances that might entangle the United States in foreign wars. Stay out of debt, Washington counseled, for public credit should be cherished.

The presidents who followed Washington expanded the powers granted by the Constitution. Between 1829 and 1837, Andrew Jackson created the first White House staff, began collecting patronage (a process his critics called the "spoils system") and developed the use of the "pocket veto" in order to defeat his Congressional opponents. Jackson was the first of the "imperial presidents"—chief executives who sometimes overstepped their constitutional boundaries.

The presidency experienced further growth under Abraham Lincoln (1861-1865) and Franklin D. Roosevelt (1933-1945), who led the United States through its greatest crises, the Civil War, the GREAT DEPRESSION, and World War II. The imperial presidency reached its peak under Lyndon B. Johnson (1963-1969) and Richard M. NIXON (1969-1974). Johnson used the Tonkin Gulf Resolution (August, 1964) to fight an undeclared war in Vietnam. President Nixon used the powers of the office to harass domestic political opponents, though such tactics proved his political undoing in the WATERGATE SCANDAL.

After Johnson and Nixon, the presidency slid into a period of decline. Although Ronald REAGAN restored a degree of confidence in the presidency during the 1980's, neither George BUSH (who lost his bid for re-

Former presidents Gerald Ford, Jimmy Carter, and George Bush with President Bill Clinton in 1993. (Reuters/Corbis-Bettmann)

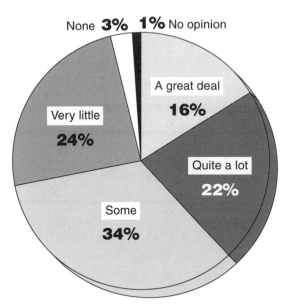

PUBLIC OPINION, 1994:
CONFIDENCE IN THE PRESIDENCY

None **3%** **1%** No opinion

A great deal **16%**

Very little **24%**

Quite a lot **22%**

Some **34%**

Percentage of respondents expressing respective degree of confidence in the U.S. presidency as an institution.

Source: George Gallup, Jr., ed., *The Gallup Poll: Public Opinion, 1994* (Wilmington, Del.: Scholarly Resources, 1995).

election in 1992) nor Bush's successor Bill CLINTON enjoyed the range of powers wielded by some of their predecessors.

SUGGESTED READING: Forrest McDonald offers a penetrating historical analysis in *The American Presidency* (Lawrence: University Press of Kansas, 1994).

President's Council on Physical Fitness and Sports: Federal program begun in 1955 by an executive order issued by President Dwight D. Eisenhower. The action was prompted by publication of an article in the *Journal of the American Association for Health, Physical Education, and Recreation* that identified "physical deficiencies" in American children in comparison to European children. Physical-fitness testing was authorized and implemented in schools by the American Alliance for Health, Physical Education, and Recreation (AAHPER). AAHPER has established various leadership, public-relations, and motivational devices to aid instructors and students in achieving physical fitness.

Pretrial publicity: Public attention given to a criminal or civil case; courts or legal counsels often assert that such publicity negatively affects the ability of judges and juries to try cases fairly. Generally, the term is used to suggest that a court will not be able to seat a jury that has not been prejudiced or biased by such publicity and therefore cannot hear evidence objectively. If pretrial publicity is sufficiently severe, the court or either party may request a change of venue to allow the trial to be held in another location.

Pretrial rights: Numerous protections of the legal status of accused offenders, often based on Constitutional principles or Supreme Court cases. These rights expanded dramatically with the case of *MIRANDA V. ARIZONA* (1966), which guaranteed such offenders the right to legal counsel even if indigent. Among the pretrial motions frequently made by defense attorneys are motions to suppress evidence, to identify informants, to change venue, and to establish a client's sanity. Some states such as California have followed the federal example of providing reciprocal pretrial discovery to both sides, thus complicating the issue of pretrial rights, as occurred in the 1995 murder trial of O. J. Simpson.

Preventive medicine: Branch of medicine that seeks to avoid diseases or other medical problems. Rather than waiting for diseases to occur and then treating them, prevention utilizes immunization to protect an individual. Instead of waiting for serious degenerative diseases to develop, prevention suggests steps that individuals can immediately take that will reduce the chances of developing the disease later. Screening programs for cancer provide a good model for prevention: Be vigilant to detect a condition before it becomes clinically apparent.

In the past one hundred years, prevention has realized some notable successes: improved personal hygiene through safe water, adequate sanitation, improved housing, and better education. Immunizations have greatly reduced the incidence of many diseases in the developed world. There are some notable problems that have resisted the best efforts: tuberculosis, AIDS,

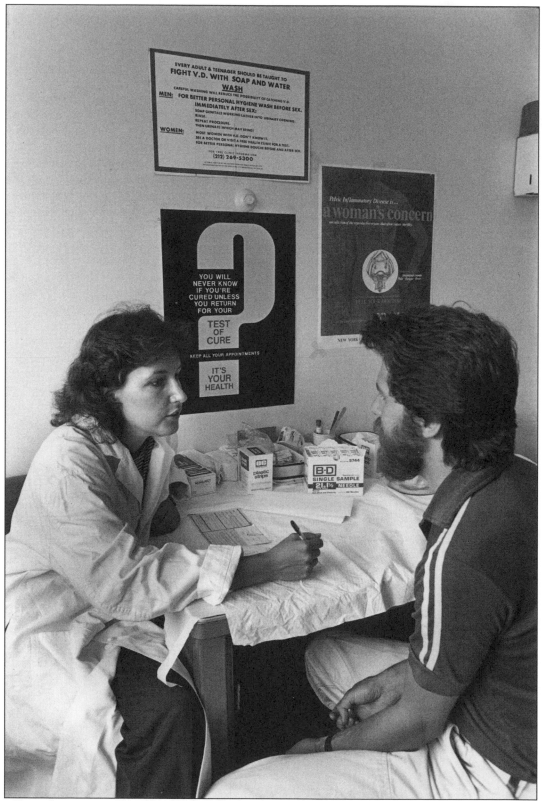

Many diseases can be prevented by following the advice of medical professionals. (Hazel Hankin)

malaria, influenza, and the common cold. The successes have been the result of hard work, scientific innovation, acceptance of new therapies, and sufficient resources, mostly monetary, to accomplish established goals. The problems are mired by incomplete understanding of the disease processes, inadequate monetary reserves, an inability to accept new modes of treatment, chemical resistance (both drugs used to treat diseases and pesticides used to control vectors), ignorance, disbelief of scientific findings, overpopulation, and a lack of financial and human resources.

Immunization is a primary weapon of preventive medicine. Since the end of the 1700's, smallpox has been eradicated. Polio, diphtheria, measles, mumps, German measles, hepatitis, tetanus, and other diseases have, in theory, been relegated to historical fact among the developed nations. In underdeveloped countries, there are inadequate funds for complete immunization. In developed countries, complacency prevents the complete elimination of these diseases.

Degenerative diseases are by-products of successes in prolonging life. However, with ongoing physical activity, appropriate eating habits, and medical surveillance, the effects of degenerative diseases such as osteoporosis, heart disease, and arthritis can be minimized.

There are three main levels of prevention activities. Primary prevention seeks to preserve health by completely avoiding disease. This can be done by removing the causes of disease (bacteria or viruses), eliminating vectors that harbor or transmit disease (rats, mosquitoes, or flies), or protecting people from the above agents through immunization. Using seat belts to protect against crash injuries is another example.

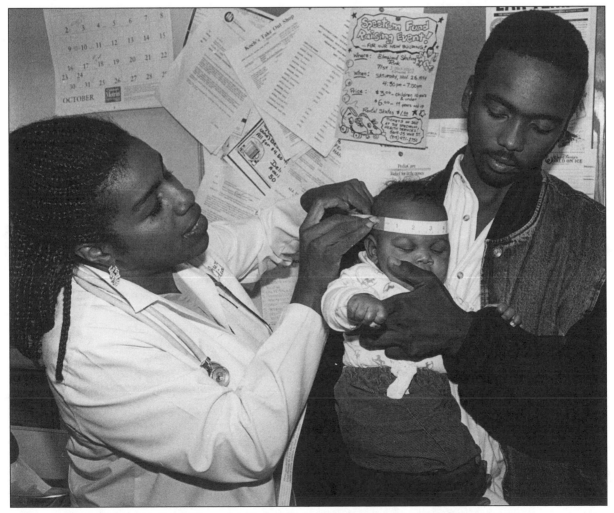

A child is examined at a preventive clinic in Philadelphia. (Impact Visuals/Harvey Finkle)

Price fixing

Secondary prevention seeks to detect and correct departures from good health as early as possible. Screening programs detect diseases before they become clinically apparent, thus allowing more time for treatment and raising the probability of a more satisfactory and long-lasting resolution of the problem. Screening programs for hypertension and cancer of the lung, breast, cervix, prostate, and colon are common. Cessation programs for addictive substances such as alcohol, cigarettes, and drugs, and programs for weight or blood-pressure reduction seek to limit the effects of the offending substance or problem. Tertiary prevention is synonymous with rehabilitation: it seeks to restore as much normal functioning as possible. Primary prevention, the most cost-effective of the three, relies on education and voluntary commitment by individuals and is the most difficult to attain. Preservation of normal function is the goal of preventive medicine. Creating and maintaining a safe environment, enhancing immunity, behaving sensibly, maintaining good nutrition, working to ensure healthy newborns, and providing sufficient health care are the main methods of preventive medicine.

Price fixing: Business practice. Price fixing, a practice that is illegal in the United States, refers to agreements by sellers of a good or service. Under a price-fixing agreement, sellers agree not to compete on the basis of price; often, the agreement specifies that each seller will charge the same price as the others. Price fixing is an attempt by multiple sellers to create what is, in effect, a monopoly, and thus to earn profits that are larger than those possible under competitive market conditions. Price fixing was made illegal by several U.S. federal laws, most notably the Sherman Antitrust Act (1890). Many national governments prohibit price-fixing practices to some degree.

Occasionally governments will mandate various forms of price fixing as a means of protecting certain groups of sellers or providing stability in a market. In these cases, the government states a price for the product or service, usually one higher than the free market would support.

Prime ministry, Canadian: Office of the individual who acts as the chief minister in Canada's parliamentary system. Although the office of the prime minister is not mentioned in Canada's original constitution, the British North America Act of 1867, it is the most important political office in the nation.

Although the prime minister is officially appointed by the governor general, the British Crown's representative to Canada, this action is little more than symbolic. Most often, the prime minister is the leader of the party that wins a majority of seats in the House of Commons; if there is no majority, the prime minister is the leader of the party that is able to win support from other political parties in Commons. In such a case, a minority government exists, and the tenure of the prime minister and his government rests upon the continued support of these allies. Except for the Unionist government formed during World War I, all prime ministers have been affiliated with either the Liberal or Conservative parties.

The influence of the prime minister on Canadian politics and society is enormous. The prime minister appoints members of Parliament to the cabinet, where they provide direction to important portfolios such as Health and Welfare, Foreign Affairs, the Environment, and Finance. As chief minister of this powerful body, a particularly capable prime minister can control its agenda and influence the directions it pursues. The prime minister also exerts control over a large number of patronage appointments, including the selection of senators to the Senate (the upper house in Canada's parliamentary system), the chief justices to all courts, the governor general, and numerous committee positions. In addition, the prime minister is the only individual who can advise the governor general to dissolve Parliament and call an election. Prime ministers have no restrictions on their length of tenure; several prime ministers have held office for more than a decade, and Mackenzie King stayed in power for more than two decades from the 1920's into the late 1940's.

The office of the prime minister often reflects the vision of the individual, particularly in the case of an especially able and powerful leader. In the late nineteen century, John A. Macdonald's backing of the National Policy was significant to the building of a transcontinental railway and, by extension, to the expansion of Canada from the Atlantic to the Pacific. Sir Wilfrid Laurier, prime minister at the beginning of the twentieth century, often expounded upon the theme that the next century belonged to Canada. His optimism manifested itself in an aggressive campaign to settle and populate the Canadian prairies and brought Alberta and Saskatchewan into confederation. More recently, Pierre TRUDEAU's concept of the "Just Society" re-

Prime Minister-elect Kim Campbell and Prime Minister Brian Mulroney in 1993. (Archive Photos, Reuters, Andy Clark)

sulted in a liberalization of laws regarding abortion, divorce, and homosexuality and in the entrenchment of the CHARTER OF RIGHTS AND FREEDOMS within the Canadian constitution.

With one exception, all Canadian prime ministers have been male. In 1993, Kim Campbell replaced Brian Mulroney as leader of the Conservative Party and became the first female to assume Canada's highest political office. After a brief tenure, however, her party suffered a massive defeat in the 1993 general election, and Jean Chrétien and the Liberal Party were propelled to power.

Prior restraint: Act by a governmental body or official to censor the exercise of the right of free press or free speech before publication or expression of the disputed material. Taking into account the original understanding of the First Amendment, the Supreme Court has usually held prior restraints to be unconstitutional. The few exceptions, which must be justified by a compelling state interest, include revelations of military secrets that would endanger the lives of troops and the dissemination of some kinds of political literature on military bases. In the well-known "Pentagon Papers" case, NEW YORK TIMES COMPANY V. UNITED STATES (1971), the Supreme Court ruled that the government could not prevent the press from publishing classified documents that do not pose an imminent threat to national security.

Prison system: Places of confinement symbolizing society's last resort (other than death) for criminals considered dangerous or deserving of lengthy punishment. Prisons reflect crime rates, politics, economics, and social problems. They suffer from overcrowding, violence, theft, and racism.

Before prisons emerged in America during the late eighteenth century, judges sentenced criminals to less humane punishments such as branding and whipping. Because prisons were seen as a better way to rehabilitate, many nations copied the American model of large walled fortresses. Canada, however, relied on probation, payments to victims, and community service. Canadian prisons are typically much smaller than their U.S. counterparts; the United States continues to build large prisons capable of holding as many as two thousand inmates. Many U.S. prisons built in the nineteenth century remain in use. The United States contin-

ues to build prisons, however, and it leads the world in the number of people under confinement. More than nine hundred state and seventy federal prisons held a population of 1,012,851 in 1994. Many more are serving time in the nation's jails (places where people are held pending trial or sentenced to a year or less) because overcrowded prisons cannot accept them.

Structure. Maximum-security prisons, which house the most dangerous criminals, have high walls, fences with razor-wire, guard towers, security cameras, cell blocks, and activity and administration buildings. Medium-security prisons, where inmates who pose less risk of escape and violence are confined, generally have razor-wire fences instead of walls. Minimum-security prisons, where well-behaved inmates stay before release, frequently have no fences or towers.

New inmates spend about a week in an orientation building separate from the cell blocks. They are interviewed, classified, and assigned according to their education and the prison's job needs. Federal prisons are particularly known for scientific classification. Most prisons do not have enough room in their school or job programs, so many prisoners go unassigned, by necessity or choice. Women's prisons generally have fewer programs than do male institutions. When inmates finish orientation, they are usually placed two to a cell; as a result of overcrowding, however, some are placed on cots in front of cells. Cell blocks are large rectangular divisions containing four or five floors on each side; each floor is typically about one hundred cells long. Mechanical devices open groups of cells, or guards can open them individually.

Inmates are let out of their cells daily for at least two mass movements: to the dining room and the exercise yard. Weekly movements include sick call and travel to chapel and the commissary, where inmates can buy toiletries, tobacco, and snacks in exchange for money deposited in their accounts by relatives or earned from low-paying jobs. Mass movement is usually one or two floors at a time. All other movement is governed by an individual pass system. At least two groups, housed in separate cell blocks or floors, are given special treatment: Prisoners in segregation units (or punishment wings) have food delivered to their cells, and those in protective custody have dining halls to themselves.

The institutional structure of a prison allows numerous opportunities for inmates to continue to indulge in criminal behavior. Violence and theft often occur during mass movement, almost every job offers material

PRISONERS IN U.S. FEDERAL AND STATE INSTITUTIONS

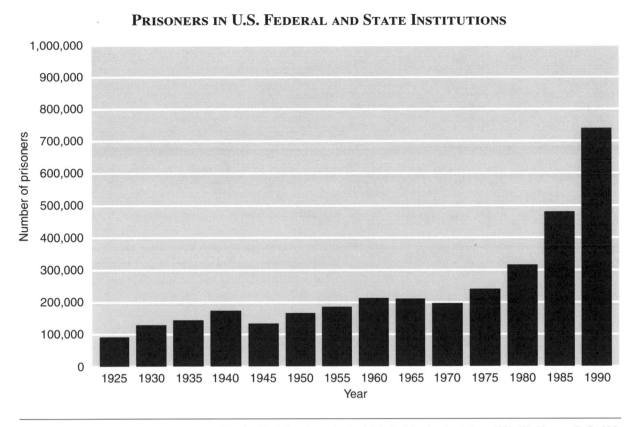

Source: U.S. Department of Justice, Bureau of Justice Statistics, *Sourcebook of Criminal Justice Statistics—1993.* Washington, D.C.: U.S. Government Printing Office, 1994.

to make weapons, and gangs require protection payments, often in the form of cigarette packages. Race takes on extreme importance in dividing inmate society. An inmate social system based on opposition to authority and inmate solidarity emerges, but some sociologists believe this code of conduct is part of the criminal culture prisoners bring with them. In any event, "prisonization" refers to the process by which prisoners from any background come to accept the inmate code, settle down to life as convicts, and try to subvert the power of authorities at every turn. Prisoners easily manipulate friction between treatment and security staff, shortages of personnel, and changes in management. In fact, many of the riots in American prisons during the years 1971 to 1986 can be related to changes in management philosophy.

Trends. Every year, a new record is set for the U.S. prison population, which grows at an annual rate of more than 7 percent. This translates into a nationwide need for about 1,143 prison beds per week. As a result of tough 1980's and 1990's laws on repeat offenders and drug violators, Americans imprison people for longer periods than any Western nation. On average, U.S. prisoners serve sentences of eight and one-half years, which is half the average of original sentences, given time off for good behavior. Debate exists over whether inmates should receive this day-for-day "good time."

Prisons are predominantly populated by poor young adult males. Women account for only 6 percent of the prison population, but their numbers are growing, as are the numbers of elderly prisoners. Nevertheless, people aged eighteen to twenty-four commit the most crime; as a consequence, most inmates are in their twenties or thirties. Those who go to prison are largely poor, have little education, come from weak families, and are unemployed. About half have offspring.

Starting in the mid-1970's, the number of minorities in prison increased. The largest group of U.S. inmates are African Americans, who constitute 46 percent of

U.S. Prison Jurisdictions with Shock Incarceration Programs

Jurisdiction	Program Length	Capacity
Alabama	3 to 6 months	180
Arizona	120 days	150
Arkansas	105 days	150
California	(a)	176
Colorado	3 months	100
Florida	3 months	100
Georgia	(b)	1,265
Illinois	120 days	430
Kansas	180 days	104
Kentucky	(c)	50
Louisiana	90 to 180 days	148
Massachusetts	4 months	256
Michigan	3 months	360
Minnesota	6 months	72
Mississippi	4 months	287
Nevada	150 days	96
New Hampshire	4 months	75
New York	6 months	1,850
North Carolina	3 months	90
Oklahoma	45 days to 5 months	430
Pennsylvania	6 months	197
Tennessee	3 months	150
Texas	3 months	400
Virginia	3 months	96
Wisconsin	6 months	40
Federal Bureau of Prisons	6 months	299

Source: U.S. Department of Justice, Bureau of Justice Statistics, *Sourcebook of Criminal Justice Statistics—1993.* Washington, D.C.: U.S. Government Printing Office, 1994. Primary source: *Corrections Compendium* (Lincoln, Nebraska, Contact Publications, 1993).

Note: Data are based on a survey; Hawaii, Idaho, Maryland, Ohio, South Carolina, and Wyoming did not respond.

(a) 3 months while in prison, 2 months of work training, 4 months on parole.

(b) 3 months for probation facilities, 4 months for incarceration facilities.

(c) 120 days plus another 6-day week.

the prison population, a total that is rising. Another growing group is Hispanics, who account for 17 percent of the total. White inmates make up 36 percent and other groups 1 percent. Some scholars argue that minorities are overrepresented not because they commit more crime but because they are more likely to receive prison terms, while whites tend to get more lenient sentences such as probation.

Inmate records indicate that half have been convicted of a violent crime. The other half represents a mixture of property crime (predominantly burglary), public-order offenses, and drug-law violations. The trend is in the direction of more violent crime. A significant part of the population (about 85 percent) has been confined before, many as juveniles. Along with this criminal record, the typical inmate also has a history of alcohol and drug abuse, and many inmates are in the risk group for the virus that causes AIDS. Two-thirds of all inmates violate conditions of their release and return to prison.

Issues. Perhaps no other condition has brought prisons into the spotlight more than overcrowding, which is defined by the federal government as two or more inmates sharing less than sixty square feet of floor space. Since the average U.S. prison cell is fifty square feet, most prisons are overcrowded. Overcrowding is accompanied by ventilation, plumbing, and food-service problems, but research on the subject shows little difference on stress levels between fifty and sixty feet. Double-celling is more stressful, and white inmates appear to have the least tolerance for this. The scientific evidence on overcrowding has yet to be conclusive and has not proven especially helpful in determining what constitutes "cruel and unusual punishment."

Prisons have been the focus of lawsuits, but recovery of damages by inmates has been rare. Understaffing, underbudgeting, and attitudes of indifference allow conditions to deteriorate. Inhumane conditions have resulted in several state systems being declared cruel and unusual in violation of the Constitution. Before the 1960's, courts generally adopted a hands-off policy toward prisons, but with increasing prisoner access to the courts, the CIVIL RIGHTS of inmates have become paramount. Prisoners sue officials over treatment, food, medical care, religious issues, access to reading material, and living conditions. Lawsuits are quite common; the successful ones most often concern issues of censorship and religion. Most prisons pay close attention to their grievance procedures in order to avoid inmate lawsuits.

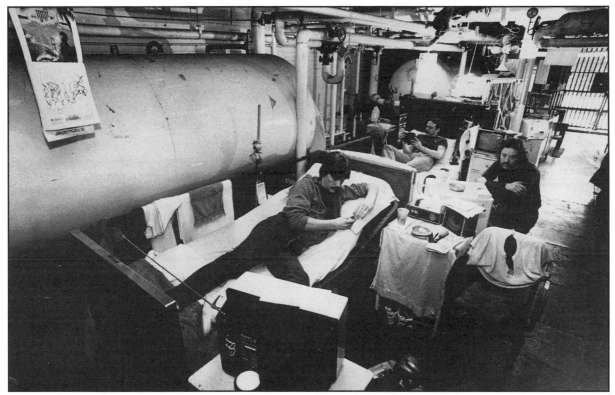

Inmates in an overcrowded Massachusetts prison are housed in the facility's boiler room. (AP/Wide World Photos)

Many officials believe that the solution is to build new prisons, but others think that this is a foolish waste of money. Constructing a new prison costs about thirty thousand dollars per bed; renovating an old prison costs about four thousand dollars per bed. Politicians are largely unwilling to burden taxpayers with these costs; many face political suicide if they attempt to raise taxes to improve inmate living conditions. Some states therefore pay private companies to take inmates; "privatization," as it is called, involves sending inmates from government facilities to institutions set up to make a profit for investors. Private prisons handle only a small part of the prisoner population, but some scholars see privatization as an alarming trend in which government is abandoning its responsibility. As an alternative, many states "lease out" inmates to neighboring states or the federal system.

The latest type of architecture to influence construction projects is the "podular" design. Its triangular style and reliance on video cameras puts inmates under constant watch. Each "pod" contains fifty individual cells that do not allow contact with each other. Guards and inmates communicate via intercom. There is little noise, as carpeting absorbs most of the sound. Podular prisons are noticeably clean and safe. Controversy exists over whether this is too "soft," and some evidence exists that it aggravates or creates mental illness. As prefabricated standard materials make such facilities relatively cheap to build, however, podular prisons are seen by many as the wave of the future.

—Thomas R. O'Connor

SUGGESTED READINGS: Issues in prison life are covered by Hans Toch in *Living in Prison* (New York: Free Press, 1977) and John DiIulio in *Governing Prisons* (New York: Free Press, 1987). Critics of the prison system include John Irwin and James Austin in *It's About Time: America's Imprisonment Binge* (Belmont, Calif.: Wadsworth, 1994).

Privacy Act (1983): Canadian federal legislation. The Privacy Act provides for the collection, retention, and use of personal information by the federal government and for access by individuals to information about them held by the government. The act applies to all federal departments, boards, and agencies and to some official corporations. The act provides that personal information may be collected and used only for

Privacy rights

operating programs or activities, specifies that personal information cannot be used for other purposes without consent, and gives a right of access subject to specific exemptions. The privacy commissioner reviews refusals to provide information and monitors the use of information by the government; refusals of information can be reviewed by the courts.

Privacy rights: Legally recognized interests in protecting personal information or behavior. The right of privacy became a public issue in 1890, when Samuel D. Warren and Louis D. Brandeis, two Boston lawyers, coauthored an article in the *Harvard Law Review*, "The Right to Privacy," which was written in protest of the publication of intimate information concerning the rich and famous by media of the day. Warren and Brandeis, later a Supreme Court Justice, proposed that the media be held liable for publishing sensitive, embarrassing, and personal information that appealed primarily to prurient curiosity rather than public interest. Such publication is distinguished from libel in that it is generally truthful. Hence, this type of invasion by the media has been often protected by the courts.

Four distinct areas of privacy have developed since the Warren and Brandeis article, three of which have little to do with the original concern. The first is "unreasonable disclosure of private facts." This area, the interest of Warren and Brandeis, is often referred to as "pure privacy." In order for a successful suit in this area, there must be publication of private facts—the facts cannot be already known—that are highly offensive to a responsible person or are an outrage to community decency and are not of public concern. While the courts recognize "intentional infliction of emotional distress," such as publishing the name and address of the target of a stalker over the protests of the victim, "newsworthiness" is a generally successful defense by the media. The fact that the media has published the story is often interpreted by the courts to indicate that there is public concern or interest in the content, and therefore it is protected. Judges have been reluctant to substitute their judgment for what is suitable to publish for the judgment of media professionals.

A "false light" invasion is similar to libel. This involves inaccurate representation of someone, although not necessarily defamation. In libel, the concern is what others think as a result of the defamation. Here the concern is the harm to the individual rather than the effect on others. "Intrusion" involves unauthorized entry of the home or office or the use of hidden mechanical devices to gather information. It is generally not allowed. The final area is "appropriation." This involves the use of a person's name or likeness without consent. This is similar to the "right of publicity," which is that individuals have the right to profit from and control the use of their names, photos, or attributes in advertising and promotional materials.

All areas of privacy were designed to protect the emotional well-being of individuals when the press goes too far. Because the courts have difficulty defining "going too far," however, only appropriation and right-of-publicity suits have been generally successful. Most states do allow "one-party consent" to gather information, although such material cannot be broadcast without consent from both parties.

Private schooling. *See* **Public versus private schooling**

Privatization: Turning public enterprises into private ones. Poor economic performance and budget realities have caused the reevaluation of many state-owned enterprises, leading many countries to examine alternatives to such state-run businesses. Privatization programs were popularized in the 1980's by British prime minister Margaret Thatcher as part of her deliberate attempt to reverse socialist policies in Great Britain. Subsequently, many developing countries adopted privatization programs. In the United States, there are relatively few privatization programs at the federal level, because few firms were nationalized in the first place. A number of state and local governments, however, have undertaken extensive privatization programs in such areas as waste management, prison management, road maintenance, and water treatment. Governments considering privatization face a trade-off of control, in the case of government ownership, versus presumed efficiency, in the case of private ownership. Programs that cost a government money potentially can earn profits if privatized, but with a risk of reduction in the quality of products or services.

Probable cause: Legal standard of proof. Probable cause is necessary for police to obtain an arrest or search warrant or to make an arrest or a search without a warrant; for prosecutors to bind a defendant over to a court of general jurisdiction during a preliminary hearing; and for a grand jury to issue an indictment. The term is a fundamental legal principle derived from the Fourth Amendment. "Probable cause" is generally held to mean that a reasonable person looking at a given set of apparent facts and circumstances would come to the conclusion that an accused person had committed an offense or that things subject to seizure would be found in a certain place.

Probate: Administration and distribution of the estate of a decedent. In probate, a court determines which creditors are entitled to funds from the estate and which persons are entitled to receive a share of the remaining assets.

Probate laws establish formal procedure for the handling, evaluation, and payment of creditors of a decedent and for distribution of the remainder of the estate to heirs or specific legatees named in the will. Probate is based on state law; generally, an estate is probated in the state in which the decedent lived at the time of death. Real estate, however, is governed by the laws of the state in which it is located, which might not be the state of domicile of the decedent. The Uniform Probate Code, adopted by twenty-nine states, resolves these and other similar conflicts by standardizing and simplifying the interpretation of inheritance rights.

The procedure for probating an estate follows some basic steps common to all states. When a person dies, all assets (bank account, stocks, bonds, and other financial transactions) are frozen until the estate is administered. If the decedent dies testate (with a will), the original copy of the will together with affidavits from witnesses are filed with the court. If the decedent dies intestate (without a will), a petition to the court of administration of an intestate estate is made. Will contests, in which the validity of the will is challenged, are resolved next. An executor (if testate) or administrator (if intestate) is appointed to oversee the assets of the estate during probate, including gathering and inventorying the assets, paying creditors, and generally keeping the assets intact until the probate court issues a final order to close the estate. Any breach of the fiduciary duty of the executor or administrator can result in criminal charges.

Allowances for living expenses for a surviving spouse or minor children are distributed according to state statute and special needs of the parties during probate. Certain property is generally exempt from probate, including the residence of the decedent, the automobile, home furnishings, apparel, and other personal items, according to state statute.

Notification to creditors of the death and pending probate is made according to each state's procedure (often publication in the classified section of the newspaper). Creditors are then given a specific time to make a claim against the estate. Occasionally, it is necessary to sell certain items of property in order to raise money to satisfy creditors' claims.

In a testate estate, many states give the surviving spouse the option of accepting his or her share under

When heirs challenge the distribution of an estate, their claims are heard in probate court. (AP/Wide World Photos)

the will or a statutorily designated percentage of the estate (the forced or elected share). A prenuptial agreement, in which a spouse agreed to waive any claim, constitutes an exception. Next, the estate is distributed according to the terms of the will. An intestate estate is distributed according to state statutes governing descent and distribution.

Pro-choice movement: Coalition of women's groups, health organizations, progressive political groups, and civil-liberty groups that advocate for reproductive freedom for women, including access to birth control and the right to ABORTION. The pro-choice movement constitutes a central part of the modern feminist movement.

In the early part of the twentieth century, it was birth-control pioneers such as Margaret Sanger (1883-1966), a U.S. nurse and author, who worked to disseminate information about birth-control methods. At the time, this was an extremely controversial activity. A staggering number of women died in childbirth or of

Pro-choice voters at a 1992 rally. (AP/Wide World Photos)

its complications. Infant mortality was considerably higher than it is today. Activists such as Sanger tried to change this picture by giving women more knowledge and control over their fertility. When the birth-control pill, the oral contraceptive, became available in the late 1950's, women for the first time were able to decide for themselves when they would conceive and how many children they would bear.

In the 1960's and 1970's, American women became more active politically than at any time since the suffrage movement of the early twentieth century. During the era of the Vietnam War and the political protest movement that accompanied it, women's rights forcefully emerged as an issue, and the birth-control movement united with the feminist movement. By the late 1960's, efforts to enact an abortion-law repeal gained steam. In *Abortion: The Clash of Absolutes* (1990), Lawrence Tribe has noted that the repeal movement "achieved credibility through public endorsement by liberal clergy, including the Episcopalians, the United Church of Christ, the United Methodist Church, and the United Presbyterian Church, and by . . . Church Women United and the YWCA." PLANNED PARENTHOOD, active in the birth-control movement, also took a public position in favor of abortion rights. Other population-control groups weighed in with support of the pro-choice position. Citizens were now ready to challenge restrictive abortion laws.

The landmark decision about a woman's fundamental right to end a pregnancy came in *ROE v. WADE*. On January 22, 1973, the U.S. Supreme Court invalidated a Georgia law restricting a woman's right to an abortion. The Court decided that this right was virtually unimpeded during the first trimester of a pregnancy. The *Roe* decision was hailed by pro-choice advocates but was roundly criticized by abortion opponents, who organized the anti-abortion, or PRO-LIFE, MOVEMENT in response. The battle between the two sides in the abortion debate was among the most visible moral and political arguments of the late twentieth century.

In 1989, the pro-choice movement received a setback with the Supreme Court's ruling in *Webster v. Reproductive Health Services*, which allowed states to require tests of fetal viability at twenty weeks' gestation before abortion is allowed. *Webster* also upheld the withdrawal of public funds to pay for abortions. Nevertheless, public opinion polls consistently showed that a majority of Americans supported abortion rights, and the pro-choice position continued to be in ascendancy.

With the development of such pharmaceutical agents as the "morning after" pill and RU 486, increasing numbers of women seem likely to gain access to abortion in private surroundings. Although such developments may make the abortion debate somewhat quieter, the pro-choice movement will likely continue to be active in ensuring women's rights to make fundamental choices about their reproductive lives.

Productivity: Economic measure. Productivity refers to the ratio of output of goods and services to an input, or factor of production, such as labor, capital, or land, or perhaps some less tangible factor such as technology, management, or organization. Productivity increases if the same quantity of an input produces more output, which usually happens when the quality of the input increases. The most commonly used measure of productivity is the ratio of output to worker hours, called labor productivity. An increase in this measure may be the result of something other than the quality or effort of workers. An individual working with a more efficient machine, for example, can produce a larger output without working harder or better. Such problems of causation confound all measures of productivity.

In the long run, increases in productivity are the underlying causes of increases in per-capita income and in economic well-being. Improved productivity also is key in fighting inflation, because it allows reductions in costs and increases in real (inflation-adjusted) wages. For those reasons, economists and government policymakers watch this economic indicator.

In the United States, the average increase in total productivity of major factors of production stood at around 1.5 percent a year during the twentieth century. About half of that total has been traced to growth in labor and capital productivity. The remainder has been attributed to such factors as education, innovation, economies of scale, and other variables. After about 1970, however, increases in total factor (or multifactor) productivity tended to be smaller. The productivity slide has been explained by the accelerated shift from a manufacturing economy to a service economy, in which technological advances are less applicable; to lower net investment spending; to environmental regulations and higher energy prices increasing costs but not output; and to reduced civilian research and development. In addition, more younger workers and women—both with less work experience than average—entered the labor force. Accordingly, policy recommendations for raising productivity have included national investment in physical and human capital; the development of new technology; improved public infrastructure such as roads, power systems, and communication systems; and the maintenance of a stable economic environment through such means as improved labor-management relations and programs to increase worker motivation.

The introduction of new technology and work processes intended to improve productivity has revolutionized many workplaces and workers' lives. Industry has seen extensive use of robots and other forms of automation and programming on the assembly line. Generalized use of such devices as computers in offices and stores, automated teller machines at banks, laser scanners at supermarkets, and audio-visual systems in classrooms has revolutionized service industries. Even farming and mining have seen innovations prompted by the computer revolution. Management techniques employing new monitoring equipment and systems have made it possible for employers to keep closer tabs on the performance—and thus productivity—of each production unit, placing real or imagined pressure on labor for various forms of "speedup."

Management also has strived to achieve higher productivity through such business reorganizations as mergers with other firms or, less frequently, the breaking up of oversized production units. These measures, as well as other forms of restructuring and streamlining, frequently have been accompanied by substantial personnel layoffs and thus reduced labor costs, with the effect of greater productivity and profitability anticipated in the future. Such layoffs, as well as management efforts to increase individual workers' productivity, have prompted labor unions to call for employers to share the cost savings or increases in profits by increasing wages and salaries.

Prohibition (1919-1933): Era in which alcoholic beverages were prohibited in the United States. Though other nations, including Finland (1919), Iceland (1915), and Norway (1919), concurrently sought to eliminate the use of alcohol, the "noble experiment" in America was to be closely monitored globally. Its failure by the 1930's caused many to feel that the regulation, not the prohibition, of liquor consumption was the best possible social policy.

Prohibitionist feeling has long run deep in the United States. Even in colonial times, the sale of alcoholic beverages was strictly licensed, and drunkenness was severely punished. The rise of a reforming fervor in the nineteenth century caused many to support the Temperance Movement, which sought public abstinence from "intoxicating spirits" and the prohibition of their manufacture and sale on the local and state levels. When prohibition became linked with an array of other reforms advocated by both the Populist and Progressive movements, it caught the imagination of the American public. By 1919, as a result of state and local laws, two-thirds of the U.S. population was living in "dry" territory. World War I (1914-1918) aided the "drys" in their war on the "wets." The association of brewers with the National German-American Alliance backfired. Drys argued that the security and safety of workers and soldiers demanded abstinence. In 1917, the Eighteenth Amendment forbidding "the manufacture, sale, or transportation of intoxicating liquors" was referred by Congress to the states; the amendment was ratified within fourteen months and went into effect on January 17, 1920. The National Prohibition Enforcement Act (or Volstead Act) of October 28, 1919, defined "intoxicating liquors" as any beverage with more than one-half of 1 percent of alcohol. Alcohol use was permitted only for industrial, medicinal, and sacramental purposes.

"This law will be obeyed . . . and where it is not obeyed, it will be enforced," proclaimed John F. Kramer, the first prohibition commissioner. The Coast Guard and the Prohibition Unit of the Bureau of Internal Revenue were the federal enforcement agencies. The law, however, was unpopular in urban, laboring, and immigrant communities. Ingenious ways were found to get alcohol. Hillside stills flourished, making illegal alcohol Appalachia's leading nonagricultural source of income. "Rum-runners" entered the United States from Canada and from offshore "booze ships," while gangs distributed "white lightning" to urban speakeasies (more than thirty thousand of which existed in New York City alone). The onset of the GREAT DEPRESSION (1929-1939) and the coming of the NEW DEAL (1933-1941) saw a shift in public opinion that resulted in the ratification of the Twenty-first Amendment, which repealed the Eighteenth, in December, 1933. The "great dry decade" was over.

SUGGESTED READINGS: Readable studies include Herbert Asbury's *The Great Illusion: An Informal History of Prohibition* (Garden City, N.Y.: Doubleday, 1950), Thomas M. Coffey's *The Long Thirst: Prohibi-*

New Yorkers celebrate the end of Prohibition in 1933. (UPI/Corbis-Bettmann)

A 1988 pro-life movement demonstration in Atlanta. (UPI/Corbis-Bettmann)

tion in America, 1920-1933 (New York: W. W. Norton, 1975), and J. C. Furnas' *The Life and Times of the Late Demon Rum* (New York: Putnam, 1965).

Project Ploughshares: Private Canadian agency founded in 1976 in Waterloo, Ontario. Project Ploughshares sponsors research, education, and advocacy to promote peaceful conflict-resolution, demilitarization, and global security based on justice and a sustainable environment. Backed by sixteen national organizations, thirty local chapters, and ten thousand members, the group also publishes a quarterly journal, working papers, and an annual *Armed Conflicts Report*. Project Ploughshares also does policy research on arms-trade control for the United Nations and Canada and sponsors citizen-diplomacy projects.

Pro-life movement: Arising in the 1960's in opposition to the call for the liberalization of ABORTION laws, the pro-life movement became a major social and political presence only after the 1973 U.S. Supreme Court decision in *ROE V. WADE*. The pro-life movement makes opposition to euthanasia and infanticide part of its campaign to protect "innocent human life."

The first permanent local group was founded in Troy, New York, in 1965, and the first permanent state group appeared in Virginia in 1967. In that year, the National Right to Life Committee (NRLC) began. The *Roe v. Wade* decision gave the movement a national focus and led to a rapid increase in its numbers. One of its few early victories was the passage by Congress in 1976 of the HYDE AMENDMENT, which barred the use of federal funds for abortions.

Until the early 1980's, the movement focused on efforts to pass a "human life" amendment to the Constitution to reverse the *Roe* decision. The election of Ronald Reagan, a pro-life sympathizer, to the presidency in 1980 seemed to promise success, especially since the Republican Party had adopted a strong pro-life policy in 1980. The defeat of even a limited anti-abortion amendment in the Senate, however, led to a new strategy that emphasized changing *Roe* through the courts. If sympathetic judges were appointed to the Supreme Court by the president, pro-lifers reasoned, victory could come there. Despite the hopes raised by the 1989 *WEBSTER V. REPRODUCTIVE HEALTH SERVICES* decision, however, this did not occur. The election of President Bill Clinton in 1992 was another blow to the

movement, but pro-lifers were nevertheless able to lobby successfully for renewal of the Hyde Amendment and were able to prevent passage of the Freedom of Choice Act.

While much of the movement worked through political channels to bring about change, others within it believed in direct action. Some picketed abortion clinics; others, such as the high-profile group OPERATION RESCUE, tried to shut down clinics by blocking clinic entrances. Violent attacks on clinics and the murders of several doctors who performed abortions were committed by a handful of pro-life zealots. Although some of these extremists were only loosely connected to the main movement, the reputation of all pro-lifers was damaged by such actions.

The pro-life movement has long been diverse. The NRLC, the largest national organization, is a single-issue group that takes stands only on the life issues of abortion, euthanasia, and infanticide. The American Life League, founded in 1979, is the second-largest pro-life organization. It sees abortion as part of a larger moral agenda that includes opposition to pornography and other perceived threats to the family. A similar view is advanced by Human Life International, founded in 1981. There are a large number of smaller groups, including Feminists for Life, which makes opposition to abortion part of a liberal program that includes opposition to the death penalty and the promotion of women's rights. While Catholics have always been a major component of the movement, substantial numbers of Protestant evangelicals have joined it, as have members of other faiths. The pro-life movement is an international phenomenon, with groups in Canada (most notably the Alliance for Life and the Campaign Life Coalition) and in many other countries.

Promiscuity: Indiscriminate or unrestricted sexual relations. Such sexual relations are usually casual, incidental, and lack premeditation.

Enduring relationships for most promiscuous youths are virtually nonexistent. The majority of youths experience difficulty, for various reasons, in establishing long-term relationships. Sex, for them, is experimental, exploratory, and used for immediate gratification. Interpersonal relationships are tenuous and are usually terminated quickly. It becomes apparent that the duration of interpersonal associations is relative to the age of those involved. Generally, the younger the person, the less likely it is that lasting relationships will be formed.

Promiscuity

Promiscuous females place themselves at high risk of pregnancy and of delivering children out of wedlock. The incidence of out-of-wedlock births rose alarmingly during the 1990's, largely as a result of increased promiscuity. The U.S. Department of Health and Human Services' *Vital Statistics of the United States* (1991) shows that a large percentage of all births in the United States during that time were to unmarried couples. As a group, unwed mothers aged fifteen to nineteen accounted for a substantial share of these births. Promiscuous youths are also at a higher risk for contracting SEXUALLY TRANSMITTED DISEASES. Syphilis, gonorrhea, chlamydia, herpes, and ACQUIRED IMMUNE DEFICIENCY SYNDROME (AIDS) reached epi-

New York City mayor Ed Koch unveils a 1986 public awareness campaign on the dangers of promiscuity. (UPI/ Corbis-Bettmann)

demic levels during the 1980's and 1990's. Reasons for the increase were largely because of increases in the number of sexually active individuals as well as nonuse or improper use of condoms.

There is ample evidence that promiscuity has been on the rise during the 1980's and 1990's. Also, sexual experimentation has been found to begin much earlier and for a greater number of people than in the past. *The Janus Report on Sexual Behavior* (1993) by Samuel and Cynthia Janus demonstrated that, among a group of Americans aged eighteen to twenty-six years of age, 70 percent of males and 68 percent of females interviewed admitted to having had full sexual relations by the time they had reached eighteen years of age. In contrast, those interviewed who were over sixty-five years of age admitted to having had sex by age eighteen at rates of 43 percent for males and 40 percent for women.

Attitudes regarding sexual abstinence have also changed. The same study reported that older respondents considered virginity to have been desirable in the past. Contemporary respondents generally considered virginity to be a burden.

The importance of media accessibility as the underlying cause of attitudinal and behavioral shifts must be considered. Numerous studies have demonstrated that sexually explicit material found on television and movies has had a profound effect on the psyche of youths and adolescents and is influential in fostering promiscuous attitudes and behaviors. Public concern regarding the matter reached a new high in the early 1990's with calls for various forms of censorship. Politically inflammatory, the topic of regulation of sexually explicit material in the media will doubtless continue to be a source of controversy.

SUGGESTED READING: Mark Baker's *Sex Lives: A Sexual Self-Portrait of America* (New York: Simon & Schuster, 1994) presents numerous interviews of individuals concerning their sexual experiences.

Pronatalism: Sociopolitical attitudes or policies aimed at increasing the birth rate of a particular population. Pronatalist attitudes may be based on religious beliefs, economic imperatives, or determined efforts to propagate a particular ethnic culture. Pronatalist governments may outlaw contraception, abortion, and nonprocreative sex, offer economic incentives (such as tax breaks or subsidies) for childbearing or child-rearing, or create social or economic penalties (such as

extra taxes) for the voluntarily childless. Critics of pronatalism charge that such policies are irresponsible in light of the world's burgeoning population.

Property rights: Property rights controversies, sometimes referred to as "takings" issues, revolve around the right of government to regulate how private property owners use their land. In the 1990's, private property owners became concerned that proliferation of land-use regulations would result in destruction of individual owners' rights.

The Fifth Amendment to the U.S. Constitution provides that private property cannot be taken for public use "without just compensation." In the past, this law was interpreted to mean that if a government agency required land to build a project, such as a highway or a school, the government had to pay the land's owners the fair market values of that property. The conflict between environment regulations and property rights differed in two significant ways from the usual condemnation procedures. First, unlike condemnation procedures involved in a highway project, in which the government actually buys the land, owners retain title to their property. Second, property owners based their claims on the loss of possible value. That is, owners argued that they should be reimbursed for income that they would have enjoyed had they been allowed to develop the land as they wished, not merely compensated for the assessed value of the undeveloped land.

Environmentalists argued that the supposed concern over the erosion of individual property rights was actually a thinly veiled attempt to weaken environmental-protection legislation on both state and federal levels. Historically, societies have long recognized that various constraints can and should be placed on individual property owners. Local units of government, such as township boards, often establish zoning codes that designate certain areas as appropriate for building homes and other areas as restricted to industry. The fact that much of the debate surrounding property rights ignored the long-established traditions of local zoning while focusing on the issue of state and federal environmental regulation lent credence to the environmentalist argument.

At the same time, however, reports of problems encountered by small property owners in trying to comply with confusing and occasionally contradictory land-use regulations suggested that the property rights movement was responding to legitimate concerns. In

Michigan, for example, one landowner who constructed a series of ponds on his rural property was simultaneously honored for his wildlife conservation efforts by a U.S. Department of Agriculture agency and charged with wetlands violations by the Michigan Department of Natural Resources. Stories in magazines ranging from *Readers Digest* to *Popular Science* detailed similar episodes, such as the story of a farmer in North Carolina who was fined thousands of dollars when he repaired an existing tidal gate, or the story of a landowner in Pennsylvania who was jailed for removing trash from a stream. In many of these cases, the problems arose not from the regulations themselves but from poor communications between government agencies and from the ignorance of zealous bureaucrats.

Few people doubt that some land-use regulations are necessary in an industrialized society. Zoning laws protect both present members of society and future generations. The message of the property rights movement, however, is that many citizens believe that land-use regulations are often confusing, contradictory, and unfair.

Proposition 48: National Collegiate Athletic Association (NCAA) regulation mandating minimum academic standards for college athletes. According to Proposition 48, scholarship athletes entering college after 1986 must have a C average in eleven high-school core courses and must score at least 700 on the Scholastic Aptitude Test (SAT) or 15 on the American College Test (ACT). Students not meeting these requirements are ineligible for athletic competition (or varsity practice) for their first year in college. In addition, when such athletes become eligible, they have only three years of eligibility remaining. Critics charge that the standards discriminate against minority and low-income students; advocates claim that such rules are necessary to preserve the academic integrity of NCAA schools.

Proposition 187 (1994): Initiative passed by California voters making illegal immigrants ineligible for publicly financed social services, education, and non-emergency health care. The legality of the measure was immediately contested; lawyers claimed that immigration issues should be decided by the federal courts.

History. Proposition 187 was passed as California and the United States were experiencing major economic changes and social problems. For example, many Californians were losing jobs as a result of cutbacks in defense spending by the federal government. People were worried about their economic future and that of their children. There also was much concern that violence, illegitimate births, welfare dependency, and, consequently, tax expenditures were increasing. In 1994, Republic politicians Dan Lungren, running for the post of California attorney general, Senate candidate Michael Huffington, and Governor Pete Wilson, running for reelection, offered similar explanations of why California's citizens were feeling economically and socially insecure: Too much tax money, they claimed, was being spent on illegal immigrants, even while many immigrants were taking jobs to which citizens rightfully were entitled.

This Republican call to limit immigration was also reflected in the platform of Republicans across the country who soon would take control of the U.S. House and Senate. President Bill Clinton also sought to limit immigration, especially of Haitians and Cubans, but he expressed strong disapproval of California's Proposition 187 because it attempted to deny illegal immigrants basic public services. Nevertheless, the measure was overwhelmingly approved by California voters on November 8, 1994.

The legislation required officials from publicly funded health, education, and social-service organizations to verify that each immigrant client or student had legal documents. Doctors and teachers, for example, would need to report anyone they suspected of being an illegal immigrant. Proponents argued that such verification was needed in order to prevent illegal immigrants from obtaining public services. Lawsuits were immediately filed, however, to prevent these and other provisions of the law from taking effect. Lawyers from the American Immigration Lawyers Association, the American Civil Liberties Union, the Center for Human Rights and Constitutional Law, and the Mexican American Legal Defense Fund were successful in getting a hold placed on most provisions of Proposition 187, at least until federal courts could examine its merits. Several religious organizations, school districts, health-care providers, cities, and unions also sought to prevent enactment of Proposition 187. The only provisions of Proposition 187 that were not blocked were those making it a felony to manufacture or use false documents.

Arguments in Favor. Proponents argued that the demand for tax-supported social, health, and educational services were escalating because legal and illegal immigration were skyrocketing in the early 1990's. Public education, burdened by increasingly overcrowded schools, was especially costly. Estimates were that illegal immigrants made up 4 percent of California's population and cost Californians more than $1 billion per year in state and local taxes. Proponents noted that most tax dollars paid by legal and illegal immigrant workers go to the federal treasury, whereas state and local governments incur most of the costs of the publicly supported services used by immigrants. Proposition 187 proponents also claimed that the measure would prevent illegal immigrants from coming to the United States to take jobs from U.S. citizens, since it would make false documentation a felony. Even

though babies born in the United States are automatically granted citizenship, the threat of arrest, proponents argued, would prevent pregnant women from illegally crossing the border to give birth.

Despite charges of racism by opponents, some members of conservative organizations such as the Federation for American Immigration Reform (FAIR) and Save Our State (SOS) raised other fears: The new wave of immigrants coming from non-European countries, such groups argued, would not easily assimilate into the dominant culture. Increasing numbers of immigrants were coming from Third World countries, and the prospect of a steady influx of immigrants with divergent languages, customs, and beliefs was not appealing to many citizens.

Arguments Against. Lawyers argued that the federal

Demonstrators show their opposition to Proposition 187 at a San Francisco march. (AP/Wide World Photos)

government, not the states, is responsible for regulating immigration. For example, the U.S. Supreme Court in PLYLER V. DOE (1981) had upheld the right of children of illegal immigrants to public-school education under the EQUAL-PROTECTION clause of the Fourteenth Amendment.

Moreover, many social scientists argued that the economic and social policies of both the United States and of immigrants' countries of origin already had and would continue to have far more impact on illegal immigration than would any law seeking to limit immigration. The proper approach, critics argued, was to examine and improve such policies rather than to create a politically popular but probably unconstitutional and economically nonsensical law. For example, Mexico, the source of most illegal immigrants, has a severely unequal distribution of income, high rates of poverty, a poor economy, and high birth rates. To sup-

port their families and themselves, Proposition 187 critics said, it was no wonder that Mexicans seek U.S. jobs; the most intelligent course of action, critics claimed, was to address such pressures at their source.

Furthermore, critics noted, U.S. policies have been responsible for the temporary or permanent migration of many Mexicans. In 1917, owners and operators of U.S. farms and railroads needed immigrant workers, and they persuaded Congress to make it easier for workers to immigrate. Still more Mexican workers were recruited between 1942 and 1964 under the Bracero Program, begun as an effort to ease wartime labor shortages but continued after the end of World War II because the supply of cheap labor was attractive to many businesses. In the 1960's, U.S. farmers and other employers successfully pressured the government to grant permanent-resident status to thousands of Mexicans whom U.S. employers wanted to hire. Programs

An anti-Proposition 187 rally in Los Angeles. (Reuters/Bettmann)

in the 1980's and immigration policy changes in 1990 also facilitated Mexican settlement in the United States. Since the economic goals of U.S. employers had brought and were continuing to bring Mexican workers and their relatives to the United States, critics argued, it would be morally wrong to deny immigrant workers and their children basic health, educational, and other social services.

Furthermore, critics noted, when people are denied basic rights, they can become a drain on the economy and fearful of authorities. Many children denied schooling, for example, end up in gangs and never acquire job skills, thereby fostering a variety of social problems. If undocumented immigrants were unable to obtain health care, their diseases could spread to the rest of the population, costing citizens both health and money.

Some argued that the NORTH AMERICAN FREE TRADE AGREEMENT (NAFTA) of 1994 would be a major factor increasing Mexican immigration. One consequence could be that more profitable U.S. industries would drive Mexican competitors out of business, thereby forcing more Mexicans to look for U.S. jobs. On the other hand, if NAFTA were to bring a net growth in businesses and jobs to Mexico, then Mexican migration could decrease.

Another argument made against Proposition 187 was that immigrant laborers make significant contributions to the U.S. economy; critics of the measure claimed that immigrants take jobs that many citizens are unwilling to take, including seasonal agricultural employment and work in textile factories, both of which typically involve low pay and poor working conditions. Proponents, though, responded that without the cheap labor provided by huge numbers of impoverished immigrants, such jobs would carry higher salaries and better working conditions, making them more attractive to citizens. Moreover, illegal immigrants often obtain false documentation to convince employers that they have the right to work; they then pay Social Security and other taxes just as other citizens. Critics pointed to studies showing that the net economic benefit of immigrants within most U.S. communities has been positive, although proponents of Proposition 187 pointed to studies demonstrating the opposite effect.

Finally, some critics raised a more humanistic argument. Most citizens voting for Proposition 187, they said, were "scapegoating" immigrants in an attempt to find a simple answer to their problems. Yet, critics said, such voters were forgetting that the United States was a nation of immigrants; the basic values underlying the nation, they argued, would not be furthered by a law breeding suspicion of foreigners or fear among immigrants. If immigration needed to be limited, it was argued, other, more humane measures should be considered. One proposal was to develop a guest-worker program allowing immigrants and their U.S. employers to reap economic benefits from migrant labor while allowing such workers access to public services for fixed periods of time.   —*Grace Maria Marvin*

SUGGESTED READINGS: Madelwyn Allen Jones provides a history of immigration dating back to 1607 in *American Immigration* (Chicago: University of Chicago Press, 1992). Thomas Muller provides evidence that immigration has meant more benefits than costs in *Immigrants and the American City* (New York: New York University Press, 1993).

Prostitution: Act or profession of offering the body for sexual relations for money. Prostitution is illegal in most jurisdictions, and both a prostitute and the person hiring the prostitute can be criminally charged and prosecuted.

Prostitutes may be males or females of almost any age. Most prostitutes begin in their early teenage years and may continue well into their adulthood. Most people who are convicted of prostitution will receive little punishment for the offense; often, a small fine or a night in jail will be all that is imposed.

There are three primary types of prostitutes: street prostitutes, drug-house prostitutes, and escorts. The most common type of prostitute is the street prostitute. These prostitutes are found on the sidewalks of busy streets in many large cities; they typically approach cars and bargain with potential clients to engage in sexual activity. They often perform the acts in the vehicles and then immediately return to the street to continue to work.

Drug-house prostitutes, who are often found in crack houses, generally have serious drug habits they are trying to support. For money or drugs, they will engage in a wide variety of sexual activity. These prostitutes earn comparatively little money and are considered the lowest class of prostitutes.

The escort type of prostitutes are often called "call girls," although they may also be males. The best-paid prostitutes, escorts often cater to wealthier clients. They are often hired through escort services, which

A prostitute works a New York street corner in 1989. (Impact Visuals, Kirk Condyles)

may be advertised in newspapers or telephone books.

Prostitution is considered a "victimless" crime, as both the prostitute and the person paying for sexual relations are assumed to engage in these acts willingly. There has thus been debate that prostitution should be legalized. In particular, supporters of legalization suggest, there are risks associated with prostitution that could be eliminated or reduced if prostitution were legalized.

Many people who hire prostitutes are victimized. They may be robbed or assaulted by prostitutes or their accomplices, and the victims then are generally reluctant to call police. Another concern relates to public health issues. Public concern about AIDS and other SEXUALLY TRANSMITTED DISEASES has focused attention on prostitutes, as they are one of the highest risk groups for such illnesses. Supporters thus often suggest that if prostitution was legalized, prostitutes could be better regulated and tested for diseases.

Another serious problem associated with prostitu-tion is the presence of pimps, people who have control over prostitutes and take most of the profits from their work. Pimps often recruit young children, especially runaways, who are very vulnerable. Pimps sometimes beat women or boys into submission or to "keep them in line." Other pimps help prostitutes to become addicted to illegal drugs in order to make them work to pay for drugs.

Supporters of legalization argue that if the business of prostitution were conducted above-board, the effects of pimps, like other societal problems associated with the business, could be curbed. Opponents of legalization typically counter that prostitution is an inherently immoral and dangerous enterprise. Legalizing prostitution, they claim, would encourage both the business and related crime and social deviance.

Protectionism: Restriction of imports. All countries have some sort of regulation on international trade, usually to protect vital or emerging industries and domestic employment. The different forms of restriction on international trade are contained in a country's commercial policy. Tariffs (taxes) and quotas (numerical limits on the amount of imports) are the most easily recognized instruments of commercial policy. More subtle, and perhaps more effective, nontariff and nonquota instruments include government purchasing policies, subsidies, and safety and technical standards, all of which tend to favor domestic firms. Protectionism as a policy intends to limit imports so that domestic industries can produce goods that otherwise would be imported, thus creating domestic jobs.

Psychics: People who claim to have extrasensory or paranormal powers of perception, typically the ability to predict future events with accuracy. Though always popular with believers, psychics in the 1990's achieved new levels of public visibility as a result of toll telephone "hotlines" that advertised psychic serv-

ices on television. Although many psychics assert the legitimacy of their abilities, critics claim that such services amount to nothing more than charlatanism.

Public Broadcasting Service (PBS): U.S. government-supported television agency. During the early stages of development of American television, only one station, WOI-TV, owned by Iowa State University, promoted educational programming as its chief objective. Since 1952, the Federal Communications Commission (FCC) has reserved more than three hundred stations for noncommercial educational purposes. Educational television, or ETV as it was called, struggled in the 1950's and 1960's to define its mission. Some educators had hopes that ETV might help universities cope with the ever-increasing numbers of students wanting access to a college education. For a variety of reasons, including high costs, efforts to establish "broadcast" education failed during the infant stages of ETV. However, two visions for educational

Psychic services are popular with believers, although skeptics assert that such operations are instances of charlatanism. (Yasmine Cordoba)

The cast of the acclaimed PBS children's show *Sesame Street* in 1970. (UPI/Corbis-Bettmann)

television did remain consistent: to supplement the public-school classroom experience with television programs for in-school use, and to provide cultural and community-interest programs during the evening.

Educational television's central problem for most of its history has been funding. Funding for educational television has come from state taxes, private donations, and gifts from commercial foundations. The most consistent supporter of ETV has been the Ford Foundation, which provided funds in 1952 for the National Educational Television and Radio Center (NET), an association of educational television stations. NET provided direction and funding for programming that all member stations shared, and this cooperative effort helped to make educational television more financially viable in the United States.

In 1967, in an effort to improve programming still further, the Ford Foundation underwrote a new organization, the Public Broadcast Laboratory. Congress joined the effort to promote educational television when it passed the Public Broadcasting Act in 1967. The act created a fifteen-person Corporation for Public Broadcasting to aid in dispensing public and private funds donated for the development of educational television. In order to administer the individual stations and programs more effectively, the Corporation for Public Broadcasting in 1969 formed the Public Broadcasting System, which has continued to coordinate educational television efforts in the United States.

PBS has been relatively successful at promoting children's educational shows as well as some adult cultural and historical programming. Most of the American public recognizes quality children's programs, such as *Sesame Street*, which reflect the ongoing effort to enlighten young children. Among the network's adult programs, Ken Burns's *The Civil War*, filmed in the late 1980's, also received widespread acclaim from critics.

Nevertheless, following the Republican victories in the 1994 congressional elections, political support and funding for PBS has waned. Political conservatives, primarily in the Republican Party, have claimed that PBS is too liberal and politically imbalanced. Such critics often claim that PBS programming reflects the social agenda of the "academic elite" in America and does not analyze social issues objectively. Conservative critics also note that much of PBS' children's programming promotes a clear social agenda that extols multiculturalism and the tolerance of a variety of cultural expressions. Although such critics typically as-

sert that they do not wish to deny PBS the right to free expression, they argue that public dollars should not be used to promote a particular social vision.

Public defenders: Attorneys retained by the state to represent persons accused of criminal offenses who cannot afford to hire their own attorneys. The Supreme Court applied the Sixth Amendment right to counsel to accused felons in *Gideon v. Wainwright* (1963) and to misdemeanants in *Argersinger v. Hamlin* (1972), concluding that indigent defendants are entitled to experienced representation at public expense. Some public defenders are paid a salary by the government to represent indigent defendants; others are private-practice attorneys who are under contract to represent defendants as needed at a prearranged fee, who are chosen by judges from members of the bar who practice in the area, or who are volunteers serving pro bono.

Public health: Branch of medicine and health that is dedicated to the common attainment of the highest level of physical, mental, and societal well-being and longevity. Individuals are the ultimate beneficiaries, but public health frequently focuses on groups within the larger context of society as a whole.

The roots of public health can be traced to antiquity, when systems for the delivery of potable water and the drainage of contaminated and septic effluent were constructed by Minoan, Greek, and Egyptian civilizations. During the Middle Ages, interest in public health, as with so many aspects of civilization, waned. However, the bubonic plague that first swept over Europe in the middle of the fourteenth century reawakened interest in the control of disease to preserve economic power. The tool of quarantine was developed at Ragusa (present-day Dubrovnik, Croatia), and the city of Marseilles enacted the first quarantine law in 1383. However, at this time diseases were widely thought to be caused by divine punishment, bad air, or bad luck. In the eighteenth century, social concern about poor working conditions, the abuse of children in the work place, and religious reform also included public health: safer working conditions, shorter hours, awareness of diseases, and the construction of improved housing. The sanitary movement originated in Europe and quickly spread to North America. Local health departments were established in the early nineteenth century in part as a response to the constitutionally based mandate to protect the public health.

Public health seeks to control or prevent the spread of disease. Communicable diseases such as measles, diphtheria, polio, and AIDS were of interest in the 1990's. Historically, scarlet fever, leprosy, bubonic plague, and tuberculosis have come under the purview of public health. Diseases are prevented by conducting immunization programs, which are offered through schools, public clinics, and hospitals. Degenerative diseases and accidents are also public-health interests. Motor-vehicle accidents, CANCER, and diabetes are examples of contemporary entities that can be prevented by public-health activities.

The condition of the environment is also important within public health. The environment is commonly taken to mean external air and water; homes and workplaces are also important environments. Externally, air is monitored for nitrates, sulfates, carbon monoxide, ozone, lead, particulates, and hydrocarbons. Monitoring indoor air is no less important but more difficult to accomplish. Carbon monoxide and lead are significant hazards that can be reduced largely by means of raising public awareness. Occupational environments are dangerous and are monitored by the Occupational Safety and Health Administration (OSHA). Temperature, noise, fumes, machinery, and radiation are some of the aspects OSHA observes. The keys to ensuring and promoting public health involve monitoring, record keeping, and instruction. Diseases that are more serious must be reported to health authorities. In this way, others can be alerted to their presence. By comparing the number of reported cases to the expected number, epidemics can be spotted and intervention undertaken in an expeditious manner. Instruction in avoiding diseases and other unsafe conditions is an ongoing need. Constant teaching is required to maintain safe environments and healthy lifestyles.

Public housing: Accommodations subsidized by the government and allocated to persons in need of affordable shelter. The history of public housing in North America has been heavily influenced by legislation and market forces.

During the GREAT DEPRESSION, the U.S. Congress passed a number of housing initiatives to satisfy the country's immediate needs. President Franklin D. Roosevelt avoided a showdown with developers when he advocated a Federal Housing Administration (FHA) in charge of insuring mortgages rather than building homes. Meanwhile, the League of Social Reconstruction planned housing projects in Canada primarily as a way to create jobs.

By the 1940's, public housing had fallen into disfavor in both countries. The Wagner-Steagall Act (1937) had created a U.S. Housing Authority (USHA) with plans to replace the nation's six million substandard dwellings. The National Association of Real Estate Boards (NAREB) and members of the building trades lobbied against the USHA on the grounds that it hoarded prime real estate to fulfill its "socialistic" goals. Businessmen learned a new phrase, "urban redevelopment," and urged legislators to revive deteriorating cities with projects combining both housing and commercial redevelopment.

It was at this point that the U.S. and Canadian strategies diverged. The Housing Act of 1949 satisfied housing advocates and business interests with language focusing on the residential and commercial redevelopment of American cities. Using a strategy later identified as "urban renewal" in the Housing Act of 1954, private-public partnerships would clear residential slums and assemble land for commercial projects, with the implicit assumption that part of each renewal budget would cover the cost of relocating displaced households. For the first time, public housing in the United States was associated with just one sector of society: the poor, predominantly black population displaced by urban renewal.

To the north, Canadian proposals incorporated comprehensive planning and commercial development into a more balanced program of urban revitalization. Rather than surrendering their cities to private development, Canadian planners incorporated redevelopment projects with innovative housing programs. Comprehensive planning also spurred talk of a subway for Toronto, Ontario, and infrastructural improvements around the country. Fiscal concerns in the late 1950's slowed construction efforts and even resulted in the transfer of several public housing developments from provincial agencies to metropolitan authorities.

The U.S. government took the opposite course during the 1950's, distancing itself from the administration of public housing and mass transit. The Federal Aid Highway Act of 1956 poured money into road construction, with the result that suburbs sprang up around most cities. Whites continued to flee the central cities and settle the peripheries, while minorities, women, and the elderly remained stuck in deteriorated neighborhoods and segregated public high rises.

Public housing built by the Habitat for Humanity organization. (James L. Shaffer)

Racial tensions stemming from such conditions wracked America's cities throughout the 1960's, with recurring violence giving Americans constant reminders of the injustices that persist in and around public housing developments. Efforts to curb dissent and reinvigorate these areas have focused on issues other than housing. Residents have fought for better access to public facilities, for employment, and for authority over their own buildings with mixed success. Much, though, remains to be done before public housing can fulfill its fundamental goal: to provide affordable shelter and community for everyone.

Public opinion polling: Process of asking people questions about various topics to find out their attitudes, beliefs, and opinions. Polls involve finding a sample of individuals to represent a population, interviewing them on topics of interest, and analyzing and reporting the results.

Uses of Polls. Polls are used by politicians, businesses, and the media to assess the attitudes of voters, consumers, and the general public. Private polling firms, universities, and government agencies conduct polls on such topics as voting choices, current issues, attitudes toward products, and television programming preferences. Politicians commission pollsters to track their campaigns and use poll results to make campaign decisions. Government agencies conduct polls to monitor the effectiveness of their programs.

Most polls are conducted for private clients outside the political arena. Elmo Roper, a major pollster, got his start as a salesman who began surveying potential customers to get a better idea of which lines would sell best. George Gallup began his work by measuring newspaper readership.

Although pollsters do many marketing surveys, polls done for political candidates and on elections have attracted the most scrutiny. Results of presidential elections since 1952 generally have been forecast correctly within two or three percentage points by major pollsters, although polls taken five or more days before the election tend to be less accurate in forecasting the actual vote. To ensure that the relevant (voting) population is represented in election polls, up to a dozen questions are asked to ensure that the person surveyed actually will vote. All major candidates for the presidency since 1960 have hired polling firms to provide advice during their campaigns.

In addition, the media subsidize polls conducted by private firms and use poll results to keep their audience informed. Network political polling began in earnest after the 1972 presidential election. *The New York Times* began conducting its own polls in 1975. Newspapers now base hundreds of stories on poll results during the course of a year. Polls are used routinely to add depth to a story, but they sometimes become the story. Reporting polls sometimes seems more important to the media than analyzing issues.

Polls are quantified almost as quickly as the data are entered into a computer. Most polls simply report the frequencies of respondents answering questions a particular way, such as how many favor a particular candidate or how strongly they favor a particular issue. Results can be analyzed according to age, education, ethnic group, gender, and income and reported as part of a trend, so that changes over time can be observed. In this way, polls can play a major role in representing public opinion.

History. Most politicians and government policymakers take public opinion into account when making decisions about campaign platforms or public policy. This concern for public opinion is especially evident in democracies, in which government is dependent on the will of the public. Jean-Jacques Rousseau, an eighteenth century French philosopher, believed that all laws are based on public opinion.

Initially, public opinion polls were based on volunteer samples, beginning with the straw poll of the presidential election of 1824. This was the first time that public opinion was measured and quantified in some way, although the importance of public opinion and its relation to public policy was discussed by the early Greeks. The poll correctly predicted that Andrew

Jackson would receive the most electoral votes, although John Quincy Adams eventually won the election in the House of Representatives.

Straw polls were used widely to forecast election results until the *Literary Digest* incorrectly predicted that Alf Landon, the Republican candidate for president in 1936, would defeat Franklin D. Roosevelt. Straw polls often were conducted by partisan newspapers and tended to exaggerate the chances of favored candidates and to downgrade the chances and ridicule the qualifications of opposing candidates.

An early method of conducting such polls was simply to estimate attendance at rallies: The greater the attendance, the greater the implied support for the candidate. Another method was to print sample ballots in the newspaper. Unfortunately, newspapers or other interested parties could stuff the collection boxes, and readers of a particular paper might have a bias toward a candidate not representative of the general public. Another method was to mail sample ballots to individuals on various lists. This method alleviated problems of ballot box stuffing but has difficulties associated with potential biases in the lists used and the "volunteer" aspect of returning the ballot. A third method, and one often found to be accurate when sufficient numbers of respondents are included, is to have interviewers "solicit" votes from members of the community. This was the precursor of the "man in the street" interviews often used to represent public opinion.

The most infamous straw poll was that conducted by the *Literary Digest* for the 1936 presidential election. The *Literary Digest* was a popular weekly newsmagazine that began conducting straw polls in 1916 as part of a strategy to increase circulation. In 1920, the magazine mailed more than 11 million ballots on which respondents indicated preferences for potential presidential candidates. In 1932, 20 million ballots were mailed.

In 1936, George Gallup, a marketing and newspaper researcher who had formed the American Institute of Public Opinion (producer of the Gallup Poll) a year earlier, predicted that his poll results would be more accurate than those of the better-known *Literary Digest* poll. He was aware of the bias in the *Literary Digest* poll resulting from sampling from lists of subscribers, telephone owners, and recent automobile purchasers, all people more likely to be Republican than Democrat. Gallup received national recognition after the success of his predictions and the misprediction by the *Literary Digest*, and public opinion polling began the process of becoming scientific. The *Literary Digest* went out of business the following year.

Types of Polls. Public opinion polls, or surveys, can be divided into two types, those based on nonprobability samples, such as the straw vote polls prevalent from 1824 to 1936, and those based on probability samples, in which selection of respondents is determined mathematically to ensure representativeness of the population.

In nonprobability samples, not everyone in the relevant population has the same probability of being included. The population is the entire group of interest, whether it is a local community or neighborhood or all the nation's or world's inhabitants. Nonprobability samples include available or convenience samples made up of readily accessible respondents. Such sampling includes surveying a group of people gathered in one place, such as people shopping in a mall. Volunteer samples consist of people who select themselves by their particular interests or feelings, often negative, about a topic. These samples include, for example, people who write letters to the editor, call in to talk shows, or respond to telephone polls soliciting input. Some organizations have used 900 telephone numbers as a means of polling, requesting that people telephone one number to express one opinion and another number to express a contrasting opinion. Such samples are not representative of the general population because they include only those people willing to spend the money to make the telephone call to make their views known.

The type of nonprobability sample that was used extensively in election polls from 1936 to 1948 was a purposive or quota sample. In such samples, respon-

A respondent answers an opinion poll. (Hazel Hankin)

dents are selected on the basis of predetermined percentages of membership in certain groups. Professional pollsters such as Gallup began using quota samples during the 1936 election. People were defined in terms of categories believed to be relevant to the topic of interest, such as political party and likelihood of voting, and demographic characteristics such as income, gender, educational level, occupation, and age. Interviewers then selected respondents who fell into the predetermined categories, stopping when the quota for that category was met.

Scientific Polls. Quota samples were used widely until after the presidential election of 1948. In that election, all the major pollsters incorrectly predicted that Thomas Dewey would defeat Harry S Truman. Various reasons were offered to explain the error. Most major pollsters switched to probability, or scientific, sampling as a means of reducing the likelihood of error.

Scientific sampling is characterized by every member of the relevant population having an equal chance of being selected. This is achieved by determining mathematically, at random, who will be chosen as a respondent. In a typical national poll, about fifteen hundred people are surveyed. Even such apparently small samples are accurate in ascertaining the attitudes of a large group because of the power of randomness. Selecting such a small number of people randomly is expensive, so some polls rely on the same group of respondents, who are polled periodically about various issues.

Once the sample is selected, individuals have to be interviewed. Questionnaires can be administered by mail, by telephone, or through personal interviews. Although mail surveys can have an adequate response rate under special circumstances, they are generally not considered a reliable technique for representing a diverse population and hence are considered suspect as a representation of a larger population. They depend on people taking the time to complete the interview form and mailing it in. This introduces a bias in that only the people who care enough about the issues addressed will take the time to return the questionnaire.

Personal interviews have the advantages of allowing additional, more complicated questions and in-depth interviews. They also make it easier to ensure that the correct person—the one selected by mathematical randomization techniques—is responding. They are, however, far more expensive to administer.

Issues of Poll Use. The widespread use and reporting of polls has led some people to examine implica-

tions of their use. The effects of polling are most noticeable in political campaigns. Early poll results that are unfavorable to a candidate can doom a campaign, because supporters looking at poll results may come to believe that the candidate has no chance of winning and may therefore switch their allegiance to another candidate. This is particularly problematic for campaign financing. It is difficult for candidates to attract financing if polls show little support for them; potential contributors are likely to see their money as being wasted on a hopeless effort. In addition, candidates shown as favored in early polls often receive more attention from the media, and increased media coverage can lead to increased support. At the least, it leads to political debates focusing on the early favored candidates, to the neglect of those not favored in the early polls.

Polls also have effects on the elections themselves. By the 1990's, television and radio stations predicted election outcomes within hours of the opening of polling places. Most of these predictions were correct. Potential voters who might have cast ballots later in the day were given the impression that elections already were decided, and it is likely that some people were dissuaded from bothering to vote by such impressions. In addition, in presidential elections, results or projected results from East Coast states are reported while West Coast polls still are open. Most radio and television stations predict the outcome of the eventual vote in the electoral college. Again, potential voters may be dissuaded from casting ballots by the perception that their votes do not matter because the election already is decided. Such arguments have led some to criticize polls and their use for undermining the democratic system by reducing voter turnout.   *—Roger D. Haney*

Suggested Readings: Herbert Asher's *Polling and the Public: What Every Citizen Should Know*, 2d ed. (Washington, D.C.: Congressional Quarterly, 1992), is a readable work that discusses types of polls, such as tracking and exit polls. Excellent cartoons are included. Norman M. Bradburn and Seymour Sudman's *Polls and Surveys* (San Francisco: Jossey-Bass, 1988) provides an explanation of how polls are conducted and a history of polls. Major pollsters, including George Gallup and Burns Roper, discuss the impact of polls on voting and society in Albert H. Cantril's *Polling on the Issues* (Cabin John, Md.: Seven Locks Press, 1980). David W. Moore's *The Superpollsters: How They Measure and Manipulate Public Opinion in America* (New York: Four Walls Eight Windows,

1992) is an outstanding history of polling presented through the biographical history of the individuals who developed the industry.

Public versus private schooling: Debates over the respective merits of public and private schools intensified in the 1980's and 1990's, giving renewed currency to an issue that is centuries old.

Contemporary with the growth of the middle class in the eighteenth century, public schools in Europe and North America began teaching commercial skills to most boys and to some girls to prepare them for roles in the workforce. After the American Revolution, pressure built for the establishment of free elementary education for the general public as a means of creating the educated electorate necessary to a democratic society. By the mid-nineteenth century, public elementary schools existed throughout the United States; by the early twentieth century, public junior high schools and high schools were becoming common. Advocates of public schooling assert that their democratic nature provides good training for life in a pluralistic society and that they can provide motivated students with educational opportunities equal to those provided by private schools.

Private schools have existed since ancient times, but public schools had become the norm by the mid-twentieth century. In the late twentieth century, however, private education made a remarkable resurgence

Private schools can offer more sophisticated classes as well as a more controlled learning environment. (Impact Visuals, Andrew Lichtenstein)

throughout North America for two primary reasons. First, private schools were free to address religious issues and to advocate religious beliefs, discussions that were generally forbidden in American public schools following court rulings that outlawed school prayer and stressed SEPARATION OF CHURCH AND STATE. In response, members of many religious groups formed their own schools to educate their children in an effort to preserve their religious traditions. Second, many parents sent their children to private schools in response to a perceived decline in the quality of American public education; advocates claim that private schools offer more direct control of content, discipline, class size, and other factors affecting the quality of education. By 1993, approximately 11 percent of American schoolchildren attended private schools. Catholic schools composed the single largest group of private educational institutions, accounting for more than eight thousand schools, or approximately one-third of the total.

Puerto Rican Legal Defense and Education Fund (PRLDEF): Community organization. The PRLDEF was founded in 1972 in New York City to protect and promote the legal rights of Puerto Ricans and other Latinos. Jorge L. Batista, Victor Marrero, and Cesar A. Perales, several distinguished community members, aided the founding of PRLDEF to increase educational opportunities for Puerto Rican youths and especially to promote their involvement in the legal professions. Active in high-profile cases involving bilingual public services, equal access to civil service employment, and voting rights and fair districting, PRLDEF has been effective in addressing and correcting the exclusion of Puerto Ricans and other Latinos from equal opportunities.

Punk rock: Abrasive, hyperenergetic form of rock music that emerged in the 1970's in England and North America. Punk was not simply a type of music but rather a whole cultural attitude expressing the alienation of the young; as early punk icon Johnny Rotten sang in the Sex Pistols' anthem "God Save the Queen," many punk fans felt they had "no future," and punk consequently challenged much of what was considered proper by the rest of society.

Both in England and North America, punk rock was an urban phenomenon. Although many would argue punk had roots in both England and North America in

the garage bands of the 1960's, English punk rock first achieved widespread notoriety in London with the arrival of the Sex Pistols in 1976. Founded and produced by avant-garde boutique owner Malcolm MacLaren and fronted by Rotten, a volatile singer and charismatic performer, the Sex Pistols managed in their frantic three-year career to outrage mainstream British society, start an "anti-fashion" revolution, and, ultimately, to change the course of rock and roll. They flouted propriety by dressing and playing sloppily, behaving anarchically, and appropriating and defiling symbols of mainstream culture. Virtually all subsequent punk and "grunge" bands, in both North America and England, are indebted in some way to the Sex Pistols. The other major British punk group was the Clash, whose songs were at once more pop-influenced, more sophisticated, and more political than those of the Sex Pistols; although the Clash was initially less celebrated, they would eventually achieve recognition as the more musically significant band.

Punk's course is more difficult to delineate in North America, where the movement was closely allied to the musical trend known as New Wave, which shared punk's iconoclasm but not its anger. North American punk flourished in various cities in the 1970's and 1980's, with each city producing its own distinctive music and subculture. In New York City, for example, punk was heavily influenced by the city's artistic avant-garde; important groups in this scene were the seminal band the Ramones and the New Wave-influenced Television and Talking Heads. Other important punk rock cities included Los Angeles (home to X and Black Flag), Cleveland (known for Pere Ubu and the Dead Boys), Athens, Georgia (home to the B-52's), and San Francisco (where the Dead Kennedys achieved notoriety). Like their British counterparts, American punks were disgusted by the bland polish of mainstream rock, by the hypocrisy and cynicism of the rock aristocracy, and by the control exerted by large record companies.

In addition to expressing angst and disillusion, punk rock returned to rock and roll a spirit of innovation and independence that had largely dissipated by the early 1970's. Punk encouraged youth to reject mass-produced music, clothing, and identities and, instead, to do it themselves—to, in short, take back rock and roll. (Some would argue, however, that punk rock itself was cynically mass-produced from the start.) Although the heyday of punk rock is long over, many of the most acclaimed rock bands of the 1980's and 1990's, including U2, Pearl Jam, and Nirvana, could

Punk rock pioneers the Sex Pistols in 1977. (AP/Wide World Photos)

The breeding of animals for sale in "puppy mills" is highly controversial. (UPI/Corbis-Bettmann)

not have come into being without it—nor, perhaps more important, could tens of thousands of screeching and bombastic garage bands the world over.

Puppy mills: Commercial dog-breeding operations that mass-produce purebred puppies for profit. Since their lineage can be traced through breeding records, the puppies are eligible for registration with the American Kennel Club, substantially increasing their value. Puppy mill operators, however, routinely pair closely related canines, producing offspring that are prone to genetic disorders. Buyers may face costly veterinary bills or the death of a puppy afflicted with congenital defects. Unsanitary and crowded housing conditions, poor diets, and overbreeding promote other health problems such as parasitic infestations and viral diseases.

Q

Qaddafi, Muammar al- (b. 1942, near Surt, Libya): Leader of Libya since 1969. Drawing upon oil income, Qaddafi built a strict Muslim state with a socialist complexion. An admirer of Egypt's Gamal Abdel Nasser, he promoted Pan-Arabic and Pan-Islamic values, condemned Western influence, and tried to fuse Muslim states into larger entities. He also supported radical movements and governments such as the Irish Republican Army (IRA), the Italian Red Brigades, the NATION OF ISLAM, the PALESTINE LIBERATION ORGANIZATION (PLO), revolutionary Iran, and—during the 1991 GULF WAR—IRAQ. Qaddafi's militant anticolonial stance and support of terrorism have generated widespread Western condemnation and prompted occasional limited military and economic retaliation against his regime.

Quantum universe: Worldview that developed as a result of the quantum hypothesis that first appeared in 1900. The development of the quantum theory radically changed the way that scientists view the experiments designed to discover the nature and behavior of matter and energy; in a broader sense, quantum theory changed perceptions of reality itself.

To explain some experimental observations that were made during the last twenty years of the nineteenth century, physicists Max Planck and Albert Einstein suggested that light energy occurred in small bundles called "quanta" (now called photons). During the same period of time, experimental investigations of atoms gave unexpected and extraordinary results. Atoms turned out to be composed of relatively vast regions of space in which particles called electrons moved around a dense nucleus. It quickly became clear that electrons were unlike the solid objects of classical physics and, in fact, appeared to have a dual nature, sometimes behaving like particles, sometimes like waves.

This duality in nature has serious implications with respect to the way that experiments are designed to ask questions of nature. Because atomic particles are so small, their behavior can only be studied indirectly, by observation of their interactions. For example, the position along a given axis of an electron traveling perpendicular to the axis might be inferred by moving a small hole along the axis and then detecting the passage of the electron through the hole. The electron, however, also behaves like a wave, and if the hole is small enough, the electron will undergo diffraction and change the direction of its travel. The experiment thus changes the system that is experimented on. Werner Heisenberg recognized this fundamental limitation on the ability to attain certitude and expressed this in a mathematical form that has become known as the uncertainty principle.

Scientists quickly recognized the impossibility of being truly objective. In a sense, the process of experimentation creates the reality that is the object of the study. The interactions are important, not the particles themselves. This change in perspective helped to foster the emergence of a worldview that is holistic and ecological. The natural and behavioral sciences have all witnessed this change in approach. Einstein recognized that matter and energy, which are separately the subject of classical conservation laws, are two manifestation of the same reality and are interconvertible (a truth expressed in his famous equation $E = mc^2$). Medical practice, psychology, and even economics have all recognized that the world is not merely a collection of individual objects but is rather a dynamic whole made up of interrelated parts. Reality can thus be understood only in terms of a systems view; the world is a dynamic, cosmic process.

SUGGESTED READINGS: A fascinating, nontechnical introduction to quantum theory and some of its philosophical implications is given by Gary Zukav in *The Dancing Wu Li Masters: An Overview of the New Physics* (New York: William Morrow, 1979). Fritjof Capra describes the transition from the Newtonian to the quantum view of reality in *The Turning Point* (New York: Simon & Schuster, 1982), which shows how this change in paradigm in the physics community has influenced other disciplines, from biology and psychology to economics.

Quayle, Dan (James Danforth Quayle; b. Feb. 4, 1947, Indianapolis, Ind.): U.S. legislator; vice presi-

Vice President Dan Quayle in 1988. (UPI/Corbis-Bettmann)

dent from 1989 to 1993. Quayle, an Indiana Republican, served in the House of Representatives from 1976 to 1980 and in the Senate from 1980 to 1988 before he was unexpectedly chosen by George Bush as his running mate in the 1988 presidential campaign. Bush and Quayle were elected by a solid margin; as vice president, Quayle worked to reform the legal system and reduce government regulations, and he headed the President's Council on Competitiveness. He became best known, however, for his often clumsy public remarks, and he was widely regarded as a liability during Bush's unsuccessful 1992 reelection campaign.

Québec separatism: A movement dedicated to achieving political sovereignty for Québec. It is based

Opponents of Québec separatism at a Toronto rally. (Dick Hemingway)

upon the belief that Québec is a "distinct society" and can protect its language and culture only by withdrawing from the Canadian federation. Although some separatists call for total independence, a majority prefer to remain economically integrated with the Canadian economy.

The Province. Québec is the largest of Canada's ten provinces, approximately three times the size of France, and its seven million inhabitants make it the second largest in terms of population. About 83 percent speak French (Francophones), 10 percent speak English (Anglophones), and the remaining "Allophones," mainly immigrants, speak the languages of their ancestors.

History. French-speaking Québecers (Québécois) believe their society is distinct from the rest of Canada by virtue of its French language, Catholic faith, French legal code, and unique culture. They reject the notion that Québec is only one of ten coequal provinces; instead, they claim it is one of the two "founding nations" (the other being English) that played a crucial role in the early history of North America and the creation of modern Canada. They perceive themselves as a nation and Québec as their homeland.

The Québécois possess a profound sense of history, much of it marked by tragedy and suffering. Their French ancestors had to tame a harsh wilderness, fight ferocious battles with Indians, and suffer military conquest by the English in 1759-1760. Well into the mid-twentieth century, Anglophones controlled the wealth of Québec, and between 1850 and 1900, some 500,000 impoverished Québecers left the province, mainly for the United States, in search of a better life. Most humiliating of all, the Québécois people were victimized for speaking their own language. They were denied jobs, refused service, excluded from organizations, and subjected to constant petty humiliations for using French. Thus, unlike English-speaking Canadians, the Québécois have emerged with a firm sense of national identity and a steely determination to survive.

Politics. The year 1960 marked a watershed in Québec history. Prior to that time, Québec was a defensive, insular, conservative society dominated by corrupt political parties and a dogmatic Catholic church. In 1960, a reform-minded Liberal Party came to power, and in a short time Québec was transformed into a confident, progressive, modern, secular society. Once the issue of reform had been met, the next obvious challenge was: How did one protect Québec culture, especially the French language, while living in an immense sea of Anglophones? Many Québécois came to the conclusion this national task could be accomplished only by separating from Canada and stopping the constant interference of the Canadian federal government. Giving urgency to this task were disturbing demographic trends. Once possessing one of the highest birth rates in the world, Québecers saw it become one of the lowest. This led to fears that separation must be accomplished while Francophones still had a comfortable numerical majority.

Québecers believed it was necessary to create a political party within the province whose principle mission was to achieve sovereignty. In 1968, René Lévesque, a respected political commentator and former Liberal cabinet minister, helped unite several small independence groups to form the PARTI QUÉBÉCOIS (PQ). Lévesque embraced the concept of "sovereignty-association," which would make Québec politically sovereign but would preserve a tight economic association with the rest of Canada. In 1976, the PQ was unexpectedly elected to power, and Lévesque was appointed premier. In the election, the PQ found support among intellectuals, the new business elite, trade unions, the poor of East Montreal, and the Saguenay region of Northern Québec, where 300,000 Francophones lived in geographical isolation. The new government passed a historic piece of legislation labeled Law 101. It made French the only official language in Québec as well as the normal language of the workplace and mandated that Québec's large immigrant influx be educated in French. The law was successful in that it increased the number of Francophones and gave them a sense of security about the future of their language, but it also—understandably—offended Anglophones in Québec and fellow Canadians. Separatists suffered a stinging defeat in 1980, however, when a provincial

Québec premier Jacques Parizeau greets supporters following the 1995 referendum on Québec separatism. (Archive Photos, Shaun Best, Reuters)

referendum on "sovereignty-association" was rejected by a decisive 60 percent to 40 percent margin.

The Constitution. Much of the following period dealt with constitutional matters. A new constitution was adopted by Canadians in 1982, but unfortunately it was the result of a last-minute backroom deal negotiated by the political elites of Canada without the participation of the Québec premier. Québecers felt betrayed by their fellow Canadians and refused to accept the legitimacy of the new constitution. Much time was then given to crafting a series of constitutional amendments that would enable Québec to accept the new document.

Prospects looked bright in 1984 when Brian MUL-RONEY was elected prime minister of Canada. Although an Anglophone, Mulroney was a native-born Québecer who spoke French fluently and sympathized with Québec's concerns. It appeared Mulroney and the provincial prime ministers had reached an understanding in the MEECH LAKE ACCORD of 1987. Québec was recognized as a "distinct society" and would be encouraged to defend and preserve its unique character. The accord also gave Québec more control over immigration, an important voice in the selection of Supreme Court justices, greater authority over federal spending programs within the province, and a veto over constitutional amendments. For the accord to become effective, the Canadian Parliament and all the provincial legislatures had to ratify it by 1990. Not all provincial legislatures did so, however, reflecting English-speaking opinion that the Accord yielded too much to Québec. After the "betrayal" of the constitution, Québecers now added a sense of rejection by English-speaking Canada to their grievances.

Prime Minister Mulroney failed to give up. Believing that it was unwise to portray any new constitutional agreement as focusing exclusively upon Québec, he broadened the issue, knowing that other Canadian provinces shared some of Québec's reservations concerning the federal government. Once again, the prime ministers of Canada and of the provinces believed they had reached an understanding, this time at Charlottetown, Prince Edward Island, in 1992. Much of what Québec had been granted at Meech Lake was renewed, including the "distinct society" clause. But there were concessions favorable to other Canadian provinces, especially in the West, and also to Canada's aboriginal peoples. The Charlottetown Accord had to be approved by referendums held in every province. Public opinion was initially favorable but

began to turn, especially after Pierre TRUDEAU, a former Canadian prime minister and a Québecer, criticized it. Many Canadians believed that the federal government would be denuded of legitimate power, and the concessions granted to Québec appeared too extensive. Ironically, the Québécois denounced the agreement for not going far enough in meeting their demands. In October, 1992, six provinces voted against the accord, including Québec, and the total nationwide vote was 54 percent against it.

An Uncertain Future. The post-Charlottetown era was marked by uncertainty and anxiety. In 1990, a new political party, the Bloc Québécois, was formed to fight for sovereignty on the federal level just as the PQ did on the provincial level. In the 1993 federal election, the Liberal Party won handily, but the Bloc Québécois won fifty-four seats and became the second-largest party in the Canadian Parliament. English Canada realized with apprehension that the "official opposition" was dedicated to pulling out of Canada. The unthinkable was now a possibility: Canada might be breaking up.

In 1994, the PQ won the provincial election, mainly because of the unpopularity of the Liberal Party rather than any marked increase in separatist sentiment. Nevertheless, the new premier, Jacques Parizeau, promised to hold a referendum on the sovereignty issue during his term of government. While public opinion polls showed a majority of Québecers against separation, political observers noted that any slight or insult directed against Québec invariably resulted in a dramatic upsurge in support. Separatists argued that not until Québecers approved a referendum authorizing separation would the province have the necessary political clout to negotiate from a position of strength. In turn, Québecers opposed to sovereignty felt uneasy that separatists had not provided specific details about separation, including such crucial matters as currency, passports, disposition of federal property, and sharing of the Canadian national debt.

In the mid-1990's, any number of scholars, journalists, and statesmen were writing doomsday scenarios of what the future might hold. The stakes involved were enormous: the survival of the Québécois people and the integrity of the Canadian state. Few Québecers or Canadians were overly confident that a solution reconciling these two apparently contradictory aspirations would readily be found.   —*David C. Lukowitz*

SUGGESTED READINGS: John Saywell's *Canada: Pathways to the Present* (Toronto: Stoddart, 1994) is a brief, readable introduction, placing Québec within the Canadian context. Sympathetic accounts of Québec's position can be found in Graham Fraser's *PQ: René Lévesque and the Parti Québécois in Power* (Toronto: Macmillan of Canada, 1984) and in René Lévesque's *Memoirs*, translated by Philip Stratford (Toronto: McClelland & Stewart, 1986). More scholarly and objective treatments are editor R. Kent Weaver's *The Collapse of Canada?* (Washington, D.C.: Brookings Institution, 1992) and Jeffrey Simpson's *Faultlines: Struggling for a Canadian Vision* (Toronto: Harper-Collins, 1993).

Queen v. Finta (1994): Supreme Court of Canada case. In *Finta*, the court upheld the validity of war-crimes statutes in Canada's Criminal Code. The defendant had been charged with having operated an investigative unit in World War II Hungary that had helped to send Jews to concentration camps. Although it ruled that the legislation was constitutional, the court announced a split decision in its reasoning that had the practical effect of making Canadian prosecutions for war crimes and crimes against humanity extremely difficult.

Queen v. Keegstra (1990): Supreme Court of Canada case. In *Keegstra*, the court upheld the validity of portions of Canada's criminal code that outlawed the willful promotion of hate. Keegstra, a schoolteacher, had been dismissed for teaching Holocaust denial and Jewish-conspiracy theories to students. The court held that the legislation represented a "reasonable limit" on the freedom of expression guaranteed in the CHARTER OF RIGHTS AND FREEDOMS.

Queen v. Morgentaler, Smoling, and Scott (1988): Supreme Court of Canada case. In the *Morgentaler* decision, the court ruled that the existing law governing the ability to obtain an ABORTION in Canada violated the Canadian CHARTER OF RIGHTS AND FREEDOMS. The Canadian abortion law, which had been passed by the federal Parliament in 1968, made abortion a crime unless a committee of three doctors determined that the mother's life or health would be endangered by continuing the pregnancy. The court concluded that these limitations violated a woman's right to life, liberty, and security of the person. The

decision left Canada without any legal restrictions on obtaining or performing abortions.

Queen v. Sullivan and LeMay (1991): Supreme Court of Canada case. The defendants in *Sullivan and LeMay* were midwives who were charged with criminal negligence after a child they were attempting to deliver died while still in the birth canal. The central issue was the legal status of a partially born child. According to Canadian law, an unborn child is considered to be a fetus until removed, living, from the mother, and a fetus is not considered to be a human being. Therefore, the court ruled, the defendants could not be charged with having caused the death of a human being.

Queen v. Zundel (1992): Supreme Court of Canada case. In *Zundel*, the court struck down a provision of Canada's criminal code against the spreading of false information. The defendant had been charged with having violated the statute by publishing a pamphlet claiming that the Holocaust of World War II was a myth promulgated by an international Jewish conspiracy. The court ruled that the law was an unconstitutional limitation on freedom of expression.

Queer Nation: Radical gay and lesbian activist organization. Founded in 1991, Queer Nation is dedicated to the "subversion of heterosexism and homophobia in all of its various cultural, political, and economic manifestations." The organization uses many high-profile nonviolent tactics to get its point across, such as press conferences, marches, vigils, and other protests. Unlike most activist organizations, Queer Nation has no hierarchy of officers yet manages to perform public services such as charity work, education, and limited research. The organization holds regular meetings and actively recruits participants.

Quinlan, Karen, case: Controversy regarding a parent or guardian's right to refuse treatment for a critically injured patient. On April 15, 1975, twenty-one-year-old Karen Ann Quinlan lapsed into a coma and was admitted to St. Clare's Hospital in Denville, N.J., where she was placed on a respirator. In July, her father, Joseph Quinlan, signed a release permitting

Joe and Julia Quinlan pose with a photograph of their daughter Karen Ann Quinlan in 1979. (AP/Wide World Photos)

physicians to turn off the respirator, but they refused. Joseph Quinlan was then appointed his daughter's guardian, with the power to discontinue all extraordinary means of sustaining vital processes. In ensuing litigation, a Superior Court judge decided in favor of the hospital; the New Jersey Supreme Court overturned the Superior Court's ruling. After she was taken off the respirator, Karen Ann lived for nine more years.

R

Rabbis, female: Rabbis serve as the spiritual heads of Jewish congregations within synagogues and in communities at large. Since ancient times, the rabbi has also served as sage, as interpreter of the Bible and religious tradition, and as a judge within the Jewish community.

Traditionally, the rabbi has always been a male. There were several reasons for this, based upon traditional interpretation of *Halacha*, or biblical law. According to this interpretation, a number of functions carried out by the rabbi were proscribed to women. For example, women were not traditionally allowed to serve as judges, as cantors, or as readers of the Torah during religious services. In particular, the question of whether a woman could serve as judge, an important role for the rabbi, precluded her ordination. A woman was also considered unqualified to be *motzi*, that is, to act as an agent in performance of obligations required among men (such as the recitation of the seven benedictions at a wedding), or to be considered as part of a *minyun*, the ten adults who must be present for a service to proceed. It should be noted that women were not considered inferior in Jewish tradition; passages in the Talmud even refer to women as more intelligent than men. A man was also required by religious law to respect his wife more than himself. Yet the obligations imposed on women were based on their status as homemakers rather than scholars.

With the evolution of conservative Judaism in the latter half of the twentieth century, and within both Reform and Reconstructionist Judaism, the interpretation of *Halacha* became more liberal. Upon becoming a *bat mitzvah* (the granting of adult status at the age of twelve), women became eligible to take on many of the duties, obligations, and privileges previously open only to men. This would eventually include ordination into the rabbinate.

As early as 1846, Reform rabbis suggested that women should be granted religious equality. Yet it was not until 1972 that Hebrew Union College-Jewish Institute of Religion, a Reform institution, ordained the first woman rabbi. Within ten years, more than seventy women had been ordained at that seminary. The Reconstructionist Rabbinical College, founded in Phila-

delphia in 1968, ordained its first woman rabbi in 1974. In 1984, the Conservative movement granted women the right to be candidates for the rabbinate. More than seventy women were admitted to the Jewish Theological Seminary in New York, and in 1985, Amy Eilberg became the first woman ordained as a rabbi within the Conservative movement.

Many Orthodox Jews, basing their beliefs upon a strict interpretation of a literal Bible, continue to maintain that women cannot be ordained as rabbis. The question has caused significant controversy even within the Orthodox tradition. Jewish feminists, many of whom consider themselves Orthodox, argue that biblical law was not meant to exclude women from many of the obligations or privileges traditionally granted to men and that interpretations of biblical law that call for such exclusion are incorrect.

Rabin, Yitzhak (Mar. 1, 1922, Jerusalem—Nov. 4, 1995, Tel Aviv, Israel): Israeli military and political

Yitzhak Rabin addresses reporters in 1988. (UPI/Corbis-Bettmann)

leader. An avid defender of Israel throughout his military career, Rabin is best known for leading Israel toward peace with the Palestinians and Arabs, an achievement for which he was awarded the Nobel Peace Prize in 1994. Rabin, who was graduated from an agricultural school, joined the Palmach, a commando unit of the Jewish Defense Force, in 1941. He fought against Vichy France in World War II and held a leadership position during Israel's 1948 war of independence. He served as army chief of staff from 1964 to 1968, playing a vital role in Israel's victory in the 1967 SIX-DAY WAR. From 1968 to 1973, he served as ambassador to the United States; in 1974, he became head of the Labor Party and his country's first native-born prime minister. In 1984, he became Israel's defense minister, and he was reelected prime minister in 1992. In November, 1995, moments after he had addressed a Tel Aviv peace rally, Rabin was assassinated by Yigal Amir, a right-wing Israeli opposed to the peace process.

Race: One of the most misunderstood concepts in American society, both intellectually and socially. From the nation's beginning, the idea of race permeated every aspect of American social, political, and economic life. The construction of an American racial ideology resulted in the subordination of ethnic and social minorities, the entrenchment of institutional racism, and the perpetuation of race-oriented conflict. Race defines many of the most contentious contemporary issues confronting American society.

History. Although the assignment of people to hierarchical social roles that are perceived as immutable coincides with the development of state systems, it was not until the eighteenth century that European scientists systematically divided the world's peoples into various racial taxonomies. The scientific division of people into racial categories parallels the evolution of empirical science, especially natural history. The rise of scientific inquiry led to hypotheses about the origin and meaning—biologically and socially—of human variation.

As early as 1684, French physician François Bernier, using facial features and body shape as criteria, classified the world's people into four basic human types. Over the next 150 years, distinguished European scientists such as Carolus Linnaeus, Johann Blumenbach, and Anders Retzius would use various anatomical measurements, particularly of the cranium,

to classify humans into distinct "races." Depending on the criteria used in defining races, scientists claimed as few as two races and as many as 150 distinct human races. Attached to these various racial taxa were a number of biological and social characteristics that were themselves viewed inseparable from various races. Myths about racial purity, racial blood, as well as numerous beliefs about racial superiority and inferiority arose in various political and economic contexts.

The construction of racial categories and theories by European scholars provided scientific evidence and justification for everything from cultural achievements to Western European exploration and colonization. Racial categories provided European colonial powers the ideological justification to exploit other people throughout the world. A similar racial ideology was exported to the United States.

In the colonization of the Americas, racial ideologies flourished to define "civilization" and "progress" in building a new nation. Initially, Native Americans were racially defined as inferior savages, making extermination not only possible but desirable. Later, racial arguments would be used to justify African slavery as well as the shaping of immigration policy in the United States throughout the late nineteenth and early twentieth centuries. It is during this time period, 1860 to 1940, that racial ideology became firmly entrenched into the fabric of American society. Americans adopted from the biological notion of race the idea that phenotypic characteristics not only define racial membership, but are often articulated with social abilities and potential achievement. Many racial minorities and ethnic groups experienced extreme prejudice and discrimination, despite their many contributions to American society.

Simultaneously, however, political and economic events at home and abroad began the process of challenging the American construction of race. The rise of African American and immigrant labor as an economic force, the racial politics of the Third Reich, the increasing importance of science to explain social issues, and other political and economic factors promoted the dismantling of the race concept.

Scientific evidence in the 1990's seemed to invalidate the notion of race as a biological reality, yet race as a sociological construct continues to exist in American society. As a "folk concept," race remains a powerful force in promoting social inequalities and limiting opportunity in every segment of American life.

The Concept. The concept of race is rooted in two

HOW ARE RACE RELATIONS IN THE UNITED STATES?

	Whites Polled	Blacks Polled
Excellent	1%	2%
Good	22%	10%
Fair	44%	45%
Poor	31%	41%

Source: The *Newsweek* Poll, February, 1995.

interconnected domains. As history suggests, the concept of race contains biological and social dimensions. From a biological perspective, human races are viewed as subspecies within the species *Homo sapiens.* Each major subcategory, it is argued, has certain inherited physical traits that distinguish that particular subpopulation. With the understanding of the process of evolution, along with the development of population genetics, those scholars who still subscribe to the concept of race identify somewhat distinct subpopulations, or races, by the frequency of hereditary traits or clusters of genotypes and phenotypes. These genetic frequencies are influenced greatly by geographic and social barriers that form relatively isolated breeding populations.

Throughout the history of the biology of race, various criteria have been utilized to discern races. Early on, scientists focused exclusively on anatomical traits. Later, blood chemistry and physiological functions were used to define racial categories. Most recently, the genetic structure of human populations has been used to identify races, but with little success.

The sociological conception of race is grounded in the political and economic reality of American life. Race as a social "fact" is based on society's material relations, which has used simplistic physical (phenotypic) or behavioral (cultural) differences to generate or maintain hegemonic societal relations. Although racial formations have shifted with the political and economic changes in the United States, using race as a form of domination drew its credibility from the idea that innate physical differences prevented some humans from achieving their full potential. In other words, social inequities are rooted in fundamental biological differences and, hence, are part of the natural order. Recent proposals about racial differences in intelligence follow this line of argument. In the United States, race as a biological and social phenomenon remains vitally important in defining access and oppor-

tunity to resources for American citizens, despite the fallacious foundations on which these race concepts are built.

Validity. Few scholars, especially anthropologists, currently accept the notion that the concept of distinct human races has any biological validity. Genetically, there is not any specific gene or cluster of genes exclusively found among one sociologically defined race; nor are "races" marked by significant differences in gene frequencies. Genetic evidence indicates that there is greater intragroup variation within a population typically labeled as a race than between the races. In addition, since the beginning of scientific inquiry about racial differences, scholars have used various phenotypic traits to construct racial typologies. All these physical traits are insignificant in defining racial differences.

The rejection of biological races within the confines of science is almost complete. Few in American society, however, are willing to discard entirely biological notions about race. Race continues to exist as a social category, incorrectly supported by the illusion of biology. From the halls of Congress to the national media, Americans are unwilling to relinquish their comprehension of race. American laws and stereotypes continue to use physical traits or attributes to categorize individuals into racial groups. Race therefore is a social construction that is perpetuated by human interaction and societal forces rather than biological fact. The American racial order continually is formulated by conflict over political and economic resources, rivalries over territory and cultural expression, and other hegemonic forces. Races as social categories, like biological races, are in a constant state of flux and are relationally constructed so as to have no meaningful independent existence. Nevertheless, the ever-changing existence of racial formation ensures the continued presence of societal oppression in the form of RACISM.

Implications. The development of racism paralleled the construction—scientifically and socially—of race as a concept. The construction of race is related to the creation of hegemonic relations in the developing American political economy. Events such as the territorial expansion of the United States, SLAVERY, and IMMIGRATION, for example, contributed significantly to the development of a racist ideology.

That ideology continues into the 1990's. Despite the challenges posed by the CIVIL RIGHTS MOVEMENT and progressive thinkers in the society, race and racism are not declining in significance. As the American political economy erodes, race and racism continue to resurface to solidify societal inequities. Across the country, there is a resurgence of racist ideologies that claim to explain physical, mental, and cultural differences, labeling some as superior and others as deficient.

Conclusions. Race is not a biological fact but a societal myth. Science has long recognized that racial categories are devoid of any real meanings. Despite the scientific retreat from the biological construction of race, race as a social category continues to gain acceptance in American society. As a social construction, race has destroyed countless lives, denying them access to resources as well as the ability to pursue societal opportunities. Contrary to popular belief about the declining significance of race perpetuated by politicians and some intellectuals, race seems likely to remain a viable oppressive force in American society until the society itself undergoes a radical restructuring of its political-economic fabric.

—*Gregory R. Campbell*

SUGGESTED READINGS: *The Mismeasure of Man* (New York: W. W. Norton, 1993) by Stephen J. Gould is a valuable introduction to the scientific development of the race concept. Audrey Smedley provides an excellent treatise on the development of the race concept in America in *Race in North America: Origin and Evolution of a Worldview* (Boulder, Colo.: Westview Press, 1993). *Human Biodiversity: Genes, Race, and History* (New York: Aldine de Gruyter, 1995) by Jonathan Marks is a wide-ranging discussion about human variation.

Eugenia Shanklin's *Anthropology and Race* (Belmont, Calif.: Wadsworth, 1994) is a concise introduction to anthropology's role in the construction and deconstruction of race. With regard to the societal implications of race in America and the world, see Michael Omi and Howard Winant's *Racial Formation in the United States: From the 1960's to the 1990's*, 2d ed. (New York: Routledge, 1994); Howard Winant's *Racial Conditions: Politics, Theory, Comparisons* (Minneapolis: University of Minnesota Press, 1994); and Melvin Leiman's *The Political Economy of Racism* (London: Pluto Press, 1993).

Race riots: Violent mob actions growing out of conflicts between groups with different racial or cultural backgrounds. In the United States, there have been many violent riots involving hostile ethnic groups, but outbreaks between blacks and whites have been most common. White-dominated riots have resulted from fears of black violence combined with the desire to maintain white supremacy. Black-dominated riots generally have been associated with resentment against long-standing patterns of racial discrimination and the desire for social change. Almost all race riots are precipitated by a violent interracial incident or by a rumor of such an incident.

Most nineteenth century riots were both initiated and dominated by whites. In several incidents before the Civil War, whites violently attacked black neighborhoods in northern cities. When SLAVERY ended, many white laborers were fearful that free blacks would undermine wages and increase unemployment, and the Conscription Act of 1863 provoked lower-class white New Yorkers to attack and kill blacks in a rampage lasting four days. During the period of Reconstruction, Southern whites, supported by the local police, resorted to riots as a means of intimidating blacks and opposing Republican policies. A riot in 1866 in New Orleans, Louisiana, resulted in thirty-six deaths in one day; that same year a riot occurred in Memphis, Tennessee, with forty-eight people killed, two of them white.

In the twentieth century, American participation in foreign wars exacerbated the dislocations and ethnic competition that produce riots; the vast majority of large-scale riots took place in the periods 1917-1919, 1942-1943, and 1965-1968. During the "red summer" of 1919, whites, often with police support, initiated some twenty-five racial incidents. There were two especially violent events: in Chicago more than thirty-eight died during a week of rioting, and in Arkansas white planters responded to rumors of black insurrection by killing as many as two hundred black sharecroppers. By the time of World War II, blacks began to initiate riots, as in the black-dominated uprisings that occurred in Harlem in 1935 and 1943. Although black youths began the Detroit riot of 1943, whites quickly counterattacked and laid siege to the black community, with the police killing seventeen blacks and no whites.

The urban riots occurring between 1965 and 1968 presented the United States with one of its historic threats to public order. During these years, an estimated half-million African Americans took part in riots in three hundred cities, resulting in some fifty thousand arrests and eight thousand personal injuries. Typically, the rioters focused primarily on looting and destroying white-owned property in black communities, leading to violent confrontations between rioters

Police struggle with a black man during a 1943 race riot in Detroit. (AP/Wide World Photos)

and police. The first major explosion occurred in the Los Angeles suburb of Watts in the summer of 1965; the most violent disturbance took place in 1967 in Detroit, resulting in forty-three deaths. Following the assassination of Martin Luther KING, Jr., in April, 1968, the nation was rocked by a wave of violent uprisings in more than a hundred cities.

The report of the National Commission on Civil Disorders of 1968, or the KERNER REPORT, emphasized the role of white racism and the isolation of the black ghetto; it concluded that the United States was "moving towards two separate societies, one Black, one White—separate and unequal." Although the waves of violent disturbances did not recur after 1968, inner-city blacks continued to be frustrated by a lack of economic opportunity and by perceptions of racial injustice, usually symbolized by police brutality against blacks. The MIAMI RIOTS of 1980 and the LOS ANGELES RIOTS of 1992, both sparked by acquittals of police officers charged with misconduct involving blacks, provided clear evidence of an enduring possibility of violent racial disturbances.

SUGGESTED READINGS: A good place to begin is with the *Report of the National Advisory Commission on Civil Disorders* (New York: Bantam Books, 1968). Allen Grimshaw includes several interpretations in *Racial Violence in the United States* (Chicago: Aldine Pub. Co., 1969). James Button gives a good summary and a useful bibliography in *Black Violence: Political Impact of the 1960s Riots* (Princeton, N.J.: Princeton University Press, 1978).

Racism: People with racist belief systems group humans into superior and inferior hereditary biological categories based on either phenotypic (color) or ethnic diversity. Frequently, racism is a cultural construct that combines popular folk prejudice and pseudoscientific explanations with legal sanctions to establish or maintain economic, political, and cultural dominance. It is not uncommon for members of minorities to use racism in order to enhance group cohesion. Only after World War II was an effective legal and scientific offensive launched in the United States against a system that had discriminated against Native Americans, African Americans, and people of Asian, Mexican, Jewish, and Southern and Eastern European descent.

Causes. Scholars have debated whether racism, like ethnocentrism, is a universal phenomenon. Carl Degler, a Stanford historian and specialist on comparative ra-

cism, suggests that prejudice based on visible biological differences is universal. By contrast, anthropologist Audrey Smedley thinks that racism is a specific cultural creation. There is also disagreement about the roots of the word "RACE." There is evidence that it emerged from the Latin root *ratio*, which refers to a kind or species. In Spanish, the word often was applied to specific breeds of horses. Not until the seventeenth century was the term "race" used in English to refer to humans. In English, the term became rigid and was applied exclusively to racial groupings.

Most ancient texts say little about the physical features of different ethnic groups. Moses Finley, a specialist on classical antiquity, argues that ancient Greeks and Romans perceived slaves as inferior by nature. The oldest sacred Hindu book, the *Rigveda*, exhorts its believers to "destroy the Dasa race." In recent decades, Indian merchants were persecuted by racist Africans in Uganda, and Chinese merchants faced discrimination in many areas of the Far East, particularly in Malaysia. From Asia to Africa to the Middle East, ethnic and racial persecution was widespread. Often, economic, cultural, and religious conflicts produced racism.

Obvious physical differences, ranging from skin color to height, also have contributed to racial antagonisms. Discrimination against people of different skin color is not a Western or American invention. For example, Hinduism, like the Judeo-Christian tradition, associates good with white and evil with black. Even in modern Indian society, there is some preference for lighter skin, although such preference is not as pronounced as in the United States. In the African kingdoms of Rwanda and Burundi, the Tutsis who ruled over the Hutu majority generally were taller and, according to anthropologist Pierre L. van den Berghe, originally had non-Negroid features. Modern ethnic conflicts have continued between the Tutsis and Hutus and have resulted in the massacre of thousands of people. As another example, in Zaria in northern Nigeria, lighter skin color was considered preferable as a racial characteristic by the dominant Fulani rulers.

There is little question, however, that Western racism has had the greatest impact on the world. Beginning with the colonial expansion of the sixteenth and seventeenth centuries, European power expanded globally. By the nineteenth century, Europeans dominated the globe. Meanwhile, Europeans created a pseudoscientific racist ideology unmatched in scope by other societies. European economic needs and racism were responsible for the diaspora of millions of Africans to North and South America. Western racism, however, did not merely affect people of color in the Third World. In Europe, for example, Nazi racism resulted in the mass murder of millions of Jews between 1941 and 1945.

The anthropologist Pierre L. van den Berghe explains Western racism by focusing on three factors. First, he believes that capitalism and the economic exploitation of Africans played a key role in fostering the growth of a racist ideology. Second, Darwinism, which stressed the "survival of the fittest," was adopted by Social Darwinists, who offered a "scientific" explanation for the inferiority of black people. Finally, in order to escape the contradiction created by the Western libertarian ideas of the American Revolution and the existence of SLAVERY, the humanity of slaves had to be denied. Berghe concludes that slaves were treated better in aristocratically dominated Latin America and in African kingdoms than in what he calls the *Herrenvolk* (master race) democracy of North America.

Types. Historically, racism in the United States was most consistently directed against people who could be identified by obvious physical characteristics. The primary objects of racism have been people of obvious Native American, African, Asian, and Mexican or other Latin American descent. At times, white ethnic Americans such as Italians, Jews, Poles, and the Irish were targets of racism. Often, racism was a product of economic competition or cultural or religious conflicts. In terms of persistence and vehemence, African Americans and Native Americans suffered the most. Some minorities focused their own racism on other minorities. For example, especially in urban areas, anti-Semitism among African Americans has been a consistent phenomenon since the 1930's.

Authorities question whether racism directed against black people preceded or followed the enactment of laws that established SLAVERY. Historians Carl Degler and Winthrop Jordan argue that race prejudice preceded such laws, but George Frederickson maintains that before the passage of slave legislation, Africans were treated much like white servants in North America. In any case, racism against black people in North America became absolute; it recognized no gradations of mixed race status, as was common in Latin America. In comparison to ethnic whites, the ability of African Americans to escape race and class barriers was limited.

White attitudes toward both Native Americans and African Americans have been attributed to the English experience with the Irish. In their attempts to subjugate the Irish, the English developed an image of a heathen savage who could be exploited and described in racial terms. This is precisely the behavior that the English applied to both Native Americans and African Americans. Many English people who had participated in the conquest of Ireland took part in the colonization of the New World.

At first, the English argued that religion and savagery justified the conquest of Indians and the enslavement of Africans. John Winthrop, a leader of the Puritans, responded to a smallpox epidemic in 1617 with the comment that it was God's method of thinning out Indians "to make room for the Puritans." Although some colonial Americans described Native Americans as "noble savages," only the image of the savage survived.

In the nineteenth century, Lieutenant Colonel George Custer, famed for his defeat at Little Bighorn, said that "nature intended him [the Indian] for a savage state." In the early twentieth century, President Theodore Roosevelt justified the seizure of Indian land by concluding that "this great continent could not have been kept as nothing but a game preserve for squalid savages." Native Americans who survived military attacks and diseases introduced by Europeans were subjected to contradictory policies of tribalization and mainstreaming.

By the end of the seventeenth century, skin color, not religion or savagery, emerged as the primary rationale for slavery. Laws were passed in Virginia and in other states that converted black servants into hereditary slaves. A well-defined racist ideology emerged gradually. This ideology was in part a direct response to the rise of abolitionist propaganda during the early nineteenth century. To justify holding black people in slavery, whites classified them as inferior. As early as 1774, Edward Long, a West Indies planter, argued that black people belonged to a separate species, and were closely related to orangutans. Developments in the field of science also contributed to the acceptance of negrophobic racism. Scientists such as Carolus Linnaeus and Johann Blumenbach in the eighteenth century began to classify humans according to various racial categories. In the nineteenth century, the influential Harvard zoologist Louis Agassiz argued that blacks and whites belonged to different species, a view that he passed on to his students. During the nineteenth century and early in the twentieth century, sci-

Black swimmers are beaten by a group of whites during a racially motivated 1964 Florida incident. (UPI/Corbis-Bettmann)

entists used a variety of measurements, ranging from the study of craniums, jaws, and foreheads to intelligence tests, to rank humans. Black people nearly always were placed at the bottom of the scale.

Racism in the Postbellum Era. The Civil War and the elimination of Southern slavery did not abolish American racism, either in the South or in the North. During the Civil War, the U.S. Sanitary Commission studied the different races in the Union Army and concluded that blacks were inferior to whites. The commission claimed that blacks had smaller brains and were closer to apes, although their good physical structures made them fit for the military. Before and after the Civil War, the majority of states outlawed racial intermarriages between whites and people of African, Asian, or Indian descent.

After the Civil War, the most important organized racist group that emerged was the KU KLUX KLAN. The Klan of the Reconstruction era was organized in the South in order to limit the political power of emancipated slaves. The Klan of the 1920's, on the other hand, attacked Catholics, Jews, and African Americans. The second clan was politically most influential in the Midwest and West. By the beginning of the twentieth century, African Americans had been effectively disenfranchised by JIM CROW LAWS in the American South and were subjected to racial SEGREGATION in much of the rest of the country.

Racist ideas permeated both the academic world and influential publications. In 1895, an article in the American edition of the *Encyclopaedia Britannica* attributed the "inherent mental inferiority of the blacks" to the "premature ossification of the skull." Some psychologists maintained that the "Nordic race" was intellectually superior. Madison Grant published a bestseller called *The Passing of the Great Race* (1916), in which he preached the virtues of Nordic superiority. He warned of the dangers of miscegenation with black people and cautioned that "inferior" white races could also contaminate the American racial elite. Grant even argued that Jesus Christ was a Nordic, not a Jew.

The Spread of Racism. Racism extended to other groups as well. As early as 1899, a writer in *The Atlantic Monthly* had argued that "to trust a Greaser [Mexican] is to take a long jump into utter darkness." According to L. L. Burlingame, a Stanford University biologist who published a book dealing with heredity and social problems in 1940, "Mexicans present the second most serious race problem" for the United States, next to that of African Americans. The American Genetics Society's journal *Eugenics* published an article in 1929 that equated Mexican "peons" with African Americans.

Mexicans were often needed as laborers in the United States, particularly during World War II. As soon as the need for labor disappeared, efforts began to deport the unwanted Hispanics. Racism affected Mexicans in the realms of education and housing much as it did African Americans. Mexicans also experienced race-related violence, notably in the Zoot Suit riots in Los Angeles, California, in 1943.

Chinese and Japanese immigrants not only faced racial prejudice but also were prohibited from entering the United States. In 1882, Congress passed an exclusion law against Chinese immigrants, and during 1907 and 1908, President Theodore Roosevelt negotiated a series of agreements, collectively known as the "Gentlemen's Agreement," with Japan to limit Japanese immigration to the United States. In both cases, the fear of the "yellow peril" was used to restrict IMMIGRATION.

Cultural and racial differences were exacerbated by economic competition with white American workers and farmers, primarily on the West Coast. People of Asian descent who remained in the United States or were born there of Asian parents were subjected to official racial discrimination. The Supreme Court decision in *Takao Ozawa v. United States* (1922) limited naturalization to white and black applicants and denied it to Asians. In another decision, *Gong Lum v. Rice* (1927), the Supreme Court agreed with a Mississippi court ruling that had ordered a Chinese student to attend a "colored" school. During World War II, Japa-

nese citizens and noncitizens were removed from the West Coast and sent to internment camps.

White immigrants and Americans who belonged to specific ethnic or religious groups also faced American "Anglo-Saxon" racism. In March, 1923, *The Atlantic Monthly* warned of the danger of Italians and Poles, because "these races at present figure so conspicuously among our immigrants." This kind of ethnic racism culminated when Congress passed new immigration laws in 1921 and 1924 that favored Northern and Western Europeans. Jews experienced similar racism in the 1920's and 1930's, facing attacks from the Ku Klux Klan and anti-Semitic publications. Most important to the emerging Jewish middle class were restrictions and quotas imposed on Jewish students and faculty members by prestigious universities and medical schools.

Racism in Canada. Canada, like the United States, has a pluralistic society, with French- and English-speaking citizens. Although Canadians have tended to be more tolerant toward multiculturalism than have Americans, they produced their share of racists. Slavery was abolished in 1834, when black people made up only 1 percent of the population. Yet American blacks who attempted to emigrate to Canada in 1911 were rejected because, allegedly, they would not be able to adjust to Canadian winters. As in the United States, Japanese citizens were interred during World War II. Italians and Jews who went to Canada also often faced nativism, and Metis, a people of European and Indian mixture, were stigmatized. The most serious racism was reserved for Asians. Chinese and Japanese people experienced violence in British Columbia, and East Indians were not allowed to enter Canada until the 1960's. Even then, they were not welcomed by Canadians. A public opinion poll in 1989 revealed growing intolerance among Canadians, and two-thirds of the respondents predicted a rise in racism over the next half century.

Social Costs. Native Americans arguably have suffered the most from white American domination. Indians represent the poorest members of American society, with average annual family incomes $1,000 below that of African Americans. Unemployment among American Indians has reached a level ten times the national average, and life expectancy is twenty years below the national average.

Not until 1968 did Congress pass the AMERICAN INDIAN CIVIL RIGHTS ACT, which granted protection to reservation Indians and recognized tribal law on reservations. Militant young Indian leaders organized the AMERICAN INDIAN MOVEMENT to advocate the interests of Indians, particularly in urban areas. Although there were signs of economic growth, especially in the business of legal gambling, years of cultural and economic deprivation still affect the lives of Native Americans.

Like Native Americans, African Americans have suffered cultural and economic hardships because of discrimination. World War II and the negative image of Nazi racism, however, helped the CIVIL RIGHTS MOVEMENT, which focused on the rights of African Americans. There has been undeniable progress, both economic and political, for African Americans since 1945. Congress passed the CIVIL RIGHTS ACT OF 1964 and the VOTING RIGHTS ACT of 1965. By measures such as the growth of the black middle class, the percentage of black college students, and the number of African American representatives in Congress, African Americans made significant gains from the mid-1960's into the mid-1990's.

On the other hand, the urban black underclass has not benefited markedly. The black underclass suffers from high rates of illegitimacy and sees limited economic opportunities. It is this class in particular that has proven most enthusiastically receptive to the anti-Semitic doctrine espoused by Louis FARRAKHAN and his NATION OF ISLAM. This organization distributed the notoriously anti-Semitic *Protocols of the Elders of Zion*, which purports to reveal a world Jewish conspiracy.

Economic competition in such urban centers as New York and Los Angeles has resulted in African American attacks on Korean-owned small businesses. Similar economic rivalry in the 1930's led to black attacks on Jewish businesses in Harlem. Some African Americans have also supported anti-immigrant nativism. California's PROPOSITION 187, a 1994 ballot proposition directed against illegal immigrants, won the support of 47 percent of black voters.

Anti-immigrant sentiments expressed during the 1980's and 1990's were a response, in part, to massive flows of legal and illegal Hispanic immigrants into the United States. Mexicans were the largest single group of illegal immigrants, but they were joined by political and economic refugees from many other Latin American countries and from around the world. Immigration flows have created a sizable Hispanic minority. In 1960, the U.S. Census recorded 3 million Hispanics. Thirty years later, 20 million were counted, although the actual number was perhaps as high as 30 million;

many may have chosen not to be counted in the census, particularly if they were in the country illegally. Like Native Americans and African Americans, Mexican Americans have asserted their cultural pride. During the 1960's, young Mexican Americans began to call themselves Chicanos, a term formerly used by whites in a derogatory sense. In 1974, partly in recognition of the size of the Hispanic population, the Supreme Court confirmed the right of Spanish-speaking students to receive education in their native language.

The economic diversity among Hispanics is great, ranging from successful Cuban businesspeople to impoverished Puerto Ricans in New York City. The Mexican American poverty rate of 20 percent in the early 1990's was far above the national average, as was the 30 percent rate for Puerto Ricans. Explanations for these high poverty rates range from racism to linguistic inabilities and family structure. Because of limited education and language skills, many young Hispanic immigrants can obtain only low-paying service jobs.

Economically and educationally, Asian Americans and Jews have been most successful in overcoming the limitations imposed by racism. Jews no longer are restricted from attending universities and professional schools. Public opinion polls between 1945 and 1981 revealed a pronounced decline in anti-Semitic prejudice, although residual anti-Semitism exists, particularly among less-educated members of society. Friction exists between groups in particular areas, for example, African Americans and members of the orthodox Jewish community in New York City. There have been numerous individual cases of black and white racist attacks on Chinese Americans and Asian Indians in urban centers. The culprits have ranged from unemployed auto workers in Detroit to Gulf Coast shrimpers.

The Immigration Reform and Control Act of 1965 opened the country to a massive influx of Asian immigrants. In 1965, 90 percent of legal immigrants came from Europe. By 1986, that figure had declined to only 10 percent. By 1990, Asian Americans numbered more than seven million. Asian Americans have been referred to as the "MODEL MINORITY" because of their rapid assimilation, economic success, and academic achievement.

The long-term economic, political, and psychological costs of American racism are still apparent. Civil rights legislation has not been able to eliminate racial perspectives and mistrust. In 1987, public opinion

An African American girl is subjected to racist taunts as she attempts to enter a Little Rock, Arkansas, high school in 1957. (UPI/Corbis-Bettmann)

polls revealed that 59 percent of whites but only 26 percent of blacks believed that blacks enjoyed equal employment opportunities with whites.

Nowhere is racial mistrust reflected more divisively than on the issues of AFFIRMATIVE ACTION and REVERSE DISCRIMINATION. A 1995 *Newsweek* magazine poll revealed that 62 percent of blacks but only 25 percent of whites believed that African Americans should receive special affirmative action support. Supreme Court decisions in 1995 that prohibited reverse discrimination and demanded a color-blind society have been answered by calls for continuation of affirmative action because the "playing field" in areas such as education and employment is not yet even. On the other side are those who argue that affirmative action has never benefited the most needy; benefits have gone largely to members of the black middle class. India presents an extreme example of a multicultural society where affirmative action has been used in an attempt to overcome a variety of forms of racial, ethnic, and religious discrimination. By 1995, half of India's population benefited from affirmative action programs; the other half was outraged to the point of rioting.

Racial dialogue in the United States has been complicated by several factors. First, the country is becoming more multicultural, with fewer than 80 percent of Americans in 1990 claiming European origins. Ironically, at the very time that racial preferences are demanded by some in the United States, many geneticists and anthropologists argued that the concept of classifying human races by using obvious physical differences makes little scientific sense. Looking at genetic data, these scientists argued that humans with obvious different physical characteristics may have more in common with one another than with members of their "own group." Perhaps if scientists, who played a key role in legitimizing racism during the nineteenth century, argue now that there is only one human race, there may be hope for the demise of racism.

—*Johnpeter H. Grill*

SUGGESTED READINGS: Analytical comparisons of racism in different societies are offered by Pierre L. van den Berghe in *Race and Racism: A Comparative Perspective* (New York: John Wiley and Sons, 1967), Martin N. Marger in *Race and Ethnic Relations: American and Global Perspectives*, 2d ed. (Belmont, Calif.: Wadsworth, 1991), and Johnpeter H. Grill and Robert Jenkins in "The Nazis and the American South in the 1930s: A Mirror Image?" (*The Journal of South

ern History*, November, 1992). Collections of primary documents on American racism include Lewis H. Carlson and George A. Colburn, eds., *In Their Place: White America Defines Her Minorities 1850-1950* (New York: John Wiley and Sons, 1972) and Melvin Steinfield, comp., *Cracks in the Melting Pot: Racism and Discrimination in American History*, 2d ed. (New York: Glencoe Press, 1973). The roots of American racism are examined by Audrey Smedley in *Race in North America: Origin and Evolution of a Worldview* (Boulder, Colo.: Westview Press, 1993) and Winthrop D. Jordan in *White over Black: American Attitudes Toward the Negro, 1550-1812* (Chapel Hill: University of North Carolina Press, 1968).

White and black racial attitudes are reviewed by Howard Schuman, Charlotte Steeh, and Lawrence Bobo in *Racial Attitudes in America: Trends and Interpretations* (Cambridge, Mass.: Harvard University Press, 1985). The prevalence of racism is emphasized by Alphonso Pinkney in *The Myth of Black Progress* (New York: Cambridge University Press, 1986). White and African American anti-Semitism is reviewed by Leonard Dinnerstein in *Anti-Semitism in America* (New York: Oxford University Press, 1994).

Radio Free Europe: U.S. government-sponsored corporation providing radio service to Eastern Europe. Radio Free Europe was founded in 1950 to broadcast uncensored news and pro-Western propaganda to citizens of Soviet Bloc nations. Radio Free Europe broadcasts in ten languages to some 25 million people in Bulgaria, the Czech Republic, Estonia, Hungary, Latvia, Lithuania, Poland, Romania, and Slovakia. Radio Free Europe spends about half of its broadcast time on news and news analysis, focusing on current events in the audience countries; the remainder is spent discussing cultural, religious, historical, economic, and political matters. Since the collapse of the Soviet Union and the end of the Cold War, critics have asserted that the service is an anachronism. Radio Free Europe merged with RADIO LIBERTY in 1976.

Radio Liberty: U.S. government-sponsored corporation providing radio service to the former Soviet Union and to Afghanistan. Radio Liberty Committee, Inc., was founded in 1951 to oppose attempts by Soviet Bloc governments to isolate their citizens from the rest of the world. Currently, Radio Liberty broadcasts in sixteen of the languages spoken in the former Soviet republics as well as in two languages spoken in Afghanistan. Many Radio Liberty programs consist of news and news analysis; other programs feature cultural, religious, historical, economic, and political matters. In 1976, Radio Liberty merged with RADIO FREE EUROPE.

Rain forests: Forests that develop under conditions of high rainfall every month of the year. Classically, the term implies tropical forests, but temperate rain forests, such as the coniferous forests of the Pacific Northwest in the United States and Canada, are also recognized. Rain forest exploitation for lumber, farming, and grazing has been questioned by conservationists. Opponents of such exploitation argue that the forests' role in global cycles and in the maintenance of biological diversity is of greater importance than the immediate economic gain from such intensive exploitation.

Rainbow Coalition: Activist organization founded 1983. Begun under the leadership of the Reverend Jesse JACKSON, the Rainbow Coalition is a multicultural effort to unify racial and ethnic groups that have been marginalized in the U.S. political process. Jackson founded the group in an effort to extend the activities of earlier CIVIL RIGHTS organizations; in the 1990's, however, the organization was torn by internal strife, as dissidents formed splinter groups or embraced mainstream Democratic Party positions.

Rainforest Action Network (RAN): Environmental organization founded in 1985. RAN is dedicated to protecting tropical rain forests and supporting the hu-

Kaiapo Indians march to protest destruction of Brazil's rain forests. (Archive Photos, Reuters, Wilson Melo)

man rights of their inhabitants through education, communication, grassroots organizing, lobbying, and nonviolent direct action. RAN has played an important role in strengthening concern for rain forest conservation by organizing and mobilizing community groups and consumers in the United States, supporting activists in tropical countries, and catalyzing educational and political activities. RAN's successes include the prompting of an influential international conference on rain forest protection, widely cited publications, and a consumer campaign that helped to persuade the Burger King Corporation to stop using beef from tropical countries, where rain forests are often denuded to provide pasture for cattle.

Rap music: Heavily rhythmic, largely African American style of popular music. Rap began as a primarily urban art form during the 1970's. New York City is most closely associated with the emergence of rap, as disc jockeys began speaking rhythmically over the records they played. They soon began experimenting with techniques such as mixing (combining musical elements from two or more records by switching

Rap star Ice-T defends his 1992 release "Cop Killer." (AP/Wide World Photos)

between two turntables) and scratching (using the hand to manipulate records and create scratching sounds to the beat). Rap music is part of hip-hop culture, which has also included GRAFFITI writing, breakdancing, and alternative forms of dress and speech.

Although artists such as James Brown had done some rapping on recordings as early as the 1960's, rap music in its own right remained an unrecorded medium until 1979. In that year, the first rap single, "Rapper's Delight" by the Sugarhill Gang, was released. The phenomenal success of that single opened the way for further efforts. Rap took on a new direction in 1982, when Grandmaster Flash and the Furious Five released their single "The Message," beginning a tradition of using rap music as a means of social commentary and criticism.

Since these early beginnings, rap has become much more popular, with record sales rivaling those of other types of music by the 1990's. It also became less identified with an urban black subculture, as whites have begun buying rap in increasing numbers. The use of rap music as a vehicle of social protest also became commonplace and has generated considerable controversy.

A number of controversies have arisen over issues raised by the growing popularity of rap music. The late 1980's saw the rise of so-called gangsta rap, with themes that were thought by many to glorify violence and promote disrespect for law-enforcement authorities. This provoked criticism by leading politicians and calls for censorship of recordings. Congressional hearings were held that focused on the standards and practices of the recording industry, with rap music being a key target of debate. Numerous police organizations, consumer groups, radio stations, and the music video channel MTV decided to boycott both songs with sexually explicit or violent subject matter and the record companies that produced them. The effects of this pressure were seen in high profile when Warner Bros. released rapper Ice-T from its label following public protests about his song "Cop Killer."

Rap has also generated controversy over the borrowing of musical elements from previous recordings. Because of the frequent use of borrowed materials, known as "samples," in rap music, composers of published works have initiated lawsuits to protect their copyrights. These have had various results. In one case, rap artist Vanilla Ice was required to pay millions of dollars for his appropriation of another artist's material. On the other hand, the Supreme Court dismissed a similar suit against the group Two Live Crew, citing the fair-use doctrine.

Many critics have also argued that rap music encourages violence, as some of the most prominent rap artists have been indicted for violent crimes, including Snoop Doggy Dogg and 2-Pac Shakur. Such incidents have kept rap in the public eye and have further politicized rap music.

Rape: Form of sexual assault. Rapes are generally classed as belonging to one of two general categories, forcible or statutory. The definition of forcible rape varies from state to state, but the crime is generally held to constitute sexual intercourse or any penetration of a body orifice of a nonconsenting person with objects or body parts by the use of force or threat of force. Statutory rape refers to sexual intercourse with a person who is below the age of consent, even though the victim may cooperate.

Historical Perspectives. In the United States, rape has traditionally been seen as occurring only to women and outside of marriage; however, in recent years, the definition has been broadened to include men and spouses as possible victims. This broadened definition is largely a result of changing attitudes toward the status of women, inside and outside of marriage. Historically, women have been seen as the property of their fathers and then of their husbands, with the female's greatest assets being her virginity as a daughter and, later, her fidelity as a wife. Therefore, rape was seen as a crime not against the woman but rather against her father or her husband. In fact, the word "rape" is derived from the Latin word for "theft." The logic that perceived women as property led to the belief that because a husband had exclusive sexual rights to his wife, it would therefore be impossible for him to rape his own wife. Such perceptions are changing, however, and by the 1990's, a husband could legally be found guilty of raping his wife.

The belief still exists that women want to be raped or that women secretly want a man to prove his masculinity and his desire by forcibly overcoming any resistance. Myths about sexual stereotypes also influence attitudes toward rape. For example, some cultures or ethnicities are seen as being more sexual than others; some women are often portrayed as "asking" for assault by their behaviors or their dress. The accusation of rape has been historically hard to prove, and some people believe that women often falsely accuse men of

Anti-rape graffiti in Minneapolis, 1991. (Avitava Kumar, Impact Visuals)

rape. However, Federal Bureau of Investigation statistics indicate that men are falsely accused of rape only about 5 percent of the time, which is the same rate as for any other felony.

In the United States in 1991, there were 124,480 rapes reported, or about eighty-three rapes for every 100,000 females. This means that about one in every eight adult women now living in the United States has been raped at least once, and it is estimated that probably one woman in four will be raped during her lifetime.

Types of Rapists. Based on a study of five hundred convicted rapists, three typologies of rapists have been profiled. The "anger rapist" is one who uses sexual assault as a means of expressing rage or anger. The rape, therefore, usually involves far more physical force than is necessary to subdue a victim. Approximately 40 percent of the five hundred convicts were in this category. For these assailants, the identity of the rape victim is insignificant; she could be any woman. However, the expression of hostility, anger, rage, contempt, hatred, or any other negative emotion is usually toward a significant woman in the rapist's life.

To the "power rapist," rape is more a means of expressing power than sexual gratification. Usually the attacker will only use the amount of force necessary to maintain control of the victim. This control enables the male to cope with his own feelings of inadequacy and insecurity. The rapist experiences anxiety, excitement, and anticipation as he plans and initiates his attack, which is often preceded by sexual fantasies. Of the five hundred offenders, 55 percent were in this category.

The "sadistic rapist" may stalk his victim, planning and waiting for the right moment to attack. Combining sexuality and aggression, this assailant may brutalize or torture his victim and may not have actual intercourse; rather, he may use an instrument such as a stick or a bottle, severely injuring or possibly causing the death of the victim. This type of perpetrator is usually mentally ill or under the influence of drugs. The sample of five hundred rapists included only 5 percent from this category.

Gang Rape. Gang rape is forced sexual intercourse with one victim, inflicted serially by several males. It may involve strangers, but recent research indicates that it is more likely to be perpetrated by acquaintances, especially on college campuses. In many cases, the victim may have had too much to drink or be under the influence of drugs. In most such cases, the perpe-

trators do not consider their behavior rape; rather, they perceive that they engaged in group sex with a willing partner. The likelihood for gang rape to occur is greater in extremely cohesive, highly motivated, tightly-knit groups. An example of this may be seen in the high incidence of gang rape by soldiers upon "conquered" enemy women during wartime.

Marital Rape. In 1985, the Supreme Court of Georgia upheld a wife's right to say "no" to intercourse with her husband. Forty-two states have made marital rape a crime; however, prosecutions for marital rape remain rare. Marital rape is attributed to two general cultural factors: the popular belief that men must express their masculinity by being able to dominate women, particularly their wives, and the long-held belief that wives cannot be raped because they are considered to be their husband's property. The husband's goal often

Activists at a 1992 New Jersey rally against rape. (Impact Visuals, Steve Latimer)

appears to be humiliation or retaliation against his wife, and physical force is usually involved.

Male Rape. Surveys at United States college campuses reveal that from 12 percent to 48 percent of male college students believe they have been forced or pressured to have nonconsensual sex. Most of this sex has been with female acquaintances who use blackmail or verbal pressure, such as pleading or threatening rather than physical force, with sodomy being the most common means of assault.

Another form of male rape is same-sex rape, where the rapists are usually heterosexual rather than homosexual. Recent research in men's prisons suggests that interpersonal sexual violence (especially as an expression of power) is relatively common, with probably about one out of every five prisoners experiencing rape. Other male-to-male rape scenarios include ones in which the assailants know their victims as their peer, coworker, subordinate, or date. The primary goal of male-to-male rape seems to be to subjugate and humiliate the victim, with the relief of sexual deprivation a secondary motive.

Generalized Factors About Rape. Although there is no "typical" rape, some factors seem to be characteristic of sexual assault in its many forms. Rapists often hold values that support a male role as sexual aggressor, such as the concept of machismo or the notion of male sexual biological needs that cannot be controlled. Another factor is the image of women as legitimate victims, for example, the belief that women need, deserve, or want to be raped. Moreover, the psychological "dating game" places stress on both males and females; the emphasis on the expression of sexuality in both male and female fashions and presentation of self promotes sexual tensions between genders; and the possible misinterpretation of intentions on the part of either victim or perpetrator presents ongoing conditions that are conducive to intense emotional reactions. Finally, the presence of alcohol appears to be a major factor in the vast majority of rapes.

There are critics who argue that it is often men accused of rape who are the victims, citing a legal system predisposed to favor a female's claim of rape. Because rape is associated with hostility, domination, and power issues, feminist scholars have suggested that when power gaps between men and women are narrowed or eliminated, rape will decrease, if not disappear.

—*Sandra Harte Bunce*

SUGGESTED READINGS: For an in-depth report on the study of convicted rapists, see Nicholas A. Groth's *Men Who Rape* (New York: Plenum Press, 1979). For more recent research on convicted rapists, read Diana Scully's *Understanding Sexual Violence: A Study of Convicted Rapists* (Boston: Unwin Hyman, 1990). For a discussion by a rape victim herself, read Susan Estrich's *Real Rape: How the Legal System Victimizes Women Who Say No* (Cambridge, Mass.: Harvard University Press, 1987).

Peggy R. Sanday offers a look at rape on college campuses in *Fraternity Gang Rape: Sex, Brotherhood, and Privilege on Campus* (New York: New York University Press, 1990). A classic on the subject of rape is Susan Brownmiller's *Against Our Will: Men, Women, and Rape* (New York: Simon & Schuster, 1975). The issue of marital rape is explored by David Finkelhor and Kersti Yllo in *License to Rape: Sexual Abuse of Wives* (New York: Holt, Rinehart, and Winston, 1985). For a study of the social consequences experienced by rape victims, see Lee Madigan and Nancy C. Gamble's *The Second Rape: Society's Continual Betrayal of the Victim* (New York: Lexington Books, 1991).

Reagan, Ronald (b. Feb. 6, 1911, Tampico, Ill.): Fortieth president of the United States (1981-1989). Whether they praise or damn President Reagan, most historians agree that he had a major impact on history. His administration weakened the progressive tax structure, lightened the regulatory burden on business, cut welfare services for the poor, and oversaw the end of the Cold War. Reagan moved the nation's political center to the right and created budget deficits that placed severe constraints on his successors.

The son of an alcoholic shoe salesman, Reagan believed that his own life proved that the United States was still the land of unlimited opportunities. In 1937, he left Illinois to became a movie and television star and by the early 1960's had developed into one of the nation's most popular conservative speakers. With the backing of conservative Republicans, he won the California governorship in 1966 and 1970. In 1980, Reagan won the Republican presidential nomination and that fall defeated Democrat Jimmy CARTER.

During his first two years in office, President Reagan subordinated everything to his economic program. He cut funds for domestic programs, raised military spending, and reduced taxes. To those who feared that this combination would lead to huge budget deficits, he promised that his economic program would unleash the dynamism of the U.S. economy. In late 1981, the

Ronald Reagan in 1987. (UPI/Corbis-Bettmann)

nation slid into a deep recession, and Reagan's popularity plummeted. He refused to change course, and his good luck held. In 1983, the economy began what proved to be the longest peacetime economic expansion in U.S. history. During his 1984 landslide victory over Democrat Walter Mondale, Reagan carried the vote in forty-nine states.

Reagan had a "hands-off" management style. He set the policy direction for his administration but left implementation to subordinates and remained remarkably disengaged from the operations of his own government. In 1985 and 1986, his lack of attention led to the IRAN-CONTRA AFFAIR. With Reagan's approval, members of his National Security Council staff tried to free U.S. hostages held in the Middle East by secretly selling arms to Iran, an anti-American terrorist state. They further violated congressional policy by diverting Iranian money to the Contra movement, which was trying to overthrow the leftist government of Nicaragua.

In November, 1986, these secret operations became public, and Reagan faced the most serious challenge of his presidency. His luck, however, held. Iran-Contra dropped from the headlines as world attention focused on the struggle by Soviet leader Mikhail GORBACHEV to move his nation toward democracy. Reagan responded to Gorbachev's overtures, and the two met five times to settle issues that divided their nations. In 1987, they signed the Intermediate-range Nuclear Forces Treaty, the first treaty that reduced the size of nuclear arsenals.

Reagan concluded his presidency on a high note. By 1989, the nation was peaceful and prosperous, and many people were getting used to the startling idea that the half-century-long COLD WAR with the Soviet Union was coming to an end. In the 1990's, however, the popular ex-president's activities were curtailed by a variety of health problems, including Alzheimer's disease.

Reality-based television: Programming that is principally based on news stories or other real-life events rather than drama. Television, like radio before it and print media before that, has long played a dual role as a provider of both entertainment and information. As a result, every major television network has devoted entire departments to news and news-oriented programming in addition to its creative divisions. In the 1980's and 1990's, "reality-based programming" grew in volume and popularity on the networks as well as in syndicated and local programming. Programs which fall into this category are both numerous and diverse.

The simplest and oldest form of reality programming is the regular newscast, which has been a part of broadcasting since the beginning of commercial radio. Besides regular newscasts, public-service announcements and community-based television have been in production for decades. In the late 1980's and the 1990's, however, commercial television moved increasingly into the "infotainment" arena, where real-life situations are examined and commented upon. Talk shows, beginning with the popular program hosted by Phil Donahue and continuing with shows starring Montel Williams, Leeza Gibbons, Maury Povich, Jerry Springer, and seemingly countless others, appeared by the dozens.

In addition to these shows, commercial programmers began to broadcast several police and law shows that attempt to depict real-life crime, such as *Cops*, *Real Stories of the Highway Patrol*, *America's Most Wanted*, and *Unsolved Mysteries*. It is perhaps these programs that are most often dubbed reality-based television. Some, such as *Cops*, aim their video cameras at the actual activities of law-enforcement personnel. Others, such as *Unsolved Mysteries*, combine documentary interview footage with dramatic recreations, and a number of commentators have noted that this blurring of the distinction between the actual and the imagined versions of events may have detrimental effects on the news media at large. For example, one controversial segment of the weekly newsmagazine program *Dateline NBC* in 1995 featured a rigged explosion of a truck's gas tank; the program failed to mention that the explosion was rigged.

Finally, with the huge expansion of cable television in the 1980's, whole networks devoted to what might be called reality-based programming came into existence. Cable News Network (CNN) broadcasts news constantly, the Weather Channel maintains round-the-clock surveillance of the weather, and Court TV has put the criminal justice system on television twenty-four hours a day. Large cable ventures such as these—and others such as ESPN, Discovery, and the Learning Channel—draw huge markets for advertisers.

Reasonable doubt: Principle of law related to the burden of proof in criminal cases. In U.S. criminal proceedings, the prosecution must prove a defendant's guilt beyond a reasonable doubt. If the prosecution fails to meet that standard of proof, the jury is instructed to acquit the defendant.

In the 1994-1995 O. J. SIMPSON case, for example, many observers believed that the defendant was factually guilty of murder charges. However, the defense was able to cast reasonable doubt in the minds of the jurors by raising questions regarding the time frame of the crime constructed by the prosecution and the veracity of the detectives who discovered and collected evidence.

Recession: Economics term. An economic recession is a period in which the GROSS DOMESTIC PRODUCT or GROSS NATIONAL PRODUCT declines for at least two successive three-month periods. A recession normally results in increased unemployment. No economic downswing since 1937 has been severe enough to be classed as a DEPRESSION, a more serious economic contraction. The U.S. economy suffered recessions in 1973-1974 and 1979, in large part as a consequence of increases in world petroleum prices, and in 1981-1982, when the Federal Reserve slowed monetary growth to halt inflation and reduce interest rates. Between 1983 and 1996, there was only one brief and mild recession, coming in 1990-1991. Social programs such as unemployment insurance can offset some of the effects of recessions on individuals.

Recidivism: In criminology, the return to criminal behavior of released and ostensibly rehabilitated convicts. Sociological and criminological research has found that within five years of release, about 80 percent of male convicts will return to prison, often for crimes more severe than those that led to their initial incarceration; such rates decrease markedly after age forty-five. Relapses are attributed to factors that include habituation to prison culture, lack of education and job skills, drug addiction, abusive family situations, peer pressure, antisocial values and personalities, racism, and inherited tendencies associated with hormones and brain chemistry. Efforts to reduce recidivism are at the heart of many debates on CRIME and the PRISON SYSTEM.

Recycling: Reuse of materials. Many materials may be used again in their original application or in new and different ways. Most metals, paper, glass, plastics, construction debris, and yard cuttings are recyclable. Economic considerations motivate most people to reuse materials, although some who recycle act out of altruistic concern for the environment.

The Need for Recycling. Humans generate wastes in virtually all of their activities. Most biological waste products are recycled through natural processes: Plants use the carbon dioxide exhaled by animals and give off oxygen as their own waste product; human wastes are transformed by bacteria into other products useful to plants. These processes have apparently evolved over millennia.

Since the Industrial Revolution, human beings have created prodigious amounts of products made from metal as well as inventing entirely new classes of molecules (such as organic chemicals and plastics). As a result of this increase in human production, bacteria have not had sufficient time to adapt processes that can use or transform these relatively new materials, and the sheer volume of these products is enormous.

Historically, people have responded to unwanted materials by discarding them. When the volume of materials was small, natural processes could treat waste without adversely affecting the environment. As the volume grew, the environment suffered. The volume of waste humans generate continues to grow. One approach to reducing the volume of waste that must ultimately be processed (discarded, incinerated, entombed, or buried in a landfill) has been recycling programs. Modern recycling programs are quite similar to ancient ones: Find a new use for something that is no longer needed.

Recycling does not occur automatically; there must be a reason for individuals to participate. For some, there is a sense of stewardship toward the planet Earth and a concern for its future condition. These people practice recycling, willingly modifying their habits: recycling discarded products from their own homes, purchasing products that are made from recycled materials, and avoiding products that generate large amounts of packaging waste. Such people are philosophically committed to the concept of recycling.

Others do not believe that there is a problem. They may look only at their own personal worlds and feel that there is plenty of space in which to dispose of trash or that other aspects of their lives have a higher priority than recycling. Legislation has been enacted to compel such people to practice recycling.

Relevant Legislation. An early attempt to recycle actually emerged in the 1970's as a means to beautify the countryside. In an attempt to deter people from discarding beverage containers in public spaces, retail sellers were compelled to collect a deposit on each container. After the contents were consumed, users

Recycling

could return the empty containers and have their deposit refunded. So-called bottle bills were initially enacted by Maine, Vermont, Massachusetts, New York, Michigan, Oregon, and California; the province of Ontario was a leader in enacting container deposit legislation in Canada. Other states and provinces continue to create legislation but container deposit laws are not universal. Such laws have been successful in cleaning up roadways and other public spaces. They have also served as demonstration projects to show the economic savings inherent with using recycled materials.

Local municipalities frequently enact ordinances designed to encourage or compel residents to recycle. Municipalities commonly provide containers to individual households and provide curbside collection services. Often associated with curbside recycling are programs that shift decisions associated with household waste removal to individual home owners. People paying for their own trash removal have an economic incentive to separate out recyclable materials, which reduces the volume of waste going to landfill sites. Because they pay to remove only the amount of waste

This mound of aluminum cans was collected by a New Jersey recycling center in a single week. (UPI/Bettmann Archive)

they generate, this saves money for home owners. Experience has shown that this economic incentive is effective. Cities such as Seattle have reduced the amount of waste going to landfills by 25 percent.

One effect of successful programs has been to generate large amounts of recyclable materials. The volume of recycled goods exceeds the industrial demand for these materials. As a result, prices for sorted recyclable materials have dropped. This has slowed the development of industries and commercial processes that use the recycled materials. Some experts have called for the enactment of new legislation to provide tax incentives for companies developing new technologies and uses for recycled materials.

Recyclable Materials. The number of materials that can be recycled continues to expand. Paper is readily recycled. An early use for recycled paper was in the manufacture of cardboard. With the advent of chemical processes that remove inks and dyes from paper, new product possibilities also emerge: greeting cards, computer papers, tissues, and similar papers.

Glass is also readily recycled. Clear glass can be ground up, remelted, and fashioned into new containers. Colored glass can also be ground and remelted, although the color cannot be removed. As a result, additional coloring materials are added, and the resulting products gradually become darker in color. The creation of beer containers is a primary market for recycling of colored glass. Alternatively, glass can be ground up and used in the manufacture of concrete. It can also be ground and added to paint, providing reflective properties to the final product.

Virtually all metals can be recycled, some more easily then others. Aluminum is initially difficult to separate. Once separated, aluminum is relatively easy to handle and process. The cost of making a product from recycled aluminum is only 5 percent of the cost of creating the same product from new materials.

Ferrous metals contain iron or steel. Because they may be separated using magnetism, metals containing iron or steel are initially easy to separate. They are then melted and other metals are removed. Complex processes have been created to accomplish this goal. Some impurities inherent in recycled iron are desirable. For example, vanadium, chromium, cobalt, and molybdenum provide strength and retard oxidation. The cost of reprocessing steel and other ferrous metals is often less than the cost of creating the same product from new materials.

Some metals are in short supply, such as chromium and palladium. It is cheaper to reprocess recycled materials containing these metals than to separate them from mined ore. In the defense industry, there are applications for some metals that may not be reliably and steadily obtained on world markets. Recycling thus becomes an important source for these critical metals. Gold, silver, and platinum are melted and recycled because of their high price. Photographic negatives and X rays are recycled to recover the silver in them.

Plastic can also be recycled. All plastics are not the same, so different types must be separated. Once accomplished, the reclaimed plastic can be melted and reused. The internal frames of some upholstered furniture are made from plastic rather than wood. Video-cassette cases are another common use for recycled plastic. A third use for recycled plastic is in the manufacture of clothing. The material in disposable diapers is also used to make lawn furniture as well as structural components for upholstered furniture.

Construction debris is added to roadbeds during initial construction. Worn asphalt is scraped off roadways, heated, and reapplied, often on the same street. Yard debris can be composted and returned as potting soil, mulch, or top dressing for lawns. Radioactive materials are recycled for safety, protecting citizens from unwanted exposure. Some sculptors recycle discards into their works of art.

Markets for Recycled Materials. There are two markets for recycled materials. The first is to sell recycled materials initially returned by consumers. The second market then sells the new products containing recycled materials to consumers.

As awareness of the need for recycling expands, the demand for products containing recycled materials will continue to expand. The need to stimulate the creation of new uses for recycled materials by the provision of tax incentives at the national level has been documented. There is a glut of some materials that have been collected by consumers for which resale is difficult. Newspaper and glass are in this category. An important aspect of paper reuse has been the presence of contamination by materials in inks, notably lead. The relatively recent introduction of soy-based inks has addressed this issue, and the backlog of recycled newspaper is slowly diminishing. Increases in the price of pulp-grade wood have accelerated the use of recycled newsprint. Increased consumer demand for computer paper has also contributed. Manufacturers of metal and plastic beverage containers have applied pressure to state and provincial governments to enact protective legislation. Often, this requires manufacturers of glass beverage containers to use unnecessarily high quantities of virgin material. This has contributed to the glut of recycled glass.

The market for recycled materials is expanding. Manufacturers have created and advertised products intended for consumers who are environmentally conscious. Stimulating demand for these products has induced other companies to create similar products or increase the content of recycled materials in existing products. Children's crafts have historically used recycled materials. These activities teach important lessons but do not create major markets for recycled materials. The conversion of soda containers into fibers that are spun or woven into clothing has been an exciting and innovative use for recycled materials. Not only are the items of clothing advertised as containing recycled materials but they also outperform similar products made from traditional materials.

Future Promises. The key to stimulating recycling and opening new markets is probably an economic one. Experience has demonstrated that only a minority of individuals are motivated to recycle by concern for the environment. For the rest, money is the motivator. It has been shown that using recycled materials is often cheaper than using virgin materials.

The outlook for recycling programs is one of promise. They will be expanded by necessity as landfill space is becoming limited and the prices for virgin materials continue to increase. They will also be expanded by demand as children are taught the importance of recycling in schools and consumers ask for products that contain recycled materials.

—*L. Fleming Fallon, Jr.*

SUGGESTED READINGS: Debi Kimball's *Recycling in America* (Santa Barbara, Calif.: ABC-Clio, 1992) is a good overview of recycling legislation. Jennifer Carless' *Taking out the Trash: A No-Nonsense Guide to Recycling* (Washington, D.C.: Island Press, 1992) contains suggestions for increasing public participation in recycling programs. William Rathje's *Rubbish: The Archaeology of Garbage* (New York: HarperCollins, 1992) is a fascinating look at landfills. The Environmental Protection Agency's *Recycling and the Consumer* (Washington, D.C.: Environmental Protection Agency, 1979) is a useful guide.

Red Cross: International humanitarian organization headquartered in Geneva, Switzerland. Its goal is to reduce human suffering caused by war, floods, earthquakes, and other calamities. The Red Cross was founded in 1863 by Jean Dunant, who had observed the suffering of wounded soldiers lying on a battlefield without medical care. The Red Cross operates ambulances and hospitals that are marked with the organization's distinctive red cross insignia. The American Red Cross has developed a successful program for children to teach them swimming and water safety. Many communities have an annual Red Cross blood drive to collect blood for emergency use.

Red Scare (1950's): Name given to widespread American fears of international communism. In the climate of the early Cold War, many U.S. citizens were attacked as communists or "communist sympathizers"; targets included some of the country's leading intellectuals, public officials, and entertainers. Senator Joseph McCarthy of Wisconsin earned notoriety as the era's leading anticommunist; after he was publicly embarrassed in a series of congressional hearings inquiring into the presence of communists in the armed forces, Red Scare hysteria abated.

Redevelopment programs: Federal, state, and local government-assistance programs designed to address the problems associated with inner-city poverty and urban decline.

Early Programs. The origins of concern over urban poverty in the United States and its causes and consequences predate the twentieth century. Until the Great Depression, however, the nineteenth century tradition of "dual federalism," or the separation of federal and local fiscal responsibilities, remained the rule. Federal involvement in urban affairs was essentially nonexistent until the mid-1930's, when large amounts of federal financial aid were allocated to cities and states in the form of grants. This type of federal aid to cities, which was thought to be temporary, involved matching funds being provided by the cities receiving money, with local agencies administering all moneys under the guidance of federal agencies. At the time, few analysts foresaw the continual growth of such federal programs.

The post-World War II perception of urban problems created a call for a continuation and expansion of federal-to-local assistance. Public debates and discussions on the decline of American cities focused on such aspects as worsening impoverishment and unem-

A Red Cross facility in Washington, D.C. (Impact Visuals/Shia Photo)

Redevelopment programs

ployment; deteriorating housing, factories, and businesses; increasing crime rates, property taxes, and concentration of minorities; and decreasing population and property values. The federal government's policy response was "URBAN RENEWAL." The 1949 and 1954 Housing Acts were promoted as being designed to clear urban slums and replace them with decent, affordable housing for the residents. Whether by design or through abuse, the real impact of these programs was to replace low-income housing with upper-class dwellings, office towers, shopping centers, and public buildings, displacing the former residents. In city after city, so-called progrowth coalitions, made up of downtown property owners and local urban-renewal agencies, used billions of dollars in federal aid toward an unintended end. The new result was the revitalization of central business districts, an increase in property values, and an exacerbation of the problems of the urban poor.

The Emergence of Redevelopment. By the 1960's, urban renewal's large-scale clearance approach had been discredited and a call for "redevelopment pro-

Redevelopment programs often involve the demolition of existing structures. (James L. Shaffer)

Homes built in New York City's South Bronx area as part of a redevelopment program. (UPI/Bettmann)

grams" was gaining support. In general terms, this meant a shift in program focus from economic revitalization at the expense of the urban poor and their neighborhoods, to addressing the causes of poverty and working toward community restoration without displacement. Under the Dwight D. Eisenhower Administration, which ended in 1960, the problems of the poor went largely unrecognized; in fact, POVERTY did not officially exist, because the government had yet to initiate a POVERTY LINE, a standard for impoverishment. The community-redevelopment vision began in earnest with the John F. Kennedy Administration's belief that overall economic stimulation would not significantly enhance the ability of the urban poor to better themselves without direct assistance at the community and individual levels. In 1963, Kennedy called for a tax cut to boost the economy and the creation of "manpower grants" to fund local vocational training, job counseling, and health-care programs for the unemployed and underemployed. After Kennedy's

assassination, President Lyndon B. Johnson initiated and expanded his predecessor's concept: The War on Poverty was announced, and the era of community redevelopment had begun.

Johnson's position was that the conventional, individual social-services approach, even with the addition of educational, vocational, and job-placement programs, should be accompanied by what he called "community action." His "GREAT SOCIETY" agenda included the Community Action Program (CAP) and Model Cities Program and the creation of the U.S. Department of Housing and Urban Development (HUD). The Office of Economic Opportunity (OEO) was created in 1964 to oversee the CAP. This federal agency created Community Action Agencies (CAAs) in each of the roughly one thousand communities receiving CAP funding to implement the program's goals at the local level. These objectives were to design and fund social services tailored to the specific needs of the community; to combine local agencies' social-service

Newark, N.J., buildings are razed as part of a 1990's redevelopment program. (Archive Photos, Mike Segar)

programs and coordinate them with new programs created by the CAA and the OEO; and to ensure the "maximum feasible participation" of local residents in designing and operating the CAP. Apparently, the CAAs experienced some degree of success in increasing the quantity and quality of community services, but the other two program objectives were more problematic. Public and private agencies that viewed their interests as being opposed resisted coordination. Residents of more militant CAAs were mobilized politically to force city governments to respond to the needs of the poor, generating criticism of the CAP.

The Johnson Administration's response to the CAP's problems was the Model Cities Program (MCP), created in 1966 with the Demonstration Cities and Metropolitan Development Act. The MCP was designed to defuse the criticism of what some viewed as disruptive, militant political activism carried out in the name of the CAP, and to expand the community-redevelopment concept. This new initiative in urban policy, directed by the recently established Department of Housing and Urban Development, featured expanded social services, physical renewal that was more sensitive to community needs, and the de-emphasis of resi-

dent participation. By 1968, 150 cities had been selected as MCP cities, and were directed to produce a comprehensive demonstration plan (CDP), a three-part process that took a year to complete. First, studies identifying local problems and proposing solutions were completed. Then a five-year plan of action and its costs were projected. Finally, a detailed accounting of administrative linkages was provided. After approving the CDP, HUD created a city demonstration agency (CDA), the local agency through which federal-action grants would be administered for the five-year implementation period. In addition, Model Cities would also be given first priority for all existing urban grant programs, and supplemental funds to pay up to 80 percent of the matching funds cities were normally required to pay. It was hoped that the combined effect of this program would be community human capital and physical infrastructure development, without clearance and displacement.

Programs Since the 1970's. The Richard M. NIXON Administration initiated an effort to shift the responsibility for many existing federal programs to states and municipalities, and to alter the focus of urban policy from providing social and human services and low-income neighborhood revitalization, to more general economic development. The culmination of this was the establishment of the Community Development Block Grant Program (CDBG) in the mid-1970's as the principal mechanism for urban assistance. Seven former urban grant programs, including Model Cities, were combined in CDBG, which allowed 100 percent of funds to be used for physical improvements and specifically prohibited more than a certain percentage from being used for education, job training, and other human services. This program featured local implementation, for example, mayors and local governing bodies decided how CDBG funds were to be used. CDBG eligibility requirements eliminated the targeting of low-income communities. These funds went to all cities with more than fifty thousand people and all counties with more than 200,000 people, and to smaller cities, on a discretionary basis. Many affluent suburban cities and counties automatically received CDBG assistance. These significant policy changes were especially troubling to their critics because the Comprehensive Employment and Training Act (CETA) of 1973 contained the same kinds of local discretion in implementation, and, although it was supposed to be a job-training and placement program for the poor and unemployed, CETA funds were mostly used to fund already-existing civil-service positions for government workers.

Upon taking office, President Jimmy CARTER expressed a desire to restructure urban policy to address more effectively the needs of the poor and their communities. Most analysts, however, feel that his options were severely limited because of economic instability and a lack of cooperation from the Congress. His administration saw reductions in social-program funding and the use of Urban Development Action Grants (UDAGs), which were given to private developers to make possible projects that might directly or indirectly affect poor neighborhoods. Retrospective analysis shows that 15 percent or less of UDAG funds had this effect, the lion's share going to build hotels and office buildings. In spite of the perceived shortcomings of CDBG in combating urban poverty, it was the only remaining federal program that the Carter Administration could use for this purpose. Its efforts resulted in a redistribution of CDBG funds to the most needy cities, but found very limited success in channeling funds to the most impoverished neighborhoods within cities because of the local implementation featured in the original legislation.

The years following the Carter presidency have not been encouraging to those who believe that an effective war on urban poverty must involve a strong federal urban policy. Since 1980, the executive branch has called for a "new federalism," which features attempts to reduce the federal-budget deficit through program cutbacks and elimination. Urban programs have been hit particularly hard, and the future of redevelopment programs for low-income neighborhoods and their residents seems especially uncertain as federal money for them has been reduced substantially while states and cities lack the funds to fill the void. —*Jack Carter*

SUGGESTED READINGS: Benjamin Kleinberg's *Urban America in Transformation: Perspectives on Urban Policy and Development* (Thousand Oaks, Calif.: Sage, 1995) provides a detailed historic examination of U.S. urban policy. *Exploring Urban America: An Introductory Reader* (Thousand Oaks, Calif.: Sage, 1995) by Roger W. Caves is a comprehensive collection of essays on urban policy, including chapters on urban poverty programs. Anthony Downs's *New Visions for Metropolitan America* (Washington, D.C.: The Brookings Institution, 1994) gives suggestions for forging more effective future urban policy.

Reed v. Reed (1971): U.S. Supreme Court case. Indeed, the Court was unanimous in striking down an Idaho law that required PROBATE judges to prefer males over females as administrators of estates. The case marked the first time the Court used the equal-protection clause of the Fourteenth Amendment to prohibit arbitrary discrimination based on gender. The decision required that gender-based policies must be reasonable, but it did not require that such policies must be justified by a compelling state interest.

Refugee Act (1980): U.S. legislation that provided a single standard admittance program for various groups of refugees who had been covered under several previous laws. The act increased the number of refugees eligible to enter the United States annually from 17,400 to 50,000. The act also brought the United States into conformity with the U.N. definition of refugees as persons unable or unwilling to return to their countries of origin "because of persecution or a well-founded fear of persecution on account of race, religion, nationality, membership in a particular social group, or political opinion." Previous laws were in-

Refugee problems and immigration

tended to aid World War II refugees and escapees from communist-controlled countries.

Refugee problems and immigration: According to long-established international agreements, a refugee is someone who has fled his or her homeland because of political persecution. Refugees are not considered to be part of normal immigration quotas, and since World War II, refugee flows to the United States and other receiving countries have increased significantly, resulting in calls for more restrictive policies.

History. Internationally organized concern for displaced persons began with the formation of the United Nations Relief and Rehabilitation Agency (UNRRA) by the Allied powers in 1943 to deal with the millions of people uprooted by World War II. UNRRA's main strategy for dealing with refugees was repatriation—sending them back to their homelands. As soon as the war ended, East-West tensions emerged, and the United States became very critical of the forced repatriation to Soviet bloc countries by the UNRRA. The United States, which provided 70 percent of that agency's funding, was instrumental in replacing it with

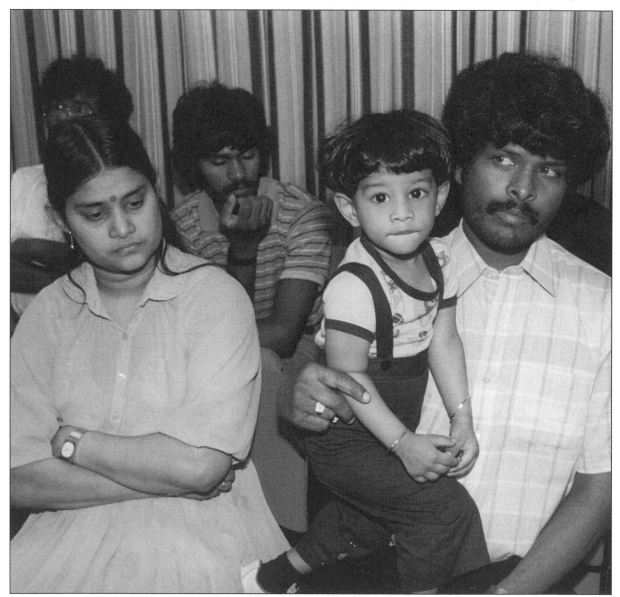

Tamil refugees discuss their 1986 flight to Canada. (Reuters/Corbis-Bettmann)

the International Refugee Organization (IRO) in 1947. The IRO's refugee policy was resettlement, not repatriation; from that point, refugees were relocated in host countries, and practically none were returned to Central or Eastern Europe, much to the dissatisfaction of the Soviets.

In 1948, the IRO, at the insistence of the United States, began aiding not only World War II refugees but also escapees from communist regimes. Since Western Europe could not resettle all those displaced by the war, overseas countries agreed to help. The United States took 400,000, 32 percent of the total, with the rest resettling in Australia, Israel, Canada, Great Britain, Western Europe, and Latin America.

Although the IRO had resettled most persons displaced by World War II, its director warned in 1950 that East-West crises—such as the Berlin blockade, successful communist revolutions in Czechoslovakia and China, and the start of the Korean War—would generate huge east-to-west refugee flows; the refugee resettlement problem was probably only beginning. In response, the United Nations created the Office of the United Nations High Commissioner for Refugees (UNHCR) to continue refugee aid efforts. In 1951, the U.N. held the Convention Relating to the Status of Refugees, which established the still-accepted definition of a refugee as someone with "a well-founded fear of being persecuted in his country of origin for reasons of race, religion, nationality, membership of a particular social group, or political opinion"; the convention also prohibited *refoulement*, or forcible repatriation. The United States was instrumental in limiting the commitment by convention signees to European refugees and in establishing persecution, not economic deprivation, as part of the official definition. This definition served U.S. Cold War interests by embarrassing new communist regimes that were generating large refugee populations. However, the United States did not sign the convention, preferring to handle asylum issues through domestic legislation, largely because it had paid for a significant part of the unexpectedly high costs of the IRO and was reluctant to enter into an open-ended commitment involving what appeared to be a growing and permanent refugee problem.

The first piece of legislation establishing U.S. refugee policy was a provision in the 1949 legislation that created the CENTRAL INTELLIGENCE AGENCY (CIA) that one hundred communist defectors per year should be recruited. The first of the Mutual Security Acts, passed from 1951 to 1961, created the United States

Escapee Program (USEP) to promote such defections. Provisions for general refugee assistance were included in the subsequent acts, but the focus was always anticommunist. Throughout the 1950's, the United States, fearing communist influence in the U.N., lent only limited support to the UNHCR and avoided making commitments to refugees that were of little political value to the United States. The ideological focus of U.S. refugee policy that developed throughout the 1950's and 1960's is illustrated by the fact that of almost a quarter of a million refugees admitted between 1956 and 1968, fewer than one thousand were from noncommunist countries.

Changes Since the 1960's. The challenges and controversies associated with contemporary U.S. refugee policies involve the broadening of the definition of those eligible for asylum to meet current realities, the escalating costs of providing such asylum, and the extension of asylum to those people fleeing governments that benefit from U.S. assistance. The internationally accepted definition of a refugee that was established by the 1951 U.N. convention makes individual governmental persecution the criterion for asylum eligibility. Those fleeing dysfunctional economies are termed "economic migrants" and are deported if they immigrate illegally. However, there is growing awareness that governmental oppression, economic malaise, and widespread social problems often go hand-in-hand, making it increasingly difficult to disentangle the reasons that people leave their homelands. The fact is, compared with the so-called convention refugees, there are many more displaced persons in the world today who are fleeing generalized reigns of terror perpetuated by their governments, ethnic conflicts, civil wars, and systematic and severe economic deprivation; these people are technically not eligible for asylum.

Although it seems clear that unprecedented numbers of forcibly displaced people are inadequately protected, the official recognition of a broader definition of "refugee" is unlikely because of the undeniable economic costs and the perceived social and cultural costs of growing refugee populations. The Western governments that established the international standards for refugee assistance have either instituted more restrictive policies or are considering doing so. International observers assert that the United States has a legitimate complaint in that it receives more refugees by far than any other industrialized nation. However, in order to understand the magnitude of the contemporary refugee problem worldwide, one must realize that refugee

Cuban refugees enter a Florida harbor in 1980. (AP/Wide World Photos)

flows to the West are small compared to those that occur within the developing world. A majority of refugees are being assisted in the poorest nations in the world. For example, in Malawi, a country with a per capita income of $170, refugees from Mozambique constitute one-tenth of the entire population. From the perspective of the United States, this would be equivalent to offering asylum to every person in Central America.

Central American Refugees in the 1980's and 1990's. Since the early 1980's, the U.S. government has become increasingly concerned about the dramatically increasing numbers of asylum seekers, especially those who enter the country illegally. For example, from 1980 to the early 1990's, hundreds of thousands of Salvadorans fled in the face of death squads that had murdered their relatives and associates; a similar situation existed in Guatemala. Yet during this period, only fifty-four Salvadorans and no Guatemalans were accepted for resettlement in the United States, in spite of the fact that Central American refugee camps could assist only a small fraction of these people. Many entered the United States illegally.

U.S. refugee policy was openly directed by Cold War considerations until 1980. From the mid-1950's through 1979, only 0.3 percent of refugee admissions were to people from noncommunist countries. Although there was some criticism of the United States' refusal to extend asylum to those fleeing the regimes of authoritarian leaders that it supported (the Shah of Iran, "Baby Doc" Duvalier in Haiti, General August Pinochet in Chile, and President Ferdinand Marcos of the Philippines, for example), the flow of refugees was controlled, and a serious domestic political backlash avoided.

However, in 1980, the Refugee Act was passed, removing the requirement that refugees be fleeing communist regimes. Soon thereafter, the Mariel boatlift brought 130,000 Cubans to America in five months. That year, 800,000 immigrants and refugees entered the United States legally. Growing sentiment for more restrictive policies emerged. The Ronald REAGAN Administration responded by reducing refugee admis-

sions by two-thirds and heavily favoring those from communist countries, in spite of the 1980 Refugee Act. The policy of forcibly returning Haitians, Salvadorans, and Guatemalans to brutal governments while admitting less physically threatened refugees from communist countries was soundly criticized in some quarters.

The George BUSH Administration continued President Reagan's policies. In 1990, new IMMIGRATION AND NATURALIZATION SERVICE (INS) regulations included a call for examining human rights violations in refugees' countries of origin, the 1990 Immigration Act created "temporary protected status," which was then given to Salvadorans living illegally in the United States for eighteen months, and a successful lawsuit forced the INS to halt the deportation of Salvadorans and Guatemalans. After the fall of the Jean-Bertrand Aristide government in Haiti created an upsurge of

Haitian refugees at a U.S. detention center in 1992. (Impact Visuals, Jim Tynan)

"boat people," however, the Bush Administration successfully petitioned the Supreme Court to lift a ban on forced repatriation, and tens of thousands of Haitians were then intercepted and returned. The Bill CLINTON Administration continued this practice and then forced the reinstatement of the Aristide government in an effort to stem the flow of refugees.   —*Jack Carter*

SUGGESTED READINGS: Gil Loescher and John Scanlan discuss U.S. refugee policy from World War II to the mid-1980's in *Calculated Kindness: Refugees and America's Half-Open Door, 1945 to the Present* (New York: Free Press, 1986). Bill Frelick examines U.S. refugee policy in the 1980's and early 1990's in "Call Them What They Are—Refugees," in *World Refugee Survey, 1992* (Washington, D.C.: American Council for Nationalities Service, 1992). A set of essays addressing refugee-related problems and policies in Western nations, including the United States and Canada, are contained in *Refugees and the Asylum Dilemma in the West* (University Park, Penn.: Pennsylvania State University Press, 1992), edited by Gil Loescher.

Refugee Relief Act (1953): U.S. legislation that established regular procedures for the admission of refugees and escapees from communist countries. Previously, presidents had admitted refugees by executive action, with the numbers of those admitted charged against the limited quotas set for immigration from Eastern European countries. The 1953 act authorized non-quota visas for 205,000 persons over a two-and-a-half-year period; each visa holder could also bring spouses and minor children outside the quota system. Immigration under this law and through later special provisions for Hungarians, Cubans, and East Asians resulted in offers of asylum to more than one million people between 1953 and 1980.

Regents of the University of California v. Bakke (1978): U.S. Supreme Court case. The *Bakke* case highlighted the tension between the desire to remedy the efforts of historical discrimination against peoples of color and the ideal of a color-blind society in which an individual's race would have no relevance.

In 1973 and 1974, Allan Bakke, a thirty-two-year-old white male, applied for admission to the University of California at Davis medical school. Applicants competed for one hundred positions. The school, however, had reserved sixteen places for minority students in an effort to encourage racial diversity on campus. Minority students could compete for all one hundred positions, whereas white applicants could compete only for the remaining eighty-four positions. In neither year was Bakke granted admission.

Bakke brought suit against the school in the summer of 1974, alleging REVERSE DISCRIMINATION and demanding admittance. He claimed that by preventing him from competing for the sixteen reserved places, the university had violated the equal-protection clause of the Fourteenth Amendment to the Constitution and Title VI of the CIVIL RIGHTS ACT OF 1964. The Fourteenth Amendment grants to each citizen EQUAL PROTECTION of the laws. Title VI prohibits the exclusion of an individual from a federally funded program because of race. Bakke noted that if minority students had been prohibited from competing for the other eighty-four positions, such a policy would be unconstitutional.

In the case argued before the California Superior Court, the California Supreme Court, and finally before the U.S. Supreme Court, university attorneys argued that using minority-group status as one factor in the admissions process was legal and constitutional. Even though a comparison of grades and standardized test scores indicated that Bakke was better qualified than many of the minority students admitted, those criteria, the university argued, were not the only relevant ones. Another important criterion, they claimed, was whether admission would increase racial diversity on campus.

In 1977, the case was argued before the Supreme Court. The following year, a highly polarized court passed down a five-to-four decision offering victory to both sides. Four justices believed the Davis program did indeed violate Title VI. On the other hand, four other justices believed that the program was constitutional and that the school was justified in its attempt to remedy past discrimination. These four justices even went so far as to argue that Title VI violated the Fourteenth Amendment. Justice Lewis Powell, who cast the decisive vote, incorporated elements from both sides in the decision he authored. Bakke, he held, had been discriminated against in violation of Title VI, and Powell ordered his admission; quotas in most situations were thus judged to be unconstitutional. Powell held that the government did, however, have a compelling need to remedy past discrimination, and could do so by utilizing racial classification as one factor in admissions procedures. The Court's decision in the Bakke case displayed how complex and nuanced were

A demonstrator urges the Supreme Court to rule against Alan Bakke. (UPI/Corbis-Bettmann)

the issues surrounding race relations, discrimination, and AFFIRMATIVE ACTION programs.

Rehabilitation Act (1973): U.S. federal legislation established to monitor the activities of the agencies identified in the ARCHITECTURAL BARRIERS ACT of 1968 and to ensure compliance with its mandates to make all public buildings accessible to the disabled. The Rehabilitation Act established the Architectural Barriers and Transportation Compliance Board, headed by the secretary of the Department of Health, Education, and Welfare. The Rehabilitation Act also asserted the federal government as a model for fair hiring and promotion practices of the disabled and extended these regulations to any federal contractor whose funding exceeded $2,500. After the establishment of the Rehabilitation Act, all fifty states and the U.S. territories enacted laws to ensure compliance with the Architectural Barriers Act's regulations.

Rehabilitation of criminals: Changing the behavioral patterns of criminals and juvenile delinquents, including their cognition, attitudes, beliefs, and social skills, to enable offenders to function in society without committing new crimes.

Criminologists (those who study crime and juvenile delinquency scientifically) often use the term "habilitation," rather than rehabilitation, to refer to the process of changing offender behavior, because those who commit serious crimes often lack the social skills needed to live lawfully in the first place. Many criminals and delinquents were not reared in environments in which they could learn the behavioral, problem-solving, and social skills needed to deal with others appropriately; in addition, most lack education and vocational training.

From this perspective, habilitation (or rehabilitation) consists of determining what difficulties offenders have, setting clear limits and restrictions on their behavior, monitoring their behavior, and carrying through individualized plans to help each offender. This perspective is influenced by social learning and cognition theories of human behavior and by the field of social psychology. Numerous studies of prison inmates show that most have little education or vocational training and have abused alcohol and drugs.

For example, an offender who steals an automobile, wrecks it, and fights police when arrested might be found to have poor control of anger and be dependent upon alcohol. The offender could be placed on intensive probation with electronic monitoring, which restricts offenders to their homes, allowing them to leave only to go to work, and meeting frequently with a probation officer. Treatment for alcohol or drug dependency and for anger control may be required, as well as testing for alcohol and drug use. The offender might also be required to pay restitution to the victim whose automobile was damaged.

Current research on habilitation using this model is encouraging; some studies show success rates of 70 to 90 percent. In comparison, without rehabilitation, as few as 20 to 40 percent of those sent to prison succeed in avoiding further serious crime. Findings vary depending upon how skillfully staff carry out a program and upon the degree to which offenders assigned to the program are appropriate to the treatment being offered. Habilitation is most likely to succeed when offenders are motivated to change, have someone willing to help them change, have goals they want to achieve, have the opportunity to take steps needed to change, and live where socially acceptable behavior may be used.

Two other perspectives are prominent in criminology. According to the sociobiological perspective, some criminals and delinquents commit crimes because of genetic, intellectual, or racial deficits, which are sometimes aggravated by social difficulties such as mental illness or poverty. Because of these basic weaknesses, some individuals who enter into crime are unlikely to be rehabilitated. Generally, research does not support this view, in that no clear distinction has been demonstrated that separates criminals or delinquents from nonoffenders. Moreover, offenders show as great a range of variations in intelligence, race, genetic makeup, health, and personality as do nonoffenders.

The crime control, or "just desserts," perspective also rejects the idea of rehabilitation, arguing that the justice system should concentrate on punishment, deterrence of further crime through fear of punishment, and incapacitation of offenders in prison. This perspective does not draw a clear distinction between adult and juvenile offenders. Nor does it, in general, address the issue of what happens to the 95 percent of offenders who return to society after serving their sentences.

Debate over rehabilitation has continued for more than a century. It has often been assumed that society must choose between punishing offenders or rehabilitating them, but many scholars do not view these goals as exclusive. They note instead that all criminal sentences involve punishment via the loss of rights and freedoms; they thus tend to view humane and appropriate punishment as an important part of rehabilitation.

Rehnquist, William (b. October 1, 1924, Milwaukee, Wis.): Chief justice of the U.S. SUPREME COURT. Rehnquist received his legal training from Stanford University's law school, from which he was graduated in 1952; he then entered into private practice in Phoenix, Arizona. Through his connections with the Republican Party in Arizona, Rehnquist was appointed as assistant attorney general for the Office of Legal Counsel during the Richard M. NIXON Administration. In 1972, Rehnquist was nominated to the Supreme

Court by Nixon; in 1986, he was elevated to chief justice by President Ronald REAGAN. Rehnquist has maintained a strict constructionist view of the Constitution and has worked for judicial restraint.

Reincarnation: Spiritual belief. Reincarnation is the ostensible process by which the essence (spiritual or material) of a person or animal migrates after death to a different body, or to a heaven, a hell, or some other state of being. Other terms for this process include metempsychosis, rebirth, and transmigration. Ancient Greeks taught that the eternal soul entered a body at conception or birth and departed at death for another body, unless the soul had been purified from sin by ascetic practices. Hindus teach that the soul migrates until it is liberated through enlightenment, devotion, or

William Rehnquist takes the oath of office as chief justice of the U.S. Supreme Court. (AP/Wide World Photos)

religious duties, while Buddhists teach that one's KARMA, the residue of one's deeds, migrates.

Relativism: View that truth is relative to individuals, societies, or conceptual systems. If truth is solely dependent on qualities that vary widely across cultures and even within the same culture, then there is no absolute universal truth.

Some claim that the existence of differences of opinion supports relativism. One person believes in capital punishment; another does not. One society believes that spirits inhabit trees; another does not. Because of such differences, some conclude that the truth in such cases is solely dependent on individual or societal opinion. A problem with this argument is that the same reasoning supports saying that the shape of the earth is solely dependent on individual or societal opinion, since there have been differences of opinion about the shape of the earth. Other relativists claim that the difficulties in finding absolute truth make it unlikely that absolute truth exists.

If relativism is construed as the view that all opinions are equally correct, since the view that relativism is incorrect is one opinion, then relativism is as incorrect as it is correct. If relativism is the view that it is absolutely true that there are no absolute truths, then relativism is self-contradictory.

Some relativists argue that they are merely saying that there are no absolute truths "for themselves"; such a defense of relativism, however, raises further questions. If "x is true for John" means "John believes x," then relativists seem to be equating belief and truth. Belief, however, seems neither sufficient nor necessary for truth, since either the world is round or it is not, regardless of what anyone believes.

Sometimes relativism impoverishes rational inquiry and discussion. Looking for the truth about whether abortion is morally acceptable by introspecting to find one's belief about it or by conducting an opinion poll in one's society is one thing. Carefully considering the evidence for and against the moral acceptability of abortion is another. Relativists tend to answer criticisms of their views with statements such as: "That may be true for you, but it is not true for me." Such a philosophy suggests that because opposing views may appear equally valid, neither can be wrong, and so there is no need to consider further whether one is more rationally defensible than the other.

If a society's believing something is enough to make it true, how can societies make mistakes? Yet such mistakes seem possible; consider genocide, slavery, torture, and intolerance. If moral mistakes were not possible, then there would be no point in attempts at moral reform: What would need changing? There would also be no such thing as moral progress, because if nothing were wrong with the old ways of doing things, they could not be improved. Most would agree, however, that substituting a society based on the dignity of all for a society based on slavery and the exploitation of women and children would be a moral advance. If one were to accept strict relativism about values, however, there would be no objective ground for claiming that an egalitarian society is better than a racist society.

Religion: The word "religion" is a generic term that can connote a wide range of social attitudes, affiliations, and actions. As such, the subject almost defies definition. In Western civilization, however, "religion" has usually meant four things: a way of believing (with an intellectual component), a way of belonging (with a strong sociological element), a way of behaving (with an ethical or moral dimension), and a way of becoming (with an influential psychological role in personal growth and maturation).

The Religious American. In spite of predictions of the "DEATH OF GOD" and of the "SECULARIZATION" of American society in the mid-1960's, the United States, on the eve of the twenty-first century, remained the most religious of Western nations as measured in terms of spiritual beliefs and behaviors. Residents of the United States are essentially traditional in their theological opinions, according to pollsters George Gallup, Jr., and Jim Castelli in *The People's Religion: American Faith in the Nineties* (1989). Conservative beliefs predominated: 94 percent of all Americans believed in God (as opposed to only 52 percent of the French); 90 percent claimed to pray; 80 percent believed they would face God on Judgment Day; 80 percent reported that "God works miracles today"; and 66 percent of men and 76 percent of women expected a life after death. It was found that 80 percent of all Americans affirmed the Bible as the literal or inspired word of God, though only one-third said they actually read the Scriptures on a weekly basis. Coupled with this was a strong sense of the supernatural, with 50 percent admitting to a belief in angels. Some 80 percent of Americans contended that there were clear

PUBLIC OPINION, 1994: HOW IMPORTANT IS RELIGION?

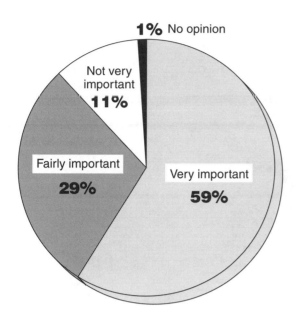

1% No opinion

Not very important **11%**

Fairly important **29%**

Very important **59%**

Respondents were asked to rate the importance of religion in their lives.

Source: George Gallup, Jr., ed., *The Gallup Poll: Public Opinion, 1994* (Wilmington, Del.: Scholarly Resources, 1995).

Analyzing the beliefs and behaviors of the "typical" religious American, Gallup and Castelli found a gender gap (women were more likely than men to hold traditional views), racial variation (with African Americans tending to be more religious than Caucasians or Asian Americans), and age differences (traditional religious views increased with age). Regional differences were also evident, with the South the most religious section, the East and West Coasts less so, and the Midwest in between.

Students of American history are divided as to why the United States has remained more religious than Western Europe (or even Canada). Some attribute it to the inherent puritanism and pietism of American Protestantism. Others detect patterns of periodical revivals, as the First Great Awakening (1740's), the Second Great Awakening (early 1800's), and a perceived Third Great Awakening (supposedly begun in the 1980's). Still others argue that the influences of immigration, the frontier, westward movement, and individualism created a demand for religious certainty and stability in the midst of rapid social change.

The Growth of Religious Diversity. In spite of the apparent continuity of American religious beliefs and behaviors in the twentieth century, major changes were becoming evident by the 1990's. One of these was the growth in religious diversity.

From its inception, the spiritual heritage of North America was inherently diverse. More than five hundred nations of Native Americans embraced mythologies and spiritualities whose richness is only beginning to be fully appreciated. Across the Middle Passage from West Africa came lifestyles and worldviews that profoundly affected the religious cultures of the Caribbean, Brazil, and the United States. From Europe came CHRISTIANITY, in both its Roman Catholic and Protestant forms. Even within the English-speaking colonies, there was Puritanism in New England, Anglicanism in the South, and a blend of Dissenter and Continental Protestantism in the Middle Colonies. The nineteenth century saw heavy Roman Catholic and Jewish immigration. By the mid-twentieth century, sociologist Will Herberg described an American faith with "three faces," as in the title of his classic study *Protestant, Catholic, Jew* (1955).

Herberg's tripartite partition of American piety remained a reality in the mid-1990's. In 1994, North America was the world's largest center of Protestantism, with 97 million Protestants; Africa was second, with 91 million; and Europe was third, with 73 million.

guidelines about good and evil that applied to every situation. Certain indicators suggested Americans were even more orthodox (in conventional Christian terms) in 1988 than a decade earlier, with 84 percent viewing Jesus as the son of God, as opposed to 78 percent in 1978.

Residents of the United States were also essentially traditional in their religious behaviors. Church and synagogue membership remained the highest in the Western world (65 percent in 1988, down from 73 percent in 1937). Worship attendance each week, at a low in 1940 (37 percent attending services weekly), rose to a peak in 1955 of some 49 percent and stabilized at 40 percent in 1972; a slight increase took place in the early 1990's. Nearly half of all Americans reported a "dramatic change of faith," and 67 percent agreed that churches and synagogues today are effective in helping people to find meaning in life. At least 70 percent of Americans contended that religious faith was important to them.

Catholic priests are ordained at a Michigan cathedral. (Jim West)

The continent was also the world's center of Judaism, with 6.8 million Jews; Asia was second, with 6.2 million. North America also had the fourth major concentration of Roman Catholics on the planet, with 97 million; Latin America was first, with 412 million; Europe was second, with 260 million; and Asia and Africa were tied for third place, with about 130 million Catholics each.

Changes, however, were evident within Protestantism in the United States. The so-called mainline churches, the product of the first wave of Protestantism in the sixteenth century (Anglicans, Lutherans, Presbyterians, and Congregationalists), and the churches of the second wave in the eighteenth century (the Methodists and the Disciples of Christ) were experiencing steady decline. Though still large, influential, and affluent, these traditions were aging and shrinking in membership. Concurrently, the so-called evangelical or conservative Protestant denominations, such as the Baptists, the Assemblies of God, and the Nazarenes, were rapidly increasing their memberships. Evangelicals grew not

only in numbers but also in influence, with three presidents— Jimmy CARTER, Ronald REAGAN, and George BUSH— self-proclaimed born-again Christians.

Changes were also evident within Roman Catholicism. Not only had Catholicism come to be regarded as "mainstream," but Catholics tended increasingly to be upwardly mobile members of the American middle class. U.S. Catholicism also continued to grow. In 1947, only 20 percent of the U.S. population identified itself as Catholic, as opposed to 28 percent by 1987. Higher Catholic birth rates and increased immigration from Catholic regions such as Latin America made it seem likely that Catholicism might someday vie with Protestantism as the dominant religious denomination in North America.

JUDAISM, like Protestantism, faced a relative decline after 1950. In 1947, some 5 percent of the American population identified itself as Jewish, in contrast to only 2 percent by 1990.

Other changes were also beginning to be seen in the tripartite paradigm Herberg had used to characterize

American religion. ISLAM was emerging as a fourth force. By 1995, estimates of the Muslim population of Canada and the United States ranged from 3.5 million to 6 million. The fastest-growing faith in the United States, Islam owed its rapid increase to immigration from the Middle East and North Africa, to indigenous expressions (such as the NATION OF ISLAM), and to conversions. By the early twenty-first century, Islam may well replace Judaism as the "third force" in American religion.

By the mid-1990's, changes were also evident in the growth of non-Abrahamic religious traditions. HINDUISM (with 1.3 million American adherents by 1993), BUDDHISM (with 500,000 American followers), and traditional Chinese faiths such as Taoism and Confucianism were rivaling in size some of the lesser Protestant denominations.

Religious Life in Canada. The religious life of North America is shared between two nations, the United States and Canada. Because of their geographical proximity, common civilization, and long historical ties, the spiritual heritage of the two states is similar. Within that similarity, however, several distinctions have emerged.

Religion in Canada flourishes in a unique physical setting. The second-largest country on earth in area (only Russia is bigger), Canada has a relatively sparse population (its 25 million people are about a tenth the population of its southern neighbor) scattered over two-fifths of North America. This population forms a rich cultural mosaic with three main sources. The original Canadians were the Native Americans (in 1986, some 331,000 Indians and 27,000 Inuit, or Eskimos, lived in Canada). The French were a second element in the making of Canada, arriving after 1534. Soon it was said that "not a cape was turned, not a river was entered, but a Jesuit led the way." By the late 1980's, 25 percent of Canada's population was French speaking. Indicative of the Latin heritage was the strength of Roman Catholicism, which claimed about half the population of Canada (the French Catholics were augmented by later immigration from Ireland, Italy, and Poland). The British were a third component, resting their claim to Canada on the landfall in Newfoundland of John Cabot in 1497 and subsequent conquest. By 1986, 67 percent of Canada's people were English speaking; among them, the largest religious traditions were the United Church of Canada, the Anglican church, and the Presbyterians.

By 1900, immigration from Europe further enhanced the mosaic of Canada, bringing new religious adherents such as Lutherans, Jews, and members of the Greek Orthodox church. Since 1983, this religious diversity has increased; most new immigrants have come from Asia, especially Hong Kong, India, and Vietnam. From 1987 to 1991, more than 190,000 immigrants arrived annually. Islam and the faiths of East Asia (Buddhism, Taoism, Confucianism) and India (Hinduism, Jainism, Sikhism) became increasingly evident.

Officially, Canada is a secular society. The separation of church and state has been a reality since 1852, when the Anglican Communion, then the official religion, became a voluntary religious association, on a level of equality with other denominations. Concurrently, the freedom of religion was proclaimed. This has meant the existence of a secular component within the population; in 1994, about 7.5 percent of Canada's people claimed to be nonreligious or atheist.

The Social Role of Religion. On the eve of the twentieth century, Social Gospel advocate Josiah Strong articulated the dilemma and opportunity facing faith as a behavior-modification mechanism in America. Strong wrote that church, state, and society all operate in the same "space" but with different "functions," explaining that "the sphere of the church includes that of the state and much more" because it is "as broad as the sphere of conscience, which is as far-reaching as all human activity." This overlap posed several major issues regarding the social role of religion.

One obvious question was the place of public piety, the proper role of religious exercises and displays in "community space." During the colonial era, there were established churches in most places: Congregational in New England, Anglican in New York and the South. While the Constitution prohibited any one established religion, it was interpreted to permit a variety of public religious practices: chaplains in Congress and the military; references to God in the Pledge of Allegiance and on the currency; and prayers at presidential inaugurations and other state occasions. The "public religion" of the United States was a blend of nonsectarian Christianity, Judaism, and what French author Jean-Jacques Rousseau called "CIVIL RELIGION." Sociologist Robert Bella has defined public piety as "a set of religious beliefs, symbols, and rituals growing out of the American historical experience interpreted in the dimension of transcendence." With references to "Providence," the "Almighty Being," and "the chosen people," the civil religion became a "celebration of the American Way of Life."

Religion

By the 1960's, however, questions flared along the frontier separating church and state. In 1962, the Supreme Court in *ENGEL V. VITALE* ruled that officials in public schools could not require their pupils to recite a nonsectarian prayer at the start of the academic day, viewing this as an unconstitutional effort to "establish religion." The issue of SCHOOL PRAYER, along with the display of religious symbols in public spaces on holy days, touched off a long-running battle. Yale University professor Stephen Carter has lamented the "gradual disenfranchisement of religious views and voices" within state and society. For Carter, the challenge is to maintain civility and "genuine tolerance" in an era of growing religious diversity, while affirming the vital contribution of spirituality to community life.

Next to public piety, the most explosive issue in American life was the public regulation of morality. In the wake of the social revolution of the 1960's, many of the issues were sexual (such as birth control, ABORTION, HOMOSEXUALITY, PORNOGRAPHY, MARRIAGE and DIVORCE, and "FAMILY VALUES") or medical (such as GENETIC ENGINEERING, EUTHANASIA, and the rationing of health services). On the questions of public piety and morality, the American religious community

A mass service at an African American Catholic church. (UPI/Corbis-Bettmann)

Members of the Hare Krishna cult perform in Minneapolis. (UPI/Corbis-Bettmann)

polarized. In the 1960's, the lead in defining social-justice issues had been taken by mainline ministers, such as the Reverend Martin Luther KING, Jr., on civil rights and James A. Pike on "the challenge of peace." In the 1990's, it was evident that the RELIGIOUS RIGHT occupied center stage, aided by an effective mastery of the media. While in the 1950's, pioneer evangelists such as Billy Graham and Charles H. Fuller had used radio to call individuals to conversion, by the 1980's, the "neo-fundamentalists" were employing television (including talk-show formats) to influence national policy. Pat ROBERTSON sometime evangelist and presidential candidate, hosted *THE 700 CLUB*, and founded

the CHRISTIAN BROADCASTING NETWORK (CBN). Jim Bakker hosted the *Praise the Lord* show and by the 1980's was buying millions in air time and opening Christian theme parks. Jerry FALWELL, an independent Baptist television evangelist who hosted *The Old-Time Gospel Hour*, founded the MORAL MAJORITY in 1979 to respond to the "political activities of feminist and homosexual groups" and to influence government decisions about abortion, religion in public schools, and regulation of private schools.

Gilles Kepel, a professor at the Institute of Political Studies in Paris, France, has contended that a "smouldering bonfire" of religious revivalism had begun in

North America is home to a wide variety of religions. (Martin A. Hutner)

the late twentieth century, as evidenced in the 1979 Islamic revolution in Iran, the resurgence of American fundamentalism, and other attempts to reverse secularism and restore traditional values. If Kepel's analysis is correct, then the cultural and moral repercussions of the "fundamentalist awakening" will last far into the twenty-first century.

Alternative Forms of Religion. For millions of Americans, conventional religion, with its models of believing, belonging, and behaving, seemed irrelevant. As such people sought alternative forms of self-actualization and becoming, it became evident that new forms of religion were evolving.

Attention to CULTS in the United States has often focused on dramatic events, such as the killing by federal agents of eighty members of the BRANCH DAVIDIANS near Waco, Texas, in 1993, or the mass suicide of Jim Jones and nine hundred of his followers from the People's Temple in November, 1978, at JONESTOWN, Guyana. Behind these bizarre manifestations lurks a constant in American piety: cult formation. A cult is a group bound together by devotion to a person or ideal, a subculture emphasizing some values neglected in the majority society. (The word "cult" is from a Latin root meaning "tilling" or "caring.")

A cult can begin with a charismatic person, a messianic vision, or a political, military, and economic purpose. Psychological stress can also generate cult formation. Within the cult, an individual may find a sense of identity, security, community, destiny, or energy—and usually a unique way of life. While not new (cults have been around since the "mystery religions" of antiquity), cults tend to become appealing in times of rapid cultural and technological change. Some cults, including the Mormons and the Christian Scientists, mature into mainstream denominations; some, like the Shakers, die out, while others, like the Amish, flourish as permanent minorities. Cults often provide a "safety valve" for society; they can also serve to emphasize views or values overlooked by the predominant culture.

The NEW AGE MOVEMENT flourished in the 1980's after long being snubbed as "do-it-yourself" religion. A generic term for many diverse principles and practices, "New Age" philosophy draws on the insights of Hinduism, Jainism, Buddhism, Chinese thought, primitive religions, alternative Western religions, and the occult, as well as on the teachings of such poet-scientists as Pierre Teilhard de Chardin. The number of "new religionists" in North America was estimated to

be slightly less than 1.5 million in 1993. With its synthesis of science and religion, recovery of folk values, integration of Eastern and Western thought, sense of millennial expectation, and concerns for peace, the environment, and human survival with dignity, the New Age movement was in many ways a reflection of modern American culture.

Conclusion. Predictions of the "death of God" and the disappearance of religion before the onslaughts of secularity and technology in the twentieth century have proven premature. In *The History and Future of Faith* (1988), Robert Ellwood speculated that the current revival of religion—in traditional and unconventional forms—was a last great reenactment of the folk religion stage of world history, a prelude to a compassionate and communitarian faith of the future. Whether one's outlook is optimistic or pessimistic, few doubt that in the United States and Canada, religion as a way of believing, belonging, behaving, and becoming remained vital at the dawn of the twenty-first century, with tantalizing patterns of continuity with the past and often startling and provocative patterns of innovation.

—*C. George Fry*

SUGGESTED READINGS: Fascinating statistical data can be found in George Gallup, Jr., and Jim Castelli's *The People's Religion: American Faith in the Nineties* (New York: Macmillan, 1989). Valuable historical continuity is provided by Frank E. Eakin, Jr.'s *Religion in Western Culture: Selected Issues* (Washington, D.C.: University Press of America, 1977). Robert N. Bellah and Phillip E. Hammond's *Varieties of Civil Religion* (San Francisco: Harper & Row, 1980) contrasts American public piety with that of other societies, such as Japan and Mexico, while Sidney E. Mead's *The Nation with the Soul of a Church* (New York: Harper & Row, 1975) places that piety in perspective. Also helpful is Robert N. Bellah's *The Broken Covenant: American Civil Religion in a Time of Trial* (New York: Seabury Press, 1975).

Controversial but useful is Stephen L. Carter's *The Culture of Disbelief: How American Law and Politics Trivialize Religious Devotion* (New York: Basic Books, 1993). Useful prognostications of the future of piety are found in Rodney Stark and William Sims Bainbridge's *The Future of Religion: Secularization, Revival, and Cult Formation* (Berkeley: University of California Press, 1985) and Robert Ellwood's *The History and Future of Faith: Religion Past, Present, and to Come* (New York: Crossroad, 1988). On the global revival of fundamentalism, see Gilles Kepel's *The Re-*

venge of God: The Resurgence of Islam, Christianity, and Judaism in the Modern World, translated from the French by Alan Braley (University Park: The Pennsylvania State University Press, 1994).

Religious Freedom Restoration Act: U.S. federal legislation enacted November 16, 1993. The act overturned a 1990 U.S. Supreme Court ruling in EMPLOYMENT DIVISION V. SMITH, in which the Court upheld the denial of employment to a Native American convicted for using peyote as part of a religious ritual. The ruling abandoned the long-accepted principle that required the government to demonstrate a "compelling state interest" to justify restricting religious practices; the new law restored the old standard. Vice President Al Gore said the new law would cover issues from autopsies to church architecture.

Religious Right: Mass movement in the late twentieth century that blended conservative politics with conservative, usually Protestant, religion. Sometimes known as the New Christian Right, this union of religious groups with political groups produced a long list of social and political concerns rooted in the moral assumptions of the Judeo-Christian heritage. The Religious Right is particularly concerned with ABORTION, traditional sex roles in society, SCHOOL PRAYER, the decline in public morality, and PORNOGRAPHY.

Background. The merger of religion and politics is not a new phenomenon in American history. For example, early nineteenth century evangelicals teamed with the REPUBLICAN PARTY to deal a death blow to slavery. Likewise, evangelicals led the assault against John T. Scopes, who was found guilty of teaching evolution in a Dayton, Tennessee, high school in 1925. In both cases, religion and politics combined their weights in an effort to affect society.

The emergence of the Religious Right, however, was different from other mass American socio-religious movements. It originated in the 1970's with numerous nationwide grassroots movements that addressed local moral issues. These issues ranged from defense of independent Christian schools to opposition of homosexual rights. However, one issue, the EQUAL RIGHTS AMENDMENT (ERA), served as a backdrop for these other movements. The Equal Rights Amendment passed Congress in 1972, but it was challenged by those who saw it as a threat to the traditional role of women in society. Phyllis Schlafly was especially critical of the ERA, and thanks largely to her determined, well-organized opposition to the measure, it was never ratified by the number of states needed to enact it into law.

The fight against the ERA attracted attention from evangelical Protestant fundamentalists and others who believed that the United States was experiencing wholesale moral decline. Further, they believed that this decline resulted from the widespread abandonment of Bible-based values. It is likely that the debate over the ERA galvanized their sundry concerns into a sense that some sort of political action was necessary in order to stem the country's perceived moral decline.

The nation's conservative political leadership took special note as evangelicals began flexing their political muscles. Coincidentally, America's liberal culture and political assumptions, which had been in place since President Franklin D. Roosevelt and the NEW DEAL, faced increasing opposition.

In 1980, these dissonant religious voices coalesced with conservative politics as the nation faced a presidential election. The incumbent, Jimmy CARTER, ran against John Anderson and Ronald REAGAN. Carter and Anderson both practiced their religious faith more openly than Reagan. Still, conservative evangelicals supported Reagan because they found his positions on domestic social issues more appealing than those of either of his competitors. When he faced reelection in 1984, Reagan again appealed to his conservative constituency, especially in the religious ranks. The Religious Right overwhelmingly supported Reagan in both elections. While the Religious Right's overall impact may be debatable, some estimate that as many as 3 million new voters registered in 1984, largely the result of its influence.

There are several reasons why conservative politics and conservative religion allied themselves into the "New Right" in the late twentieth century. In addition to the nation's perceived moral decline, political conservatives chafed at the excesses of what they considered to be government interference in both the economic and private sectors of American life. Conservative religious groups could scarcely disagree with this contention, given the government's tendencies to be sympathetic to the social issues they opposed. Consequently, "big government," or more specifically, the perceived excesses of a big, liberal (socially and economically) government, became the nexus between politics and religion. The religious element of the New

Right blamed the American government for implementing social policies that they believed were contradictory to biblical principles. Meanwhile, they left the politically conservative element of the New Right to pursue reforms in the economy and foreign relations. In either case, the existing governmental structure and the DEMOCRATIC PARTY in particular became convenient targets for these groups.

Issues. Bolstered by their success in the battle against the ERA, the religious leaders who would form the core of the Religious Right began to speak out against other issues, especially "secular humanism." A precise definition of secular humanism is elusive; although the Religious Right maintains that it is a philosophical assumption that humanity is superior to deity and that humanity's chief end is to glorify itself rather than God. Thus, there is a tendency on behalf of the new Religious Right to see "secular humanists" as

agents of Satan, out to rid society of all vestiges of religion. Further, the Religious Right tends to see public institutions, particularly elementary and secondary schools, as the chief propagators of secular humanism.

Despite the fact that the Religious Right addresses numerous issues, it may be too much to say that it has a precise agenda. In foreign affairs, the New Right staunchly opposes communism because it is associated with ATHEISM. In the wake of the Soviet Union's collapse, the Religious Right generally remains suspicious of former Soviet allies. It also tends to support or oppose issues in the foreign arena according to how it perceives related domestic issues.

On the domestic scene, the Religious Right vigorously defends the pro-life movement, arguing that abortion is murder. In fact, since *ROE V. WADE* legalized abortion in 1973, the Religious Right has advocated a constitutional amendment that would ban abortions.

Religious Right leader Ralph Reed with Newt Gingrich in 1995. (Archive Photos/Reuters/Jiminez)

Religious Right leader Jerry Falwell addresses a 1981 Kansas rally. (AP/Wide World Photos)

The Religious Right also supports voluntary prayer in public schools and a tax VOUCHER PROGRAM that would allow parents to send their children to the school of their choice. They also defend traditional sex roles in society, as well as the primacy of the traditional nuclear family. Some in the New Right believe that the United States is a Christian nation, while others believe the country has a Judeo-Christian heritage. In either case, both assert that the nation should return to biblically based values.

Organizations. Because the Religious Right has no precise agenda, it has no single organization that articulates its position. Rather, there are a number of institutions that raise issues relating to the Religious Right's concerns. The MORAL MAJORITY was among the first of these organizations. Established in 1979 by Jerry FALWELL, the Moral Majority sought to unite individuals, regardless of their particular religious affiliation, who believed that American society had abandoned God. Falwell challenged his followers to voice their concerns over school prayer, creationism, declining moral standards, and any other issue that would restore a sense of public morality. The Moral Majority disbanded in 1989, but it was succeeded by the Liberty Foundation, an organization that lobbies Congress on moral issues.

The Religious Right has also advanced its cause through the media, especially television. Falwell's church, the Thomas Road Baptist Church in Lynchburg, Virginia, sponsors *The Old-Time Gospel Hour*. This show is usually a rebroadcast of services held at Thomas Road Baptist Church. Consequently, Falwell has a forum via which he may simultaneously admonish both his congregation and his viewing audience.

Yet Falwell was not necessarily a pioneer in using television to merge politics and religion. In 1960, Pat ROBERTSON established the CHRISTIAN BROADCASTING NETWORK (CBN). Like Falwell, Robertson was concerned about declining moral standards, especially in television programming. One of CBN's most noteworthy shows, *THE 700 CLUB*, employs a talk-show format to disseminate information on culture, society, politics, and economics. Robertson drew considerable attention from both the religious and nonreligious sectors when he ran unsuccessfully for president in 1988. Organizations that reflect the Religious Right's concerns are too numerous to mention; it is safe to say, however, that they provide their supporters with information pertinent to the issues of public morality. This interconnectedness helps provide a sense of political and cultural solidarity that helps transcend denominational differences and facilitate interdenominational cooperation.

Conclusion. The Religious Right is "new" in the sense that it successfully galvanized religious and political sentiments into a sustained national movement. Whereas early religious and political issues may have drawn passing attention, the Religious Right has built an impressive, although largely informal, organizational structure. Moreover, by attaching itself to conservative Republican Party politics, the Religious Right probably ensured a longevity for itself that it may not have otherwise obtained.   —*Keith Harper*

SUGGESTED READINGS: For a thorough statement of the New Right's social and political agenda, consult Newt Gingrich's *To Renew America* (New York: HarperCollins, 1995) and *Contract with America* (New

Religious Right leader Pat Robertson addresses the 1986 National Right to Life Convention. (UPI/Corbis-Bettmann)

York: Times Books, a division of Random House, 1994), by Gingrich et al. For a statement of the religious concerns of the New Right, see Jerry Falwell's *"Listen, America!"* (Garden City, N.Y.: Doubleday, 1980) and *Strength for the Journey: An Autobiography* (New York: Simon & Schuster, 1987). Secular humanism is Robert E. Webber's topic in *Secular Humanism: Threat and Challenge* (Grand Rapids, Mich.: Zondervan, 1982). Editors Robert C. Liebman and Robert Wuthnow's *The New Christian Right: Mobilization and Legitimation* (Hawthorne, N.Y.: Aldine, 1983) is an especially perceptive sociological analysis of the New Right. Matthew C. Moen's *The Transformation of the Christian Right* (Tuscaloosa: The University of Alabama Press, 1992) is a brief yet helpful examination of the Religious Right from a political-science perspective.

Religious Roundtable: Christian political organization founded in 1980. Ed McAteer, a Southern Baptist organizer for Howard Phillips' Conservative Caucus, founded Religious Roundtable in an effort to attract mainstream Baptists, Presbyterians, and others who had ideological differences with the MORAL MAJORITY and the other chief RELIGIOUS RIGHT organization of the time, Christian Voice. Enlisting popular television evangelist James Robison as his vice president, McAteer launched his organization with a gathering of prominent conservatives. A similar convocation after the 1992 Republican convention was a "who's who" of right-wing luminaries eager to demonstrate support for George BUSH and the REPUBLICAN PARTY.

Remarriage: Entering into another marriage after one's spouse dies or is divorced. Recent studies show that almost half of all U.S. marriages are remarriages; the success rate is about the same as for first marriages. As a result of the high rate of remarriage, a large percentage of American children live with a stepparent and, often, stepsiblings. Both the breakup of the marriage of a child's biological parents and subsequent remarriage often have traumatic effects upon the child involved.

Remedial education: Programs set up to assist students having difficulty in school or who are labeled as being "at risk" of having difficulty in the future. These programs are alike in seeking to remedy a problem or deficit that individual students or groups of students are thought to have.

There are many problems experienced by schoolchildren that are manifested in poor school performance. Among such problems are poverty, hunger, having a "deficient" family life, having a first language other than English, having a learning disability, being alienated from school, and being a behavior problem in school. Since the 1960's, remedial-education programs have attempted to counter some of these roadblocks to learning. School breakfast and lunch programs, HEAD START, Follow Through, Title I remedial reading and math programs, bilingual-education programs, after-school job-related programs, desegregation programs, learning centers, special-education programs, and grants for school districts having high concentrations of poor children are some of the established programs.

There are several ways of looking at remedial education. The most widely accepted view is that remedial programs are needed in order to "level the playing field." This perspective suggests that groups of chil-

A remarriage ceremony for a New York couple. (Don Franklin)

dren (for example, the poor or minorities) who suffer from deficits that put them at a disadvantage in schools can be identified. It is argued that these children can and do benefit from programs that "compensate" for their deficits. In principle, this is accomplished by remedying the problem, followed by withdrawing the student from the remedial program. The student is then thought to be ready to reintegrate into mainstream classes, able to learn and compete effectively with other students.

Critics of remedial education agree in theory with the philosophy of these programs, but have concerns about their implementation. Some observers argue that they fail to reach all or most of those who qualify for them. Others argue that even when remedial programs reach those in need, they are often ineffective because they lack adequate funding and staffing.

Critics also argue that remedial programs divert attention away from the real problems of schooling. They comment that one of the major accomplishments of remedial education is to segregate poor students from their classmates. They argue that this is a consistent policy of the government, suggesting that officials are primarily interested in segregating poor learners from good learners, thus enabling the latter to learn without interference. It is also said that remedial education programs "blame the victims" by embarrassing participants of such programs, thus reinforcing their sense of difference or inferiority to other students. Blaming the victims also diverts attention away from closer examination of mainstream educational subject matter and school organization. From this perspective, the inflexibility of curricula, the organization of schools, and the competitive nature of schools create a climate in which it is inevitable that some students fail to thrive. Hence, these critics argue that the problem lies with the organization of schools rather than with those who fail to succeed within such flawed institutions.

Reno, Janet (b. July 21, 1938, Miami, Fla.): U.S. attorney general. In 1993, Reno became the first fe-

U.S. attorney general Janet Reno in 1994. (AP/Wide World Photos)

male attorney general in U.S. history. In 1978, she became state's attorney for Dade County, Florida, holding that post until nominated as U.S. attorney general by President Bill CLINTON. Reno is known for her concerns in the areas of children's rights, juvenile justice, and drug abuse. She became the center of controversy over the assault by federal agents on the Waco, Texas, compound of David Koresh's BRANCH DAVIDIAN cult on April 19, 1993, an assault she had authorized.

Repressed memory: Active but unconscious mental process that makes certain mental material unavailable to conscious awareness. Repressing memories is a frequent defense mechanism of victims of incest and sexual molestation. Debate exists over whether memories from childhood can be "recovered" and brought to consciousness or if this is actually "false consciousness."

The term repression was first used by Sigmund Freud to explain frequent memory gaps, particularly those related to early childhood. He observed in his patients that less pleasant material is the most difficult to recall.

INCEST, sexual relations between close relatives, is not allowed in most cultures. Sexual molestation of a child, forced physical and sexual contact between an adult and a child under the age of eighteen, is against the law. In a child experiencing incestuous relations, repressed memory may become exaggerated because recollection of the sexual event exerts a profound effect upon the individual's personality. Children who have been sexually victimized by adults experience such disturbances as hysterical reactions and repressed memory.

Psychotherapists often use hypnosis and other techniques to probe their patients' minds in an attempt to uncover repressed memories of incest or sexual molestation. They have found that trauma from these events can be totally forgotten (repressed) for decades. Therapists claim that by allowing the person to talk through his or her problems, the repressed memories can be recovered and an account of the event is possible. Attempts have been made to use the account of these events to prosecute the offenders in court.

The use of the contents of repressed memory as evidence for conviction in incest or molestation cases is difficult. First, the period of time between the incest or molestation and its recollection may be years. The ac-

cused adult could be disabled or dead. Second, the relationship that exists between the perpetrator and the victim may be damaged by prosecuting such a case. Finally, the likelihood of a conviction is reduced by the questions raised about "false consciousness," memory of events that are partially or totally untrue. A likely defense for charges of incest or sexual molestation would be to challenge the legitimacy of psychotherapy. In 1993, Martin Gardner suggested that a false premise exists in repressed-memory therapy—one must first believe that people are able to block unpleasant occurrences from consciousness. Such a premise rests on personal accounts of memories that cannot be proved or disproved in a court of law.

Many psychotherapists insist that repressed memory is a natural and likely reaction to traumatic incestuous events in childhood. They argue that until society accepts the reality that the sexual molestation of children occurs, and until society commits to deal with the structural changes necessary to end the sanctioning of child sexual abuse, the damage to children will continue. They further argue that groups of people desperately search for other explanations to avoid the truth of incest and child molestation because the possibility of such events is too painful to accept.

Reproductive issues: Factors considered in decisions to engage in sexual intercourse. Among these issues are childbearing, contraception, ABORTION, utilization of technological advances, recourse to surrogacy, and INFERTILITY. Reproductive issues are among the most hotly contested and politically and socially divisive issues of the late twentieth century.

Reproductive Freedom and Culture. Women's search for autonomy and gender equality is interwoven with cultural definitions of who women are, the importance of bearing children, and the value of family life. The ability to reproduce strongly influences the way girls are raised to become women and the political and social consequences of women's role in society. The right to choose whether to bear children, together with the social and moral implications of that decision, are part of the liberal climate of the last decades of the twentieth century.

The traditional role of women as companions to their husbands, bearers of children, and helpmates to their families evolved as women entered the workforce in increasingly large numbers. Women's need for self-identification and the recognition that they had the legal right to control their own bodies led to a decrease in fertility and a delay in childbearing. The women's movement broke down barriers to women's social and economic inequality and highlighted the fact that the traditionally subordinated status of women was outmoded.

Demographic concerns also affect the nature and meaning of decisions concerning reproduction and the technology used to accomplish it. Moreover, class and culture are important determinants of the use and acceptance of contraceptives as well as the new technological innovations often unavailable to women of lower socioeconomic status. Such inequities in society deny low-income women equal access to the choices available to those in other social and sociocultural sectors. A dearth of educational information concerning health and reproduction coupled with a lack of access to prenatal and postnatal care, an absence of quality medical services and health insurance, and low Medicaid reimbursements often interfere with the reproductive choices of poor women and women of color. Other deterrents to free reproductive choice include a denial of federal funding of abortions for Native Americans living on reservations, language barriers and other communication breakdowns that are the result of misunderstanding or misinterpretation especially among the Hispanic population, and inadequate or absent informed consent about invasive procedures. Coerced sterilization or late-term abortion are often the only options available to this group of women.

Changing Roles. Many social critics argue that in the permissive and narcissistic culture of the 1990's, with its emphasis on appearance over substance, sex has become a commodity and sexual relationships devalued. Sexual and emotional intimacy have become dissociated and, as a result, a variety of forces have exerted pressure on both sexes. Among them are an increased level of personal and social expectations from intimate relationships and a consumer mentality in which each person feels entitled to "have it all." Anything less is unacceptable. Marriage has become shrouded in a fairy-tale mystique, with each partner's expectations derived from his or her own early familial relationships and perceptions. At the same time, there is a power struggle between the sexes, as the masculine mystique based on toughness and domination is pitted against women's claim to sexual fulfillment as an integral part of their existence, separate and apart from their traditional procreative role. As women become more assertive and establish their place in the world outside the home, the boundaries between work and family life have been redrawn.

Because the contemporary male is often driven by the need to prove himself through wealth, power, and status, a decreased capacity for intimacy has resulted. Fear of submission leads to a compulsion to win. Consequently, men tend to separate sexual and emotional needs, which generally remain synonymous to women. Partly as a result of the interpersonal differences, women are marrying later and less often, and instigating divorce more often than in earlier generations. Those with the greatest income and education are most likely to divorce and least likely to remarry. In contrast, the wealthiest and best-educated men are most likely to stay married or remarry quickly.

The 1960's brought the advent of change in society's perception of intimacy. An increase in college education for both sexes extended adolescence and delayed the transition to adulthood. A heightened emphasis on career delayed the age of first marriages and shifted the focus of intimate relationships from procreation to sex. The 1970's brought a heightened appreciation of the emotional risks associated with intimacy; marriage often became regarded as a "trap" in which men feared losing control and women wished a commitment to legitimize their newly discovered sexuality.

More conservative courtship practices prevailed during the 1980's. Concern bordering on fear over SEXUALLY TRANSMITTED DISEASES such as ACQUIRED IMMUNE DEFICIENCY SYNDROME (AIDS) as well as venereal disease (syphilis and gonorrhea) affected attitudes about dating and sex. Initially considered a disease of gay men, AIDS was quickly established as more far-reaching, evolving into a deadly worldwide epidemic of immense magnitude. Lack of education and poor dissemination of information about the dangers of sexually transmitted diseases and the social and physical consequences of intercourse remain problematic.

Popularity and concern about one's image prevailed in the 1990's. Health clubs proliferated, coupled with an emphasis on diets, cosmetics, and clothing, which emerged as central to social value and popularity within many groups. Present was a rising tide of anorexia nervosa and bulimia nervosa on college campuses, considered to be symbolic of social and emotional isolation and fear of loneliness and disillusionment. Date rape increased alarmingly, while sexual activity at younger and younger ages surged.

The rising out-of-wedlock birth rates point to a tre-

Planned Parenthood clinics are among the biggest providers of birth-control information and services. (James L. Shaffer)

mendous decline in the stigma that society once attached to such births. Teenagers, who once accounted for half of the unwed births, bore fewer than one-third of the 1.2 million babies born out of wedlock in 1992. Most teenage pregnancy is related to POVERTY. Pregnant teenagers generally do not have access to contraception, often come from a low-income, single-parent family, drop out of school, and ultimately go on welfare. The highest out-of-wedlock birth rates in 1992 were among unmarried Hispanic women (95.3 per 1,000) followed by African American women (86.5) and white women (35.2). The rise from 1980 to 1992 was sharpest among women age twenty and older.

Issues of Marriage. Marriage before the Industrial Revolution was linked to notions of the family as a basic social unit and of mutual cooperation for the common good. The family was a rigid institution, resistant to change and dedicated to maintaining the status quo. The Industrial Revolution caused a new urban industrial culture to emerge, breaking down old institutions and substituting new patterns and changes in goals. Marriage became the primary means by which an individual's need for comfort and support, love and understanding could be satisfied.

The contemporary concept of marriage as a partnership is a radical break with tradition. Patriarchy and the hierarchical distinction between husband and wife, with husband being omnipotent and wife compliant and obedient, has been eroded. Companionship and the idea of a harmonious union of two individuals have emerged in its place. The sexual revolution and changing ideas about premarital chastity have resulted in a reevaluation of sexual morality and the acceptance or rejection of social or religious values.

Parenthood, once characterized by unquestioned obedience and conformity by children, consisted of molding offspring in a manner deemed appropriate by those in authority. Autonomy and self-reliance, prevalent in the latter part of the twentieth century, came about through mutual cooperation between parents and children. Nontraditional families, stepfamilies, same-sex relationships, divorce, and single parenthood have changed and impacted the traditional family structure.

The choice to remain childless often begins as a decision to defer childbearing until certain goals are achieved or obstacles overcome, such as graduation, purchasing a home, saving a nest egg, or getting out of debt. Disadvantages of childbearing are debated until a number of childless years have passed and the commitment to childlessness becomes permanent. Other reasons for childlessness involve infertility and advancing age. Consideration of a viable adoption alternative points up the fact that relatively few newborns are available. Adoption records, once sealed and inaccessible, are now made available for examination by adoptees who desire information concerning the birth parents and medical histories.

Most young singles have not given up on marriage but have merely postponed it. Moving in large numbers to urban areas, they seek employment, living arrangements, and friends. Without the support of a marital partner with whom to shape their lives, they enjoy the freedom, economic self-sufficiency, sexual experiences, and personal development afforded by friends and support groups. Such groups include men's and women's groups, political and social groups, therapy groups, and organizations formed around specialized interests, all of which help to validate the single lifestyle. Often, age thirty is the line of demarcation at which point singles decide whether to continue their lifestyle or to marry. A study by the U.S. Census Bureau reveals that only 60 percent of women who are single at age thirty will marry and that the percentage decreases sharply with increasing age. Part of the reason is demographic: Women outnumber men, giving women relatively fewer marriage prospects. Conversely, men who marry after age forty-five usually marry women only about four years younger than themselves. Women who marry for the first time after age forty generally have a high degree of self-confidence and often lack the traditional feminine identity.

The decision to marry may stem from multiple interrelated emotional, psychological, religious, and societal factors. Marriage may represent permanence, trust, reliability, commitment, legitimization of children, pressure from parents or peers, economic security, and feelings of love and dedication. Childbearing is important for many reasons: continuity of lineage, proof of adulthood and its connection to families and communities, pressure from society, and a desire to fill a void in one's life. A child is born generally within the first five years of marriage. In communities of color, childlessness is a very serious concern. As a result of cultural norms and restricted professional or career opportunities for women, motherhood and family life are highly valued. Losing the option of procreating and parenting can be devastating to low-income women or women of color.

Interfaith marriages are actively discouraged, and in some cases forbidden, by most major religions in society because of a fear of disruption of family life. Three-fourths of all persons marrying for the first time have religious ceremonies, as do 60 percent of divorced people who remarry. Catholic intermarriage is invalid in the view of the Church. A Catholic who wishes to marry a non-Catholic and remain in a state of grace must first receive dispensation from a priest, promise to remain faithful to his or her religion, and have all children baptized and brought up in the Church. Orthodox Judaism regards interfaith marriage as a sin, and most orthodox and conservative rabbis will not officiate at weddings for mixed couples. Some reform rabbis are more lenient, performing ceremonies without insisting on the conversion of the non-Jewish partner.

Although interracial marriage has been recognized by the Supreme Court since 1967, the incidence of those marriages is statistically negligible (1.6 percent of all U.S. marriages in 1983). Interracial couples are often targets for bigotry in American society. Reasons for these marriages are probably the same as those of traditional couples, but other factors such as a desire to defy cultural prejudices or to rebel against parental authority may motivate interracial couples to marry.

Choice of Contraception. The women's movement reflected the changing social environment and growing emancipation and independence of women. Birth-control technology and capability expanded rapidly, providing women additional freedom. Methods range from intrauterine devices (IUDs) and birth-control pills to injectable contraceptives (DEPO-PROVERA), reversible subdermal implants (Norplant), and "morning after" pills.

The birth-control pill was first approved for use in June, 1960, a time when rapid population growth was coming to be viewed as a threat to the global environment and the economic and social health of many countries, especially those of the Third World. It revolutionized contemporary birth-control methods as a result of its simplicity, accessibility, and effectiveness. Within twenty years of its advent, an estimated 10 million to 15 million American women and 80 million to 100 million women worldwide were using oral contraceptives for birth control. Oral contraceptives are used chiefly by women under age thirty because of possible cardiovascular side effects among those over age thirty-five. Misinformation about the possible health risks from the pill discourages many young women and teens from using it. Because of side effects, IUDs are being prescribed only for women in monogamous relationships who have at least one child. Other methods such as the condom and the diaphragm, less effective than the IUD or the pill, are unattractive to many couples.

The right of contraception was formally recognized by the Supreme Court in *GRISWOLD V. CONNECTICUT* in 1965, which declared unconstitutional a Connecticut statute that outlawed contraceptives and made their use a criminal offense. (In the same case, the Court recognized a constitutional right of privacy and gave it legal protection.) The immediate consequence of the decision was the repeal of birth-control statutes in Connecticut and thirteen other states and a dramatic increase in the number of women who gained access to birth-control devices and counseling. *Griswold* was confined to traditional notions of contraception by married persons. The privacy guarantee was extended to contraception for single persons in 1972 and for minors in 1977.

Birth-control methods include sterilization, which is totally effective and generally not reversible; pills, which are 95 percent to 99 percent effective and cause fewer side effects; and a mini-pill with no estrogen, available to women who are breast-feeding or smokers over age thirty-five. IUDs are 98 percent to 99 percent effective, but carry an increased risk of pelvic inflammatory disease (PID). The Dalkon Shield, a type of IUD, has been associated with PID, subsequent infertility, and even death. The condom, readily available, offers good protection against sexually transmitted diseases, particularly if coated with spermicide. The failure rate of 3 percent to 15 percent is generally attributable to careless use. The diaphragm has a failure rate of 2 percent to 20 percent because of improper or inconsistent use. Its side effects are generally negli-

gible, but users may become allergic to the spermicide used with it. It can also cause urinary-tract infections. Norplant, an implant diffusing a low dose of medication directly into the bloodstream, contains no estrogen but can cause menstrual irregularity. When surgically inserted in capsule form under the skin of the arm, it offers contraceptive protection for five years. Other contraceptive methods that are easy to obtain and use are sponges, foams, creams, jellies, and vaginal suppositories. Their failure rate ranges from 3 percent to 21 percent. The cervical cap, similar to a diaphragm but without the risk of urinary tract infection, is available primarily in large population centers. A generally flagging interest in the United States concerning contraceptive development has resulted from insufficient funding, decreased concern about population growth, regulatory hurdles, and the prevalence of product litigation, which has severely impacted the pharmaceutical industry.

Abortion. The right to reproduce also includes the right not to reproduce through ABORTION, contraception, or sterilization. Pro-choice advocates support the rights of women to control their own bodies and decide whether to bear children. Right-to-life supporters argue that abortion is murder and a threat to the foundations of the traditional roles of motherhood, the American family, and religious and moral precepts. The biological partner has also raised the issue of his right to have a voice in the abortion decision.

In January, 1973, the Supreme Court in *ROE V. WADE* ruled that a woman has a constitutional right to choose to terminate her pregnancy based on two principles: the woman's fundamental right of privacy, and the status of the fetus. The Court wrote that because the right of privacy is fundamental, only a compelling reason will allow the government to interfere with the exercise of that right. The Court also answered the claim that abortion destroyed life when it explained that the unborn was not a person entitled to the constitutional guarantees of life and liberty, stating that "person" in the Fourteenth Amendment is used in the postnatal sense only.

Abortion calls into question differing beliefs about the roles of the sexes, the meaning of parenthood, and human nature. Approximately 90 percent of all abortions occur in the first trimester. Those that are not are often performed on young, poor, or minority women who lacked access to help at an earlier stage. Contraception and abortion are special moral issues for Catholics. Consistent with nineteenth century Catholic

Abortion is the most controversial reproductive issue. (Reuters/Corbis-Bettmann)

theology forbidding abortions during all periods of pregnancy, in 1869, Pope Pius IX stipulated excommunication as the penalty for anyone procuring an abortion. Because of the Church's belief that life begins at conception, the Vatican's *Instruction on Respect for Human Life in Its Origin and on the Dignity of Procreation* (1987) states that no moral distinction can be made among any stages of embryonic development; the absolute sanctity of human life makes it impossible to discard early embryos or use them for research.

Technology and Infertility. Pregnancy-inducing technologies include *IN VITRO* FERTILIZATION (IVF), first available in 1978, gamete intra-fallopian tube transfer (GIFT), artificial insemination, treatments for stimulating ovulation, and fallopian tube reconstruction. These procedures are costly and often not covered by medical insurance, making them inaccessible to many, and stressful for those who can afford them, requiring multiple visits to the fertility clinic with no assurance of success. Moreover, because they are not attached to established medical centers, fertility clinics are often selective with very specific screening preferences: poor,

unmarried, disabled, and lesbian women are often not accepted for testing. Of the 3 million births annually in the United States, thirty thousand to forty thousand are the direct result of technological conception.

In 1988, the National Center for Health Statistics reported that at least 2.3 million couples experienced infertility. This was an increase from 4 percent to 7 percent in young women in their early twenties, largely as the result of the spread of sexually transmitted diseases. The physiological causes of infertility include an absence of ovulation, sperm deficient in number or in ability to reach the egg, and damage to fallopian tubes, uterus, or cervix. Scar tissue from inflammatory infections can affect the functioning of the tubes and uterus. In men, such infections may impair sperm quality and production. Reasons for infertility can be found through testing in the majority of cases. As new technologies become available, making it possible to choose an embryo's gender or to alter its genetic structure, ethical questions arise. Prenatal testing that reveals certain diseases, such as sickle-cell disease, adds an emotional and moral burden to the situation.

Reproductive technologies

Surrogacy raises moral and practical questions concerning the potentially conflicting rights of the child, the surrogate, and the biological father and his wife. The role of the unborn fetus as a patient for whom therapies are being developed is also being debated; a fetal-rights movement has resulted. —*Marcia J. Weiss*

SUGGESTED READINGS: Judith Rodin and Aila Collins have edited *Women and New Reproductive Technologies: Medical Psychosocial, Legal, and Ethical Dilemmas* (Hillsdale, N.J.: Lawrence Erlbaum, 1991), which presents a multidisciplinary approach to reproduction and how it is viewed on the threshold of the twenty-first century. Sherrill Cohen and Nadine Taub have edited *Reproductive Laws for the 1990's* (Clifton, N.J.: Humana Press, 1989), a project of the Working Group on Reproduction at Rutgers University, which assesses the effect of technology on reproductive issues. Suzanne Wymelenberg's *Science and Babies: Private Decisions, Public Dilemmas* (Washington, D.C.: National Academy Press, 1990) describes the understanding of human fertility and related issues, such as teenage pregnancy and prenatal care, and addresses ethical concerns in human reproduction and public policy. *Marriage and Family in a Changing Society*, 4th ed. (New York: Free Press, 1992), edited by James M. Henslin, contains a series of articles dealing with sociological approaches to the study of marriage and family life.

Phil Brown's *The Death of Intimacy: Barriers to Meaningful Interpersonal Relationships* (New York: Haworth, 1995) is a social commentary encompassing psychology, sociology, and feminist theory. Robert Blank and Janna C. Merrick's *Human Reproduction, Emerging Technologies, and Conflicting Rights* (Washington, D.C.: Congressional Quarterly, 1995) examines the controversial and complex issues surrounding reproduction from a public policy perspective, focusing on the degree to which emerging technology has reshaped the debate. John A. Robertson's *Children of Choice: Freedom and the New Reproductive Technologies* (Princeton, N.J.: Princeton University Press, 1994) examines the consequences of reproductive technology and its possible ethical and legal implications.

Reproductive technologies: Medical interventions used in the treatment of infertility. The term refers particularly to those methods by which fertilization is achieved through some method other than sex-

ual intercourse. This creates options for infertile couples, but also gives rise to ethical and social dilemmas.

Reasons for Treatment. The specific treatment depends on the cause of infertility. Extensive testing of both the woman and the man must precede medical intervention. Criteria used to determine infertility are strict. Most physicians will not begin testing unless a couple has attempted pregnancy for a year, or if three or more miscarriages (spontaneous abortions) have occurred. Causes of infertility are equally common in men and in women and have been as easily treatable as advising men to stop wearing tight jeans. Most infertility treatment attempts to allow "normal" fertilization through sexual intercourse. Hormonal or surgical efforts may attempt to increase sperm count in the man or ovulation in the woman or to remove blockages such as scarring covering the woman's fallopian tubes. In a small percentage of couples, fertilization through intercourse cannot occur or is deemed unlikely or risky.

Common Technologies. Artificial insemination (AI) is the most common technology in use and is a component of many other reproductive technologies. Owing to relatively low risk and invasiveness, AI may be used without diagnosed infertility. AI involves collecting a male's sperm and then implanting the sperm in a woman's uterus. In cases of male infertility, a couple may use sperm from a donor. Hormone treatments are often used with the woman to guarantee timing of ovulation. Sperm can also be frozen, using cryotechnology, for later use. Men facing surgery that might affect their fertility have done this. In at least one case, a man dying of cancer had his sperm frozen, and his wife conceived and bore his child after his death.

The greatest publicity has revolved around *in vitro* fertilization (IVF). The first "test-tube" baby, Louise Brown, was born in England in 1978. IVF does not occur in a test tube, however, but in a petri dish. It is used to treat women with healthy ova whose fallopian tubes are blocked, disallowing normal fertilization. Sperm are collected from the male partner and ova from the woman. This latter procedure is invasive, requiring hormonal manipulation of the menstrual cycle and surgical removal of ova (using laparoscopy). The sperm and ova are combined in a petri dish with a medium to nourish their development. When the resulting embryo reaches the eight-cell stage, it is reimplanted, via catheter, in the woman. A number of improvements in the procedure have been developed, notably the GIFT procedure, gamete-intra-fallopian transfer, where fertilization actually occurs in the fal-

Louise Brown, the first "test-tube" baby, in 1979. (UPI/Corbis-Bettmann)

Reproductive technologies

lopian tube. Success rates for IVF have been very low, with 25 percent success rates being high; GIFT success is as high as 40 percent, but the method is not appropriate for everyone. Success rates are higher at some clinics than at others; the above rates are higher than most. Successful pregnancies typically require multiple attempts (in new, induced menstrual cycles), and often involve experiences with spontaneous abortions.

IVF results in the fertilization of multiple embryos.

Because of the invasiveness of the procedure and high failure rates, multiple embryos are typically implanted in the woman. "Excess" embryos are discarded, or frozen for later use. Freezing embryos, like freezing sperm, creates options for delaying conception.

IVF technologies create additional possibilities. Women without healthy ova can now make use of ovum donors. A new conceptus can be removed from one woman and, through embryo transfer, implanted in

A Colorado couple proudly displays their baby girl conceived via the GIFT procedure, a controversial reproductive technology. (UPI/Corbis-Bettmann)

another woman to develop in her uterus.

Some combination of these technologies has been used in surrogate parenting. A couple desiring parenthood can take the man's sperm for AI with a woman who has contracted to undergo the pregnancy and to deliver the baby as the contracting couple's at delivery. When the intended mother can conceive but not withstand pregnancy, her own ova may be used to create the pregnancy, again borne by a surrogate, using embryo transfer.

Ethical Concerns. Legal and ethical debates have proliferated along with the proliferation of reproductive technologies. Beyond distaste with "playing God," a more concrete issue concerns the involvement of reproductive technologies with eugenics, the use of genetic selection to improve the human condition. AI is not merely used to treat infertility; clinics have advertised sperm from "superior" donors. In addition to usage by eugenicists, these clinics may be used by non-married women seeking pregnancy.

The disconnection of genetic from social parenthood is at the core of a range of problems emerging in the 1980's and 1990's. The most publicized have been legal cases stemming from surrogate parenthood. In 1986, Mary Beth Whitehead changed her mind about giving up a baby she gave birth to (as the genetic mother) on behalf of William and Elizabeth Stern. In resolving the "Baby M" case, the Supreme Court of New Jersey ruled that surrogate contracts involved the illegal sale of a human being.

The often unforeseen dilemmas vary with the procedures used. The most emotional issues stem from the production of multiple embryos using IVF. Pro-life activists typically oppose IVF because of concern with unused embryos. In addition to the destruction of "excess" embryos, freezing embryos for future use has created dilemmas, as when the couple has died in an accident, or when the couple has divorced and one partner no longer wants a pregnancy to develop from the embryos. Finally, multiple embryo implants lead to an increase in multiple fetuses, which, by definition, create high-risk pregnancies, even when "only" two fetuses are involved.

Questions of parenthood have also arisen with AI. Men have sued for parental rights after a child is born. While superficially similar to cases of surrogate mothers, the physical and emotional investment is far lower with AI, and most such efforts have not been successful. In 1995, however, a court in Louisiana ruled that a child who was conceived after her father's death (using frozen sperm from her mother's dying husband) was entitled to Social Security benefits, as a child whose "natural" father had died would be.

Reproductive technologies have developed faster than the ability to regulate them. In 1995, a scandal erupted involving the prestigious infertility clinic at the University of California at Irvine. Couples sued the clinic, claiming that ova or embryos taken from women for their own infertility treatment were donated without authorization to other couples.

Implications for Women. Reproductive technologies create an increased range of choices for women. Besides the obvious benefits for the infertile, the availability of treatment grants security to young women who delay childbearing while establishing careers, thus avoiding premature decisions. The potential for childbearing beyond menopause would mean that women are no more bound by age than men are. The image of post-menopausal mothers, however, arouses critics.

Critics are concerned with the health risks to older pregnant women. In addition, there is concern that cultural pressures for women to have children, with motherhood the only sanctioned female role, are increasing. Women are no longer allowed to "give up" on attempts to bear children. The long years and the emotional and especially physical stresses borne largely by the women undergoing infertility treatment heighten these concerns. Custody fights over embryos were predictable; couples undergoing infertility treatment experience enormous marital strain.

Advocates of reproductive technology respond that freedom and choice always create stress. Men have always had the reproductive freedom the new technologies grant women. Advocates hope for medical and social advances to cope with emerging problems.

Implications for Children. There are concerns with the children as well. Will a generation of older mothers increase the likelihood of orphaned children? Will there be an increase in the numbers of children born with chromosome and other birth defects? Finally, technologically "produced" children may have different relationships with their parents, one of whom may be the genetic parent, the other "bypassed" as deficient. Will parents pressure children that much more to be worth the time, effort, and money invested in their birth?

Conversely, advocates respond, parents may be that much more grateful for their child's existence. Stepparents and adoptive parents already cope with nontra-

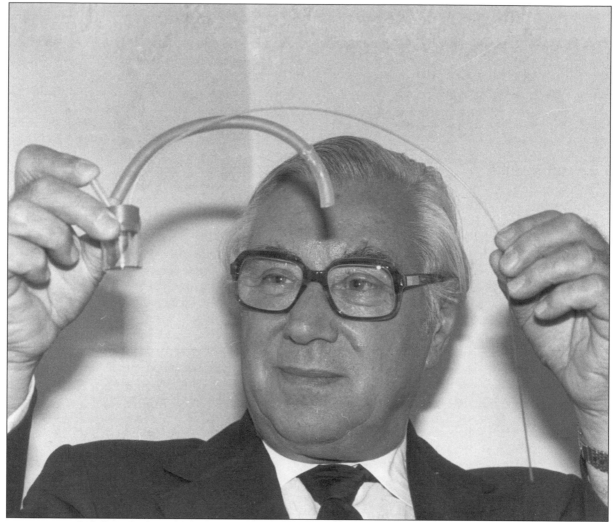

A doctor displays a suction device used to transplant human eggs. (UPI/Corbis-Bettmann)

ditional parent-child relationships. Men have never been asked not to bear children in their fifties because they might die during their offspring's childhood.

Certainly, reproductive technologies have created as many new problems as choices and options. Arguments can be expected to continue about which methods are appropriate. As knowledge increases, so does the realization that not everything that can be done should be done. The opposite is not automatically the case either. —*Nancy E. Macdonald*

SUGGESTED READINGS: More detail on medical options can be found in Barbara Eck Menning's *Infertility: A Guide for the Childless Couple*, 2d ed. (New York: Prentice-Hall, 1988). Essays exploring ethical problems can be found in a volume edited by Elaine Hoffman Baruch, Amadeo F. D'Adamo, Jr., and Joni Seager, *Embryos, Ethics and Women's Rights: Exploring the New Reproductive Technologies* (New York: Harrington Park Press, 1988). Sharp criticism of reproductive technologies can be found in Gena Corea's *The Mother Machine: Reproductive Technologies from Artificial Insemination to Artificial Wombs* (New York: Harper & Row, 1985). For a look at the personal costs of surrogate motherhood, see Elizabeth Kane's *Birth Mother: America's First Legal Surrogate Mother Tells the Story of Her Change of Heart* (New York: Harcourt Brace Jovanovich, 1988), which provides a firsthand account.

Republican Party: U.S. political party founded in 1854. Created as a political organization that opposed the expansion of slavery into the West, the Republican Party has evolved through several stages to become the major force for conservatism in American politics.

Origins. The 1850's were a turbulent decade in the United States, as the nation repeatedly wrestled with the question of slavery and the possibility of Southern secession. One of the by-products that emerged from the maelstrom of events leading to the Civil War was the creation of a new political organization known as the Republican Party.

On February 28, 1854, a group of Whigs, antislavery Democrats, and Free-Soilers met at Ripon, Wisconsin, to discuss their opposition to the possible passage of the Kansas-Nebraska Act, which would allow the expansion of slavery into the Western territories. These "anti-Nebraska" delegates decided to coalesce their disparate factions around the idea of abolition, and they called themselves "Republicans." When the Kansas-Nebraska Act became law, many of these Republicans called a second meeting at Jackson, Michigan, in July, 1854, resulting in the formal organization of the party. The early Republican Party based its philosophy upon abolition of slavery in the District of Columbia and the repeal of two laws: the Kansas-Nebraska Act and the Fugitive Slave Act.

Early Successes. In 1860, the Republicans gave their presidential nomination to Abraham Lincoln, an Illinois abolitionist and former Whig. Lincoln condemned slavery as "a moral, a social and a political wrong"; for fear of alienating the South, however, he denied the equality of blacks and refused to pursue immediate emancipation of slaves if elected. The Republican platform similarly vacillated on the crucial issues of the day. While it supported the idea that "all men are created equal" and opposed attempts to reopen the slave trade or allow the "peculiar institution" in the Western territories, it still reaffirmed a state's rights to continue such operations where they already existed. On less controversial issues, the Republicans supported the intercontinental railroad, high tariffs, homesteading, and the lowering of immigration barriers.

Lincoln described Republicans as being "for both the man and the dollar, but in case of conflict, the man before the dollar." This philosophy dominated during the postwar period known as Reconstruction (1865-1877), when Radical Republicans controlled

The 1992 Republican National Convention in Houston. (AP/Wide World Photos)

Delegates cheer President George Bush at the 1992 Republican National Convention. (AP/Wide World Photos)

the Congress that produced the Thirteenth, Fourteenth, and Fifteenth Amendments to the Constitution. These amendments outlawed slavery and guaranteed the civil and voting rights of African Americans.

In 1877, however, the party mostly abandoned its radical ideology and returned to its older, more conservative Whig tradition of promoting the laissez-faire philosophy of its Eastern corporate faction. Not all Republicans, however, agreed with the shift, and the resulting tension between "Main Street" and "Wall Street" occasionally fractured the party throughout the twentieth century.

During the half-century following the Civil War, the Republicans controlled the presidency. Only one Democrat, Grover Cleveland, captured the White House between 1860 and 1912. The party followed a policy known as the "Republican Theory of the Presidency," according to which the executive branch typically allowed Congress, which the party frequently controlled, to dictate probusiness policies such as high protective tariffs, low taxes, and antiunion laws. Republican presidents, congresses, and courts generally ignored regulatory laws such as the Interstate Commerce Act of 1887 and the Sherman Anti-Trust Act of 1890.

When the free-enterprise trend became abusive of basic human rights near the end of the nineteenth century, Republican reformers such as Theodore Roosevelt, William Howard Taft, and Robert M. "Fighting Bob" LaFollette led the Progressive Movement, which replaced the party's conservative, probusiness old guard. Roosevelt, who was president from 1901 to 1909, was an ardent imperialist who greatly strengthened the institution of the presidency; he also secured the first major prosecution of a monopoly (the 1904 Northern Securities case) and successfully managed the first national labor negotiation during the 1902 anthracite coal strike. Taft, president from 1909 to 1913, was more conservative than his predecessor; he nevertheless expanded Roosevelt's antitrust and land-conservation activities. LaFollette, governor of Wisconsin from 1901 to 1906, introduced the first income tax in U.S. history.

These Republican progressives contested each other for the party's 1912 presidential nomination. Roosevelt ran under the banner of the newly formed Progressive Party, and his candidacy caused a split with the Taft faction, costing the Republicans the presidency and Congress when Woodrow Wilson and the Democrats came to power. In 1920, disillusionment with Wilson's brand of progressivism and internationalism

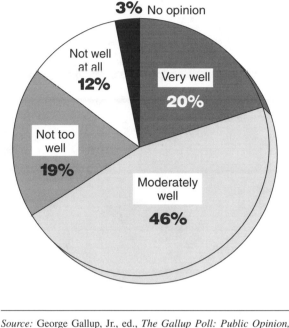

PUBLIC OPINION, 1994: HOW WELL DOES THE REPUBLICAN PARTY REPRESENT YOUR VALUES?

- 3% No opinion
- Very well 20%
- Moderately well 46%
- Not too well 19%
- Not well at all 12%

Source: George Gallup, Jr., ed., *The Gallup Poll: Public Opinion, 1994* (Wilmington, Del.: Scholarly Resources, 1995).

afforded the Republicans another opportunity. When Republican Warren G. Harding captured the White House by promising a "return to normalcy" in the wake of World War I, he carried both houses of Congress with him.

Harding's victory initiated a new period of conservative Republican domination and a renewal of the laissez-faire programs popular in the late nineteenth century. Andrew Mellon, Harding's secretary of the treasury, reduced taxes on millionaires by one-third and introduced the "trickle-down theory," which became a staple of twentieth century Republican economic philosophy. Calvin Coolidge, Harding's vice president and president from 1923 to 1929, expressed the party's dominant philosophy when he stated that "the chief business of America is business." These entrepreneurial Republicans also favored prohibition and opposed immigration and crop supports. When the Republican leadership failed to solve the problems created by the GREAT DEPRESSION of the 1930's, voters rejected such arguments and relegated the Republicans to the status of a minority party. The Democrats won

Republican Party leaders Bob Dole and Newt Gingrich clasp hands in 1995. (AP/Wide World Photos)

seven of the next nine presidential elections and frequently controlled both houses of Congress from 1930 to 1994.

Defeated but not destroyed, the Republican Party refused to concede total victory to the Democrats. Western conservative Republicans joined with Southern Democrats during the late 1930's to oppose what they perceived as "New Deal Socialism" exemplified by Franklin Delano Roosevelt's policies. This new conservative coalition remained intact during the years of Democratic domination and steadily gained influence throughout the late twentieth century.

Nevertheless, these Republican conservatives remained a minority throughout the 1950's and 1960's. During the 1950's administration of Republican President Dwight D. Eisenhower, conservatives expressed disappointment over Eisenhower's moderate ideology, his refusal to dismantle New Deal programs, and his enforcement of the racial integration mandated by the Supreme Court in its landmark 1954 ruling *BROWN V. BOARD OF EDUCATION OF TOPEKA, KANSAS.* Conservatives cheered the 1964 Republican presidential nomination of Arizona senator Barry Goldwater, but his landslide loss in the general election to Lyndon B. Johnson rep-

resented another major setback for the party's right wing.

When Richard M. NIXON won the presidency in 1968, he shocked conservatives in the party with his announcement that he was a Keynesian economist who supported unbalanced budgets, guaranteed family income, and a federal environmental protection agency. He placated the right wing by appointing a staunch conservative, Maryland governor Spiro Agnew, as his running mate, pursuing a tough law-and-order agenda, and escalating the war in Vietnam. This strategy proved generally successful until bribery scandals ended Agnew's career in 1973 and Nixon's cover-up of the WATERGATE break-in led to his resignation in 1974.

Contrary to criticisms expressed by disgruntled conservatives, Nixon had turned the party to the right by routing federal money into the suburbs, where most of his supporters lived. Although the Watergate scandal disgraced Nixon and his advisers and assisted the Democrats' victory in the 1976 presidential election, it did not deal a mortal blow to the Republican Party.

After defeating incumbent Democrat Jimmy Carter in the 1980 election, right-wing Republican Ronald

REAGAN achieved a political revolution during his tenure in Washington. Reagan pursued the conservative agenda more vigorously than any president since Herbert Hoover. Determined to undo what he perceived as socialist government policies, Reagan combined huge tax cuts with massive increases in military expenditures. He neglected antitrust regulatory policies, civil rights programs, and other remnants of the old liberalism. Although personally popular with the American people, the former actor supported policies that generated great political controversy. Reagan's influence also extended to the Senate, which the Republicans controlled from 1981 to 1987, and contributed to the election of his vice president, George Bush, as his successor. Bush, a moderate Republican, excelled at foreign policy but raised taxes, failed to halt a troublesome recession, and lost handily to Democrat Bill CLINTON in 1992.

During the 1990's, Republicans hoped they could realign American government. Massive deficits, a menacing crime rate, and public dissatisfaction with Democratic leadership provided a golden opportunity for Reagan's disciples in Congress, led by Georgia Republican Newt GINGRICH and Texas Republican Richard Armey. Armed with their "CONTRACT WITH AMERICA," the Republicans in 1994 captured both houses in Congress for the first time in forty years. Promising a balanced budget, tax decreases, and welfare reform, the Republicans won an overwhelming victory, and the party's new ascendancy seemed likely to exert a powerful political impact well into the twenty-first century.

—*J. Christopher Schnell*

SUGGESTED READINGS: A good starting point for anyone interested in Republican politics is Donald A. Ritchie's *The Young Oxford Companion to the Congress of the United States* (New York: Oxford University Press, 1993). Wilfred E. Binkley's *American Political Parties: Their Natural History* (New York: Alfred A. Knopf, 1958) and Charles Jones's *The Republican Party in American Politics* (New York: Macmillan, 1965) are also useful.

Reserve Officers Training Corps (ROTC): Programs maintained at civilian colleges by the U.S. Army, Navy, and Air Force that allow students to earn

ROTC members practice a flag ceremony. (UPI/Corbis-Bettmann)

a military commission while attending college. Officer training at U.S. civilian colleges began at Norwich University in 1829. The government became involved during the Civil War in the Land-Grant Act, also called the Morrill Act, which included provisions for military instruction at institutions that received federal land grants. In the National Defense Act of 1916, the War Department received more control over the system, allowing honor graduates to serve on active duty. By the late twentieth century, ROTC programs supplied about 70 percent of all U.S. military officers.

Responsibility: Accountability for something that has been done or something that should be done. The concept of responsibility is relevant to many different areas of human life, and several different types of responsibility can be distinguished. The literature on responsibility is dominated by discussions of moral responsibility and legal responsibility, but one can also talk meaningfully about job-related responsibilities, parental responsibilities, the responsibilities of a citizen, and so forth.

Moral responsibility, as it has evolved in Western culture, derives from Aristotle's account. According to Aristotle, a person comes to bear moral responsibility for what he or she has done, except in cases in which the person acts under externally imposed compulsion or out of ignorance. Of course, not all ignorance serves to excuse a person, and Aristotle carefully explains which types of ignorance excuse a person from responsibility.

In general, this account yields the conclusion that human beings are morally responsible for some of what they do but not all of what they do. Further, human beings are generally morally responsible for the kinds of persons they turn out to become. It is true that some people are unable to overcome certain addictions or dependencies, but Aristotle insists that if such people are responsible for having entered such states in the first place, they are still responsible for what they have become. Western conceptions of legal responsibility are likewise in large part based on these ideas.

Some thinkers subscribe instead to a theory of determinism, according to which human beings lack free will. In this view, there is no room for ascribing responsibility, for neither freedom nor responsibility is present without the other. If all of one's actions are determined by forces beyond one's control, then there is no basis for ascribing responsibility to human beings.

Those who reject determinism can still maintain that people lack responsibility for their actions in significant areas of life. For example, persons who suffer from mental illness or extreme senility are frequently judged not responsible for their actions on the grounds that they are ignorant of what they are doing. More controversial is the contention that those who grow up in abusive or dysfunctional families have not had an opportunity to learn right from wrong and cannot be held responsible for their subsequent behavior.

In all discussions of responsibility, it is important to distinguish between prospective and retrospective responsibility. One has a prospective responsibility to do something in the future, and one has retrospective responsibility for what has happened in the past. It is also important to distinguish between individual and collective responsibility. No individual person might bear responsibility for certain problems and injustices in society, but it can be argued that, in some cases, people are members of groups or collectives that bear responsibility for these problems. In addition, some writers have proposed that moral responsibility can be borne by nonhuman entities such as corporations.

SUGGESTED READING: A cogent overview of relevant issues is provided in *The Spectrum of Responsibility*, edited by Peter French (New York: St. Martin's Press, 1991).

Retirement: Workers retire by leaving the paid labor force permanently. Retirement has become institutionalized, in part through creation of publicly funded elderly support programs that provide economic incentives to retire and disincentives for not doing so. In addition, some companies mandate that employees retire when they reach a certain age, commonly sixty-five in the United States. This institutionalization of retirement has become the focus of debates because of the social and economic consequences of retirement.

History. The origins of institutionalized retirement in the United States can be traced to the nineteenth century and the rise of industrialization. Industrialists instituted discriminatory hiring and firing practices and restrictive management policies in their attempts to employ only the strongest, most physically able workers. By the 1920's, 45 percent of businesses with fewer than twenty-five workers and 95 percent of businesses with more than one thousand workers had open policies of not hiring anyone over the age of forty. Firing older workers solely on the basis of their age

Retired couples may use their increased leisure time to pursue hobbies or enjoy the company of friends and family members. (Cleo Freelance Photo)

became a common practice. Older workers who survived the purges tended to be clustered in seasonal and unskilled jobs with low pay.

Social reformers of the early twentieth century defined aging as a "social problem" because so many elderly people became indigent as a result of mandatory retirement and the absence of adequate pensions. This marked the beginning of the push for publicly funded support for elderly persons, particularly those who had been in the paid labor force.

The Social Security Act of 1935 was the first comprehensive legislation concerning issues of retirement benefits. The GREAT DEPRESSION exacerbated the plight of the elderly. Millions of workers lost their jobs and their pensions (if they were lucky enough to have them), and many lost their life savings because of bank failures. The idea that people became impoverished

through their own fault no longer was credible.

SOCIAL SECURITY provided publicly funded assistance to retired persons who participated in the program and to selected other groups; participation in the program expanded over the next several decades to become almost universal. The purpose of the program was to change the status of unemployed elderly people to "retired" and to encourage older workers who still held jobs to retire in order to make way for younger workers.

The Institutionalization of Retirement. Social Security and the emergence of more, and more generous, private pension plans resulted in the institutionalization of retirement. The setting of formal and informal rules regarding retirement altered relationships between people and their jobs and the government. As late as the early 1950's, a majority of workers thought

Despite stereotypes, relatively few senior citizens move to warm-weather retirement communities. (UPI/Corbis-Bettmann)

that only physical infirmity justified retirement. By 1960, however, most workers viewed retirement, with a publicly funded pension, as a right earned by working during one's young adult and middle years.

The promise of paid retirement has come to be seen as the motivation for enduring many years at a repetitive industrial or bureaucratic job that offers little personal meaning or fulfillment.

Many sixty-five-year-olds can look forward to a decade or more of relatively good health, and the average retirement age is falling as more workers take "early" retirement. The idea that it is not only socially acceptable but also desirable for able-bodied adults not to hold paid jobs has become an integral part of America's social structure and culture. What started as an attempt by the federal government to address the effects of age discrimination and regulate the labor market has come to be viewed as an earned and cherished right.

Debates. Early debates on retirement focused on whether it was beneficial for retirees. Questions of the effects on society were considered later, when the institutionalization of retirement through Social Security and mandatory retirement was debated as a conscious domestic policy strategy for dealing with UNEMPLOYMENT and other problems. When critics of retirement policies suggested that retirees' best interests were not being served, conservative social theorists of the late 1950's and early 1960's developed "disengagement theory," which openly supported the recently engineered policies. This theory stated that in industrialized societies, withdrawal of elderly workers from the labor force and other important social institutions is inevitable, as well as beneficial and desirable both to society and to elderly workers.

Critics of disengagement theory responded by claiming that the withdrawal of America's elderly had been neither natural nor inevitable but carefully orchestrated; altruism had not been the motivation. They further asserted that political and economic goals were served at the expense of the elderly, who lost their major source of self-esteem and social status. Some critics attributed ill health and premature death of retirees to the stress and depression associated with loss of important roles and the attendant lowered standard of living. To these critics, disengagement theory was an apologist position for institutionalized age discrimination.

A third position in this debate came from retirees themselves, who participated in social scientific studies, the best known of which was conducted for a ten-year period from 1952 to 1962. These respondents' statements and life histories generally indicated that retirement did not cause stress, depression, poor health, or death. Although many retirees reported reductions in income, most claimed that their standard of living had improved. Some saw retirement not as a separation from society but as an earned entitlement and a new set of active roles, lasting perhaps as long as or longer than labor-force participation.

The focus of retirement-related debates shifted from a focus on its effects on retirees to its effects on society as a whole. Labor-force participation rates and the average age at retirement of Americans declined dramatically over the course of the second half of the twentieth century. Because retirees are in better health, have longer life expectancies, and are better educated than ever before, a significant amount of productive potential is lost to society. Longer life expectancies also added to the cost of providing pensions and retirement benefits beginning at the age of sixty-five. When the original Social Security legislation was passed, relatively few people survived for more than a few years beyond that age. Such concerns have prompted calls to increase the age at which retirees begin to receive full benefits. Some changes were made in the forms of institutionalized retirement. Mandatory retirement was abolished in 1986, and the age of eligibility for full Social Security benefits was increased to sixty-seven.

At the heart of arguments supporting the need for changes in the institutional form of retirement is the changing "elderly dependency ratio," the number of retired workers in relation to the number of people in the labor force. That ratio has been rising as a result of several demographic forces, including longer life spans and a trend toward smaller families. Proponents of change in the retirement system predict future disaster as it becomes difficult and then impossible to con-

tinue current retirement policies and practices without irreparably damaging the national economy.

Those who foresee problems in funding retirement benefits often advocate "work life extension" and a higher age of retirement. As of the early 1990's, 75 percent of workers over the age of sixty-five held white-collar service jobs. It is argued that they could remain employed longer with minimal hardship, as the jobs do not impose physical strains. Other versions of this position endorse flexible or phased retirement, with older workers reducing their work hours gradually over a long period of time. Their pensions would increase the longer they remained employed. This would represent a reversal of policies prominent in the 1980's, when workers were encouraged to take early retirement so that jobs would be available to younger workers.

Those who oppose significant changes in retirement claim that although the elderly dependency ratio will increase, the child dependency ratio may well decrease, and that other factors may operate to reduce economic pressures. They suggest that continuing increases in female labor-force participation (until it equals or almost equals male labor-force participation) are almost certain to prevent labor shortages, and they point out that labor shortages anticipated in the early 1990's did not materialize. They also prescribe both private and public investment in "human capital," such as continuing education and vocational training programs. Ongoing training may be needed to reverse trends toward creation of jobs that workers are not qualified to fill because they are unfamiliar with new technology.   *—Jack Carter*

SUGGESTED READINGS: Mandatory retirement before the passage of Social Security legislation is discussed in Judith C. Hushbeck's *Old and Obsolete: Age Discrimination and the American Worker, 1860-1920* (New York: Garland, 1989). Several contributions relating to modern retirement are found in Irving Bluestone, Rhonda Montgomery, and John Owen's edited volume *The Aging of the American Work Force* (Detroit: Wayne State University Press, 1990).

The debate over publicly funded retirement programs is examined in *Retirement and Public Policy* (Dubuque, Iowa: Kendall/Hunt, 1991), edited by Alicia H. Munnell. The institutionalization of retirement as a valued stage of life is the focus of Michael L. Teague and Richard D. MacNeil's *Aging and Leisure: Vitality in Later Life*, 2d ed. (Dubuque, Iowa: Brown & Benchmark, 1992). Winfried Schmahl presents ideas on how to restructure the institution of retirement in *Redefining the Process of Retirement* (New York: Springer-Verlag, 1989).

Retirement Equity Act (1984): Major reform of U.S. pension plans. On August 23, 1984, President Ronald Reagan signed a bill that lowered the age at which employees had to be allowed to participate in pension plans from twenty-five to twenty-one. Several provisions especially benefited women. Pension plans were required to provide survivors' benefits to spouses of vested employees even if the employees died before retirement age. With some restrictions, the law also permitted employees to leave and return without sacrificing pension accumulation. The act also prohibited pension plans from counting one-year maternity or paternity leaves as breaks in service.

Retribution: Recompense for one's actions. The term frequently applies to reward or punishment after death; when it carries a temporal referent, it typically means punishment. Two primary issues arise with regard to retribution. First, on what grounds is retribution justified? Some people argue that retribution serves as a deterrent to wrong action, while others emphasize that justice requires the rectification of wrongs. Second, how far should retribution go? Aristotle taught that retribution should be proportionate to the offense, and the Bible limited it to an "eye for an eye." Some cases, for example rape, have sometimes carried more extreme penalties, such as death.

Reverse discrimination: Discrimination against members of a majority group. Typically, charges of reverse discrimination are leveled in regard to formal attempts to rectify past discrimination against members of various minority groups. Most commonly, opponents of AFFIRMATIVE ACTION programs argue that any program that grants preferential treatment to a designated minority group is discriminatory to members of the majority.

The issue of reverse discrimination presents an apparent conflict among three ideals, justice, equality, and freedom. Justice holds that a wrong must be rectified. American history is filled with examples of injus-

A Little Rock, Arkansas, restaurant owner practices reverse discrimination in 1982. (UPI/Corbis-Bettmann)

tices against various minorities, from the enslavement of African Americans, to the removal of Native Americans from their land, to the internment of Japanese Americans during World War II. Rectifying such injustices causes the system to conflict with another ideal, equality. Equality holds that every citizen should have equal access to the public goods and should receive equal treatment under the law. When any program is adopted that seeks to redress past wrongs by establishing quotas or giving preference in some way, the ideal of equality is undermined. The value of freedom suggests that citizens should be free from the arbitrary exercise of authority. When affirmative action policies are enforced, such enforcement often means that some individual's or group's freedoms are denied. It is not surprising, then, that the courts have had a difficult time dealing with the concept of reverse discrimination.

The issue of reverse discrimination has been addressed by the U.S. Supreme Court on several occasions. Two of the most significant cases were *Regents of the University of California v. Bakke* (1978) and *United Steelworkers v. Weber* (1979). In the first case, Allan Bakke, a white male, had been denied admission to a medical school because of a university policy that established yearly quotas for the admission of certain minority groups. The court ruled that such quotas were unconstitutional. In the *Weber* case, however, an agreement between an employer and a union to reserve a percentage of spaces in a job-training program for minority applicants was found to be constitutional. The effect of the two decisions was to maintain that quotas were not acceptable as means to redress past wrongs but that "goals" to achieve racial balances were.

The issue became further confused when the question was raised as to who the victims of discrimination were. Were they actual victims of past discrimination? The Court decided in *Johnson v. Transportation Agency, Santa Clara County* (1987) that employers can act to remedy past discrimination without admitting to a history of past discrimination. Johnson, a white male, was denied a promotion in favor of a white female. At the time, all the agency's 238 skilled positions were held by men. The Court ruled in favor of the white female and, therefore, in favor of the agency's policy.

In the 1990's, sympathy toward victims of past discrimination appeared to decline, and affirmative action and related "reverse discrimination" programs became among the most volatile of political issues. As the twentieth century neared its end, the mood of both the U.S. Congress and the executive branch seemed to be moving toward satisfying the will of the majority.

Richmond v. J. A. Croson Company (1989): U.S. Supreme Court case. In 1983, Richmond, Virginia, adopted a minority set-aside program for city contracting, according to which 30 percent of all city construction subcontracts were to be granted to minority-owned business enterprises. The J. A. Croson Company, which had been low bidder on a city project, sued the city when its bid was rejected in favor of a higher bid submitted by a minority-owned firm. The Court ruled that race-conscious affirmative action programs are valid only where there has been past discrimination by the state government itself. The decision thus cast doubt on the legality of race-conscious affirmative action programs.

RICO statutes (1970, 1986): U.S. federal legislation. These statutes, contained in the U.S. Code chapter 18, sections 1961-1968, are known formally as the Racketeer Influenced and Corrupt Organizations statutes. They originated in Title IX of the Organized Crime Control Act of 1970, amended in 1986. The laws were intended to give federal law-enforcement agencies, specifically the Federal Bureau of Investigation (FBI), more power to investigate typical criminal activities of organized crime groups. Many such investigations previously had been handled by state or local agencies. Racketeering activity is defined in the statutes as two or more offenses committed within a ten-year period by a criminal group. This definition puts many criminals under the definition of "organized crime."

The government can seize all assets and property belonging to those convicted under the statutes and can issue temporary restraining orders freezing the use of certain assets. The laws were meant to be used to prosecute those involved in organized crime, but threat of prosecution under the RICO statutes also has been used as a means of persuading some accused persons to plead guilty to crimes. Such use was prominent in some cases of alleged white-collar crimes in major financial markets, particularly the Chicago Board of Trade, in the 1980's. Successful prosecution under the RICO statutes would have cost some defendants millions of dollars in seized assets, and use of temporary restraining orders could have put them out of business. Some defendants chose to plead guilty to lesser crimes rather than take the financial risks involved in a trial on charges under the RICO statutes. Some observers of the judicial system saw such cases as abuses of the intent of the statutes.

Right-to-die movement: Coalition advocating the legalization of physician-assisted suicide in cases involving individuals who are suffering from severe or terminal illnesses. The right-to-die movement began organizing in the United States after World War I. The Euthanasia Society of America, founded in 1938, drafted a proposal to legalize the termination of human life by painless means for the purpose of avoiding unnecessary suffering. The cause stalled immediately after World War II, however, since the word "euthanasia" was too closely associated with Nazi Germany. The movement gathered momentum again during the 1960's. In 1967, the Euthanasia Society started a tax-exempt Euthanasia Education Fund and also opened discussion of the "living will," documents in which people may record their desire not to receive treatment for late stages of illness. The society changed its name to Choice in Dying in the mid-1970's.

The first legislative and judicial moves toward liberalization involved comatose patients. In 1976, the New Jersey Supreme Court gave permission for Karen Ann Quinlan's parents to disconnect the respirator to which their comatose daughter was attached. Also in 1976, the California Natural Death Act was passed, giving living wills legal standing. The founding of the Hemlock Society in 1980 by Derek Humphrey and others marked the beginning of a more vigorous engagement in the movement. In the 1990's, the right-to-die movement received support not only from the Hemlock Society and Choice in Dying but also from such organizations as ERGO!, Americans for Death with Dignity, Compassion in Dying, and the World Federation of Right to Die Societies, among others. Dr. Jack KEVORKIAN, a retired Michigan pathologist, assisted in more than twenty suicides and became one of the most outspoken proponents of the right to die.

There are essentially six degrees of euthanasia under discussion in the right-to-die movement. The most basic involves the simple discontinuation of artificial life-support systems for a patient in an irreversible coma who cannot live without such intervention. The second involves discontinuing feeding or hydration of a comatose patient who does not require any other artificial support. The third involves the withholding (at the patient's request) of treatment that can extend the life of but that will not cure a severely or terminally ill patient. The fourth involves providing pain relief to someone in great pain while knowing that the pain medication may hasten the patient's death. The fifth involves giving patients access to means that they may use to kill themselves in order to escape from severe or terminal illnesses. The sixth and most controversial involves the administration of a lethal injection (at the patient's request) to a patient who is severely or terminally ill. Involuntary euthanasia, which occurs when someone ends another person's life without that patient's explicit knowledge or consent, is outside the right-to-die debate.

Oregon's Measure 16, also known as the Oregon Death with Dignity Act, went into effect on December 8, 1994. It enables Oregon physicians to write prescriptions for lethal doses of medication for use by qualified terminally ill adults who meet the act's specific requirements. Similar measures have been battled in the courts in other states. The people of the state of Oregon thus legalized physician aid in dying for the first time anywhere in the world.

The movement's primary opposition comes from the leadership of the Roman Catholic church. Members of the Unitarian church and the United Church of Christ are at the forefront of religious support for euthanasia.

Rightsizing: Business term. Companies periodically make adjustments to operate more efficiently. Related to "upsizing" and "downsizing," rightsizing involves several strategies to ensure corporate efficiency by changing the size of the business. Many companies do internal assessments on a regular basis, often producing rightsizing changes. Rightsizing often occurs when mergers are done and corporatewide assessment reveals the need for changes to structure, staffing, and production methods in the combined entity. Many times, certain departments or functions are redundant. Many employees fear rightsizing because of the frequency of downsizing during the 1980's and 1990's, resulting in layoffs. Rightsizing, when done carefully and sensitively, can yield better job security and corporate growth and success.

Robertson, Pat (Marion Gordon Robertson, b. March 22, 1930, Lexington, Va.): Religious broadcaster and politician.

Pat Robertson at a 1992 press conference. (Archive Photos, Reuters, Steve Jaffe)

Robertson, a leader of the RELIGIOUS RIGHT in the United States, got his start as religious broadcaster in 1959 when he bought a tiny television station in Portsmouth, Virginia. On this station, he created and directed *THE 700 CLUB*, a Christian talk and variety show that was to catapult him to fame and fortune. Robertson pioneered the "telechurch" phenomenon and formed the massive Christian Broadcasting Network (CBN). He campaigned unsuccessfully for the Republican Party's presidential nomination in 1988.

Robinson, Jackie (Jan. 31, 1919, Cairo, Ga.— Oct. 24, 1972, Stamford, Conn.): Baseball player. Robinson, the first African American to play modern organized baseball, desegregated U.S. professional team sports. He starred as an infielder with the Brooklyn Dodgers from 1947 to 1956, braving the taunts of teammates, opponents, executives, and spectators. The six-time all-star helped the Dodgers win six National League pennants and one World Series. The 1947 rookie of the year, Robinson led the National League in batting in 1949, earning most valuable player honors. He batted .311 lifetime, twice leading the National

Jackie Robinson steals home during a 1952 game. (UPI/Corbis-Bettmann)

Sue Rodriquez, the plaintiff in _Rodriguez v. British Columbia_, is escorted into a 1992 press conference. (Reuters/Bettmann)

League in stolen bases. In 1962, Robinson became the first African American elected to the National Baseball Hall of Fame.

Robinson-Patman Act (1936): Legislation. Named for Congressman Wright Patman of Texas and Senator Joseph T. Robinson of Arkansas, this law sought to control the spread of chain stores. It banned such practices as giving discounts for quantity purchases (a form of price discrimination) and other devices through which chain stores could offer lower prices than small, independent competitors. The measure was written in such vague terms that enforcement was difficult. It has had little economic impact on the spread of chain stores. The law reflected the animus against economic bigness that existed within Congress during the New Deal.

Robotics: Science and technology dealing with mechanical devices (robots) that operate automatically. Robotics involves designing robots to complete tasks by following a set of instructions stored in the robot's computer control center. Robots can perform a wide variety of tasks, including welding, drilling, and painting automobile body parts; producing plastic food containers and wrapping food items; and assembling electronic circuits and watches. Most robots are stationary structures with a single arm capable of lifting objects and using tools. Mobile robots equipped with television cameras for sight and electronic sensors for touch are being developed for scientific purposes such as seafloor and planetary exploration.

Rodriguez v. British Columbia (1993); Supreme Court of Canada case. In *Rodriguez*, the court upheld the validity of a provision of Canada's criminal code outlawing medically assisted suicide. The plaintiff, a woman suffering from the terminal disease amyotrophic lateral sclerosis, had sought the court's approval of the assistance of a physician in ending her life. The court, however, ruled that the ban on assisted suicide did not violate the guarantees of the CHARTER OF RIGHTS AND FREEDOMS.

Roe v. Wade (1973): U.S. SUPREME COURT case. *Roe v. Wade* established that a pregnant woman has a constitutional right to seek an ABORTION in the first trimester of pregnancy.

Roe v. Wade sprang from the attempt of Norma Jane McCorvey (known as "Jane Roe" in subsequent litigation) to terminate her pregnancy by means of abortion in Texas in 1970. At that time, Texas statutes forbade abortion except for the purpose of saving the life of the mother. Roe's life was not endangered by her pregnancy. With the encouragement of her attorney, Sarah Weddington, Roe decided to challenge the Texas statute on constitutional grounds. A federal district court suit was brought against Henry Wade, the district attorney of Dallas County, asking that he be enjoined from enforcing the Texas abortion statute on the ground that it unconstitutionally interfered with a pregnant woman's right to personal privacy. The district court agreed with Roe, and Texas appealed to the U.S. Supreme Court. The case was first argued on December 13, 1971, reargued on October 11, 1972, and decided by the Court on January 22, 1973.

The fundamental issue in *Roe v. Wade* is whether "personal privacy" rights reach the abortion decision. By 1971, the Supreme Court had extended the idea of "liberty," protected under the CONSTITUTION'S DUE-PROCESS clause, to include some marital and personal privacy rights. The most important precedent had been *GRISWOLD V. CONNECTICUT* (1965), in which the Court held that there is a right to receive and use contraceptive devices and information. The same right had been extended to unmarried persons in *Eisenstadt v. Baird* (1972). These cases rested on the Court's assumption that some existing constitutional rights established a "zone of privacy" that reached private marital and sexual decisions. The guarantees of the First, Fourth, Fifth, and Ninth Amendments were all cited by the Court.

The Court's decision in *Roe v. Wade* was written by Justice Harry Blackmun for a seven-to-two majority. The Court held that a pregnant woman does have the right to an abortion on demand in the first trimester of pregnancy. In the second trimester, the state is free to place some restrictions on the right in order to protect the health of the mother; in the third trimester, after the child has "quickened," the state may have the power to prohibit abortion altogether. The opinion balances the interests of the state governments against the personal privacy rights of women. The state's interest is to protect unborn life and the safety and health of pregnant women. Roe's interest is what the Court called "the fundamental right of single women and married per-

Norma McCorvey (left), the "Jane Roe" of *Roe v. Wade***, leaves the Supreme Court with attorney Gloria Allred after a hearing in a 1989 case that threatened to overturn the 1973 ruling.** (AP/Wide World Photos)

sons to choose whether to have children." By tying the right to an abortion to the right to choose whether to have children, Blackmun brought the case more squarely within the precedent established by *Griswold v. Connecticut*.

Roe v. Wade is enormously controversial. Since the case was decided, there have been constant efforts by its opponents to overturn it and by its supporters to protect the rights it established. Occasionally, the passions raised by this case have resulted in violence, and the issue is nearly constantly before the Supreme Court in one form or another. Because the decision in the case appeared to many people to be political rather than judicial in character, there have been many demonstrations at the Court itself.

Rose, Pete (b. Apr. 14, 1941, Cincinnati, Ohio): Baseball player and manager. A major league star from 1963 to 1986, Rose in 1989 was banned from organized baseball for life for betting on major league games including games involving his own Cincinnati Reds. In 1990, Rose pleaded guilty to filing false federal income tax returns, and he was fined and served a five-month prison sentence. Although he holds numerous records, including the major league record for most hits in a career (4,256), Rose is ineligible for election to the National Baseball Hall of Fame; nevertheless, numerous journalists and former players have pressed for his induction.

Roth v. United States (1957): U.S. Supreme Court case. Upholding a federal conviction of Samuel Roth for selling pornographic materials, the Court ruled that "obscenity" enjoyed no constitutional protection because it was "utterly without redeeming social importance." At the same time, the Court insisted on a narrow definition of OBSCENITY and required that prosecution must be based upon the influence that the work as a whole had on an average person of the community. The decision was the first time that the Court significantly limited government's prerogative to criminalize materials considered obscene. Two liberal dissenters argued that the First Amendment protected all forms of expression, including obscenity.

Royal Canadian Mounted Police (RCMP): Canadian federal police force. Except in Ontario and

Pete Rose dives into a base during the 1975 World Series. (AP/Wide World Photos)

Royal Canadian Mounted Police officers escort a refugee to an immigration facility. (Reuters/Bettmann)

Québec, the force also acts under contract as a provincial force. Founded in 1873 and originally known as the Northwest Mounted Police, the force was set up to enforce an orderly settlement of the Canadian West to ensure that the "Wild West" atmosphere of the American frontier would not be duplicated. The term "Royal" was added to the name in 1904 to recognize the service of the unit's officers in the Boer War. The present name was assumed in 1920 when the organization merged with the Dominion Police. The scarlet dress uniforms of the Mounties, as the RCMP's officers are known, are recognized throughout the world.

Royal Commission on Aboriginal Peoples (RCAP): Canadian federal investigatory body. The RCAP was established August 27, 1991, by Prime Minister Brian MULRONEY. At roundtable discussions with aboriginals, the RCAP examined a range of issues with the goal of securing full participation of aboriginal peoples in Canada's economic prosperity and political life. The commission investigated such issues as the history of relations between aboriginals and the Canadian government; aboriginal self-government; land claims; and socioeconomic, cultural, educational, and justice issues of concern to aboriginal peoples.

RU 486: Drug used to terminate unwanted pregnancies. Developed in France and gaining acceptance in other regions, RU 486 has several medical applications, but its use is fervently opposed by antiabortion activists.

RU 486 was first synthesized in 1980 at the pharmaceutical works at Roussel-Uclaf in Romainville, France. Researcher Georges Teutsch constructed steroid compounds that did not exist naturally and submitted them to researcher Daniel Philibert for testing. One of the compounds bound strongly to progesterone receptors. Progesterone is a natural hormone that is secreted by the corpus luteum, the tissues left over when an egg erupts from the ovary. Progesterone maintains the lining of the uterus. This lining is important to allow a fertilized egg to implant and develop a placenta. Progesterone also relaxes the uterus, reducing contractions that might expel the embryo, and keeps the cer-

Members of the Christian Defense Coalition and the Feminist Majority Foundation express conflicting views on the legalization of RU 486. (Reuters/Corbis-Bettmann)

vix, or opening of the uterus, from expanding.

An artificial steroid that occupies a progesterone receptor site could either mimic the action of progesterone or be an "antagonist" and seal the receptor sites and produce the opposite effect of progesterone. This new compound turned out to be a strong antagonist. Although the Roussel-Uclaf facility was not actively seeking a birth-control drug, it was immediately apparent that a progesterone antagonist administered before the implantation of a fertilized egg could prevent the uterine lining from maturing and accepting the new embryo. After implantation, RU 486 could fill up the progesterone receptor sites and prevent the lining from being maintained; when the endometrium eroded, the embryo would also be expelled. Experiments with non-pregnant monkeys showed that both oral and injected doses of RU 486 triggered a premature menstrual period, and even at high levels the doses were not toxic. The first clinical trials began in 1981. Success in terminating pregnancy led to large-scale studies in 1985, which expanded to include women in Great Britain, China, and Sweden. Passing test criteria, Roussel-Uclaf was granted permission to market RU 486 in France in September of 1988.

RU 486 is available to French women who wish to terminate a pregnancy, up to forty-nine days into pregnancy, counted from the last day of the menstrual period. Named mifepristone, RU 486 is delivered in tablet form combined with prostaglandin, a compound that speeds up uterine contractions to expel the embryo. One-third of French women utilize RU 486 to terminate an early pregnancy rather than use surgical abortion.

This drug is also a potential treatment of cancers that carry progesterone receptors, including some breast cancers, and may have clinical uses in triggering delivery and production of milk. Opponents of ABORTION consider RU 486 to be a chemical substitute for surgical abortion. Proponents point out that more than one-third of conceived eggs naturally fail to implant or spontaneously abort, and that this chemical manipulation of the biological system is a relatively safe and noninvasive mechanism for individual birth control as well as a tool to meet the challenge of world overpopulation.

Ruby Ridge incident (1992): Bloody standoff involving excessive force by the FEDERAL BUREAU OF INVESTIGATION (FBI), followed by attempts at a cover-up. Randy Weaver, a Christian fundamentalist who believed that a biblical Apocalypse was imminent, lived with his wife, Vicki, and their four children in an isolated cabin on Ruby Ridge, near Naples, Idaho. The Weavers were affiliated with the Aryan Nations and other right-wing groups committed to white supremacy; they opposed most governmental regulations, especially limits on the ownership of firearms. In spite of their extreme views, the Weavers appeared to be good neighbors and responsible parents.

Randy Weaver's conflicts with the law began in 1986 when he sold two sawed-off shotguns to an informer of the Bureau of Alcohol, Tobacco, and Firearms (ATF). The ATF tried to pressure Weaver to report on the neo-Nazi underground in the area; after his refusal, he was arrested and charged with selling illegal weapons. With the support of his wife, Weaver refused to appear at the federal trial scheduled in February, 1991. The result was an armed standoff that lasted for more than a year. U.S. marshals monitored the cabin but were reluctant to use force that would endanger the lives of the four children. Members of the Aryan Nations and neo-Nazis encouraged Weaver by holding a nearby vigil.

On August 21, 1992, marshals got too close to the cabin and accidentally ran into the Weavers' teenage son, Sammy, and a visiting friend, Kevin Harris. After the marshals killed the boy's dog, a confused gunfight left two people dead: Sammy Weaver and Deputy U.S. Marshal William Degan. Both parties claimed the other side initiated the shoot-out. The FBI was called in with its Hostage Rescue Team, and a siege began with more than one hundred federal and state officers surrounding the cabin. FBI supervisors in Washington, exaggerating the threat, prepared special "rules of engagement" that instructed agents, contrary to a Supreme Court ruling, that they "could and should" use deadly force against any armed adult. On August 22, a sniper, perhaps following the unconstitutional directions, wounded Harris and accidentally killed Vicki Weaver while she was holding her infant daughter. Ten days later, Randy Weaver surrendered to authorities.

In 1993, Weaver and Harris were tried on charges of murder and conspiracy, but an Idaho jury, faced with inconsistencies in ATF and FBI accounts, acquitted both men. Weaver served only a four-month sentence for his failure to appear for the earlier trial on the weapons charge. The family sued the government for the wrongful death of Vicki Weaver, and after long negotiations, in 1995 the Department of Justice agreed

Kevin Harris testifies at hearings on the Ruby Ridge incident. (Archive Photos, Reuters, Mike Theiler)

to pay an out-of-court settlement of $3.1 million.

FBI and ATF agents were widely criticized for their actions during the siege, and an FBI report later revealed that several FBI agents had concealed evidence about their actions in the affair. In early 1995, FBI director Louis Freeh disciplined twelve agents for misconduct. Although Freeh reprimanded his friend Larry Potts, who had overseen the Ruby Ridge operation, he then promoted Potts to deputy director of the FBI in May. A subsequent Justice Department probe in July found that many documents had been changed or destroyed, and Freeh suspended Potts and four others who held headquarters jobs. The matter was turned over to the U.S. Attorney's Office for possible criminal prosecution.

A subcommittee of the Senate Judiciary Committee, chaired by Senator Arlen Specter, held hearings on the Ruby Ridge affair in 1995. The committee report of December 21 criticized the ATF for giving a false impression about the threat posed by Weaver; the report also denounced the FBI for its unconstitutional rules of engagement and for its sloppy record keeping. Even before the report was issued, the FBI announced that henceforth agents would never be authorized to use deadly force without strong evidence that either they or others faced imminent threat of death or serious injury.

SUGGESTED READING: Jess Walter gives a fascinating journalistic account in *Every Knee Shall Bow* (New York: HarperCollins, 1995).

Runaways: Children and teenagers who leave home without permission and do not return within a reasonable length of time are considered runaways. Several issues of public concern relate to runaways, including the potential danger to young people who leave home and the legal considerations, which may be adjudicated in juvenile court.

The number of runaways in the United States is unknown, because circumstances under which young people leave home vary widely. The Missing Children's Assistance Act of 1983 defines missing children as those age thirteen or younger whose disappearances could be the result of kidnapping or other illegal abduction. Estimates of missing children vary between one million to more than two million each year. Not included in these estimates are cases in which parents or guardians force young people to leave home; such cases are termed instances of "throwaway children."

Other cases involve teenaged runaways who are never reported to police. Some have moved to the homes of their divorced parents without getting permission; in many cases, however, divorced parents take their children without going through court to obtain legal custody. Some runaways leave home to escape conflicts between family members or to end physical, psychological, or sexual abuse by family members. Most leave to seek adventure or adult freedoms or to escape some problem that they do not know how to solve.

Public concern about dangers runaways face are well founded. Because runaways are legally not adults, they have difficulty obtaining employment, housing, and transportation needed to survive on their own. Many are homeless, broke, and without proper food. Their relative lack of life experience makes them vulnerable to adults who may take advantage of them. Case studies and social research have documented numerous incidents of runaways becoming involved in drug dealing, prostitution, burglary, and other crimes, or becoming victims of crimes or diseases such as ACQUIRED IMMUNE DEFICIENCY SYNDROME (AIDS).

Juvenile courts in the United States hear approximately 11,800 runaway cases each year, making such incidents one of the most common status offenses, or violations of laws for minors. Usually, courts try to help runaways find better ways to cope with family problems, but courts also restrict runaways' freedom. If runaways violate other laws while on the run, they may be sent to institutions or out-of-home placements.

One error that contributes to public fear about runaways is that solved cases are often not removed from files on missing children, leading to overestimates of the number of missing children. Most runaways leave home for a brief period and return unharmed. Many communities have organized shelters where runaways can receive clean clothing, meals, a safe place to sleep, and help to work out problems with their families. Regardless of the outcome, however, running away is a signal to parents and children that it is important to talk openly to resolve their differences.

Rushdie, Salman (b. June 19, 1947, Bombay, India): India-born English novelist, critic, and nonfiction writer. Rushdie's novels are distinguished by an irreverent, self-reflexive, and fragmented style and by an intimate knowledge of Indian, British, Muslim, and Christian cultures. He became an international figure when the Ayatollah Ruhollah KHOMEINI decreed in

Islamic protesters call for Salman Rushdie's death. (Reuters/Bettmann Newsphotos)

Russia and the United States

1989 that Rushdie should be killed for blaspheming against Islam in his 1988 novel *The Satanic Verses*. Rushdie has since lived in virtual seclusion guarded by the British government. His persecution sparked a worldwide controversy over freedom of expression and artistic license. His other books include *Midnight's Children* (1981), *Shame* (1983), *Haroun and the Sea of Stories* (1991), and *East, West: Stories* (1995).

Russia and the United States: Relations between the newly independent Russian Federation and the United States developed in the dual context of the legacy of Cold War Soviet-American relations and the intention of both powers to make a new beginning following Russia's independence from the former Soviet Union.

Background. The COLD WAR came to a gradual conclusion during the late 1980's and early 1990's. Although it is impossible to pinpoint a single date, the opening of the Berlin Wall in November, 1989, was frequently viewed as the Cold War's symbolic end. Various separate developments contributed to its decline. The Soviet decision during the era headed by Mikhail GORBACHEV (1986-1991) to approach foreign policy in a new way, namely via Gorbachev's policy of "new thinking" (*novoe myshlenie*), influenced the changing climate between the United States and the Soviet Union in the late 1980's. Gorbachev's emphasis on mutual interdependence, rather than the Soviet emphasis on international class struggle, was a major component of the new policy. The new approach was derived in part from recognition that the arms race was depleting the Soviet economy. Similar conclusions

U.S. president Richard M. Nixon and Soviet premier Leonid Brezhnev at a 1974 summit meeting. (UPI/Corbis-Bettmann)

may have influenced American opinion during the administrations of Ronald Reagan and George Bush. In both countries, the arms race had resulted in a neglect of domestic concerns and huge budget deficits, problems that were more apparent in the less-developed Soviet economy.

Beginning with the 1985 Summit Conference in Geneva, relations slowly improved between the two nations. By the time the Berlin Wall fell, relations between the United States and the Soviet Union were cordial. During the last years of Gorbachev's rule, the countries actively cooperated in numerous areas, and the United States supported Boris YELTSIN's efforts to defeat the anti-Gorbachev, anti-reform coup of August, 1991.

Post-Soviet Russian-American Relations. When newly independent Russia inherited the foreign-policy apparatus of the Soviet Union, Russia proudly announced a new beginning to its foreign policy, stating that Russia had no enemies. For Americans, it was relatively easy to accept the NEW WORLD ORDER, although at times it was hard to forget forty-five years of Cold War. For Russians, the end of the Cold War was more cataclysmic because it resulted, first, in the loss of the Soviet sphere of influence in Eastern Europe and, later, in the breakup of the Soviet Union (1991). The resulting sense of "loss of empire" could be compared to that

accompanying Great Britain's loss of its empire after World War II.

The rapprochement between the new Russia and the United States in the post-Cold War era was neither uncomplicated nor consistent. In the post-Cold War era, both military superpowers were diminished in power and influence. With the loss of its fifteen republics and its painful transition to a market economy, Russia's power significantly declined, although the country remained a military superpower. The economic weaknesses were far more obvious than in the Soviet era. The United States, although the preeminent global power, faced growing economic competition from Japan, continued budget deficits, and a sense of declining influence in the world.

In the post-Cold War era, instances of Russian-American cooperation in nuclear nonproliferation and in other scientific and technological areas were positive developments. In 1995, a joint space mission involved participation of an American astronaut in a long space journey with Russian cosmonauts and the docking of Russian and American space vehicles in outer space. The United States emerged as Russia's ally in its attempt to consolidate control in the Russian government of former Soviet nuclear weapons deployed in Kazakhstan, Belorussia, and Ukraine. Ukraine emerged as the power least likely to agree to

U.S. president Ronald Reagan and Soviet premier Mikhail Gorbachev sign an arms-reduction treaty in 1988. (Reuters/Corbis-Bettmann)

Russian control of its nuclear weapons, since Ukraine feared that, without nuclear power, it could face threats from Russia in the future.

Russian-American relations in the post-Cold War era existed in a global, as well as a bilateral, context. One context was Asia, where the other principal players were Japan and China. Russia and the United States had both common interests and differences in their approach to China. Both Russia and the United States had highly developed economic relations with China. The dire straits of the Russian economy, however, led its defense establishment to seek the sale of arms and nuclear reactors to China to save its dwindling defense industry. The sale of strategically important items to China and Iran evoked strong American concern. Despite their economic links with China, Russia was wary of the Chinese, their neighbors and rivals along a long, often tense border. The United States, although engaged in multidimensional economic relations with China, was concerned about the possibility of China becoming a strong military power in the future.

In the Middle East, there were differences in policy toward various countries, especially Iran and Iraq. In the aftermath of the GULF WAR of 1991, the United States was inclined to retain a harsh embargo against Iraq, whereas Russia was more inclined to readmit Iraq into the international economy, since Iraq owed billions of dollars to Russia for aid that had been rendered by the Soviet Union. Iran posed another dilemma in Russian-American relations. Russia maintained cordial relations with the fundamentalist Iranian regime while other Western powers, especially the United States, were estranged from Iran. Russia's willingness to furnish nuclear reactors to Iran, ostensibly for peaceful purposes, met strong objections from the United States, which argued that Iran's oil reserves made it unnecessary for Iran to develop atomic power for nonmilitary use.

Another context in which American-Russian relations functioned was the consortium of industrialized nations, known colloquially as the GROUP OF SEVEN, or G-7. Russia's interest in becoming part of the group of industrialized powers had some apparent support on the part of the American president, who treated the Russian president as an equal at G-7 meetings. The G-7 states were reluctant to admit Russia as a full partner, however, because of the weakness of Russia's domestic economy. Russia's relationship to the NORTH ATLANTIC TREATY ORGANIZATION (NATO) was another aspect of the international context. NATO was created in 1949 as part of the post-World War II efforts to contain Soviet expansion. Although its purpose evolved over the years, NATO's role in the post-Cold War era was not easily definable. The NATO powers offered the states of Eastern Europe auxiliary membership in the "Partnership for Peace." Although Russia initially protested the move, it eventually accepted membership in the Partnership for Peace.

American-Russian relations in the post-Cold War years were heavily involved with aid and investment. American aid to post-Soviet Russia took several forms. Private philanthropy to Russia involved charities, religious groups, and the efforts of groups especially created to aid Russia. Aid at the governmental level was channeled through the INTERNATIONAL MONETARY FUND (IMF), the G-7 nations, and specific American-Russian projects supported by international agencies. The aid pledged by the IMF was greater than that actually sent because Russia was often unable to meet the necessary preconditions for receiving aid. Private American investment in Russia was extensive, and, by 1995, greater than that of any other industrialized nation.

Although post-Cold War relations were generally regarded as cordial, internal pressures in both countries prevented a closer relationship. In Russia, strong nationalist and neo-Communist forces attacked the initial Russian foreign policy conducted by Boris Yeltsin, the president of Russia, and Andrei Kozyrev, his foreign minister, who were accused of serving Western interests. The rise of the militant nationalist Vladimir Zhirinovsky intensified attacks on the pro-Western foreign policy of President Yeltsin. The proliferation of political parties in Russia complicated attempts to have a unified foreign policy since the parties could not generally agree on a common agenda. Even among those committed to the path of reform, there was little common ground. The war in Chechnya in southern Russia, which began in 1994, further split Russian political forces. Although treated as a domestic issue, the war in CHECHNYA had international ramifications and tended to reflect the foreign policy positions of the major political forces. The war in Chechnya occa-

sioned concern in the United States, but it was also recognized that Chechnya was part of Russia. Russia's increased involvement in the affairs of the former Soviet republics, referred to as the "near abroad," also evoked American concern, although the United States tended to maintain its distance from problems in the former Soviet republics.

In the United States, an intense struggle between the Republicans and the Democrats for control of Congress and the White House began in the mid-1990's. Although their attention was focused primarily on domestic issues, budgetary differences among rival political factions affected foreign policy and foreign aid. There was pressure on the American president to reduce attention to foreign-policy issues in favor of domestic concerns and to make deep budgetary cuts in all areas. The conflict indirectly affected all countries to whom the United States wanted to give foreign aid.

The Balance Sheet. Russian-American relations in the post-Cold War era could be described in cautiously optimistic terms; the two countries had few, if any, direct areas of conflict, and both countries shared a desire to contain the proliferation of nuclear arms. De-

PUBLIC OPINION, 1994: IS RUSSIA A SIGNIFICANT THREAT TO THE U.S.?

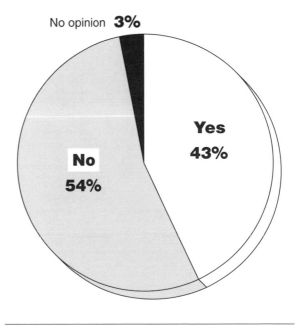

Source: George Gallup, Jr., ed., *The Gallup Poll: Public Opinion, 1994* (Wilmington, Del.: Scholarly Resources, 1995).

spite such cooperation, however, there were also disagreements between Russia and the United States in respect to their policy in Bosnia, the expansion of NATO, Russian strategic-arms sales to Iran and China, policy toward Iraq, and other international issues. The early post-Cold War period set the pattern for the years ahead. The two post-Cold War powers were likely to engage in various cooperative arrangements, yet also experience conflict in areas of rivalry or disagreement.

—*Norma Corigliano Noonan*

SUGGESTED READINGS: Security interests of the late Soviet Union and post-Soviet Russia are the subject of Mark Galeotti's *The Age of Anxiety: Security and Politics in Soviet and Post-Soviet Russia* (London: Longman, 1995). The evolution of Russian foreign policy is treated in editor Peter Shearman's *Russian Foreign Policy Since 1990* (Boulder, Colo.: Westview Press, 1995). Russian-American relations in the larger context of Russian-American-Japanese-Chinese relations is the subject of editor Michael Mandelbaum's *The Strategic Quadrangle* (New York: Council on Foreign Relations, 1995).

Rust v. Sullivan (1991): U.S. SUPREME COURT case. In the *Rust* decision, the Supreme Court ruled on regulations the Department of Health and Human Services had imposed on family-planning programs set up under Title X of the 1970 Public Health Service Act. These regulations stated that medical personnel at Title X projects could not counsel patients "concerning the use of ABORTION as a method of family planning," make referrals to abortion clinics, or undertake any activities that "encourage, promote, or advocate abortion." A group of clinic workers and doctors challenged these rules in court and lost. Deciding in favor of the Department of Health and Human Services by a five-to-four margin, the Supreme Court in effect stated that a gag rule could be imposed on anyone accepting money from the federal government for any purpose.

S

Safety net: Term coined by Ronald Reagan in the early 1980's to describe his legislative proposals for social welfare. In the face of his efforts to cut federal social spending on such programs as FOOD STAMPS, AID TO FAMILIES WITH DEPENDENT CHILDREN (AFDC), and MEDICARE, Reagan assured the U.S. public that the poor would still be protected by a basic safety net of social services. Although many legislators, government officials, and concerned citizens questioned the effectiveness of the safety net, Reagan, who enjoyed considerable popular and congressional support for his legislation, was successful in reducing federal spending on many social-welfare programs. One may argue that a measure of Reagan's success is that the term "safety net" has continued to be used in public discourse.

St. Francis College v. Al-Khazraji (1987): U.S. Supreme Court case. After St. Francis College denied tenure to a teacher who was a U.S. citizen born in Iraq, the teacher claimed that he had been discriminated against because of his ethnicity. The teacher sought judicial relief based on the Civil Rights Act of 1866, a law dealing only with racial discrimination. The problem before the Court was that both parties were classified as belonging to the same race. The Court ruled that the term "race" was commonly used to refer to many classifications when the law was drafted and that Congress had intended to protect all classes of people from "discrimination solely because of their ancestry or ethnic characteristics."

Salinas lettuce strike (Aug. 24, 1970-Nov. 10, 1971): Labor conflict. The Salinas strike was initiated by César CHÁVEZ's UNITED FARM WORKERS union (UFW) for better wages and working conditions for the largely Hispanic fieldworkers, who struck against the growers of rowcrops, including lettuce, in California's Salinas Valley. The growers, particularly larger ones such as Interharvest and Bud Antle, resisted the UFW's attempts to organize and refused to negotiate, while the Teamsters Union competed to organize the same workers. The UFW picketed the fields and attempted to organize a boycott of the products involved, and Chávez conducted a hunger strike. Only a few growers signed contracts, however, and by November, 1971, the strike ended unsuccessfully.

Salk, Jonas (Oct. 18, 1914, New York City—June 23, 1995, La Jolla, California): Physician and medical researcher. Salk developed a vaccine providing immunization against poliomyelitis, a viral disease that can cause paralysis and death in children and young adults. The effectiveness of the Salk vaccine was demonstrated in a 1954 nationwide test involving nearly two million schoolchildren. In 1963, the Salk Institute for Biological Studies was established in La Jolla, with

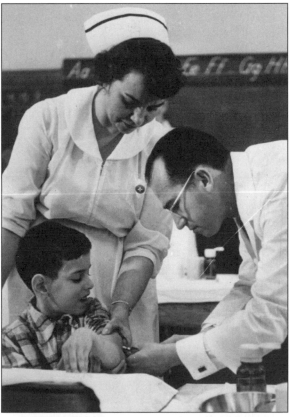

Jonas Salk administers polio vaccine to a child in 1954. (AP/Wide World Photos)

Salk as its director. Salk was working on a vaccine against the AIDS virus at the time of his death.

Sampling: Process of creating new songs using musical elements of previous recordings or live sounds. Sampling involves electronically capturing specific sounds, which are then combined with new melodic, harmonic, or rhythmic arrangements. It is most frequently used by rap artists, and its increasing use has raised issues of musical originality and PROPERTY RIGHTS to commercially released music. Normally, the use of a sample must be cleared with the composer or publisher of the previous recording through a formal licensing agreement specifying the terms of the sample's use and the royalties to be paid. Nevertheless, sampling has spawned numerous lawsuits alleging improper use.

Sanctuary movement: Nationwide attempt by U.S. churches and other religious organizations to challenge government policy concerning victims of Central American conflicts. The 1980's witnessed new waves of refugees entering the United States in order to escape the violence of civil war in such nations as El Salvador and Nicaragua. Immigration laws stated that refugees from political persecution could, upon application, be granted temporary residence in the United States; however, the Ronald Reagan Administration, which had ties to one or another side in several Central American wars, argued that most such escapees were refugees from economic hardship only and were thus not eligible for residency status. As a consequence, the overwhelming majority of Central American refugees were detained as illegal immigrants and deported back to their home countries.

Two local Christian leaders from Tucson, Arizona—the Reverend John Fife, a Presbyterian, and James Corbett, a Quaker—believed that the immigration laws were being abused. Both had attempted to assist refugees with applications to the IMMIGRATION AND NATURALIZATION SERVICE (INS). Fife and Corbett, however, found that in each case the applications were denied, despite what they considered to be ample evidence of political persecution. Drawing upon biblical and historical traditions of Christian hospitality, the two men decided to offer "sanctuary"—housing within the walls of a church—to the refugees on the assumption that the federal government would not violate the sanctity of a church building. The first refugees were housed at Fife's Southside Presbyterian Church in Tucson. Other churches across the Southwest soon followed his example.

Church organizations across the United States eventually joined the Sanctuary movement, providing links in a chain that resembled the Underground Railroad of the pre-Civil War era. Families would initially be housed in churches in California, Arizona, New Mexico, and Texas, then moved to other sanctuaries in the American heartland, and finally to urban areas, where they would be assisted with jobs, housing, and other essentials. While scores of churches from many denominations considered themselves to be part of the movement, not all provided actual shelter to refugees; some raised funds, provided food and clothing, or recruited attorneys to defend various Sanctuary workers against criminal charges filed against them by state and federal authorities.

The Ronald Reagan Administration took a strong stand against the Sanctuary workers, charging many of them with violations of federal immigration laws. Fife, who was dubbed by government authorities the "general" of the movement, accused the government repeatedly of violating his and his congregation's civil rights by infiltrating church worship services and Bible studies, maintaining surveillance on church members, and tapping church telephones. Eventually, Fife and several other Sanctuary leaders in the Southwest were arrested and brought to trial, where they were convicted under federal immigration laws and given suspended sentences or jail terms. One particular element of the government's case was that Sanctuary workers actually "recruited" refugees by traveling to Central America and escorting them across the border to churches in the United States, a charge that was publicly denied by the movement but that a number of Sanctuary workers privately admitted to be true.

After their convictions, Fife and many of the "first generation" of the Sanctuary movement no longer participated actively in the sheltering of refugees, but they continued to speak out against what they considered to be the government's violations of its own laws. As for the refugees themselves, many chose to return to their native countries as the civil wars in Central America began to die down.

Sanger, Margaret (Margaret Louise Higgins; Sept. 14, 1879, Corning, N.Y.—Sept. 6, 1966, Tucson,

A Sanctuary movement speaker addresses a Madison, Wisconsin, crowd. (Mary Langenfeld)

Birth-control pioneer Margaret Sanger is gagged with adhesive tape before a 1929 Boston meeting; Sanger was permitted to address the crowd only by writing on a chalkboard. (UPI/Corbis-Bettmann)

Ariz.): Founder and leader of the United States birth-control movement. In the early twentieth century, Sanger distributed birth-control information advocating the right of women to control their bodies and determine whether and when they would bear children. She established birth-control clinics and founded the organization now called Planned Parenthood. A former nurse, Sanger traveled to Europe to learn about birth control. She was influenced by socialist concerns about population size, "free love" advocates seeking freedom from Victorian sexual restrictions, and feminists who believed that women should be free from constant worry of unwanted pregnancy. Sanger is credited with coining the phrase "birth control."

Satanism: Worship of Satan as a religious deity. A historically ancient practice, Satanism often involves associated activities such as attempts at black magic, sorcery, or calling on demons or the dead. Satanic rituals often mirror traditionally accepted religious practices but blend other rites with such ceremonies. These rituals, sometimes referred to as "Black Masses," are intended to both worship Satan and mock conventional religion. Practices associated with Satanism can also include perverse sexual acts and other behaviors, sometimes involving animal sacrifice and, rarely, human sacrifice. In the 1980's and 1990's, rumors of large networks of Satanists involved in the kidnapping of children and others for sacrifice alarmed many Americans. Investigations by law-enforcement agencies, however, failed to confirm the existence of such networks, and such rumors were generally dismissed as fantasies.

Satellites: Natural or artificial bodies that orbit a planet in the same way that planets orbit the sun. In popular usage, the term usually refers to artificial satellites in orbit around the earth, although spacecraft have also been placed into orbits around the moon and a number of planets. The orbit of a satellite results from a balance between its inertial tendency to continue in a straight line and gravity, which pulls the satellite down.

An earth satellite is typically launched vertically to clear the earth's atmosphere as quickly as possible. Once the rocket has reached sufficient altitude, it tilts into a path parallel to the earth's surface and continues accelerating until the satellite is traveling fast enough to remain in orbit. Satellites must orbit at least 150 kilometers above the earth's surface or else friction with the outer atmosphere would soon slow them down. Satellites in such low orbits travel at about 29,000 kilometers per hour (eight kilometers per second) and circle the earth in about ninety minutes. Satellites in higher orbits travel more slowly and take longer to circle the earth. At a distance of 35,000 kilometers, satellites take twenty-four hours to orbit the earth; seen from earth, they appear to remain fixed in the sky (such orbits are termed "geosynchronous").

Many forces disturb the orbits of satellites, including the gravity of the sun and moon, gravitational effects from the nonspherical shape of the earth, atmospheric drag, and even the pressure exerted by sunlight. Satellites within a few hundred kilometers of the earth eventually reenter the atmosphere. At their high speeds, friction with the air causes incoming satellites to break up and largely vaporize, though surviving fragments frequently reach the surface.

Many classes of satellites are in use. Weather satellites include both geosynchronous satellites for continuous and global coverage and low-orbit satellites for more detailed coverage. Communications satellites are usually geosynchronous, so antennas can remain pointed at them continuously. Military reconnaissance satellites provide photographic coverage from low orbits and monitor electronic communications from geosynchronous orbits. Earth-observation satellites provide photographic coverage from low orbits. Scientific satellites of many types make use of space to escape the limitations imposed by the earth's atmosphere; perhaps the most famous scientific satellite is the HUBBLE SPACE TELESCOPE.

Weather satellites make possible improved weather forecasts and tracking of dangerous storms. Military reconnaissance satellites provide military intelligence and verification of arms-control agreements. The ubiquitous satellite dishes on buildings testify to how dependent global communications are on satellites. One of the most controversial effects of satellites is their capacity to allow foreign governments and corporations to observe a nation's internal affairs or resources without that nation's knowledge or consent. Moreover, some satellites use radioactive materials as power sources while in orbit, and these materials have occasionally survived reentry to contaminate the earth's surface. Some proposed uses of satellites—to display advertisements, reflect sunlight to illuminate the ground at night, or to collect and transmit solar energy

1393

to earth—have generated opposition because of their possible environmental or aesthetic effects.

Savings and loan bailout (1991): Federal recompensation of investors and institutions that lost money in the bankruptcy of many of the nation's savings and loan associations.

Originally, savings and loans were cooperative banks or building and loan associations that loaned funds for the purchase of real estate or the funding of building construction, primarily loaning funds on home mortgages. These organizations accumulated the savings of their members and invested the money in loans, mortgages, and other securities. These activities were permitted and regulated by law. In the late 1970's, savings and loans began losing customers to money market funds that paid higher interest rates.

In order to allow savings and loans to remain competitive, Congress passed a series of deregulations designed to help the industry by allowing it more flexibility. These included the Depository Institutions Deregulation and Monetary Control Act of 1980, which lifted interest caps on deposits, the Garn-St. Germain Depository Institutions Act of 1982, which permitted savings and loans to make business and commercial real estate loans, and a 1988 sanction that allowed deferral and amortization.

Deregulation led to abuses throughout the industry. Brokerage houses began investing in savings and loan associations. The increase in cash flow and the new opportunities from deregulation presented savings and loans with opportunities in unfamiliar investment areas. Experienced, conservative managers were often replaced by managers with bolder investment strategies. By the late 1980's, approximately one-third of the

Depositors wait to withdraw their money from a savings and loan rumored to have management problems. (AP/Wide World Photos)

three thousand savings and loan associations were losing money. Some industry experts assert that one-half of that third were insolvent. By 1986, the Federal Savings and Loan Insurance Company (FSLIC) had run out of money. In 1987, the Treasury Department tried to recapitalize the savings and loans through the Competitive Equality Banking Act, the Federal Savings and Loan Insurance Recapitalization Act, and the Thrift Industry Recovery Act.

Between 1988 and 1991, the savings and loan bankruptcy reached a crisis point. The Financial Institutions Rescue, Recovery, and Enforcement Act of 1989 allocated $50 billion and provided increased federal regulation of savings and loan organizations. Additionally, the Resolution Trust Company was created to oversee the bailout. Initial estimates of the expense of the bailout were far below what the recompensation plan will actually cost. As a result, in 1991, an additional $55 billion swas dedicated to the effort. The General Accounting Office estimates that the total cost, including interest, could run as high as $500 billion.

SUGGESTED READINGS: Michael Waldman's *Who Robbed America?: A Citizen's Guide to the S&L Scandal*, with an introduction by Ralph Nader (New York: Random House, 1990) provides a comprehensive overview of the scandal and its effect on the taxpayer. Paul Zane Pilzer's *Other People's Money: The Inside Story of the S&L Mess* (New York: Simon & Schuster, 1989) chronicles the bankruptcy of the savings and loan organizations. Michael Robinson's *Overdrawn: The Bailout of American Savings and Loans* (New York: Dutton, 1990) explores the effect of the bankruptcy on taxpayers, government, and the industry's future.

Scabs: Workers who defy LABOR UNIONS. The most common use of the term is in reference to workers who take the jobs of striking workers. They may be union members themselves who refuse to strike or who go back to work before a strike ends, or they may be nonunion workers who replace strikers. The term also can refer to workers who take employment at less than the union wage or who refuse to join a union. Scabs reduce the power of unions because they offer employers an alternative to hiring union workers and negotiating with unions.

Scalia, Antonin (b. March 11, 1936, Trenton, N.J.): U.S. Supreme Court justice. Scalia attended Georgetown University, from which he was graduated summa cum laude in 1957. He obtained his law degree in 1960

U.S. Supreme Court justice Antonin Scalia listens to questions during his 1986 Senate confirmation hearings. (AP/Wide World Photos)

from the Harvard University Law School. After his graduation from law school, Scalia served in private practice and in public-service positions during the Richard Nixon and Gerald Ford administrations. Scalia also taught at university law schools, including the University of Chicago and the University of Virginia. In 1986, he was nominated by President Ronald Reagan to the Supreme Court. Since his appointment, Scalia has proven to be one of the Court's most colorful and conservative members.

Schenck v. United States (1919): First U.S. Supreme Court decision to define the limits of the freedoms granted by the First Amendment to the Constitution. Charles Schenck was arrested under the 1917 Espionage Act for distributing handbills that counseled resistance to the draft during World War I. The decision in the case was not reached until after the war was over, but the Court upheld Schenck's conviction and found that speech and the press could be restricted if such materials created "a clear and present danger." The "clear and present danger" doctrine was struck down by the Supreme Court in 1969.

Scholarships: Financial or instrumental assistance given to individuals for the purpose of furthering their education or other scholastic or extracurricular training. Scholarships customarily are given in response to an individual application for assistance or, alternatively, in recognition of a special talent, ability, or achievement. They are typically provided in the form of cash or as a loan to be used for a specific purpose. Tuition, travel, book, and housing costs may be covered as part of a scholarship. Also known as grants, awards, stipends, endowments, or fellowships, scholarships may be provided by federal, state, and local governments, as well as by private organizations.

Scholarships, race-based: Financial assistance provided to minority students on the basis of race. In the aftermath of the end of legal SEGREGATION, many institutions created special scholarships to attract minority students. Such scholarships began as part of AFFIRMATIVE ACTION programs designed to rectify centuries of DISCRIMINATION during which the vast majority of scholarships and educational opportunities had been limited to whites. Race-based scholarships

made up only about 5 percent of all scholarships available at American colleges and universities in 1991. Courts have debated the legality of such scholarships, occasionally restricting their use; although the vast majority of scholarships are awarded on the basis of need, critics have characterized such rulings as blows against diversity in higher education.

School prayer: National debate about whether prayer should be allowed in public schools in the United States. Groups that wish to restore the United States to its "Christian roots" often advocate legislation or amendments to the Constitution to guarantee a time of prayer in the regular school day in one form or another, usually voluntary or nondenominational prayer or a moment of silence. Opponents typically argue that any sort of prayer backed by the state or its agents (for example, a school board) is inevitably coercive and a violation of the First Amendment's SEPARATION OF CHURCH AND STATE.

History. The issue emerged with the rise of public schools in Massachusetts, though it was seldom recognized as a problem. The earliest secondary schools in Massachusetts, called Latin grammar schools, were typically founded to prepare children for college and "for the service of God, in church and commonwealth." The Old Deluder Satan Act of 1647, which required towns in Massachusetts of fifty or more households to provide for the education of youth, had as its chief rationale to teach children to read the Bible. Even with the passage of the First Amendment to the U.S. Constitution, with its "establishment clause" prohibiting the founding of a state church, the possible applicability of that prohibition to prayers in the few public schools in existence was not appreciated. Between 1800 and 1850, public schools finally came to outnumber private schools, but they retained morning devotions with few changes. Until the late nineteenth century, the motive, curriculum, and administration of elementary education were partly religious. Indeed, even in the twentieth century, long after other objectives for public education had been adopted, a school day, especially at the elementary level, might still begin with a scripture reading or a prayer, either by the teacher or by a student.

The practice of religious exercises in public schools was one thing; statutory provision for such actions was another. In 1900, only Massachusetts actually required morning prayer or Bible reading. Many other states

An Alabama man stands outside the U.S. Supreme Court as the Court hears his 1984 challenge to a state law permitting school prayer. (UPI/Corbis-Bettmann)

either allowed them or left the question open, perhaps to be addressed by local boards. The Baltimore law requiring Bible reading or prayer, which became the focus of a Supreme Court ruling in 1963, was not passed until 1905. After 1910, eleven states joined Massachusetts in requiring one or the other, including Pennsylvania in 1913. Pennsylvania's law is interesting because in 1843 the Philadelphia School Board had exempted children whose parents objected from having to participate in religious exercises. During the 1850's, the superintendent of schools of New York decreed that prayers could not be required in public schools. Between 1890 and 1930, six states found such religious practices in violation of their own constitutions. By 1962, thirteen states had found Bible reading or prayer to be legal, while seven had found them to be unconstitutional.

Supreme Court Decisions. In 1962, the Supreme Court made its first ruling on the issue of required prayer. A local school board in New Hyde Park, New York, required every classroom teacher to begin each school day by supervising the students as they recited aloud the following prayer: "Almighty God, we acknowledge our dependence upon Thee, and we beg Thy blessings upon us, our parents, our teachers, and our Country." In the 1962 case *ENGEL V. VITALE*, the Supreme Court held that the requirement breached the "wall of separation" between church and state on the grounds that "it is no part of the business of government to compose official school prayers for any group of American people to recite as part of a religious program carried on by government." Indeed, Justice Hugo Black, who wrote the opinion for the majority, noted that early Americans had fled England to escape just such a use of civil power over religious matters.

In 1963, the Supreme Court ruled unconstitutional two laws impinging on school prayer in the decision entitled *Abington School District v. Schempp*. On December 17, 1959, the Commonwealth of Pennsylvania had amended its Public Law 1928 by requiring that each public school should be opened each day with the reading of ten verses of scripture. The other case involved a rule passed in 1905 by the board of school commissioners of Baltimore City, directing that schools hold opening exercises primarily for the "reading, without comment, of a chapter in the Holy Bible or the use of the Lord's Prayer." Madalyn Murray and her son William, both professed atheists, objected to the requirement and initiated legal proceedings to have the rule rescinded.

The *Schempp* decision directly affected an estimated 42 percent of American public-school children, and reaction was prompt and angry. A constitutional amendment was introduced in the House of Representatives to overturn the decision, but it never got out of committee. Candidates for office sometimes raise the issue, as do special-interest groups. President Ronald Reagan endorsed a constitutional amendment that would overturn the court's ruling and allow voluntary prayer in schools. Many school districts attempted to comply with the ruling, but some have continued to require Bible reading or prayer. Confusion also followed about exactly what was allowed or forbidden. One example of such confusion is the offering of prayers at graduation ceremonies. In 1992, the Supreme Court, ruling on an appeal from the Ninth Circuit Court of Appeals, barred schools in that circuit from allowing students to offer prayers during the ceremonies. One basis for such an action would be that school boards cannot empower students to do what the boards themselves cannot do. In 1995, however, the Supreme Court lifted that ban without addressing the issue itself.

Arguments Against School Prayer. The basic argument against school prayer is that prayer is an inherently religious act, so by ordering or allowing group prayer in schools the considerable weight and influence of the state is made to favor religion over nonreligion and, one might add, theism over nontheism. Also, the practice of excusing nonreligious children from school prayer forces them to state publicly their disbelief with at least two observable consequences. The first, according to the Supreme Court of Wisconsin, "the excused child loses caste with his fellows, and is liable to be regarded with aversion, and subjected to reproach and insult." Secondly, the fear of losing status with peers and teachers may prevent nonconsenting children from exercising their constitutional rights. In addition, prayers like that of the New Hyde Park School Board may be objectionable to very religious students, precisely because of their nonsectarian flavor.

Arguments in Favor of School Prayer. Several arguments have been adduced in support of prayer in public schools. The first deals with tensions within the Constitution and its amendments. A study of American history shows, as the Supreme Court itself recognized in *Zorach v. Clauson* (1962), that the country's founders and their institutions recognized a Supreme Being. It, therefore, cannot have been their intention to preclude the exercise of religion in public life. In addition, a

Advocates of school prayer at a 1984 rally on the steps of the Capitol. (UPI/Corbis-Bettmann)

large majority of Americans are church members, while only a few are professed atheists. Prohibiting school prayer restricts the rights of the overwhelming majority and amounts to hostility against religion, which the First Amendment also prohibits.

Other arguments in defense of school prayer admit that sectarian prayer is unconstitutional, but contend that other types are permissible. Nondenominational prayer, such as that composed by the New Hyde Park School Board, was defended on the grounds that it was based on America's spiritual heritage widely conceived and did not favor one religion over another. Hence, it did not violate the First Amendment's prohibition of establishing religion. If a minority of students or their parents object, those students could be dismissed from class during the time of prayer. If even nondenominational prayers are barred, a moment of silence can be observed by all persons, during which nonreligious children may meditate on other worthwhile subjects.

Another defense of school prayer holds that while it may be admitted that the offering of prayer is an inherently religious act, starting the school day with prayer serves other purposes of a purely secular benefit that justify the continuance of the practice. In the Baltimore case, the superintendent argued that the acknowledgement of the existence of God establishes a tone of discipline that constrains behavior. Others have argued that prayer enhances harmony among students.

Ongoing Controversy. This issue has not been settled. On the one hand, some religious people have come to believe that the Supreme Court has adopted an antireligious stance that can only be corrected by an amendment to the Constitution specifically enfranchising school prayer. On the other hand, modern American culture is becoming even more religiously mixed. The participation in American education of Christians of various denominations, Jews, Native Americans, Muslims, Buddhists, Hindus, and people of no faith at all militates against an acceptable compromise.

—*Paul L. Redditt*

SUGGESTED READINGS: Decisions and supporting data for the two major Supreme Court decisions, *Engel* and *Schempp*, are available in editors Charles Aikin and Victor Jones's *Leading Decisions of the United States Supreme Court* (San Francisco: Chandler, 1962 and 1963). Books that set the issue of school prayer in its larger constitutional context are Martha M.

General Norman Schwarzkopf explains troop movements during the 1991 Gulf War. (Archive Photos, Reuters, Jonathon Bainbridge)

McCarthy's *A Delicate Balance: Church, State, and the Schools* (Bloomington, Ind.: Phi Delta Kappan Educational Foundation, 1983) and Ralph A. Rossum and G. Alan Tarr's *American Constitutional Law, Volume 2: The Bill of Rights and Subsequent Amendments*, 4th ed. (New York: St. Martin's Press, 1995). In *Introduction to the Foundation of American Education*, 9th ed. (Boston: Allyn and Bacon, 1993), James A. Johnson et al. provide chapters on the law and American education and on the history of education in America.

Schwarzkopf, H. Norman (b. Aug. 22, 1934, Trenton, N.J.): U.S. Army general. The son of a brigadier general, Schwarzkopf was graduated from the U.S. Military Academy at West Point in 1956; he served two tours of duty in Vietnam in the 1960's. In 1983, he was promoted to general and oversaw the U.S. invasion of GRENADA. In 1988, Schwarzkopf was appointed commander in chief of the U.S. Central Command, overseeing military operations in eighteen countries in Africa and Asia. He rose to fame in January and February of 1991, when he directed U.S. forces in a rout of Iraqi troops during the Persian GULF WAR. Schwarzkopf retired from the Army in August, 1991.

Science Council of Canada: Agency formed in 1966 to advise the Canadian government on science and technology policy. Originally composed of a mix of appointed scientists and senior federal civil servants, the council increasingly set its own research and policy agenda and eventually became composed exclusively of scientists from outside the government. The council championed university research, assumed a role in public education, advocated a national industrial strategy, and acted as an early-warning body to anticipate problems and opportunities. Despite its effectiveness, the council was eliminated as a result of federal budget cuts, and its functions were subsumed by Industry Canada.

Science for Peace: Private Canadian agency established at the University of Toronto in 1981 for research and education. With many members working in natural or social science, the group addresses military, defense, environmental, and economic issues, working "toward a just and sustainable world." Through public lectures, conferences, workshops, and policy advice to governments and parliamentary bodies, Science for Peace lobbies for disarmament and global security. The group also publishes periodicals and books on such issues as the impact of militarism on the environment, disarmament verification, and world security.

Scientology, Church of: Self-development organization incorporated in 1953. Founded by the science-

fiction writer L. Ron Hubbard (1911-1986), Scientology is a controversial worldwide organization, often in conflict with government agencies, that advocates techniques to train members to rise beyond their conditioning and remember their true selves. Hubbard created the organization to promote the teachings of his bestselling book *Dianetics: The Modern Science of Mental Health* (1950). The organization has aggressively defended itself against lawsuits brought by the Internal Revenue Service (IRS) and former members and has many celebrities as adherents. The group claims to have trained 7 million people, mainly in English-speaking and European countries.

Scopes trial (1925): Landmark academic freedom case. Also known as the "monkey trial," the Scopes case occurred when John Thomas Scopes (1900-1970), a substitute biology teacher in Dayton, Tennessee, tested the state's Butler Act, which prohibited the teaching of the theory of evolution in public schools. The trial pitted the famous civil libertarian Clarence Darrow, who argued for the defense, against three-time presidential candidate and religious fundamental-

Clarence Darrow addresses the court during the 1925 Scopes trial. (UPI/Corbis-Bettmann)

ist William Jennings Bryan, who argued for the prosecution. Over its course, the eleven-day trial became a public debate about the SEPARATION OF CHURCH AND STATE. Though Scopes was convicted of the actual offense and was fined one hundred dollars, the trial was widely viewed as a victory for academic freedom over religious fundamentalism.

Sea, laws of the: Principles for the orderly use of the world's oceans. Countries have long recognized the need for such rules, and to this end the international community has established treaties and customary laws to govern interrelations on the seas. For centuries, the principle governing the law of the sea was the "freedom of the seas" doctrine. Countries had a right to navigate the high seas for purposes of commerce, fishing, discovery of new territory, and promoting national security. Only along their immediate coasts, to a limit of three miles (the distance a cannon could shoot from shore), could states claim territorial jurisdiction over fishing, trade, and matters affecting coastal security. During the twentieth century, with the discovery of oil on coastal state continental shelves and of rich deposits of manganese nodules on the deep-sea bed, pressures to claim access to such resources grew, and countries began to exert broader claims to the coastal seas and continental shelves.

To manage the growing and competing claims, governments negotiated the Law of the Sea Treaty over an eight-year period from 1973 to 1982. This treaty attempted to codify existing customary rules, regulate access to the mining of deep-sea resources, establish mechanisms for the resolution of disputes, update and harmonize rules for management of coastal fishing resources, promote marine scientific research, and better regulate marine pollution. The effect of the treaty was to extend the territorial sea jurisdiction of coastal states from three to twelve miles, and to further extend jurisdiction over natural resources to two hundred miles. Beyond this, especially in matters concerning deep-sea mining, the international community would have the capacity to regulate national claims to access.

Worried that the International Supervisory Authority to be created under the treaty would stifle free enterprise, U.S. president Ronald Reagan refused to support the treaty, and the United States, together with other countries possessing deep-sea mining technology, set out to establish rules among themselves to regulate mining claims. The part of the Law of the Sea Treaty that dealt with deep-sea mining was renegotiated during the early 1990's, however, and free-market principles were introduced, thus answering many U.S. objections.

The Law of the Sea Treaty addresses many other important issues. It regulates access to coastal state fisheries, encouraging scientific research and conservation measures to be taken to preserve fishery resources. It reiterates the right of innocent passage, which was especially important because the treaty, by permitting extended coastal territorial sea claims, caused more than two hundred international straits to fall under complete coastal state jurisdiction. Preserving the right of states to navigate through formerly international waters, then, was important for facilitating ocean commercial traffic. Rules for demarking the territorial claims to bays, archipelagos, and continental shelves were regularized. Machinery for resolving territorial disputes and disputes over deep-sea mining claims was established in an effort to avoid conflict.

The law of the sea has taken monumental strides in the twentieth century. Still, many disputes exist among various countries and interests, and the building and refining of this law are ongoing processes.

Sea Shepherd Conservation Society: Environmental and animal rights organization founded 1977. The Sea Shepherd Conservation Society was founded by Paul Watson, a former member of Greenpeace who grew dissatisfied with that organization's commitment to nonviolence in defense of the environment. Watson believed that the use of nonharmful force, particularly against property, could be justified to protect life. In the summer of 1977, therefore, Watson and several friends established an organization they at first called Earthforce. Headquartered in Vancouver, the group was dedicated to the use of direct action to protect the world's animals; its first mission was to travel to East Africa to document the illegal slaughter of elephants.

Earthforce soon ran into financial problems, and Watson turned for assistance to Cleveland Amory, a well-known writer and historian who gave Watson the $120,000 he needed to buy a retired English fishing ship. With the help of a grant from the British Royal Society for the Prevention of Cruelty to Animals, he equipped the ship with supplies and a crew and rechristened it the *Sea Shepherd*, a name taken from a sixteenth century poem; the organization also took the new name. With their new equipment, Watson and the group inaugurated a new era of environmental activism, intervening to protect baby seals that were being slaughtered for their fur and even ramming and sinking whaling ships. By the 1990's, the organization, which had grown to more than fifteen thousand members, was operating a fleet of antiwhaling vessels and had established its own intelligence agency. Opponents accused the group's members of being fanatics who employed terrorist tactics; Watson, however, would reiterate with pride that the society's actions had never harmed a human being.

Search and seizure: Examination or impounding of property or persons by law-enforcement officers who are seeking evidence. Under U.S. law, no person or property can be searched without probable cause,

and items can be seized only if they are contraband, fruits of a crime, or used to commit a crime. The Fourth Amendment and numerous court decisions specify in greater detail specific requirements for various types of searches and seizures.

Secondhand smoke: Smoke added to the air by smokers and then breathed in by other persons. After noting that a large percentage of persons with certain serious health problems were smokers, scientists studied hundreds of thousands of persons to determine whether or not the use of tobacco contributed to those diseases. In 1964, the U.S. surgeon general reported that cigarette smokers were several times more likely than nonsmokers to die of lung cancer, respiratory dis-

Nonsmokers have objected to exposure to cigarette smoke in public places and to violations of no-smoking regulations. (Reuters/Corbis-Bettmann)

eases, and circulatory disease (such as heart attacks and strokes). In 1993, federal authorities concluded that the use of tobacco caused 420,000 deaths annually.

These reports aroused much controversy. Smokers and tobacco companies denied that these charges had been proved. As late as 1977, half of all smokers refused to believe that smoking tobacco was harmful. However, the *Harvard Medical School Letter* concluded that the evidence that cigarettes were killing smokers was "rock solid."

New evidence indicated that smokers injured not only their own health but also the health of persons around them. The children of smoking parents, it was found, had far more lung cancers and respiratory illnesses as children of nonsmokers, and the spouses of smokers, on the average, had a 30 percent higher rate of lung cancer and died four years younger than the spouses of nonsmokers. In 1992, the Environmental Protection Agency reported that secondhand smoke annually caused 300,000 cases of respiratory infections, aggravated up to 1 million cases of asthma in infants, and triggered forty thousand deaths annually from heart disease. In 1993, the director of the National Cancer Institute estimated that secondhand tobacco smoke killed fifty thousand persons annually.

The percentage of American men who smoked fell from 66 percent in 1955 to 26 percent in 1995, but more than a million teenagers began smoking each year. Smoking would thus apparently remain, in the U.S. surgeon general's words, "the largest single preventable cause of death in America."

The World Health Organization called for bans on tobacco advertising, and England, France, Germany, Norway, Sweden, Denmark, Switzerland, and other countries outlawed all cigarette advertising. The United States banned cigarette advertising on radio and television and required cigarette advertisements and packages to bear the warning that smoking was "dangerous to your health."

Smokers have a choice, but inhaling secondhand smoke is not a voluntary risk. By 1978, federal law required interstate buses, trains, and airplanes to provide no-smoking areas. The U.S. Labor Department proposed a ban on smoking in the workplace. Many restaurants, including the giant McDonald's chain, put up "no smoking" signs. Universities banned smoking in dormitories and classrooms. By 1992, forty-four states required no-smoking areas in public places, such as restaurants and libraries, and increasingly outlawed all smoking in public places. Polls in 1994 showed that

80 percent of the public considered secondhand smoke a health risk, and 67 percent favored a ban on smoking in all public places. These measures had some effect, and estimated U.S. deaths from secondhand smoke dropped from sixty-two thousand in 1985 to forty-seven thousand in 1994.

Secularization: Process of social change in which rational, scientific ways of knowing and understanding the world gradually replace religious explanations. Through this process, religious faith, with its emphasis on the supernatural, loses its influence to science, with its emphasis on objectivity and proof.

There has been considerable debate over whether the secularization process has led to a decline in religion or whether it has strengthened religion. Some analysts believe that it has led to religious decline. They argue that society's constructed worldview (beliefs, values, and symbols used to make sense of life) is very fragile. Science-oriented society encourages a plurality of worldviews that essentially makes all worldviews relative. Thus, religion becomes one of the many possible worldviews from which to choose. Proponents of this argument believe that secularization has caused a de-emphasis of nonrational religious experience in favor of more rational forms of religion.

Others argue that religion is actually strengthened by the secularization process. They believe that secularization has affected religion by making it a more private affair. They argue that this is good because people can "choose" religious outlooks, and thus religion might be more important to individuals. In addition, they agree that secularization has prompted a reduction in religion's emphasis on supernaturalism, but they believe that by de-emphasizing the "other world," religion is led to focus on "this world." Consequently, religion serves less to legitimate society and more to critique and to promote social change.

When church membership figures are used as indicators of whether religion has declined, there is support for both sides of the debate. Those who argue for religious decline point to drops over the past decades in the percentage of the U.S. population who say they are members of a congregation. According to a 1945 Gallup Poll, approximately 76 percent of respondents said they were members of a congregation; in 1995, the total had dropped to 68 percent. Those who say that religion has not declined argue that these short-term figures are deceptive. In 1776, only 10 percent of the U.S. population were members of congregations. This is evidence that a long-term examination of membership shows an increase in religious participation.

There is little debate over whether secularization exists. Worldviews have been increasingly shaped by a rational, utilitarian, scientific approach. Social institutions such as government, education, and medicine do depend less on religion for their legitimation. The emphasis on supernaturalism and otherworldliness has decreased. Have such changes led to a decline in religion? The debate will continue for some time.

SUGGESTED READINGS: Peter Berger argues that secularization has led to religious decline in *The Sacred Canopy* (Garden City, N.Y.: Doubleday, 1967), while Robert N. Bellah argues that religion is strengthened by secularization in *Beyond Belief: Essays on Religion in a Post-Traditional World* (New York: Harper & Row, 1970). For empirical data on the question of membership decline, see Roger Finke and Rodney Stark's work *The Churching of America: Winners and Losers in Our Religious Economy* (New Brunswick, N.J.: Rutgers University Press, 1992).

Securities and Exchange Commission (SEC): U.S. government agency responsible for oversight of securities markets and transactions. The Securities and Exchange Commission was created in 1934 with the passage of the Securities and Exchange Act. The commission is responsible for the administration of federal securities designed to provide for the protection of investors and for ensuring that securities markets are maintained in a fair and honest manner. The SEC is vested with quasijudicial powers in order to enforce securities laws through sanctions if necessary. The SEC's powers include the right to impose sanctions to ensure compliance and to prosecute persons who violate federal securities laws.

Activities of the SEC include the registration of all securities offerings as required by the Securities Act of 1933. The act requires entities issuing securities and their controlling persons to file registration statements containing financial and other pertinent data about the issuing entity and the security being offered with the commission when making public offerings of securities. Some issuers are exempt from this requirement, such as government securities, nonpublic offerings, and some offerings of less than $1.5 million. The purpose of this registration process is not to guarantee investors against loss, but to provide potential buyers with information in order to make an informed decision as to the value of the securities in question. Filing of annual reports and other reports by companies whose securities are listed on the exchanges and by companies with assets in excess of $5 million and five hundred or more shareholders is also required. These reports must contain fiscal and other data as required by the commission. The SEC also requests disclosure of transactions or intended transactions involving large shareholders, officers, and directors of companies, or persons acquiring at least 5 percent of certain securities.

The commission is also charged with broad regulatory responsibilities over securities markets, persons who conduct business in securities, and the self-regulatory agencies within the industry. The SEC also oversees the Municipal Securities Rulemaking Board, which seeks to adopt rules intended to promote just and equitable principles of trade and to protect investors.

Regulation of mutual funds is also the responsibility of the SEC, as stated in the Investment Company Act of 1940. The act requires that these companies register with the commission and covers sales load, management contracts, composition of boards of directors, and capital structure, all in an effort to protect investors. The act prohibits investment companies from making certain types of transactions until approved by the commission and determined to be fair to investors. The SEC may initiate court action to block mergers and other transactions if they are determined to be unfair to stockholders.

Sedition: Illegal attempts to disrupt or overthrow a government. Unlike TREASON, which involves an overt act as part of an attempt to overthrow or hinder the government, "sedition" refers more specifically to preliminary stages of such actions. The crime of seditious libel involves communications advocating the overthrow of the government; in the United States, however, the ability of prosecutors to bring seditious libel charges is severely limited by the First Amendment. Charges of sedition thus usually involve both seditious libel and the CLEAR AND PRESENT DANGER that such activities will be carried out.

Segregation: Separation of people by RACE, religion, or ethnicity. There are two different types of segregation, de jure (by law) and de facto (by custom,

Segregation

Pro-segregation demonstrators in New Orleans, 1960. (UPI/Corbis-Bettmann)

tradition, or attitude). Segregation has existed throughout human history in every society and civilization. Examples include the caste system in Hindu nations, apartheid in South Africa, and the system of race relations found in the American South from 1865 to 1965.

Racial segregation appeared in the United States in 1619 when the first slave ship arrived in the Virginia colony. Slave laws were based on race, as slave owners defended the institution by proclaiming white supremacy. Africans, it was argued, were an inferior, uncivilized race and had to be kept separate from whites.

When the Civil War brought an end to SLAVERY in 1865, Southern whites reconstructed segregation by passing laws known as Black Codes. Everything was segregated legally, from schools, hospitals, and churches to graveyards and swimming pools. The Supreme Court found such separation constitutional in *PLESSY V. FERGUSON* (1896), arguing that public facilities could be separated by race as long as the different facilities were maintained equally. This "SEPARATE BUT EQUAL" doctrine legitimized a rigid system of segregation throughout the South until 1954. In that year, the

Court reversed *Plessy* in BROWN V. BOARD OF EDUCATION OF TOPEKA, KANSAS, insisting that dividing children by race, for whatever reason, was unconstitutional. The Court ordered school systems to desegregate with "all deliberate speed."

Many white citizens in the South responded with violence and called for the impeachment of Chief Justice Earl Warren. *Brown* helped set off the CIVIL RIGHTS MOVEMENT, which by 1965 overturned all systems of legal segregation. But as late as 1990, school DESEGREGATION remained an unmet goal. More than 60 percent of black students in the United States attended schools in which they were more than 90 percent of the student body. This de facto segregation proved far more difficult to remedy than did legal segregation. Federal courts attempted to use BUSING to break down segregated school boundaries, but that method proved unpopular and was rarely used.

Canada's blacks have accounted for less than one percent of the country's total population for most of its history, yet it, too, has a history of racial segregation. The two provinces with the highest black population, Ontario and Nova Scotia, developed systems of separate public schools. The Court of Queen's Bench ruled in 1884 that blacks could legally be sent to separate schools. This segregation remained the accepted system in Ontario until 1964. Canadian Americans shared the patterns of PREJUDICE found in the United States. Blacks were refused service in hotels, expelled from churches, and kept from getting high-paying jobs. The only difference between Canada and its southern neighbor was that blacks in Canada had always remained equal in the eyes of the law. They served on juries, voted, and could testify against whites in court.

Both the United States and Canada outlawed legal segregation in the 1960's, though DISCRIMINATION in employment and education continued. Large gaps in income existed, with black families averaging about one-quarter the income of the typical white family.

Self-defense: Legal doctrine that permits individuals who are unlawfully attacked to take reasonable steps to defend themselves. The doctrine is premised on the belief that greater social harm will result if an unlawful aggressor is permitted to kill an innocent

Supporters of subway gunman Bernhard Goetz argue that he acted in self-defense. (UPI/Corbis-Bettmann)

victim than if the victim is allowed to use force to defend against the aggressor. Society protects individuals' rights to self-help and bodily integrity. By using unlawful force against an innocent victim, courts have typically concluded, an aggressor effectively forfeits the right to bodily integrity.

Self-esteem: Confidence and satisfaction in one's self. People with high levels of self-esteem and positive self-concepts tends to behave in appropriate ("nurturing") ways; people with low levels of self-esteem and negative self-concepts tend to behave in inappropriate ("abusive") ways. The terms "self-esteem" and "self-respect" are sometimes used interchangeably.

Self-help books and videos: Written and filmed materials focusing on self-improvement. While self-help books generally outnumber self-help films, both formats concentrate on promoting psychological and physical wellness. By offering prescriptive advice on problem development, prevention, and solutions, both serve to foster physical and mental health as well as personal growth.

Self-help books and videos can be obtained at bookstores, public libraries, and commercial video stores. They may be used independently by individuals striving to alter their own problematic behavior or by couples or families seeking to make collective changes. Additionally, they may be used as adjuncts to therapeutic activities directed by professionals, such as physicians, psychologists, or psychiatrists. Known as bibliotherapy, or book therapy, the use of self-help books is a primary vehicle for health education and health care. Self-help books and films address a wide variety of problems, including conditions such as anxiety, depression, divorce, romantic problems, chemical dependency and substance abuse, family violence, and serious personal illnesses. For people dealing with these problems, such resources may provide an introduction to understanding a problem and beginning the task of solving it. Alternatively, for other individuals these materials may be used for facilitating the development of more positive life events and help to encourage a change in strategies, such as improved diet and exercise, adaptive ways of coping with life changes, improving social relationships, the learning of new parenting skills, and even enhancing personal or marital sexuality and skills. In this way, these materials foster

health maintenance, restoration, and fulfillment.

Self-help materials often begin with a good description of the problem to be solved or the goal to be achieved. The person seeking information is given a mental outline of how to understand, think about, and define the problem or goal. Different strategies for solving the problem are then described in detail or through examples of what others have experienced. Some books and films feature mental, social, or physical exercises that may be used to facilitate change. Others provide workbooks that individuals can use to help them work through concepts or very specific aspects of personal problems.

Self-help approaches to problem solving have existed for centuries for health and social problems. Though they are a worldwide phenomenon, self-help solutions are most popular in the United States, as they appeal to individuals wanting autonomous means of solving problems. It should be emphasized, however, that the success of any self-help approach often relies on high personal initiative and the quality of the self-help materials. When motivation to change is low or in conflict with other concerns, often professional help can be the most appropriate course of action. For many individuals, however, self-improvement strategies are sufficient, and self-help materials can provide an important resource for accomplishing positive, lasting change.

Self-segregation: Tendency of people of different races to remain separate socially and institutionally despite the absence of legal barriers to INTEGRATION. The term is usually applied to efforts by African Americans to maintain institutions that are predominantly black or to form organizations within integrated institutions specifically for blacks. The phenomena of "WHITE FLIGHT" from cities and white abandonment of public schools are generally not referred to as instances of self-segregation.

Since the 1960's, the amount of interaction between African Americans and whites has greatly increased. The integration of institutions such as workplaces and schools has led to greater social interaction. However, substantial de facto SEGREGATION remains in housing and public schools. In addition, many whites and blacks still harbor elements of hostility toward people of other races and cultures. As a result, members of minority groups in integrated institutions often feel a degree of hostility and pressure; such entities as employee organizations, student groups, and fraternal organizations are thus often designed generally for minority group members only. These groups serve as ways of asserting minority interests, as support groups, and as social organizations. Other social organizations such as FRATERNITIES AND SORORITIES are also often culturally and racially exclusive; many observers defend such groups as necessary and praise them for creating a sense of community among minority group members. Critics, however, attack such organizations as socially divisive.

Perhaps even more contentious has been the drive to maintain and expand predominantly black institutions of education. Some African Americans argue that integration has failed to provide educational opportunities for many blacks; they assert that the often unconscious hostility of many whites means that in predominantly white institutions of education, blacks are never treated fairly or given truly equal opportunity. Blacks in these institutions thus become alienated and at risk of dropping out. Efforts to further desegregate higher education by merging historically white and black colleges thus often meet with strong resistance from African Americans.

Critics of self-segregation, especially in education, counter that integration has not failed but has never been truly tried. They point to continuing patterns of residential segregation and resulting educational segregation and to studies showing that blacks who attend integrated schools generally have higher college graduation rates than those that attended still segregated schools. Such observers typically argue that white resistance to DESEGREGATION causes most of the problems seen by blacks in integrated institutions.

Selph v. Council of the City of Los Angeles (1975): (1975): U.S. district court case. Jacqueline Selph, a paraplegic permanently confined to a wheelchair, asserted that the city's failure to provide polling places accessible to wheelchairs was a violation of the equal-protection clause of the Fourteenth Amendment. The district court, however, ruled that the city did not have an obligation to modify all of its polling places but merely needed to make reasonable accommodations for the handicapped, such as providing accessible, centrally located polling places.

Senior citizens: Persons older than a certain age. In North America, the term "senior citizen" (or simply "senior") is applied to various age groups fifty-five and above. Many restaurants and entertainment facili-

Senior citizens are an important force in American politics. (UPI/Bettmann)

ties offer "senior discounts" to patrons over the age of fifty-five, for example, and sixty-five was long considered the appropriate retirement age. However, more people than ever are working well past sixty-five, even into their seventies; it is now illegal in most businesses for an employer to force a person to retire because of age. A large and growing segment of society, senior citizens are sought after for their wisdom, wealth, and votes. Overall, senior citizens contribute a cultural stability in most segments of society. However, increased life spans, growing medical costs, and falling income create difficulties for many older citizens. The AMERICAN ASSOCIATION OF RETIRED PERSONS (AARP), a public-service group and lobbying organization for the rights of older persons, provides many services for senior citizens.

Separate but equal: U.S. legal doctrine used to justify racial SEGREGATION. The Fourteenth Amendment, adopted in 1868, guaranteed newly freed slaves "equal protection of the laws"—that is, statutes had to treat blacks and whites the same. Several Southern states responded with a series of segregation laws that required separation of the races in schools and other public facilities. In 1896, the U.S. Supreme Court ruled in PLESSY V. FERGUSON that facilities had only to be equal, not integrated. Thus, the "separate but equal" concept allowed the South to maintain a rigid segregation system until the 1954 BROWN V. BOARD OF EDUCATION OF TOPEKA, KANSAS, decision, which dismissed "separate but equal" treatment as "inherently unequal."

Separation of church and state: Originally, the transfer of church property to the civil government, and the policy of toleration of religious diversity by the state in early-modern Europe associated with the process of SECULARIZATION. Today the phrase has a

Orthodox Jews protest a 1994 Supreme Court ruling that the creation of a special school district for disabled Jewish children violated the doctrine of separation of church and state. (Reuters/Corbis-Bettmann)

more general meaning, referring to legal limits on the influence of religious beliefs on state functions such as education and the maintenance of public places.

From the seventeenth century in Europe, governments began to tolerate minority religious groups, such as Protestants (Huguenots) in France, Catholics in England, or Jews in both countries, for "reasons of state"—that is, as part of the government's mandate to preserve civil order and promote general prosperity. In the United States, the experience of religious liberty in the Colonial period led to the expression of religious beliefs by one denomination that often insulted the beliefs of another, mainly among Protestants. In order to preserve religious liberty, Thomas Jefferson called for "a wall of separation" between church and state. This principle subsequently led to the First Amendment to the U.S. Constitution, banning laws that promote the "establishment of religion" and prohibiting laws that restrict the "free exercise" of religion.

Today, most governments around the world recognize some version of the separation of church and state. "Separation" is always a matter of degree, however, and it has never been absolute. One way the intertwining of political and religious realms has been recognized by social scientists is by introducing the concept of "civil religion." This concept refers to cultural meanings that inform politics but are not explicitly delineated in the law; rather, such meanings are provided by the historical experience of society, usually rooted in a religious tradition.

With recognition that a literal "wall of separation" has never existed, however, come sharply contrasting demands from different constituencies either that the separation be enforced or that a religious grounding of state policies be legalized.

Debates over whether local governments can sponsor nativity scenes in public parks or whether public schools can require prayer in the classroom involve consideration of positions along the spectrum of these two extremes, as do debates over the fundamental purposes of government—debates that have led to important social changes around the world. Such major shifts in the understanding of the constitution of the state as the Iranian revolution and the Nicaraguan revolution, both in 1979, and the growth of the Solidarity movement in Poland in the 1980's, where Catholic clergy were prominent, are examples.

SUGGESTED READINGS: Thomas Robbins and Roland Robertson have collected a number of interesting studies comparing U.S. debates to debates over the issue elsewhere in the world in *Church-State Relations: Tensions and Transitions* (New Brunswick, N.J.: Transaction Books, 1987).

Separation of powers: Division of responsibilities among legislative, executive, and judicial branches of government. The purpose of such separation is the prevention of the abuse of power by any branch; abuse is prevented by ensuring that the same individual or body does not make, enforce, and adjudicate the law. Under the U.S. CONSTITUTION, power is also shared among the three branches through a system of checks and balances. Separation of powers has its origins in the ancient idea of "mixed government" and in the ideas of John Locke and Baron Montesquieu.

Service economy: Economic sector dependent on service industries or jobs. Since the 1950's, the service sector (including business, personal, governmental, and educational services) has grown faster than any other economic sector, especially in industrialized nations such as the United States and Canada.

Experts disagree on why growth in service industries has occurred. Early conservative theorists speculated that the growth in services marked the beginnings of a shift to better working and living conditions for all people, especially in advanced capitalist countries where the expanding service sector was said to be the inevitable result of the free market. Others trace the rise to economic changes that began in the 1970's, including deindustrialization (the closing of manufacturing plants and the relocation to poorer nations or regions), which led areas hardest hit by the loss to search for alternative sources of revenue and jobs. Others, using a more analytical perspective, discuss the rise of services in relationship to the capitalist quest for profits and the "cheapening" of the labor force.

The change from predominantly agricultural and manufacturing production to services has profoundly affected the ways women and men consume and produce. Consumption activities, such as food preparation and dining, that until the mid-1950's occurred almost exclusively in the home, now frequently occur away from home in restaurants, fast-food outlets, and other public dining facilities.

In addition to the changed patterns of consumption

in families, these widespread economic, social, and cultural changes continue to affect patterns of employment. Unlike factory or farm work, which involves production for the market and little direct daily contact with the consuming public, members of the labor force who sell services work closely with the purchasing public. A worker in a meat-packing plant who prepares hamburger patties for future sale is a manufacturing worker, but a restaurant cook who microwaves the hamburger for purchase by a waiting customer would be considered a service worker.

Service workers may be self-employed, hired by privately owned small or large businesses, or employees of the government or public sector. Broadly, service occupations can be broken down into two areas: advantaged or "primary" and disadvantaged or "secondary." Primary services are higher-status jobs that are also better paying and usually more stable than secondary jobs. They include positions in management, finance, real estate, insurance, and state and local government. Although some people claim that these are the areas that have grown the most, thereby opening more lucrative job opportunities for all, the shift to service employment has not uniformly benefited the workforce. Instead, the jobs that are fastest growing fall within the secondary sector, including janitorial and food services. Secondary jobs are often stigmatized and undervalued, low-paying, lacking in medical or vacation benefits, and are characterized by unhealthy and stressful working conditions. The increase in the numbers of working poor in the United States and other industrialized nations is attributed, in part, to the rise in these limited-opportunity jobs.

700 Club, The: Religious television program. The flagship program of the Reverend Pat ROBERTSON's CHRISTIAN BROADCASTING NETWORK (CBN), *The 700 Club* can claim to have been the first Christian talk show. Originally devoted to prayer and counseling, the show eventually adopted a magazine format that includes celebrity interviews, news features, and entertainment. It was on *The 700 Club* that Jim and Tammy Faye Bakker rose to fame before forming their own television ministry, the scandal-ridden *PTL*. According to John B. Donovan, Robertson's biographer, the show "has four basic goals: to give information from a different perspective; to give hope and inspiration so people can face the future; to minister directly to persons through prayer; and to meet the felt needs of viewers." The show also provides a bully pulpit for host Robertson's political views.

Sex and sexuality: The various ways in which individuals express and experience themselves as functioning sexual beings. Although the majority of individuals in all cultures are heterosexual, or sexually attracted to members of the opposite sex, a substantial number of individuals identify themselves as homosexual or bisexual. The prevalence of widespread misconceptions and biases has added urgency to the search for factual information about all aspects of human sexuality, including sexual identity, sexual orientation, gender, and sexual behavior.

U.S. Population by Sexual Preference. The most extensive reports on sexuality in the United States were conducted by Alfred C. Kinsey between 1938 and 1949. Kinsey reported that 37 percent of the males interviewed had at least one homosexual encounter, as had 13 percent of females. His findings were later interpreted as suggesting that 10 percent of the U.S. population was exclusively homosexual. Subsequent, and probably more accurate, surveys estimated the prevalence of exclusive HOMOSEXUALITY at 5 percent. Despite these differences in prevalence rates, it is clear that many individuals identify themselves as exclusively attracted to same-sex partners. Societies vary tremendously in their tolerance for alternative sexual orientation; however, there is no known culture in which adult homosexuality is openly encouraged or the preferred orientation of all but a significant minority.

Legislation Regarding Sexual Orientation. Legislation regarding sexual behavior has its origin in the Judeo-Christian tradition. Sodomy laws declaring homosexual practices illegal exist in twenty-four states and the District of Columbia. Sodomy laws ban "unnatural" (nonprocreative) sexual acts, especially between males. These acts include anal and oral genital contact, even among consenting adults and regardless of their sexual orientation. These laws also include sexual acts considered unacceptable in most Western cultures, such as child molestation. Equal application of these laws would extend to heterosexuals who engage in the illegal sexual acts, but the vast majority of sodomy prosecutions have involved homosexual men. In Canada (where sodomy is referred to as "buggery"), any sexual behavior between consulting adults in private is acceptable.

The landmark U.S. case regarding sodomy, *Bowers v. Hardwick* (1986), was upheld by the Supreme Court.

Homosexuals have been widely discriminated against on the basis of their sexual preferences. (James L. Shaffer)

This case involved a male who was charged with committing sodomy in a private residence with another consulting adult male. The Court indicated this law had constitutional merit and could be enforced under Georgia law with a maximum prison term of twenty years. Although the prosecutor decided not to prosecute the defendant, the ruling set a precedent for other cases.

Cases that have centered on the civil liberties of homosexuals include *Rosenberg, District Director, Immigration and Naturalization Service v. Fleuti* (1963) and *Boutilier v. Immigration and Naturalization Service* (1967). Both of these cases were brought before the U.S. Supreme Court under the IMMIGRATION AND NATIONALITY ACT OF 1954, which states that alien homosexuals defined as "aliens afflicted with psychopathic personalities," are "ineligible to receive visas and shall be excluded from admission into the United States." These rulings by the Court were not based on constitutional grounds. Because of the lack of a definite ruling, the lower courts have generally decided to admit homosexuals who are considered to be of good "moral character" and who have never lied about their sexual orientation on their visa applications.

Most of the major professional health-care organizations have issued statements endorsing the decriminalization of homosexuality. The American Psychiatric Association removed homosexuality from its list of mental disorders in 1973; the American Psychological Association followed suit in 1975. Despite these decisions, the courts continued to refuse to grant equal rights to homosexuals.

Discrimination against homosexuals extends to job security. The CIVIL RIGHTS ACT OF 1964 encompasses minority groups such as African Americans, Hispanics, women, religious minorities, the elderly, and handicapped individuals. It provides them with the right to obtain employment and safety from workplace discrimination based on their status. The United States Court of Appeals, however, has denied homosexuals the status of "class" within the meaning of civil rights statutes in the case of *Life Insurance Co. of North America v. Reichardt* (1979). According to the decision, Title VII of the 1964 act prohibiting employment discrimination on the basis of "sex" was based on the traditional meaning of gender, not sexual orientation. Because of the lengthy history of viewing homosexuality as a sin, sickness, and vice, U.S. courts have been reluctant to provide protection to homosexuals as has been done in Canada and Great Britain.

In the past, a U.S. Department of Defense directive supported the laws of sodomy and indicated that homosexuality was incompatible with military service. It prohibited the enlistment of homosexuals into the armed services. If a homosexual did enter the service in spite of this prohibition, the individual was discharged in a timely manner. This regulation was based on admittance of homosexuality alone, and proof of homosexual acts was not required.

Under the auspices of gay-rights activists, the Supreme Court again heard arguments about discrimination against homosexuals in the military. In 1990, the Court upheld the military's right to ban gays from serving in the armed forces. This statute was later relaxed by the Bill CLINTON Administration, which instituted a "don't ask, don't tell" policy in which soldiers were not asked about their sexual orientation; in turn, they were required to remain silent about their sexual preference.

There have been some breakthroughs for homosexual rights, such as the Hate Crimes Statistics Act that Congress passed in 1990. This act provided a special status to gays and lesbians by providing legal protection from hate-motivated crimes. This may provide little consolation after a crime has been committed, but is viewed as a positive step toward gaining equal rights for homosexuals.

Nature Versus Nurture in Sexual Identity and Orientation. The determinants of sexual identity and sexual orientation have been hotly debated. The controversy centers on whether sexual orientation is determined by biological or environmental factors. If it is shown that sexual orientation is determined by biological factors, this would challenge religious and legal positions that view homosexuality as a freely chosen preference. Thus, the debate about the origins of homosexuality has wide-ranging implications.

Biological evidence of sexual identity and orientation is substantial. With respect to sexual orientation, genetic studies have been the most useful. The typical methodology in genetic studies involves identifying gay men who have either a monozygotic (identical) or dizygotic (fraternal) brother in order to determine the prevalence of homosexuality among twins. The concordance (agreement) rate of homosexuality is then examined among the sets of twins. Because identical twins share 100 percent of their genes, a high degree of concordance for homosexuality would represent evidence supporting the importance of heredity. Fraternal twins share only 50 percent of their genes and a lower

Scientists continue to debate the influence of environment on the development of a child's sexual identity. (James L. Shaffer)

concordance rate is expected in this case. In virtually all genetic studies of homosexuality the concordance among identical twins is higher than that for fraternal twins. In other words, the greater the genetic similarity among subjects, the higher the concordance or similarity in their reported sexual orientation.

Researchers at the National Cancer Institute found preliminary evidence of biological determination by connecting a particular region on the X chromosome to homosexual orientation. It was found that gay men had a higher incidence of gay male relatives on the maternal side of the family than the general population. This was in contrast to the limited number of gay male relatives on their paternal side of the family. Further examination of X-chromosome similarities among family members led to the preliminary identification of identical DNA markers in male, nontwin brothers. Thirty-three of forty pairs of brothers were found to have this marker. This is significantly higher than would normally be found in the general population (50 percent) and further points to a biological predisposition toward homosexuality for some men.

Research comparing the brain structure of homosexual and heterosexual males and females has provided additional information about potential biological aspects of sexual orientation. Several researchers have compared the size of one brain structure, the hypothalamus, among individuals of differing sexual orientations. The hypothalamus has been implicated in regulating sexual behavior among many species. A number of studies have reported significant structural differences in the brains of homosexual and heterosexual men and women. Researchers in the U.S. reported that one region of the hypothalamus was smaller in gay men than in heterosexual men. Additionally, this brain region is relatively small among heterosexual women.

A growing body of evidence reveals that one pathway to adult homosexuality is nonconformity to societal gender expectations. Very feminine boys have a much higher probability of developing a homosexual orientation than masculine boys. Some boys display feminine characteristics at a very young age, suggesting the underlying factors are present well before the individuals reach puberty and identify themselves as sexual beings.

Indirect evidence of biological factors in sexual orientation came from a study of native Dominican Republican males. Because of a genetic error, these boys were born without male genitalia. Their parents erroneously assumed they were females and socialized them accordingly. Entering puberty, however, their penises began developing and they changed their sexual identity from female to male. This came without any socialization regarding their new-found gender and was adopted readily in their pubescent stage of life. Thus, these males who thought of themselves as females prior to puberty readily adapted to a new gender. Despite having been reared as girls destined to marry men, they made the transition to becoming males who would marry women. This again established a dominant role played by biology in sexual identity and orientation.

If sexual orientation were largely determined by social factors, such as early sexual experiences and upbringing, one would expect relatively high rates of adult homosexuality in cultures that condone or encourage same-sex sexual activity in adolescents. In fact, this does not appear to occur. One New Guinea culture that encourages ritualized homosexual behavior among its young males is an example of biological drives overriding socialization. The young Sambian males are taught that female bodies are unattractive, poisonous, and to be avoided. Boys are expected to perform fellatio, or oral sex, on adult men as a necessity for achieving masculinity in adulthood. Even in this particular outline of homosexual behavior, the boys mature into adults who seek female sexual partners and are predominantly heterosexual.

Clearly, any genetic determination of sexual orientation involves complex interactions among multiple factors. After all, the parents of the vast majority of homosexuals are themselves heterosexual. However, most homosexual men and women report being aware of their homosexual feelings early in life, generally prior to or during adolescence. Many also report repeated failures to change their orientations despite intense internal and external pressure to conform to a heterosexual culture in which homosexuality is stigmatized. Efforts to change sexual orientation through therapy have consistently been ineffective. It appears that biology, whether heredity, prenatal factors, or other influences, sets a predisposition toward a particular sexual orientation. Perhaps the social experiences of the individual determine how the genetic predisposition is manifested and how sexual orientation ultimately evolves.

Gender Roles and Gender Differences. Gender roles refer to the traits and behaviors expected of males and females in a specific culture. In the U.S. and Canada, the socialization of gender roles begins at the moment of birth. Parents treat male and female infants very differently, from the choice and color of clothing to the ways in which boys and girls are held and stimulated. Based on cultural expectations, women are expected to be more gentle, dependent, kind, and submissive. Conversely, men are socialized to be more aggressive, protective, and competitive. These fairly rigid societal expectations of the desirable characteristics for each gender are called gender-role stereotypes.

Numerous societal forces shape and reinforce existing gender roles and stereotypes. Although the focus has predominantly been on the impact of parents in gender-role socialization, other agents include teachers and peers. The popular media has been especially influential in shaping gender-role stereotypes. Historically, men were depicted in traditional masculine occupations, such as police officers, attorneys, and physicians. Women were more likely to portray such traditional roles as schoolteachers, secretaries, and nurses.

It is well established that gender roles in many Western cultures have been changing. For example, the traditional view of the woman as a housewife has gradually given way to that of working mother and wife. An increasing number of families consist of a man and woman, both of whom are employed outside of the home. Consequently, more and more girls are being exposed to career-minded role models. Additionally, more parents are encouraging their daughters to pursue advanced studies and careers. Conversely, sons are being encouraged to assume a more equitable role in raising their children and in assuming household responsibilities. These developments are gradually reflected in the popular media as growing numbers of men and women are depicted in nontraditional roles.

Increasing evidence points to the importance of cultural and societal factors in creating gender differences in roles, abilities, and traits. Early studies suggested that males surpassed females in visual-spatial skills (such as mathematical ability), while females excelled in verbal, or language, skills. Subsequent studies revealed that these differences were in fact quite modest, were based on group differences, and may have resulted from cultural expectations. Despite obtained differences in groups of boys and girls, countless numbers of girls exceed the performance of the "average" boy in mathematical tests and countless boys outperform the "average" girl in verbal skills.

Males in many Western cultures are described as inherently more aggressive and competitive than females; however, cross-cultural comparisons reveal that this is not a universal phenomenon. Among the Mundugumor of New Guinea, both men and woman are aggressive. In the Tchambuli tribe, men are responsible for rearing the children, while the women are the primary providers for the family. Additionally, women are more sexual and aggressive than men in that culture. Although men and women of all cultures share the same biological makeup, extreme cultural differences exist in gender roles. It appears the gender roles and stereotypes are more a product of society than of biology. These findings may lead one to reconsider the meaning and value of existing gender roles.

Social Effects of AIDS and Other Sexually Transmitted Diseases. Sexually transmitted diseases (STDs), formerly known as venereal diseases, are diseases that are spread through sexual contact. There are numerous sexually transmitted diseases that are classified as either bacterial, such as gonorrhea and syphilis, or viral, including herpes and HUMAN IMMUNODEFICIENCY VIRUS (HIV). Prior to the discovery of antibiotics in the nineteenth century, syphilis had reached epidemic proportions in Europe and North America. A drastic reduction in the incidence of syphilis and gonorrhea followed the discovery of effective treatments. These two STDs were considered extremely rare until the 1980's, when it was discovered that STD infection rates had again dramatically risen. Additionally, such comparatively uncommon STDs as herpes and genital warts were found to be widespread. Researchers estimated that one in four Americans would contract an STD at some time in their lives. Although some STDs produce few obvious symptoms, their long-term consequences can be devastating. For example, chlamydia, a common bacterial infection, can produce infertility in women if untreated, and syphilis can be fatal without treatment.

Most alarming are the findings about the prevalence of HIV, the virus that causes ACQUIRED IMMUNE DEFICIENCY SYNDROME (AIDS). AIDS represents the most deadly of all STDs. The disease and its cause were not identified until the early 1980's; the worldwide number of cases of persons diagnosed with AIDS grew dramatically thereafter. The earliest reports of AIDS erroneously attributed it to homosexual behavior, earning it the title of the "gay plague." As a consequence, governments and health organizations were initially slow to respond to the epidemic. Some claimed that AIDS represented a just punishment for immoral sexual behavior, thereby justifying their reluctance to implement

1417

HIV-prevention programs. Not until the full extent of the epidemic became known did governments and health agencies implement HIV risk-reduction campaigns. Critics argued that such efforts were underfunded and ineffective.

In the U.S. and Canada, the majority of cases affect men who have sex with men and those who use intravenous drugs. However, any activity involving the exchange of bodily fluids, especially semen and blood, involves some risk of HIV infection if one participant is a carrier. Thus, AIDS is most accurately viewed as a disease caused by certain behaviors rather than by certain groups of people.

Because AIDS was originally associated with certain stigmatized groups, namely gay men and drug abusers, it came to be viewed as a shameful disease. Further, because heterosexual men and women did not belong to the presumed high-risk groups, many devel-

oped a false sense of invulnerability. Believing AIDS to be a gay disease, heterosexual men and women continued to engage in risky sexual behaviors. Consequently, the incidence of HIV infection continued to rise significantly in these groups. Although many gay and bisexual men adopted safer practices, thereby reducing their risks of HIV infection, heterosexual men and women did not consistently show the same changes. Such findings instilled a sense of urgency to achieving a better understanding of the various factors associated with sexual behavior in general and sexual risk-taking in particular. As with all diseases, AIDS risk-reduction requires a knowledge of how to avoid the disease and a motivation to implement necessary behavior changes.

Sex Education. SEX EDUCATION is mandated in twenty-two states, but the curriculum and context vary widely from state to state. Most sex-education pro-

Elderly people often retain sexual drives. (Jim Whitmer)

grams focus on the biological and reproductive issues and are inclined to ignore the more sensitive sexual issues such as masturbation, sexual orientation, abortion, and areas of sexual experience. Fewer than 10 percent of teenagers receive comprehensive sexual education according to the Sex Education and Information Council of the United States.

Although the actual number of sex-education programs has increased, the primary source of information regarding sexual activity remains the peer group. This generally results from the uncomfortable feelings associated with talking to one's parents. The second-most cited source of information comes from assorted readings. Both of these sources are questionable in their reliability in offering accurate information about sexuality.

One popular sex-education program promotes abstinence as the primary means for preventing pregnancy. This approach became popular in the United States during the Ronald REAGAN and George BUSH administrations and received major funding from the federal government. The impact of these abstinence-only programs has been less than desirable. In a follow-up study, it was found that the participants in these classes actually increased their sexual interactions as compared to a control group that did not receive any sexual education. The latest trend has been to emphasize postponement and protection in sex-education classes. These programs show more promise in preventing pregnancies and sexually transmitted diseases.

Aging and Sexuality. Because of increases in life expectancy, the fastest-growing segment of the population is the sixty-five and older group. A long-standing myth is that elderly individuals lose their desire and capacity for sexual activity. There are certain changes that occur in the aging process that may inhibit coitus, but generally individuals who were sexually active in young adulthood will remain so into late adulthood.

Despite these physical changes, it is reported that nearly half of the sixty- to ninety-one-year-olds surveyed reported engaging in sexual activity on a regular basis. Although coital frequency and masturbation decline with age, the overall sexual satisfaction reported by the older adults did not differ greatly from that of their younger counterparts.   *—Alice M. Sigley*
Richard D. McAnulty

SUGGESTED READINGS: A comprehensive overview of human sexuality is found in Jeffrey S. Nevid, Lois Fichner-Rathus, and Spencer A. Rathus' *Human Sexuality in a World of Diversity*, 2d ed. (Boston: Allyn &

Bacon, 1995). Another good source of general information about human sexuality is Albert R. Allgeier and Elizabeth R. Allgeier's *Sexual Interactions*, 4th ed. (Lexington: D.C. Heath, 1995). A thorough overview of the history of sex research is provided by Vern L. Bullough's *Science in the Bedroom: A History of Sex Research* (New York: Basic Books, 1994). A sex survey by Robert T. Michael, John H. Gagnon, Edward O. Laumann, and Gina Kolata, *Sex in America: A Definitive Survey* (Boston: Little, Brown, 1994) provides interesting information about the reported practices of a U.S. sample.

Many of the controversial issues in sexuality are debated in Robert T. Francoeur's *Taking Sides: Clashing Views on Controversial Issues in Human Sexuality* (Guilford, Conn.: Dushkin, 1994). Susan Bunting's *Annual Editions: Human Sexuality 95/96* (Guilford, Conn.: Dushkin, 1995) provides reprints of articles on such topics as cross-cultural perspectives on sexuality and sexual violence. Opposing viewpoints on such controversial issues as sex education, homosexuality, and teenage pregnancy are presented in *Teenage Sexuality: Opposing Viewpoints*, edited by David L. Bender and Bruno Leone (San Diego: Greenhaven Press, 1994).

Sex-change operations: Surgical operations available for transsexuals, individuals who feel psychologically trapped in the body of the wrong sex. The procedure takes a long time and is very expensive; outcomes are mixed.

A small number of people, for unknown reasons, feel that they are trapped in a body of the wrong sex. Most of these individuals have an intense desire to relieve the perceived mismatch of their mind and their body, and, if they have enough money, may undergo surgery to alter their genitalia and legally change their sex. The male-to-female procedure is more successful and more commonly done than the female-to-male.

Male-to-female sex change involves removing the scrotum, testes, and penis, and creating an artificial vagina from some of the remaining tissue. Male-to-female transsexuals also have their facial hair removed and undergo hormone treatment to enlarge their breasts and soften their skin. After surgery, male-to-female transsexuals have a fully functioning vagina and can even reach orgasm through coitus; because they have no ovaries and the uterus is incomplete, they cannot bear children. The surgical techniques for this

Sex education

operation have been perfected to the point that it is impossible to tell a male-to-female transsexual from someone who is born female without a gynecological exam to reveal the absence of ovaries and fallopian tubes.

Female-to-male surgery involves removal of the ovaries and uterus, and the addition of an artificial penis and, sometimes, scrotum. Female-to-male transsexuals take hormones to increase growth of muscles and facial hair, but breasts do not shrink from hormone treatment and short individuals cannot grow any taller. Unlike male-to-female surgery, the outcome of female-to-male surgery is not very realistic. The skin that is used to create the penis is taken from the thighs or the belly and is not very sensitive. Also, it is impossible to create artificial erectile tissue or to reroute the urinary opening; thus, the resulting penis is positioned on the lower abdomen, above the pubic bone, and is nonfunctional (although it may include an artificial implant to simulate an erection).

Either way, transsexual surgery is accomplished in many steps over a period of years; psychosocial adjustment, too, must be slow and gradual. Some individuals manage both transitions well—and even go on to marry and adopt children. Others, however, find it difficult to cope with the stresses of repeated surgery, the financial drain, and the anger, confusion, or prejudices of their friends, family, and coworkers. Because of these psychological risks, physicians generally require that surgical candidates undergo a preoperative psychiatric evaluation and practice living in the other gender role for several months before any surgical steps are taken.

Although sex change has become a viable medical and legal option, there are many who deem it unethical for philosophical or religious reasons. The resultant debate, like virtually every other controversy involving sex, politics, and religion, is unlikely to disappear.

Sex discrimination *See* **Sexism and sex discrimination**

Sex education: A movement to add biological and family-life-oriented sex education to the public-school curriculum made minor progress in the "liberal" 1960's and 1970's. Later, the perception of ACQUIRED IMMUNE DEFICIENCY SYNDROME (AIDS) as a fatal, sexually transmitted disease compelled more states to develop guidelines and even require sexuality education focused on disease prevention and behavior modification.

Background. Although American society had long relied upon parents to provide basic "facts of life" sex education for children, the increasing complexity of both medical developments and basic biological knowledge began to push the answers to sex questions beyond the scope of many parents' understanding by the 1960's. Increases in divorce rates, single-parent families, availability of a birth-control pill, and more open discussion gave the appearance of a "sexual revolution." Although Alfred Kinsey had offered an elective basic sex education course for underclassmen at Indiana University in the late 1930's, in the 1960's atmosphere it became legitimate to offer formal educational programs at both college and public school levels in some regions. The surge in sex-education courses was a result of both dedicated teachers and eager students. University of Houston psychology professor James Leslie McCary, starting with 185 students in his first class, filled his university's largest lecture hall with more than 1,100 students four semesters later.

Well-trained secondary biology teachers began to provide coverage of human reproductive biology equivalent to coverage of other systems in classes that were often required of all students and in a coed setting. Home-economics teachers expanded coverage of childbirth, childcare, and the basics of menstruation, birth control, and even sexual response. Health education was not commonly separated from physical education, however, and sex education was often limited to the single-period locker-room film-and-question sessions by the coach or physical education teacher, limited to single-sex classes only.

"Sex education" from this era focused on reproductive biology. A growing group of sex educators and counselors, however, expressed disdain for education that focused on "mere plumbing," and sex education gradually moved to "sexuality education" by decreasing biology content and adding substantial coverage of culture, psychology, health, personal skills, and relationships. Whenever any form of sex education was offered separate and distinct from biology or home economics, religious and conservative opposition made school officials uneasy. As a result, only one state actually mandated sex education from this time period, and most states were readily exempting students from class sessions under the general religious-objection opt-out. A movement away from sexual free-

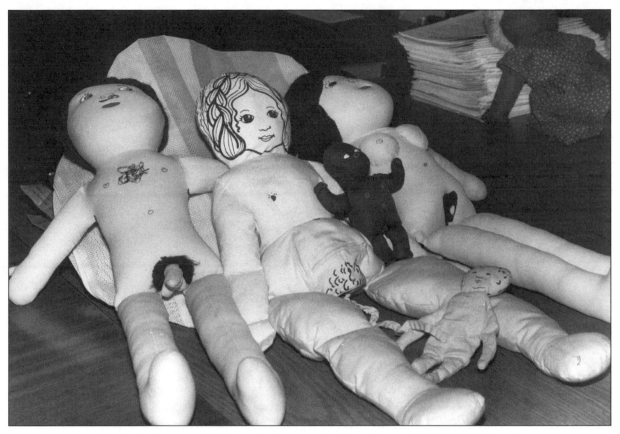

Anatomically correct dolls made for sex-education classes. (UPI/Corbis-Bettmann)

dom and toward more conservative values in the late 1970's and early 1980's made additional sex education unlikely.

The discovery of acquired immune deficiency syndrome (AIDS) dramatically altered public perceptions of the need for sex education. Since AIDS appeared to be eventually 100 percent fatal, and both homosexual and heterosexual contact were major modes of transmission, a sense of urgency led many state school boards to risk controversy and mandate some level of sexuality education that always included information on the prevention of AIDS transmission. By 1986, New Jersey, Kansas, and the District of Columbia had joined Maryland in mandating sexuality education. By 1993, seventeen states required sexuality education, and thirty more encouraged it with recommended guidelines.

Sex-Education Advocates. Proponents of sex education contend that the topic should be covered just as thoroughly, and just as naturally, as other social and biological topics. Advocates claim that the personal quality of students' lives is higher when they under-

stand their sexuality and that rates of ABORTION, unwanted pregnancy, and SEXUALLY TRANSMITTED DISEASES would be substantially higher without current sex-education programs.

Advocates of sex education claim that the sexuality knowledge needed today far exceeds the basics most parents understand and that many parents fail to educate their children on this topic. They cite survey data indicating that nine out of ten parents want their children taught sex education in schools. They point to the fact that thirty states have state advisory committees to review the sex-education materials and programs; this provides community input and support and reduces negative reactions.

Proponents contend, however, that the quality of school programs varies so widely that surveys of the effectiveness of sex education are likely to show no clear-cut differences. Educators note that most states do not mandate coverage of sexual behavior, abortion, condoms, masturbation, sexual identity and orientation, and sexuality and religion. Sex educators also push for far more coverage at an earlier age, contending that much sex education comes too late. It is obvious that state guidelines often omit controversial topics that are still vital to students, including abortion and birth-control methods. Local school administrators are likely to dilute their interpretation of such guidelines even further to avoid local controversy.

Sex educators also note that certification for teachers delivering sex education is uncommon, with only nine states requiring specific training. In addition, few states monitor schools to assure state regulations are implemented. In view of these limitations, proponents contend that it is difficult to assess the effectiveness of sex education.

Sex-Education Opponents. Most opponents of sex education are politically conservative or religiously fundamental. Some contend that parents hold the sole responsibility for educating their children and dismiss the need for detailed understanding of anatomy, disease symptoms, and cultural attitudes at variance with the Judeo-Christian norm. State and community advisory committees may be viewed by such critics as liberal efforts to force sex education on communities.

Opponents assert that classroom teaching and discussion of sexual topics do not prevent but instead encourage premarital sex. They note that rates of premarital sex, childbirth out of wedlock, and sexually transmitted diseases have not decreased in spite of sex-education programs.

In those states where sexuality education has been mandated, opponents often promote the adoption of a "sex respect" program that concentrates on student activities aimed at reinforcing "just say no" and abstinence, and which contains little information on sexual anatomy, birth control, or behaviors necessary to avoid contracting AIDS and other sexually transmitted diseases.

Six states prohibit the teaching of specific topics within sex education. Virtually all states give parents the option of excusing their children from any part or all of a sex-education class. The parental opt-out in most cases was written into the sex-education mandate or relevant state board regulations to defuse opposition and gain its acceptance. Some teachers report that students eager to learn sex education do not relay the course content to parents they know will object, and usage of such opt-outs is uncommon. A shift to more conservative and religious values in the mid-1990's, combined with lessening concern over an AIDS epidemic, resulted in the dismantling of several state sex-education mandates.

Summary. In spite of a substantial increase in sex education following the arrival of AIDS, sex education coverage varies widely. Teachers are rarely trained for teaching sex education, and the issue remains highly controversial in nearly all states and communities where it is mandated.   —*John Richard Schrock*

SUGGESTED READINGS: *Human Sexuality*, by James Leslie McCary (New York: Van Nostrand Reinhold, 1967), was the classic pioneer sex-education textbook for college-level students; meticulously researched with all facts referenced, the book went through four editions and found its way into most libraries. *Guidelines for Comprehensive Sexuality Education, Kindergarten-12th Grade*, by the National Guidelines Task Force (New York: Sex Information and Education Council of the United States, 1991), established a model for sexuality education with input from the American Medical Association, the March of Dimes Birth Defects Foundation, Planned Parenthood Federation of America, the National Education Association, the American School Health Association, and the National School Boards Association.

Unfinished Business: A SIECUS Assessment of State Sexuality Education Programs, by Alan E. Gambrell and Debra Haffner (New York: SIECUS, 1993), surveyed sex-education efforts in light of the key concepts promulgated in the national guidelines above. *Education for Sexuality: Concepts and Programs for Teaching*, 3d ed. (New York: CBS College Publishing, 1985), by John J. Burt and Linda Brower Meeks, was a guide widely used by teachers throughout the 1970's sex-education era and the 1980's AIDS-education era. Accompanied by overhead masters, the outlines represent more detail than is usually covered in local school curricula.

Sex roles: Sex-based traits and behaviors that each culture assigns to males and females. Socially imposed sex-role stereotypes create inequality by prescribing certain qualities, behaviors, and opportunities and prohibiting or discouraging others.

Background. People have always been assigned social roles based upon their biological sex. These social roles have never been equal; in most societies, males have been accorded the highest status, held the most prized offices, and controlled the basic resources. Throughout the history of the United States and Canada, men have been more valued and considered more rational, competent, and entitled to privilege than women. In the 1800's, women were not allowed to own property, gain professional training, or vote.

The traditional view of sex roles grew out of this male-dominated culture and was supported by various theories. One of the best known is that of sociologist Talcott Parsons, who believed that highly contrasting gender roles were essential for society. In his book *Family Socialization and Interaction Process* (1955), he asserts that society requires that men be "instrumental" and women be "expressive." The man's instrumental role was to be the wage earner, the manager, and the leader; the women's expressive role was to take care of the emotional well-being of people, providing nurture and comfort. For nearly two decades, Parson's theory dominated sociology; however, it has been attacked by numerous critics and is no longer widely accepted. Critics charged that his theory stereotyped masculine and feminine traits, reinforcing differences and denigrating women.

The contemporary view of sex roles holds that both sexes are capable and can be successful in a variety of roles at home and at work. Women can exhibit traditional male characteristics of being independent, strong, logical, and task oriented. Males, in turn, can exhibit traditional female characteristics and be nurturing, sensitive, cooperative, and detail oriented. In many ways, American and Canadian societies have been and are continuing to move away from male dominance toward egalitarian sex roles.

Evolution of Egalitarianism. The move from traditional sex roles to contemporary sex roles has been slow and full of controversy. Two distinct ideologies have been involved. One ideology, called liberal, enlightenment, or minimalist, holds that women and men are basically alike and equal in all important respects; therefore, they should have access to the same roles, rights, privileges, and opportunities to participate in various aspects of life. The other ideology, called cultural, structural, or maximalist, holds that men and women are essentially unlike one another, and different roles, rights, and activities should be assigned accordingly. Most people believe one or the other of these conflicting ideologies. These different viewpoints have been in place since the 1840's, when the first wave of the women's movement occurred. The first wave centered on the single issue of voting rights, and both ideologies were united, for different reasons, in the common goal of granting women the vote. The liberal feminists wanted the vote because they saw universal suffrage as fair and equitable. The cultural feminists believed that, compared to men, women were more pure, moral, nurturing, concerned about others, and committed to harmony. They gave speeches that argued that women should be allowed to vote because this would curb the corruption of political life and women's moral virtue would reform the political world that was debased by the control of immoral men. While the combined force of cultural and liberal feminists was necessary to win suffrage, the deep ideological chasm between these two groups was not resolved.

The second wave of the women's movement began in the 1960's and created even more factions, such as radical feminists, liberal feminists, separatists, structural feminists, lesbian feminists, revalorists, womanists, and antifeminists. Some women believe that traditional sex roles should be the norm; some women (separatists) believe that males and females differ so radically that women must create and live in their own women-centered communities; and some women (liberal feminists) believe that women should have the same economic, political, professional, and civic opportunities and rights as men.

Work and Home Roles. According to Ronald Stover and Christine Hope in *Marriage, Family, and Intimate Relations* (1993), there are growing expectations that married mothers should help provide for the family. By the 1980's, a majority of adults in the United States approved of the earning of money by married women, and the majority of married women were employed outside the home. The debate over women working has not ended, however, and in many cases this role expansion created role conflicts and role strain. "Role conflict" refers to situations in which fulfilling the demands of one role keeps one from fulfilling the demands of a second role. According to Stover and Hope, more so than women in earlier generations, modern mothers face potential role conflicts in trying to balance employment roles with parental roles. A large proportion of mothers believe that parental care is best for preschool children, yet 56 percent of all mothers of preschoolers are employed full-time.

Mothers who stay at home and care for their children full-time are not immune from potential stress either. The emerging cultural image of motherhood envisions mothers both as fully involved parents and as full-time workers, so many stay-at-home mothers feel they are not living up to this cultural image. Oftentimes, this creates role strain. "Role strain" occurs when different people expect different behaviors

Many researchers believe that children are socialized to play certain sex roles. (UPI/Corbis-Bettmann)

within the same role. Stover and Hope assert that mothers inevitably suffer guilt, ambiguity, and stress regardless of the choices they make about child care.

Most researchers believe that traditional male roles have undergone much less change than traditional female roles—as the female role has expanded to include the role of breadwinner, the male role has remained the same. In *The Second Shift* (1989), Arlie Hochschild found that only 20 percent of men share housework and child care equally with their working wives. She found that women who are employed tend to suffer chronic exhaustion, low sex drive, and more frequent illness. However, women who are not employed also suffer negative aspects. Because of the change from traditional sex roles to contemporary sex roles and the perception of new opportunities for women, Hochschild says that the status of the full-time housewife has been eroded and the role of housewife has lost its allure. These women have also been burdened with extra tasks that the employed women are not home to do—collecting delivered parcels, letting in repairmen, or watching the children of neighboring mothers who work. Often times, Hochschild says, this results in resentment on the part of the stay-at-home woman.

Women's Role as Caregiver. In the United States and Canada, caregiving to infants, children, and the elderly is almost exclusively the responsibility of women. Elizabeth Janeway states in *Man's World, Woman's Place: A Study in Social Mythology* (1971) that the maternal role is the area where questioning of woman's role has made the least impact. Two extreme positions have emerged regarding women and caregiving. One viewpoint, often assumed by politically liberal individuals, argues that women have been assigned virtually exclusive responsibility for taking care of others. Those holding this position also claim that caregiving is not highly valued by society as a whole and is not accorded substantial status or prestige or salary. Thus, women's continuing to be the primary caregivers serves to perpetuate their already subordinate place. A second position, often assumed by people who believe in traditional sex roles, holds that caregiving is an essential and sacred activity for which women are particularly well suited and at which they are particularly skilled. This argument entails a view of women as having a kind of essential goodness, purity, compassion, and empathy that sets them apart from men and suits them naturally to attending to others.

—*Karen Anding Fontenot*

SUGGESTED READINGS: Sex-role socialization in the family and schools is discussed in Judy Mann's *The Difference: Growing Up Female in America* (New York: Warner Books, 1994). Perceptions of the sexes are explored from both a historical perspective and future projections in Marie Richmond-Abbott's *The American Woman: Her Past, Her Present, and Her Future* (New York: Holt, Rinehart and Winston, 1979) and Carol Tavris and Carole Wade's *The Longest War: Sex Differences in Perspective* (New York: Harcourt Brace Jovanovich, 1984).

The role of the media in perpetuating and changing sex-role stereotypes is explored in Cynthia M. Lont's *Women and Media: Content, Careers, and Criticism* (Belmont, Calif.: Wadsworth, 1995). Male socialization and its effect on personal and professional relationships are discussed in Joseph Pleck and Jack Sawyer's *Men and Masculinity* (New York: Prentice-Hall, 1974). In *Who Cares? Women, Care, and Culture* (Carbondale: Southern Illinois University Press, 1994), Julia Wood discusses various theories explaining the female role as caregiver. Arlie Hochschild explores the expanding female role, and many of the negative effects of this expansion, in her book *The Second Shift* (New York: Avon Books, 1989).

Sex therapy: Treatment of sexual dysfunctions and the exploration and understanding of methods that will increase sexual satisfaction. The goal is to improve overall sexual functioning and to eliminate behaviors or attitudes that act as obstacles to positive sexual interaction.

By the 1990's, sexual dysfunctions came to be viewed as complex problems that may be personal or interrelational, but this is a relatively new approach. Before the 1960's, sexual difficulties were generally viewed as symptomatic of emotional conflicts from childhood and were treated with psychoanalysis. This allowed the patient to gain insight into the origins of the dysfunction, but did not necessarily guarantee a solution to the problem.

In 1970, William Masters and Virginia Johnson authored *Human Sexual Inadequacy*, which offered new ideas about sexual difficulties and their treatment. They viewed anxiety, especially anxiety about sexual performance, as the major cause of sexual problems. Thus, Masters and Johnson believed that if the patient could learn new sexual skills or improve existing sexual behaviors, the anxiety would be reduced, and satisfying, natural sexual activity would be the result. Their program, which consisted of a two-week intensive workshop with a sex-therapy team teaching new sexual techniques, produced successes that were remarkable at the time.

While their two-week workshops are still popular, and now combine relationship skills with sexual issues, and while some therapists still rely on the behavioral techniques Masters and Johnson developed, in general there is less enthusiasm for their approach. This is largely because of the 1990's view that sexual problems are more than the results of performance anxiety. In addition to anxiety, sexual dysfunction is understood to be the result of interactions between physical, psychological, and interpersonal factors. Thus, societal attitudes toward sexuality and treatment methods for sexual issues have changed considerably over time.

Many therapists practice "psychosexual therapy," an approach developed in the 1970's by Dr. Helen Singer Kaplan, which combines behavioral (task-oriented) and psychoanalytic (insight-oriented) methods to treat sexual dysfunctions. Her 1974 book, *The New Sex Therapy: Active Treatment of Sexual Dysfunctions*, has become a classic in the field.

In 1989, Sandra Leiblum and Raymond Rosen coauthored *Principles and Practices of Sex Therapy: Update for the 1990's*, which describes the major trends that characterize sex therapy. First, there is an appreciation for biological factors that may influence sexual functions such as erections, orgasms, or desire. Health conditions, organic problems, hormone levels, medications, and drug abuse are considered as possible agents contributing to dysfunction. Second, there is an increasing emphasis on the use of medications to treat some specific sexual problems. Third, especially as a result of Kaplan's work, is the interest in sexual desire. Instead of focusing only on the actual physical sexual dysfunction, sex therapy concerns itself with some patients who experience either low-level or no sexual desire, which inhibits sexual interaction or expressions of sexual interest. Finally, a major focus is on the interpersonal relationships of the sexual partners, how their individual sexual attitudes developed and presently contribute to their sexual relationships.

Sexism and sex discrimination: Sex discrimination can be defined as the differential treatment of women and men on the basis of sex. The term was coined to refer to discrimination against women; when discussing discrimination against men, one usually speaks of "reverse" sex discrimination. Sex discrimination has historically taken place in the workplace, in education, in the courts, and in nearly every arena of life. The ideological basis for sex discrimination is called sexism, a term that came into use in the late 1960's and early 1970's but that describes attitudes and behaviors that have long been a part of most cultures. Sexism is based on the belief that women are inferior to men in important ways and that women's primary purpose is to serve men.

Sexism is built into the social system of patriarchy, in which men have the primary control over families, the economy, politics and government, and other cultural institutions. Virtually all human cultures of any size are patriarchal to at least some extent; although how and when this situation began is debated, most scholars agree that patriarchy is at least thousands of years old.

Sexism, then, is a modern term to denote a long-standing situation. Although there have been a few voices over the centuries speaking against what has since become known as sexism (for example, Christine de Pizan objected to sexist practices in fifteenth century France), male dominance and discrimination against women, along with an underlying sexist belief system, was largely taken for granted as a normal and appropriate part of human relations until the nineteenth century. Since then it has been questioned and opposed by feminist movements, which began in the United States and Europe but which are spreading to all parts of the world.

Economic Discrimination. A major area in which the effects of sexism are felt is economic discrimination. Women do the largest share of the work of the world, much of it unpaid and unvalued as work because it revolves around care of home and family. This unpaid work is not counted in the gross national products or gross domestic products of the countries of the world. In countries where women do most of the agriculture, even their farming, which is done to provide food rather than a cash payment, is seen as domestic labor and therefore is not counted as work.

The 1980 United Nations Conference on Women held in Copenhagen reported that women do between two-thirds and three-fourths of the world's work and produce 45 percent of the world's food but earn only 10 percent of the world's income and own only 1 percent of the world's property. By the end of the United Nations Decade for Women in 1985, the report on the decade's progress concluded that although women made some gains in education, health, employment, and politics, they still bore most of the responsibility for labor in their families and their countries, while men had most of the power.

Approximately 35 percent of European women work for wages; in the United States, the number is above 47 percent. This, however, is in addition to responsibility in most cases for care of the home and family. In industrialized countries, women work an average of fifty-six hours a week in their homes. This compares, in the United States to eleven hours for men; in Japan, men are reported to spend eight minutes a day on work in the home. In Africa, women do 75 percent of the farming, plus the cleaning, cooking, childrearing, and gathering of wood and water that sustains their families.

When they became independent of Western powers, many Third World nations began work on "development," which aims at improving cash-based industry. Because of sexist assumptions about work, grants of foreign aid were aimed at men, often helping them to gain economic power at the expense of women, whose work continued to be ignored. Land-reform programs, moreover, typically gave men title to land even when women were the ones who worked it, and even though women in many African societies had traditionally held control of the land.

In the United States, the increasing impoverishment of women and their dependent children is sometimes

An unusually overt example of sex discrimination. (James L. Shaffer)

referred to as the "feminization" of poverty. The largest and fastest-rising percentage of the poor are women and their children. In the first year after divorce, it has been estimated, a man's standard of living is likely to rise by 43 percent on average, whereas a woman's will go down by an average of 75 percent. The feminization of poverty is exacerbated by the facts that women on the average earn less than men (in the United States, women of all races on average earn less than men of any race), that women are often discouraged from entering lucrative jobs and professions, and that women must often juggle both paid labor and primary responsibility for care of their homes and families.

Political Discrimination. This kind of economic inequality is not simply unfair economically; it also hurts women in other arenas of life. When women are kept at an economic disadvantage, required to work at home with neither recompense nor acknowledgement that what they are doing is work, often while also supporting themselves and their children economically in low-paying jobs, they have little leisure for outside activities. The result is that they also become politically disadvantaged, because they do not have enough extra time or energy to fight for their rights on the political scene. This is one reason women have traditionally had so little voice in government and politics.

While some women have risen to political prominence in their nations, they are so few that they are anomalies; Margaret Thatcher of Great Britain, Indira Gandhi of India, Benazir Bhutto of Pakistan, Golda Meir of Israel, and a handful of others are notable examples. Moreover, in 1989 women made up only 12.7 percent of the membership of the world's parliamentary bodies, even though women make up slightly more than half of the world's population. In addition, women who have had important public roles in the past have often disappeared from view because women's history has until recently been ignored or derided as trivial and unimportant.

Legal discrimination against women, while increasingly being challenged, still exists throughout the world. Even when women have legal rights, these are often easily ignored because political and judicial power is largely in the hands of men. For example, women in Kenya are legally protected as heirs in their husbands' estates; in reality, however, land still commonly goes to the eldest son. In Muslim countries such as Iran, women are required to be completely veiled in public; in Saudi Arabia, women are not even allowed to drive cars.

Sexism in Language. Even the languages most of the world's people speak are sexist. Almost all are gendered in some way; in most cases, this gendered language is value-laden. For example, the masculine forms of words are usually treated as the generic, or "normal," forms. If a group made up of both males and females is discussed, or if the gender of an antecedent is unknown, the masculine pronoun is almost invariably used. This holds true both in Indo-European languages and in Semitic languages, two of the largest language groups of the world. What this usage indicates is that the masculine is widely regarded as normative, the feminine as derivative.

Violence as an Enforcer of Sexism. Sexism is also often characterized by violence against females; violence is seen by feminists as a major enforcer of sexist norms. People who must constantly fear violence naturally tend to become submissive. The most common forms of violence against women include rape and other kinds of sexual assault, DOMESTIC VIOLENCE, SEXUAL HARASSMENT at the workplace and elsewhere, sexual slavery or forced prostitution, PORNOGRAPHY or the pictorial depiction of sexual dominance and violence, and genital mutilation.

Most of these are epidemic throughout the world. Some forms of violence against women, however, are more specific to certain areas. An example is the recent rise in "sex tourism," in which men are encouraged to travel to countries such as Thailand, the Philippines, and South Korea for sexual services at special brothels set up for this tourist trade. The prostitutes are often young girls who have been sold by their poverty-stricken families. Incredibly, this phenomenon was first proposed as a development strategy by such international aid agencies as the World Bank, the International Monetary Fund (IMF), and the U.S. Agency for International Development.

Another practice, once common in Europe and America but now mostly localized to nations in Africa, Latin America, and Asia, is genital mutilation. It is estimated that more than twenty million living women have been genitally mutilated. This process usually involves CLITORIDECTOMY, the removal of the clitoris and parts of the labia minora, and often also includes infibulation, the sewing together of the labia majora. The first process curtails sexual pleasure and makes intercourse painful; the second ensures a woman's sexual fidelity. Both are dangerous, can cause death from the surgery or later infection, and increase danger in childbirth. There is great international debate about this issue, however, because proponents insist that the practice is a cultural custom that must be respected.

Theories About Sexism. Many feminists have sought to understand sexism by putting it into a theoretical framework. Writing in the 1950's, Simone de Beauvoir, argued that the primary cause of the oppression of women was motherhood, the necessary binding to home and family, which keeps women in an inferior position. Later theorists, however, have made other suggestions. Historian Gerda Lerner has argued that patriarchy's rise can be documented in the Middle East over the past six thousand years as part of the rise of a class system based on hierarchy of men over women and of free men over slaves. Marilyn French argues that sexism can be explained as a war against women designed to maintain and retain control over women's bodies and labor. The radical feminist philosopher Mary Daly has attempted to document male dominance over and hatred of women throughout society. Susan Brownmiller believes that RAPE is at the center of the oppression of women, asserting that once men found they could control women through sexual assault, they did so.

Efforts to Eradicate Sexism. Feminist reactions to sexism, however, are not limited to issues of scholarship. People in the nations of Western Europe and the United States have been involved in the feminist struggle for more than a hundred years. In the nineteenth century, American feminists such as Susan B. Anthony and Elizabeth Cady Stanton believed that political sex discrimination was the key to the whole problem. They and many other activists spent their lives working toward attaining women's suffrage, or the right to vote. Yet it was not until 1920 that sex-based voting discrimination was ended in the United States with passage of Nineteenth Amendment to the Constitution.

Once the right to vote was won, however, the feminist movement in the United States nearly died out. Suffragists were hopeful that, with the right to be part of the political process, women would be able to change the laws and customs that had discriminated against them. Most women, however, tended to vote with their husbands; there was no "female bloc" as the feminists had hoped. Furthermore, women's rights soon took a back seat to other national concerns, especially the Great Depression of the 1930's and World War II. American women joined with men to face these problems, and the issue of women's rights faded into the background.

During World War II, American women were asked to enter the workplace to replace men who had gone to war. This request was presented to women as their patriotic duty, and they gladly took on the challenge. Many women experienced economic independence and the other benefits of paid jobs for the first time, and many were reluctant to give them up at war's end. With peace and the return of the soldiers to the job market, however, women were expected to give up their jobs just as gladly and return to their previous lives as homemakers.

The 1950's brought the period characterized by what author Betty Friedan called the "feminine mystique." Women were idealized as wives and mothers, and sex discrimination against women in education, in the workplace, and in other arenas was considered to be appropriate and based on women's natural roles. This situation continued until the late 1960's, when a revived feminist movement began.

Clearly, winning the vote had not been enough. Women also needed other sorts of legal protections against sex discrimination. During the 1960's and 1970's, a number of laws were passed that sought to curtail sex discrimination. In 1963, the EQUAL PAY ACT was passed, requiring that men and women doing the same job be paid equally. The following year, the CIVIL RIGHTS ACT was passed; Title VII of that act prohibited sex discrimination in hiring, promotions, working conditions, and firing. This act legally put an end to such long-held traditions as posting separate want-ads for women and men and refusing to promote women on the grounds that they would soon marry, have children, and quit their jobs. Interestingly, the word "sex" appeared in the antidiscrimination provisions of the Civil Rights Act as a joke in an attempt to discredit the entire act. Yet the category of sex was included in the forbidden types of discrimination, and the whole act passed. Yet the EQUAL EMPLOYMENT OPPORTUNITY COMMISSION (EEOC), developed to enforce the law, had little funding and therefore little power until the 1970's; the law thus had little effect for several years.

Two important laws were passed in 1974. The EDUCATIONAL AMENDMENTS ACT required that males and females be treated equally in any educational institution receiving federal funds. Since 1974, therefore, females have had the right to participate in school athletics on the same basis as males. In addition, the 1974 EQUAL CREDIT OPPORTUNITY ACT was passed to prohibit sex discrimination in lending.

In 1972, Congress finally passed the EQUAL RIGHTS AMENDMENT (ERA) to the Constitution, which had

Sexism and sex discrimination

first been proposed in 1923. By the following year, thirty-one states had ratified the ERA, with only seven more required for ratification. In the next several years, however, a well-financed and highly publicized anti-ERA campaign took effect, and it became clear that full ratification would not occur by the deadline of March 22, 1979. The deadline was extended to 1982, but by then a conservative mood had overtaken the country, and the amendment was not ratified.

In the United States, the effort to eradicate sex discrimination has also included changes in the arena of higher education. When the university system first began in Europe in the late Middle Ages, women were specifically denied admission because of their sex, a policy that was extended into the New World. It was not until 1821, when Emma Willard opened the Troy

A San Francisco woman celebrates her 1981 victory in a sex-discrimination suit against the U.S. Forest Service. (UPI/Corbis-Bettmann)

Female Seminary in upstate New York, that American women had an opportunity for anything like a college education. In 1832, Oberlin College in Ohio became the first college to admit both women and men; women were originally admitted so that they could do housework for the male students, whose educational experience included agricultural work. Although many critics decried the process, more and more colleges, both coeducational and women-only, opened their doors to women in the late nineteenth and early twentieth centuries.

The number of women receiving U.S. college degrees rose to about 40 percent of the total in the 1930's and 1940's, but the percentage declined during the postwar period, when women were expected to limit their ambitions to the domestic sphere. Since the 1960's, however, the figure has consistently risen; in 1987, for the first time, more than half of all U.S. degrees earned were granted to women.

Several nations experimenting with socialism have attempted to include equality for women in their national agendas, although with mixed success. Most communist countries removed legal barriers to women's full participation in the workforce but failed to remove underlying sexist belief systems. Women in these nations were thus left with traditional domestic responsibilities and typically continued to be treated as subordinates in family and private lives. When most formerly communist countries threw off socialism in the late 1980's, it was an easy step, therefore, to return to traditional gender practices.

The modern nation of Israel was founded on a socialist model in which women were allowed and expected to participate fully alongside men, both in productive labor and in protecting their constantly endangered new homeland. As time went on, however, women were increasingly relegated, even on the communal farms called *kibbutzim*, to the traditional women's tasks. Further, marriage and divorce in Israel are under the jurisdiction of the rabbinical courts, and only men can initiate divorce.

The lesson of such experiments seems to be that it will be difficult, if not impossible, to remove discrimination against women, either in the workplace or in politics and law, without first removing the sexist notions that domestic work is women's special province and that women are subordinate to and should serve the needs of men. Feminist organizations exist around the world, however. Although the fight against sexism began in the United States and Europe, women throughout the world have organized to attack sexism. GABRIELA in the Philippines and the Women's Information Centre in Thailand have been set up to help victims of forced prostitution. Vimochana in India helps battered women. Development Alternatives with Women for a New Era (DAWN), an international organization based in India, connects Third World women working on economic and political rights. The Nicaraguan Women's Association fights male violence against women. In Brazil in 1991, the São Paulo State Council for Women's Rights finally won an end to the legal murder of wives for infidelity. In Africa, the Uganda Association of Women Lawyers and Women's Legal Aid Clinic was developed to help uneducated poor Ugandan women, and feminist groups in Nigeria fight genital mutilation.   —*Eleanor B. Amico*

SUGGESTED READINGS: One of the classic early analyses of sexism is Simone de Beauvoir's *The Second Sex* (New York: Alfred A. Knopf, 1952). An extremely radical feminist analysis can be found in Mary Daly's *Gyn/Ecology* (Boston: Beacon Press, 1978). A well-documented treatise exposing what the author calls an actual war on women is Marilyn French's *The War Against Women* (New York: Summit Books, 1992). The classic that galvanized a generation of white, middle-class women in the 1960's is Betty Friedan's *The Feminine Mystique* (New York: Dell, 1963). An analysis of sexism from the perspective of an African American is Bell Hooks's *Feminist Theory: From Margin to Center* (Boston: South End Press, 1984). Two books by Gerda Lerner document the history of patriarchy and feminism: *The Creation of Patriarchy* (New York: Oxford University Press, 1986) and *The Creation of Feminist Consciousness* (New York: Oxford University Press, 1993). A volume that deals in depth with the reality and meanings of sexual assault is Susan Brownmiller's *Against Our Will: Men, Women, and Rape* (New York: Simon & Schuster, 1975). An analysis of sexism from a male perspective is offered by John Stoltenberg's *Refusing to Be a Man: Essays on Sex and Justice* (New York: Breitenbush Books, 1989).

Sexist language: Use of words and phrases that unfairly or unnecessarily single out the sex or gender of a person or group, most often about or directed toward women.

Sexism in language is evident as the deliberate use of words to demean another person based on gender,

Sexual abuse

but it is also built into the English language via grammatical conventions. English contains what is called the neutral male standard, in which a representative person is called "he" or in which all men and women grouped together are referred to as "man" or "mankind." The use of the male as the standard to represent all people inherently assumes that the not-male (that is, the female) is the nonstandard or deviant. Such an assumption relegates women to a secondary status. Terminology such as occupational titles, while claiming to use the neutral male, often reflects the conventional roles prescribed for men and women in the workforce. Studies have shown that words such as "policeman" and "chairman" connote a male-centered occupation to most people, yet gender-neutral terminology such as "police officer" or "chair" suggests the availability of the profession to both genders.

Sexism may also be seen in the irrelevant reference to a person's gender or sexual status. Referring to a physician as a "woman doctor" or a driver as a "lady driver" calls undue attention to the gender of a woman, while the same would not be done for a man. In another example, the imbalance between the titles of "Mr." and "Miss" or "Mrs." suggests that the marital status of men is not important, while that of women is. While a man retains the title of "Mr." whether he is married or single, women's titles distinguish them as married or single. Use of the alternative title "Ms." suggests that the marital status of a woman is as irrelevant as that of a man.

Sexism is further evident in references to women as children, in insults referring to men as women, and in references to sexual activity. Use of terms such as "baby" or "girl" for an adult woman suggests that she carries the same status as a child, and in a patriarchal society is therefore subject to adult males. In addition, insults such as calling a man a "sissy" suggest that women are of less value than men. Many derogatory terms used to describe sexual intercourse characterize women as sexually passive or even victimized and portray men as the sexual aggressors, reinforcing the idea that women are less powerful than and under the control of men.

Central to the issue of sexist language is whether language shapes or reflects reality. If language reflects reality, then a society's language can change only by altering its actions and beliefs to reflect an egalitarian relationship of the sexes. Some suggest that changing one's words is merely a superficial move to placate the oppressed group. On the other hand, if language

shapes perceptions of reality, then by changing language a society can increase awareness of the oppression of particular groups, make an effort to effect social change, and express sympathy for the oppressed.

Sexual abstinence. *See* Abstinence, sexual

Sexual abuse: Maltreatment of others by forcing sexual activities upon them or by engaging in sex with those who are not mentally competent or mature. Sexual abuse can consist of any of three basic forms of victimization: sexual molestation of children; INCEST (sex acts between closely related family members); and RAPE (nonconsensual sexual intercourse). These types of sexual abuse violate one or more of the guidelines typically held to govern the proper expression of sexuality, which mandate that sexual relations must be mutually understood, voluntarily consented to, and legally sanctioned.

Sexual molestation involves a variety of forms of sexual contact between a child and an older person, usually an adult. According to a 1993 study, as many as 11 percent of men and 23 percent of women report having been sexually molested as children. The actual incidence may be even higher; infants and toddlers are unable to speak for themselves, while somewhat older children may not realize that the sex is wrong, and their stories of reported abuse are often not believed. Pedophiles, adults who sexually prey on children, may use threats, deception, or blackmail to silence their victims.

Incest, though prohibited in virtually every society, is estimated to affect approximately 10 percent of American children. Some studies report that sex between fathers or stepfathers and daughters represents approximately 75 percent of all incest cases; other scholars have disagreed, however, contending that the most common types of incest involve cousins and siblings. What is not a matter of disagreement is that incest is a family disorder that harms victims and weakens the bonds of security and trust that keep families together.

According to a 1991 Senate report, rape is thought to affect approximately 20 percent of American women. DATE RAPE involves the use of a dating situation to manipulate another person into sex; STATUTORY RAPE occurs when a person has sexual relations, whether consensual or not, with a person who is under

Rape is among the most serious forms of sexual abuse. (UPI/Corbis-Bettmann)

the legal age of consent; gang rape is a serial assault on a victim by two or more individuals. All such forms of rape may involve physical violence; what all forms of rape have in common is that they usually involve psychological harm to the victim.

Sexual victimization can lead to long-lasting psychological scars. Traumatic sexualization, caused by the distorted conditions in which the sexual abuse occurred, may lead to repressed sexuality or promiscuity; moreover, some victims may in turn sexually abuse others. Sexual abuse also usually involves a betrayal of trust that can lead to prolonged distrustfulness, inhibited intimacy, anger, and hostility. Victims also often find themselves stigmatized by the shame and guilt associated with the abuse. Such victims, who are often blamed for their own victimization, may struggle with their self-esteem and engage in self-destructive behaviors. A final common product of sexual abuse is a feeling of powerlessness to ward off assaults. This powerlessness may heighten a victim's fear and anxiety and can impair the ability to cope with the abuse or with future threatening circumstances.

Sexual ethics: Rules or norms for sexual behavior and sexual practices. Sexual ethics have changed radically in the United States since World War II. Scientific research findings in the field of sexology, the development of the birth-control pill, secularization, and the increased pluralism of values and beliefs in American society contributed to the transformation of sexual mores.

Historical Trends. Norms or rules for behavior, including sexual behavior, change over time. Norms and ethics are shaped by the experiences and acquired knowledge of both the individual and the community. Sexual ethics also change over time and in particular social contexts. For example, sexual intercourse outside of marriage used to be a criminal offense punishable by imprisonment or fine. Adultery was against the law. Traditional American sexual norms are based on the Judeo-Christian ethic and were written into many American laws. According to this ethic, the only acceptable sexual behavior is heterosexual intercourse for procreation and to express love within the context of legal marriage.

Redefining Behavior and Ethics. Until the twentieth century, this was the dominant ethic in Western culture. However, secularization and increased diversity of belief systems led to the decline in support for religiously defined values. The shift was continued by the spread of scientific findings from the field of sexology. Starting with Sigmund Freud (1856-1939), sexologists explored and attempted to explain scientifically, the biological nature and social aspects of sexuality. Research by Alfred Kinsey (1894-1956) in the 1940's and 1950's revealed a diversity of sexual practices among Americans. The work of William Masters and Virginia Johnson in the 1970's furthered the understanding of women's and men's sexual behavior and sexual responses. The National Opinion Research Center at Chicago conducted a major national survey in 1992 on American sexual practices that supported the evidence of a continued trend toward liberalization and diversity in the area of sexuality.

Social scientists, supported by data from sexological research, redefined behavior that used to be called "perversions." Attempting to maintain an objective, nonjudgmental attitude, sexual practices outside the norm of heterosexual intercourse are now called "paraphilias" or different ways of loving. These include loving objects rather than people (fetishism) and mild sado-masochism between consenting adults. Cross-dressing (transvestism), voyeurism, and exhibitionistic displays are perceived more as minor public nuisances than as moral aberrations. This viewpoint is a major shift from earlier attitudes that defined these behaviors as sinful or criminal.

Feminism and Gay Rights. Ethicists studying sexual behavior and norms also locate the redefinition of sexual ethics in the context of contemporary multicultural movements for liberation. The feminist and gay rights movements also support the trend toward diversity and tolerance. Just as women are asserting more independence in the workforce, they are also changing norms regarding sexual behavior. Changes in women's roles are encouraging women to take the sexual initiative and to communicate their sexual desires to their partners. The development of the birth-control pill and other CONTRACEPTIVE DEVICES that reduced the risk of pregnancy also contributed to liberalizing attitudes and behavior. Without fear of pregnancy, women were freer to engage in sexual intercourse to a comparable degree with men.

The GAY RIGHTS MOVEMENT also supports and encourages scientific research related to homosexuality. Such research led the American Psychological Association to remove HOMOSEXUALITY from its list of sexual dysfunctions. Most social scientists understand homosexuality to simply be another way of loving. Research shows that homosexuals and homosexual activity existed throughout human history and in every human culture and society. Zoologists find animals engaged in sexual activities with the same sex. Continued research may show that homosexuality is genetic, or at least as difficult an orientation to change as is heterosexuality. Therefore, attitudes about the morality of homosexual behavior are changing. Some religious traditions are more tolerant of homosexuals than in the past, ranging from not condemning gays and lesbians as long as they remain celibate to complete acceptance, ordaining them, and allowing them to be church leaders and teachers.

Unethical Sexual Behavior. Although there is more tolerance for diversity and many sexual behaviors that were once considered immoral have been decriminalized, some behaviors are still considered deviant. Many define sexual intercourse with animals and with dead people as abnormal and deviant. PROSTITUTION, even between consenting adults, is illegal and participants are labeled as criminals. Critics maintain that if prostitution were legalized, prostitutes could be licensed and prostitution could be regulated as any other business. This is done in other countries, notably The Netherlands. Licensing and regulation would cut down on AIDS and other SEXUALLY TRANSMITTED DISEASES. This commodification of sex is perceived by some to continue the exploitation of women, treating them as sexual objects.

Coercive sexual behavior such as RAPE or sex with under-age children is also illegal. Sex can be abusive, and violence against women is expressed through all forms of rape, including marital and DATE RAPE. Sexual relationships with children are defined as either incest if the adult is related to the child or STATUTORY RAPE if the adult has sexual realtions with an underage child. Since children cannot give full consent to sexual acts because they cannot fully comprehend the consequences nor the meaning of the act itself, sex with adults is viewed as an abuse of power as well as an act of violence.

Effect of AIDS and STDs on Sexual Behavior. Despite liberalization of attitudes and behavior over the last fifty years, sexual behavior and practices are also affected by the AIDS epidemic and the increased number of sexually transmitted diseases (STDs), especially those most resistant to medical treatment such as new strains of syphilis. Communication in sexual relationships is now a moral obligation: Does one tell one's partner that one has AIDS or is HIV positive? Since AIDS kills, is a person guilty of murder if he or she has AIDS and knowingly has unprotected sexual intercourse with another person? Does neglecting to use a latex condom constitute the same crime as murder? Does one tell one's partner one has herpes or that one has or had gonorrhea or syphilis? Are health-care workers obligated to tell the partners of their patients that they have AIDS or STDs? Should the state test everyone before marriage for AIDS and STDs? Many states had dropped the blood-test requirement before the spread of AIDS and new STDs.

Other Controversies and Debates. Debates rage over how much the state can interfere in the private lives of its citizens, especially in the area of sexuality. Can the state regulate the number of children women can have? Can NORPLANT, a long-term contraceptive implanted under the skin, be forced on women? Abortion and women's rights to choose to be mothers remain an unresolved debate as the Supreme Court and states attempt to wrestle with informed consent, waiting peri-

ods, and fathers' rights. New reproductive technologies such as IN VITRO FERTILIZATION raise issues involving donor eggs and sperm, surrogate mothering: who are the "real" parents in such cases? The state wants to regulate some sexual practices, especially those that include children, suspected coercion, and procreation. Sexual liberals believe that the state should not regulate any aspect of sexual life between consulting adults. Some feminists and religious groups feel that women and children still need protection against men and abusive adults. The issue of PORNOGRAPHY is particularly controversial. Are women and children exploited by pornography? Is pornography considered free speech and, therefore, protected by the Constitution? Conservatives believe that the state should and must regulate sexual behavior because it goes to the heart of the family and the socialization of children. These are moral or ethical dilemmas that compound the continuing questions of adultery, incest, and rape. One very important issue is SEX EDUCATION: How much should children be told and when? Is it the parents' prerogative, or should schools play a role in sex education?

Sexual ethics are part of the network of wider social norms that societies create for themselves. Sexuality is personal and private yet at the same time very political. Most ethicists approach these questions through education and helping people analyze the complexities of modern life so that they have sufficient information to make informed choices about what is best for themselves, for their sexual partners, for their families, and for their communities.   —*Susan A. Farrell*

SUGGESTED READINGS: For an excellent account of changing sexual mores, see John D'Emilio and Estelle B. Freedman's *Intimate Matters: A History of Sexuality in America* (New York: Harper & Row, 1988). Edwin Schur discusses modern sexuality in *The Americanization of Sex* (Philadelphia: Temple University Press, 1988). In *Sexuality and Its Discontents: Meanings, Myths, and Modern Sexualities* (London: Routledge and Kegan Paul, 1985), Jeffrey Weeks describes and analyzes current controversies and the rise of the new moralism in light of social-science research. *Sex in America: A Definitive Survey* (Boston: Little, Brown, 1994), by Robert T. Michael et al., is the published findings of the National Opinion Research Centers' 1992 survey on American sexual behavior.

Sexual harassment: Unwelcome sexual advances, requests for sexual favors, or other verbal or physical

Anita Hill is sworn in before the Senate Judiciary to answer questions related to charges of sexual harassment she had made against Supreme Court nominee Clarence Thomas. (AP/Wide World Photos)

conduct of a sexual nature. Sexual harassment, which emerged as a major social issue in the 1980's and 1990's, can be legally actionable if it occurs in the workplace or other regulated setting.

Numerous statutes deal with sexual harassment, including Title VII of the CIVIL RIGHTS ACT OF 1964 and the Civil Rights Act of 1991. Many states also have anti-harassment legislation. Some statutes cover specific situations; Title IX of the EDUCATION AMENDMENTS ACT of 1972, for example, covers universities and their students and applies to all educational institutions receiving federal assistance. In addition, victims of sexual harassment may file common-law claims for compensation.

EQUAL EMPLOYMENT OPPORTUNITY COMMISSION (EEOC) guidelines define two types of harassment: *quid pro quo* harassment, in which a victim's submission to advances is used as a basis for employment decisions, and "hostile environment" harassment, in which unwelcome sexual conduct unreasonably interferes with job performance or creates an intimidating, hostile, or offensive working environment.

At first, courts denied that sexual harassment was covered under Title VII. In *Williams v. Saxbe* (1976), however, a circuit court ruled that the conduct of the plaintiff's supervisor "created an artificial barrier to employment which was placed before one gender and not another." Subsequent decisions have also held that sexual harassment can constitute discrimination under Title VII.

The next stage in the evolution of the legal doctrine of sexual harassment was the establishment of *quid pro quo* harassment (so called because in a *quid pro quo* arrangement, something is given in exchange for something else). In *Barnes v. Costle* (1977), a District of Columbia circuit court suggested two criteria for determining the existence of *quid pro quo* harassment: disparate treatment of women as opposed to men and tangible employment consequences. The court further held that employers can be found liable for damages in such cases if they knew or should have known of such behavior and failed to take corrective action. Other significant *quid pro quo* cases include *Henson v. City of Dundee* (1982), *Katz v. Dole* (1983), and *Carrero v. New York City Housing Authority* (1989).

The key "hostile environment" case was *Meritor Savings Bank v. Vinson* (1986), in which the plaintiff was terminated from her job at a bank. The plaintiff had sexual intercourse with her supervisor. The plaintiff alleged that early advances were rebuffed but that she accepted later advances for fear of losing her job. The Supreme Court ruled that sexual advances need only be "unwelcome" to constitute possible harassment; the fact that the victim participated "voluntarily" cannot be used as a defense. The Court also elaborated on the definition of "hostile environment," which must include more than trivial and harmless behavior, even if such behavior is annoying; such behavior must be sufficiently severe as to "alter the conditions of the victim's employment and create an abusive working environment."

In *Harris v. Forklift Company* (1993), the Supreme Court used the "reasonable person" test to determine whether a particular behavior constitutes sexual harassment. If a reasonable person would find certain unwelcome sex-related behavior to be offensive, the Court reasoned, such behavior does constitute sexual harassment. Therefore, while merely offensive behavior is not prohibited, an employer would be in violation of the law if a reasonable person would find the workplace so filled with sexual improprieties that it had become a hostile and abusive environment, even if there was no evidence of physical or psychological harm to victims.

Since 1990, more than ten thousand charges of sexual harassment have been filed each year. About 98 percent of the people charged with harassment are men, and more than 90 percent of the adult victims are women. Approximately 65 percent of all such cases are filed after dismissals, and 16 percent are filed after people quit voluntarily.

SUGGESTED READINGS: Alba Conte's *Sexual Harassment in the Workplace: Law and Practice* (New York: Wiley Law Publications, 1990) is a good basic source for legal and historical information. Arthur Gutman's *EEO Law and Personnel Practices* (Newbury Park, Calif.: Sage, 1993) provides a more thoroughly legal perspective. Nancy J. Sedmak and Michael D. Levin-Epstein's *A Primer on Equal Employment Opportunity*, 5th ed. (Washington, D.C.: Bureau of National Affairs, 1991), is a good overview of the topic.

Sexual identity: A person's privately experienced feeling—also known as gender identity—of being male, female, or sexually ambiguous. Conservative factions view sexual identity as a matter of choice, while clinicians find it to be a complex of factors originating with chromosomal inheritance, resultant sexual anatomy and physiology, sex-role assignment

Many gay activists argue that sexual identity revolves around freedom of choice. (UPI/Corbis-Bettmann)

by society, and development of sexual self-awareness in a complex society.

Generally, development of male or female anatomy is determined by whether a sperm carrying a Y chromosome or an X chromosome fertilizes an egg, which carries one X chromosome. The resulting XX combination in a fertilized egg produces a girl; an XY combination produces a boy. It is generally correct to assert that the sperm determines the sex of the child.

In the early embryo, undifferentiated gonads can become either testes or ovaries, and accessory ducts are ready to develop into the male and female reproductive systems. A gene complex on the Y chromosome, identified by research efforts in the 1980's, carries a "testes-determining factor," which causes gonadal tissue to differentiate into testes. In its absence, the gonads develop into ovaries. Development of testes or ovaries and their resultant hormones triggers the development of appropriate ducts and tissues, such as the vas deferens and scrotum in a male or the oviducts and labia in a female. Unusual hormone balances and other factors can result in XX infants developing male anatomy or XY infants possessing female anatomy. Ambiguous genital development produces hermaphroditic or intersex variations between male and female; in very rare instances, both an ovary and a testis develop.

Sex-role assignment is usually based on apparent sexual anatomy. Family, friends, and society respond to a child based on their culture's unique expectations for boys and girls. However, as a child develops an awareness of a sexual self, this may or may not align with the chromosomal sex, sexual anatomy, or society's gender assignment. The physiological and social factors that influence the development of a person's private sexual identity are a complex of nervous system and socialization differences still under study. Clinical work with patients who are ambiguous indicates that sexual identity is heavily determined by biological factors, with social models, interactions, and rehearsals important in finishing sexual identity differentiation. Sexual identity is not a simple matter of "will"; a person does not consciously select which sex will provide sexual arousal and imagery.

Sexual identity becomes controversial in the areas of sex-change operations and the belief that sexual identity is a matter of free choice. Most people develop normal male or female anatomy, are comfortable with their sexual role, and are aroused by the opposite sex. A few are physiologically ambiguous and may require surgery and hormonal and psychological therapy. Although a private matter mainly of concern to appropriate medical personnel, sex-change operations attract much publicity in the tabloid press. Homosexuals and others who do not fit conventional heterosexual roles face condemnation by those who feel it is merely a matter of choice.

Sexual revolution: Shift in sexual attitudes and behaviors in American society. A decade of significant social and cultural turmoil, the 1960's also witnessed a new openness toward various sexual behaviors and a willingness to discuss sexual topics in public. While some commentators argue that these new attitudes marked a revolutionary change in American society, others claim that despite expanded discussion about sex at that time, American sexual values did not change significantly.

Historians note that American sexual attitudes had changed markedly well before the 1960's. In the nineteenth century, most Americans considered sex appropriate only in the context of marriage and only heterosexual behavior was acceptable. Discussion of sex was limited to moral exhortation. By the middle of the twentieth century, however, the popularity of motion pictures suggesting sex outside of marriage, the use of both female and male sexuality in advertising, and the growth of urban areas that allowed for anonymity in the practice of sexual behaviors considered deviant all signaled new attitudes toward sex in America. The 1960's saw an acceleration of these historical trends. Topics formerly considered taboo captured the public imagination, and discussions of premarital sex, extramarital sex, and HOMOSEXUALITY became common. Behaviors such as living together, which had previously earned condemnation, became socially acceptable.

Several events led to the shift in attitudes at that time. Wide distribution of effective CONTRACEPTIVE DEVICES, especially the birth-control pill, reduced the risk of pregnancy and allowed for an emphasis on the pleasures of sex apart from the responsibilities of parenthood. The successes of the Civil Rights movement encouraged some Americans to question conservative sexual mores, which many protesters claimed contributed to the dominance of heterosexual white males. Feminists argued that these sexual mores limited women to the roles of housewives and mothers. Gay activism in the late 1960's brought attention to homosexuality and raised questions as to what constituted sexual deviance. Finally, media entrepreneurs recog-

Provocative films such as those starring Brigitte Bardot reflected the changing social mores of the sexual revolution.
(AP/Wide World Photos)

nized that sex brought increased profits. The numerous men's magazines and the proliferation of X-rated theaters kept sex in the forefront of American culture.

Though the concept of a sexual revolution having occurred in the 1960's gained popularity, several social scientists hold that no such revolution ever happened. They argue that increased media attention to sex merely made it seem as though a significant shift in values had occurred. Pointing to numerous polls and studies about American sexual behaviors and attitudes, they argue that Americans remained largely conservative in their personal beliefs regarding sex. They point to the conservative movement of the 1980's as evidence that the 1960's were not as revolutionary as some have argued.

SUGGESTED READINGS: John D'Emilio and Estelle B. Freedman offer an assessment of the sexual revolution in the final chapters of their *Intimate Matters: A History of Sexuality in America* (New York: Harper & Row, 1988). Hubert J. O'Gorman has edited *Sex and Morality in the U.S.* (Middletown, Conn.: Wesleyan University Press, 1989) a sociological study of sexual behavior.

Sexuality. *See* **Sex and sexuality**

Sexually transmitted diseases (STDs): An STD is any infection that is passed through sexual contact of any type. STDs range in severity from causing simple discomfort, such as genital itching, to causing infertility, shortened lifespan, and serious harm to newborns. They are among the most common infections in all societies.

In a sexually active person, an STD should be suspected if the person has symptoms such as unusual itching in the genital area or a change in genital appearance such as color (redness), discharge, odor, or sores (blisters, warts, or ulcers). Such symptoms do not necessarily mean that an STD is present—sometimes even normal bodily functions can cause some of these symptoms—but they should prompt a person to seek medical attention. Physicians and other healthcare professionals are required to provide consultation and care in a strictly confidential manner, even to teenagers.

STDs are extremely common. At least 12 million Americans acquire an STD each year, and more than half of all Americans will have had an STD by age thirty-five. It is not unusual for a person to have more than one STD simultaneously.

Chlamydia and Gonorrhea. Chlamydia is a bacterium that can cause pus to be discharged from the cervix (the opening of the uterus into the vagina). In men, it causes painful urination and discharges of pus from the urethra (urine tube). Many people with chlamydia have no symptoms. Approximately 3 million to 5 million Americans acquire a new case of chlamydia each year. About 10 to 20 percent of sexually active female teenagers are infected with chlamydia, but only 30 percent of these have symptoms. Only about half of the male partners of infected women will have symptoms. These symptoms are also found in other common STDs including candida ("yeast" infection), trichomonas, and gonorrhea.

Treatment of chlamydia in men and women is simple and quick with modern oral antibiotics, resulting in a cure in about a week. All sexual partners, even those without symptoms, should be treated to prevent reinfection. If chlamydia in men is not treated, the infection can move into the prostate gland or even the scrotum. This will produce fever, pain on urination, pain in the back or groin, or even scrotal pain.

Untreated chlamydia in women can be more serious than that in men. Untreated chlamydia in women can move into the uterus and fallopian tubes and involve the ovaries and other abdominal organs. Approximately 1 million American women each year experience an attack of pelvic inflammatory disease (PID), and chlamydia causes about 30 percent of these cases. PID is experienced as strong pains in the lower belly accompanied by high fever. Treatment may require hospitalization. Even with successful treatment, PID can leave a woman infertile.

Infants born to a woman infected with chlamydia may develop an eye infection or pneumonia. The eye infection develops within two weeks of birth. The pneumonia develops four to eleven weeks after birth. These infections are not serious if treated promptly.

Gonorrhea is another common bacterial STD. Nearly 1 million Americans become infected each year. Gonorrhea often accompanies an infection with chlamydia. Like chlamydia, it is easily treated with antibiotics. Untreated women can develop PID or infection of other organs including the meninges (brain sac), liver, and heart. Infants born to women infected with gonorrhea may develop infection of the eye or other organs; this can be prevented by prompt antibiotic treatment of the mother and of the baby at birth.

Herpes. Herpes is a family of viruses that causes "fever blisters" around the mouth. One member of the virus family, herpes simplex type 2, is transmitted mainly by sexual intercourse. It causes about half a million Americans to seek medical help each year. The main symptom of herpes is painful "water blisters" that form on male and female genitals, especially mucous membranes and surrounding skin. These blisters appear two to seven days after exposure and may last for a month. The affected areas are inflamed and are so painful that persons try to hold their urine for as long as possible. Small blisters close together will merge, forming large ones. In addition to the blisters, the patient usually will have flulike symptoms of chills, fever, headache, nausea, and generalized muscle soreness. Eventually the blisters break and form sores that heal without scars. The fluid in the blisters is highly infectious.

There is no cure for herpes. The virus remains in the body for the life of the infected person and usually

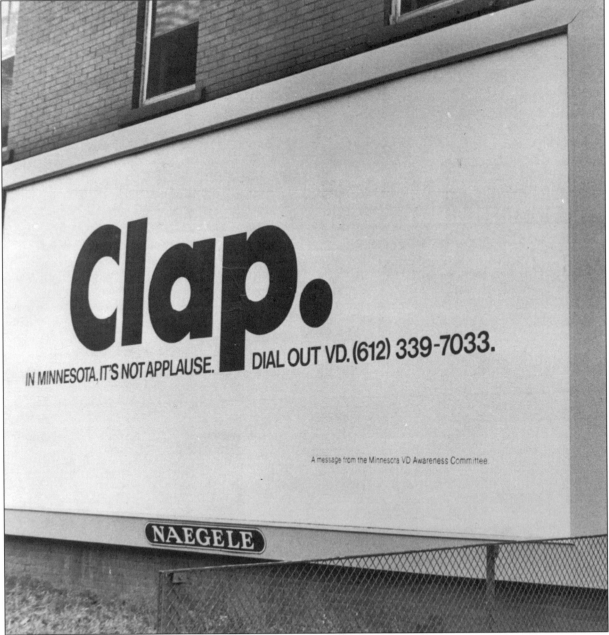

A 1972 Minnesota campaign to fight the spread of sexually transmitted diseases. (UPI/Corbis-Bettmann)

breaks out periodically to repeat the symptomatic phase of the disease. Repeat bouts of herpes are not as unpleasant as the first. During the active phase of the disease, aspirin may provide the patient with some pain relief. A medicine called acyclovir may shorten the active phase but does not prevent further recurrences.

Active vaginal blisters during childbirth put the baby at high risk (50 percent) for infection with herpes. An infected newborn develops blisters and sores over his or her entire body. If untreated, herpes on the baby's skin may spread to the baby's nervous system and kill the child. The risk of herpes infection to the baby from the mother is greatly reduced by a cesarean delivery.

A woman who has been infected with herpes has a greater risk for cancer of the cervix than a woman who has not been infected. This kind of cancer can be detected early by a pap smear and nearly always can be cured, so women with herpes should have pelvic examinations with a pap every six months.

Genital Warts. Genital warts are caused by a virus and are probably the most common STD in America. They cause nearly 2 million patient visits to physicians yearly. The disease is seen mostly in sexually active persons sixteen to twenty-five years old. The contagious warts are of different sizes and shapes. They appear about three to eight months after infection. They may begin on the genitals as several soft, pink, painless "risings" that may grow together and then look like cauliflower or a bunch of grapes. In women, they may appear on the external genitals or on the cervix. Cervical warts are a special problem because they may be asymptomatic, noticed only during a pelvic exam. If left untreated, genital warts may disappear on their own, may grow larger, or may become infected. Most likely, however, the untreated wart will become cancerous. The usual treatment for genital warts is painless and effectively removes the wart and the risk of cancer.

AIDS. The ACQUIRED IMMUNE DEFICIENCY SYNDROME, better known as AIDS, is an STD caused by the HUMAN IMMUNODEFICIENCY VIRUS (HIV). Sexual transmission and transmission at birth are major, but not the only, ways a person can become infected with HIV. After the initial infection, it may be three weeks or even three years before there is evidence of infection, and that evidence consists of changes in blood proteins detectable only by laboratory tests. This means that some people infected with HIV will never know the source of their infection. Many of the 2 million Americans estimated in 1996 to be infected are unaware of their status.

An infected person can transmit the virus to another person almost immediately, but symptoms of the infection may not occur for three to ten years. The virus works by destroying the immune system so that the person eventually dies of infection or cancer. There is no cure for AIDS. The drug zidovudine (ZDV, also known as AZT) inhibits the virus and prolongs life but does not kill the virus.

Conclusions. STDs are contagious infections transmitted by social interaction, as are many other diseases. Some STDs cause relatively trivial irritation; others are lethal. The possibility of contracting an STD or passing on an STD to someone else has social implications regarding one's responsibility to other persons, especially to infants. The risk of an STD may be great enough or important enough to discuss in a new relationship before sexual involvement. Public health campaigns urge the necessity of practicing "safe sex," using a latex condom. Anyone becoming sexually active needs to consider the possibility of contracting an STD. —*Armand M. Karow*

SUGGESTED READINGS: A historical record of the social and medical responses to changes in prevalence and treatments for STDs from the late nineteenth century through the late twentieth century is given by Allan M. Brandt in *No Magic Bullet: A Social History of Venereal Disease in the United States Since 1880* (New York: Oxford University Press, 1985). Medical aspects of STDs in adolescents and adults in various geographic areas of the world are presented concisely by Mahmoud F. Fathalla, Allan Rosenfield, Cynthia Indriso, Dilup K. Sen, and Shan S. Ratnam, in *Reproductive Health: Global Issues*, volume 3 of *The FIGO Manual of Human Reproduction*, edited by Allan Rosenfield and Mahmoud F. Fathalla (Park Ridge, N.J.: Parthenon, 1990). Eve K. Nichols, with the assistance of the Institute of Medicine, National Academy of Science, gives a balanced presentation of the AIDS epidemic and its social impact in *Mobilizing Against AIDS* (Cambridge, Mass.: Harvard University Press, 1989).

Shaare Tefila Congregation v. Cobb (1987): U.S. Supreme Court case. After a Jewish synagogue in Silver Springs, Maryland, was painted with anti-Semitic slogans and symbols in 1982, synagogue members filed a federal suit alleging that the desecration of its building was an act of racial prejudice covered by the Civil Rights Act of 1866. The court of appeals ruled that the law did not apply because Jews were not a "racially distinct group." The Supreme Court, however, reversed the ruling and unanimously affirmed that the law was intended to protect any identifiable classes of persons who are subject to intentional discrimination "solely because of their ancestry or ethnic characteristics."

Shame: Negative emotion typically caused by the violation of a rule or expectation. Such disobedience might involve a moral rule or merely a social expectation (as in table manners, a dress code, or rules of common courtesy). One may embarrass or be embarrassed by oneself or by family members, friends, or others with whom one identifies. The avoidance of shame is a powerful motive, causing people to obey and to encourage others to obey rules and expectations.

Shelter movement: Movement dedicated to providing safe havens and services for victims of domestic abuse. From fourteen hundred to twenty-five hundred women are killed every year by their domestic partners, and more than 100,000 hospital stays (as well as some thirty thousand emergency room visits) a year are attributed to DOMESTIC VIOLENCE. Two to four million incidents of domestic violence are estimated to occur each year. The women's shelter movement is an obvious outgrowth of this terrible social situation. Few governmental agencies are dedicated to this problem, and the police are powerless to protect women before they are hurt; therefore, the shelter movement—women addressing the needs of women—has set up "safe houses" for battered women, who often have to flee dangerous situations quickly. Besides providing safe havens for women, the shelter movement has established telephone hotlines and attracted public attention to the issue.

Sick building syndrome: Symptoms of ill health brought on by exposure to chemical and biological pollutants present in buildings. As many as a fourth of all office workers experience symptoms they connect with their places of work.

Symptoms of sick building syndrome are wide-ranging and can include recurring flu-like symptoms, headache, digestive disorders, respiratory and skin problems, neurological problems, menstrual irregularities in women, fatigue, and exacerbation of allergies and sensitivities to commonly used chemicals. Often, the sufferer initially notices symptoms only in the culprit building, but with repeated exposure, symptoms can become constant or lead to chronic illness.

In recent decades, awareness has grown about the harmful effects of indoor pollution on health, especially in new buildings, in which air may contain many times more toxins than the most polluted outside air. A common chemical pollutant is formaldehyde, which is emitted by pressed wood products, plywood, building insulation, upholstery foam, carpet underlay, and fabric finishes. Formaldehyde is a suspected human carcinogen and is believed to "sensitize" people to other contaminants and foods. Other sources of chemical and particulate pollution include combustion sources such as gas, oil, coal, wood, and tobacco smoke; wall-to-wall carpeting; asbestos-containing insulation; vinyl flooring; and cleaning fluids. New carpets, which are treated with dozens of chemicals, are implicated in many cases of sick-building syndrome. Pesticide spraying is also frequently linked with the onset of illness.

Biological contaminants include dust mites, molds, pollens, and bacteria. Common effects on health are eye, nose, and throat irritation, shortness of breath, dizziness, lethargy, fever, asthma, and digestive problems. Infectious diseases such as influenza and Legionnaire's disease can be transmitted by air conditioning and heating systems. Other sources of biological contaminants are ventilation and heating ducts, carpets, and air conditioners.

Measures to prevent and cure sick-building syndrome include keeping windows open; ensuring that air-conditioning brings in outside air; favoring hardwood or tile floors over carpeting or vinyl; favoring solid wood or metal furniture over pressed wood; avoiding the use of toxic bug sprays and cleaning fluids; having furnaces checked for leaks; and having ventilation ducts cleaned regularly by a nontoxic method.

Simpson, O. J., case: Widely billed as the "trial of the century," the O. J. Simpson double-murder case began in June of 1994 with the discovery of the stabbed and slashed bodies of the former football star's ex-wife, Nicole Brown, and her friend Ronald Goldman outside Brown's condominium. Before the trial ended with Simpson's acquittal on October 3, 1995, the case had mesmerized the nation, brought wide attention to the issue of DOMESTIC VIOLENCE, and ex-

posed deep racial divisions in the perception of the American justice system.

Before surrendering to police several days after the murders, Simpson was briefly a fugitive in a low-speed vehicle pursuit seen by millions on national television. Thus began an unprecedented barrage of pre-

O.J. Simpson tries on the blood-stained gloves at his 1995 murder trial. (Archive Photos/Sam Mirovich/Reuters)

O.J. Simpson exults as he hears the not-guilty verdict in his 1994-1995 murder trial. (AP/Wide World Photos)

trial publicity exceeding that of all previous high-profile cases. The trial began in January, 1995, in a circus atmosphere dwarfing even that of the 1925 SCOPES "monkey trial" in which Clarence Darrow confronted William Jennings Bryan. The fame of the participants in the Simpson case soon approached or exceeded such levels, largely because the entire trial was televised to an enormous viewing public. Along with Simpson and Judge Lance Ito, prosecutors Marcia Clark and Christopher Darden and "Dream Team" defense attorneys F. Lee Bailey, Johnnie Cochran, and Robert Shapiro became household names, as did controversial witnesses such as Los Angeles police detective Mark Fuhrman and Simpson's onetime houseguest Kato Kaelin.

Relying heavily on physical evidence and other circumstantial factors, since they had neither an eyewitness nor a murder weapon, the prosecutors introduced numerous calculations based on DNA analysis to establish that blood found at the crime scene belonged to Simpson. Prosecutors also argued that tests had established that blood from the victims had been found on both a glove and a sock found at Simpson's house and also in his automobile.

To confute such evidence and raise doubts in the jurors' minds, the defense suggested a racist conspiracy by police to plant evidence against Simpson and offered an alibi for Simpson's whereabouts at the time of the crime. The defense was aided in its presentation by what most observers regarded as two major blunders by the prosecution: Reliance on the testimony of Fuhrman, who was later shown to have lied on the witness stand about his use of racial epithets, and a disastrous attempt to demonstrate that the "bloody glove" recovered at the crime scene fit Simpson. When Simpson tried on the glove at the prosecution's request, it appeared not to fit him, an episode that may have proven fatal to the prosecution's case.

Little about the Simpson trial was not controversial. Even the length, cost, and conduct of the trial itself became issues, as did the credibility of the Los Angeles Police Department, which had already been severely tainted by the Rodney KING case and the 1992 LOS ANGELES RIOTS. Fuhrman's alleged RACISM became a public symbol for his department's alleged racism and for police racism in general, while the Simpsons' stormy marriage became a public symbol for the emerging legal and social issue of domestic violence.

Moreover, the jury's swift acquittal of Simpson on all counts in a matter of only a few hours led to broad criticisms of the jurors themselves. Critics asserted that the jury could not possibly have discussed even the major portions of the months of evidence in its brief deliberations, leading to wide speculation that the jurors had improperly discussed the case beforehand. The defense team's use of the "race card" was also criticized by many analysts, who argued that the emotional issue of racism had been effectively used to obscure the facts of the case. Most notable, perhaps, was the broad racial split in the perception of the verdict: Surveys consistently showed that a large majority of whites believed that Simpson was guilty, while a large majority of African Americans believed him to be innocent. Numerous observers remarked that such surveys raised troubling questions about race and justice in the United States; many others commented that the trial highlighted the power of wealth to confound justice, as few even of Simpson's supporters denied that a defendant of lesser means might well have been convicted on the same evidence.

After his acquittal, Simpson continued to draw media attention, but he consented only to prearranged interviews with journalists who agreed to limit their questioning. Critics pointed to such behavior as further evidence of Simpson's guilt, while his attorneys maintained that such discretion was necessary to protect Simpson's rights in a civil suit brought by Brown's and Goldman's relatives after the criminal trial, in which the victims' families sought millions of dollars in damages for wrongful death.

Sin: Religious transgression. Historically, the concept of sin is rooted in the Judeo-Christian belief in the fallen nature of humankind. According to this belief system, the first man and first woman were created in God's image and were in union with Him. They were, however, tempted to do what they were not supposed to do, acting against God's law; as a result, their disobedience brought separation and alienation from God and changed the world into one in which pride, self-deception, and the human impulse toward evil were unleashed. In general, sin can be described as the voluntary disregard of established moral customs.

Singapore caning case: International punishment dispute. Michael Fay, an American teen living in Singapore, was sentenced to four months in prison, a $2,200 fine, and six lashes with a cane after he and

Michael Fay leaves a Singapore prison after receiving corporal punishment for a 1994 vandalism incident. (Reuters/Corbis-Bettmann)

another juvenile were convicted of spray-painting several cars in the city. President Bill CLINTON and some members of Congress came to the boy's aid after public outcry at the severity of the punishment and the family's requests for political intervention. International objections to the punishment were based on the perceived cruelty of the caning process: The offender is brought to a public square, where blows are delivered using a split wooden pole to administer sharp blows across the lower back or buttocks. With each blow, the skin is broken, leading to bleeding and lifelong scarring.

Singapore's strict laws prohibiting such acts as chewing gum, spitting, and failing to flush public toilets were brought to the attention of Americans when the Fay situation became public. Heavy fines, jail sentences, and caning are common punishments for such crimes in the small country, where murder, rape, and other serious and violent crimes are virtually nonexistent by American standards. Lee Kuan Yew, the man given credit for the creation of modern Singapore, believes that the indiscriminate acts of individuals who disregard the rules of the society will eventually undermine the order of that society. He and others in Singapore's government believe that the importing of Western values and ideas into the city-state could mean an end to their near-ideal society, and Singapore's leaders have acted to discourage the infiltration of Western values and disorderliness into their society.

Fay's parents argued that their son's confession was coerced and that vandalism was not serious enough a crime to warrant such severe punishment. Although Fay was known to belong to a gang of troublemakers and had often gotten into trouble at the Singapore American School, Fay's family thought that an outcry by the American public would force the authorities in Singapore to commute the sentence. American support of the teen, however, waned following the initial upsurge. While polls showed that a slim majority of Americans were against the sentence, a much more vocal minority argued that the harsh punishment had proven to be an effective deterrent in Singapore and might prove an effective and inexpensive means by which to deal with rising crime among American youth.

Singapore authorities pointed out that Fay was fortunate not to have received the maximum punishment of eight cane strokes and that being a citizen of the United States in no way meant that Fay had any kind of immunity from the laws of Singapore and the consequences of breaking those laws. Following the intervention and appeals by President Clinton and other leaders, however, authorities in Singapore did agree to reduce the number of cane strokes. Fay was permitted to return to his family home in Ohio shortly after completion of his sentence.

Single mothers: Women who by choice or circumstances raise one or more children without a partner. Single parenthood has been identified as a social issue within the last twenty-five years, as rising numbers of women raise children on their own.

Single parenthood includes children born to unmarried women, many of whom are teenagers, women who are divorced or widowed, or women who choose to have a child on their own. As of 1970, 9.9 percent of families were headed by women; by 1987, the proportion of female single-parent households had increased to 16.2 percent of all American families. Disadvantaged groups have a higher rate of lone-parent families headed by women. In Canada, the 1961 census data revealed that 8.4 percent of Canadian families were headed by a single parent (the majority of whom were women); by 1991, this figure had increased to 9.8 percent. In the United States, the figures for children born to an unwed woman are 18 percent for white women and 64 percent for black women; in Canada, 23 percent of children are born to unmarried mothers.

Of greatest concern is the fact that children born or raised in one-parent families headed by mothers are more likely to live in poverty. In 1992, the number of single mothers in the United States reached 9 million, of whom 4 million lived below the POVERTY LINE. In response to the lack of affordable accommodations, single mothers spend a disproportionate amount of their resources on housing. Young single mothers may not be able to acquire the necessary educational skills to allow them to compete for entrance into the labor market. Additionally, divorced women experience a substantial drop in their standard of living. As a result, children living with single mothers have to overcome substantial barriers to break the cycle of poverty. Furthermore, the current economic climate in which welfare benefits are under attack and child-care subsidies are reduced works against a single mother having the opportunity to seek employment opportunities or receive wages that enable her to provide for the needs of her children.

A different group of single mothers includes a small but growing proportion of career women who post-

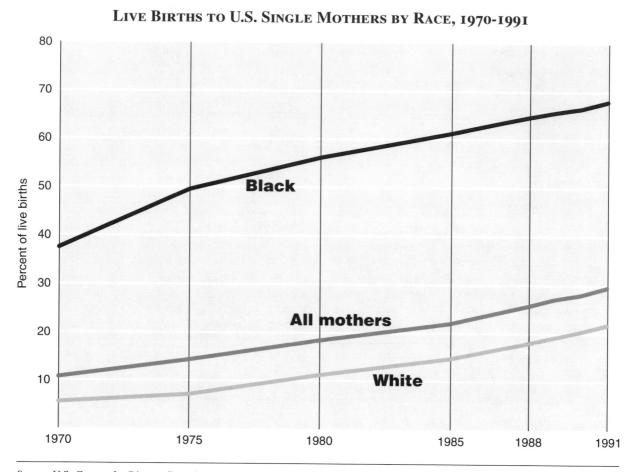

LIVE BIRTHS TO U.S. SINGLE MOTHERS BY RACE, 1970-1991

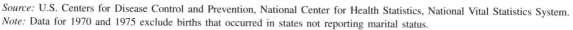

Source: U.S. Centers for Disease Control and Prevention, National Center for Health Statistics, National Vital Statistics System.
Note: Data for 1970 and 1975 exclude births that occurred in states not reporting marital status.

pone childbearing and then choose later in life to raise a child alone; some of these women choose artificial insemination or adoption. These single-parent women differ from most single mothers in terms of economic stability and the circumstances surrounding their decisions to become mothers.

Sit-ins: Protest strategy. Used without much success before the 1960's, sit-ins attained popularity during the heyday of the CIVIL RIGHTS MOVEMENT as nonviolent protests against segregated public facilities. The modern Civil Rights movement is sometimes dated to February, 1960, when four black students from a local college "sat in" at the lunch counter of a Greensboro, N.C., Woolworth's store. Within a year, about seventy thousand protestors had participated in similar actions,

more than three thousand had been arrested, with many physically attacked by white mobs. Many facilities were desegregated as a result, and the tactic soon began to be used in other social movements, notably the anti-VIETNAM WAR movement.

Six-Day War (1967): Arab-Israeli conflict in which Israel achieved a stunning victory over Egypt, Syria, and Jordan, winning the Sinai Peninsula and Gaza Strip from Egypt, the Golan Heights from Syria, and the West Bank from Jordan. A series of military maneuvers and alliances led to the war. In May, 1967, Syria announced that Israel was massing troops at the Syrian-Israeli border. Showing support for Syria, Egyptian president Gamal Abdel Nasser called for the withdrawal of U.N. security forces from the Egyptian-

A 1971 sit-in by Jewish activists protesting business dealings with the Soviet Union. (Archive Photos)

Israeli military vehicles occupy Nativity Square in Bethlehem during the 1967 Six-Day War. (UPI/Corbis-Bettmann)

Israeli cease-fire lines and closed the Strait of Tiran to Israeli shipping. Jordan's King Hussein then signed a defense pact with Nasser, which convinced Israel that its Arab neighbors were preparing to attack. Led by Defense Minister Moshe Dayan, the Israeli Air Force on June 5 sabotaged the Egyptian Air Force, the Arab nations' most capable military force. Israel then led an offensive against Egyptian ground troops; when Jordan entered the war, Israel retaliated on the Jordanian and Syrian fronts. On June 11, the U.N. Security Council secured a cease-fire on all fronts, ending the war.

Skinheads: Originally referring to any persons with close-cropped hair, the term has come to designate white males belonging to various youth gangs espousing neo-Nazi beliefs. In the United States, skinheads were at first associated with such racist groups as the KU KLUX KLAN and the White Aryan Resistance, but many later formed their own groups. Unlike members of most other youth gangs, skinheads frequently come from upper-class and middle-class neighborhoods; many are the products of dysfunctional families. Skinheads have been accused of racist vandalism, ethnic intimidation, and violence, usually directed toward minorities, Jews and Jewish institutions, and homosexual groups.

Slander: Spoken defamation that causes public scorn, derision, or disrepute of another person. Slander may also be defined to include "transitory gestures," a phrase connoting public gestures with known negative interpretations, such as thumbing the nose or other similar expressions. In either case, a resultant direct harm must be provable in order for a plaintiff to sue successfully for slander. As in cases of LIBEL, the written counterpart of slander, intent and actual damage caused by slander must be proved by a plaintiff before a defendant can be found liable for damages by a court.

Slavery: Social institution that binds individuals in involuntary servitude. Slaves are regarded as the physical property of the owner, and their labor is obtained by force or coercion. The United States is still suffering from the lingering effects of some two hundred and fifty years of slavery within its borders.

History. Slavery was almost universal in the ancient world. It began to decline in Europe during the Middle Ages, when it was largely replaced by the less-binding system of serfdom. Slavery began to revive in the fifteenth century as Europeans explored the west coast of Africa. Most Europeans believed that Africans were inferior beings because they were not Christian. Therefore, Europeans believed, enslaving Africans was justified, and it fulfilled a moral obligation to bring them the benefits of Christian society. The numbers of Africans enslaved remained relatively small until 1501, when the Spanish began to import African slaves to fulfill their agricultural needs in the West Indies. During the next three hundred years, approximately ten million Africans were brought to the Americas as slaves.

In North America, English colonists at first preferred to use indentured servants rather than slaves. As agriculture in English colonies expanded in the seventeenth century, however, so did the need for labor. The first Africans arrived in Jamestown, Virginia, in 1619. By 1700, a slave system was firmly established in most Southern colonies. Slavery was never widespread in the Northern colonies, though all of them allowed it.

The American Revolution spread new ideas about democracy, equality, and freedom in the colonial population. After the war, Northern states, responding to ideas espoused in the Declaration of Independence, began to outlaw slavery. By 1804, all the Northern states had abolished it.

In the Southern states, the institution of slavery was revived by the invention of the cotton gin in 1793. This device made it possible to process more cotton, and as cotton production rose dramatically, more slaves were needed to work in the cotton fields. By 1860, there were nearly four million slaves in the United States.

The importation of slaves was outlawed by the U.S. government in 1808, but their sale within the country remained legal in fifteen Southern states until after the Civil War. Opposition to the institution of slavery grew along with the numbers of slaves in the South. By 1860, the rift between North and South had deepened; when Abraham Lincoln, an advocate of the gradual abolition of slavery, was elected president in 1860, several Southern states seceded from the Union to protect their right to maintain the slave system.

In 1863, Lincoln issued the Emancipation Proclamation, which actually freed only a handful of slaves but which signaled his intention to abolish the institution. When the war ended, slavery was officially abolished by the Thirteenth Amendment to the Constitution.

The proprietor of a museum devoted to slavery displays some of his exhibits. (UPI/Corbis-Bettmann)

After the Civil War, it was necessary to provide for the needs of the freed slaves, who had been utterly dependent on their masters. The congressional Reconstruction Acts put the South under military control and helped to ensure that the rights of the newly freed slaves were protected. When Reconstruction ended in 1877, many former slave owners returned to positions of power. While blacks had made progress during the Reconstruction period, those gains were wiped away once control was returned to Southern whites.

The return of the white power structure in the South led to the passage of increasingly restrictive state laws. These were called "black codes" or JIM CROW LAWS. They restricted the rights of blacks to own property, allowed them to work only in certain jobs (usually in agriculture or domestic service), and segregated almost all public facilities. Laws requiring citizenship tests and poll taxes kept most poor blacks from voting. These laws were upheld by the U.S. Supreme Court in such decisions as *PLESSY V. FERGUSON* (1896). Southern whites also employed terrorism to keep blacks from making economic, social, or political progress. The

KU KLUX KLAN and other groups used lynching and other mob violence to secure black cooperation.

In the early twentieth century, nearly one million Southern blacks moved North to look for work and improve their chances for a better life. The move from a rural Southern society to an urban Northern environment was traumatic for many blacks, and their sense of dislocation was intensified by the fact that they were often no more welcome in the North than they had been in the South. During the 1920's, there was a resurgence of the Ku Klux Klan, and its influence spread outside the South to the Midwest and the West. Ironically, there was at the same time a resurgence of black culture, often called the Harlem Renaissance, and a new appreciation, even among white Americans, for black music, art, and literature.

The Great Depression of the 1930's hit African Americans very hard. They were discriminated against in hiring and wages, and unemployment rates for blacks were significantly higher than those for whites. The NEW DEAL programs of President Franklin D. Roosevelt did little for them. The Social Security system at first excluded farmers and domestics, who made up 65 percent of all black workers. President Roosevelt did appoint several blacks to positions in his administration.

World War II increased the need for black labor, and racial barriers began to fall as the country pulled together for the war effort. Once again, blacks moved in large numbers to the North and West, where most government jobs were located. The influx of blacks to new areas resulted in conflicts over jobs and housing in several cities.

Increasingly in the 1930's, 1940's, and 1950's, African Americans challenged discrimination in the courts. In BROWN V. BOARD OF EDUCATION OF TOPEKA, KANSAS (1954), the Supreme Court unanimously struck down segregation in public schools. This decision signaled the beginning of an all-out effort to eradicate the lingering effects of slavery in America. From 1955 to 1970, demonstrations, marches, and legal challenges tore down many racial barriers. The federal government passed the CIVIL RIGHTS ACT in 1964 and the VOTING RIGHTS ACT in 1965, both of which were largely designed to protect the rights of African Americans.

African American rage at more than three hundred years of slavery and discrimination began to spill over in the late 1960's. Beginning with the Los Angeles Watts riots in 1965, there was a long period of unrest in black neighborhoods across the country.

By the 1970's, African Americans began once again to focus their attention on changing the system from within. Black studies programs were instituted in most American universities, and increasing numbers of blacks began to attend college. By 1980, black mayors had been elected in 318 U.S. cities, and there were more than seven thousand black elected officials. Nevertheless, many problems directly attributable to the legacy of slavery remained.

Problems of the Black Community. The cycle of poverty begun during the era of slavery has had many negative effects in the African American community. Sociologists agree that family stability is dependent on economic stability, and about one-third of all black families today live below the POVERTY LINE; only 11 percent of U.S. white families live in poverty. Inferior education systems in poor neighborhoods do not adequately prepare urban blacks to enter the labor force; while African Americans represent 12 percent of the population, they account for 17 percent of the nation's service workers and 15 percent of its blue-collar work-

ers, but only 6 percent of its managers and professionals. Median family income for blacks remains at about half what it is for whites. The UNEMPLOYMENT rate for blacks is double that for whites.

Economic opportunity is closely tied to educational opportunity. Largely as the result of cuts in federal programs, the percentage of African Americans attending college fell from 9.2 percent in 1980 to 8.9 percent in 1990. Most analysts agree that without drastic improvements in educational opportunities, African Americans will never be able to achieve true economic equality.

Cultural Achievements. When they were forcibly brought to the Americas from Africa, black slaves brought with them their traditional cultures. African dialects have given such words as "tote" and "corral" to the language. BLACK ENGLISH is today recognized as a separate dialect of American English with origins in African languages and the slave culture. Slang expressions such as "jive" and "cool" have found their way into the everyday vocabularies of millions of Americans.

Music is perhaps the field in which African Americans have made their greatest contributions. The music the slaves used to cheer themselves as they worked was African in form. The slave calls and hollers gave way to spirituals, and, later, the blues. All used the rhythms and patterns of African music. These forms, which sustained the slave communities in troubled times, eventually evolved into gospel, jazz, rhythm and blues, rock and roll, and rap. African Americans have been among the pioneers and leading artists in all these fields.

Increasing numbers of African Americans are entering the middle class and achieving the American Dream, yet thousands continue to live in the poverty and alienation that has been the inevitable legacy of the institution of slavery. Americans continue to address the problems stemming from hundreds of years of slavery and more than a century of its lingering effects.
—*Deborah D. Wallin*

SUGGESTED READINGS: The history of minorities in America is thoroughly explored in Ronald Takaki's *A Different Mirror: A History of Multicultural America* (Boston: Little, Brown, 1993). *The Autobiography of Malcolm X* (New York: Ballantine Books, 1992) provides insights into being black in America from the 1930's to the 1960's. *The Content of Our Character: A New Vision of Race in America* (New York: HarperCollins, 1990), by African American author Shelby

Slumlords

Steele, is a controversial collection of essays that explores the recent progress of race relations.

Slumlords: Individuals who own or manage substandard housing. The term "slumlord" is an emotionally charged word typically used to convey derision for an insensitive property owner who does not maintain adequate facilities for residents. Slumlords can be convicted of criminal negligence, endangerment, or dereliction of duty and sentenced to fines; in extreme cases, slumlords have been sentenced to jail time or house arrest. Courts can also order such individuals to make improvements to their rental properties.

Small Business Administration: Government agency. The Small Business Administration was created by the Small Business Act of 1953, and it has authority created by several other laws, including the Equal Opportunity Act of 1964. The agency's mission is to aid, counsel, assist, and protect the interests of small businesses, including helping them to receive a fair portion of government contracts. The agency also participates in loans given by other lenders and guarantees loans to businesses unable to obtain financing on their own. This service has enabled many would-be entrepreneurs without financial resources or a record of success to start their own businesses. Particular emphasis is given to businesses owned by socially or economically handicapped individuals and those owned by or employing individuals with physical handicaps.

Smith, Susan, case (1994-1995): Murder of two South Carolina boys by their mother. In November, 1994, Susan Smith reported that her two young sons, aged three and one, had been kidnapped during a carjacking. Nine days later, Smith confessed that she herself had rolled her car into a lake with her boys strapped inside. The car, with the bodies of the boys in it, was soon recovered. Widespread attention was given to the story of Smith's troubled life, which had included incidents of sexual molestation, suicide at-

The Small Business Administration assists individuals who want to open enterprises of their own. (James L. Shaffer)

Susan Smith is led from the courthouse during her July, 1995, murder trial. (AP/Wide World Photos)

tempts, and a failed marriage. She was found guilty of murder in August, 1995, and sentenced to life imprisonment.

Smog: Photochemical mixture of chemicals that occurs when air pollutants interact under the influence of solar radiation. This interaction produces new materials. There may be more than one hundred different chemicals in smog, but it usually contains large amounts of ozone, which is harmful to most forms of life. Photochemical smog may occur almost anywhere but is more common in large cities with many automobiles and certain climatic characteristics. Cities such as Los Angeles, Mexico City, and Buenos Aires, located in warm, dry climates with many sunny days, are especially subject to smog outbreaks.

Smoking and tobacco: In 1994, one of out every six deaths in the United States was related to smoking. Tobacco is responsible for more deaths each year than alcohol and drug abuse, infectious disease, poisonings, firearms, and automobile accidents combined. During the 1980's, an average of 430,000 Americans died each year from smoking-related diseases; medical costs for treating American smokers averaged $68 billion a year in the same decade. Such statistics have fueled a powerful movement to restrict or even outlaw tobacco sales and smoking, a movement that has been hotly contested by tobacco companies and smokers'-rights groups.

History. In 1560, Jean Nicot, a Frenchman, introduced tobacco to the European world. Native Americans had shown Spanish sailors in Cuba how to smoke the plant, and the sailors brought some back to the Old World. Nicot announced that it had cured diseases and was useful in promoting good health. Others who came across the substance, however, denounced it as a foul and smelly weed. After the English colony in Jamestown began exporting tobacco to London in 1612, King James I attempted to have it banned from his court because it made people cough and left a foul odor. Something about the weed caught on, however, and it became faddish to smoke it in pipes and cigars.

In 1857, the first medical study of the effects of smoking appeared in the British medical journal *The Lancet.* A scientist reported that tobacco caused people to become inactive and lazy, interfered with their ability to think clearly, caused coughs, and irritated smok-

ers' throats and lungs. The report caused little reaction, perhaps because smoking was still somewhat uncommon. The popularity of smoking, however, grew rapidly after the introduction of cigarettes in the early 1900's. By 1963, companies produced 4,345 cigarettes annually for every person in the United States.

Regulation and Medical Risks. In 1890, twenty-six U.S. states had laws prohibiting the sale of tobacco to children under eighteen. The Anti-Cigarette League pushed for even tighter restrictions, and by 1909, fifteen states had prohibited cigarette sales and consumption. This early success ended with World War I. Tobacco companies began giving their products away to soldiers, and General John J. Pershing, the commander of U.S. forces in Europe, publicly proclaimed, "What do we need to win the war? Tobacco as much as bullets." Cigarettes were alleged to give soldiers courage, dignity, and strength, and the success of the campaign virtually ended the antitobacco crusade.

In 1939, medical researchers published the first findings linking smoking to major health problems and shorter life spans. The results of surveys of health records demonstrated that smokers died from lung cancer at much higher rates than did nonsmokers. Smokers also were found to suffer from other chest illnesses and breathlessness far more often than nonsmokers. From 1950 to 1954, fourteen more studies were published that found a connection between smoking and heart and lung disease. A 1964 Public Health Service report on the health of 1,123,000 men found that smokers were seven times more likely to die of heart and respiratory illnesses than were nonsmokers. In that year, however, more than 50 percent of U.S. adult males smoked.

In a historic 1964 report entitled *Smoking and Health*, Surgeon General Luther L. Terry stated for the first time that smoking was "the most important" cause of chronic bronchitis, emphysema, coronary artery disease, and lung cancer. Congress responded to the report by passing the Cigarette Labeling and Advertising Act of 1965, which required cigarette packages to carry the warning, "Caution: Cigarette Smoking May Be Hazardous to Your Health." In a victory for the industry, however, Congress did not require any other warnings on package labels until 1969.

About 35 percent of Canadians over the age of fifteen smoke regularly; almost one in four (23 percent) of Canadians under fifteen smoke, percentages that are slightly higher than the comparable figures for the United States. The government of Canada does not

A commuter in New York protests the ban on smoking on his train. (UPI/Corbis Bettmann)

Phillip Morris chief executive officer William Campbell tries to convince Congress that cigarette smoking is not addictive. (Reuters/Corbis-Bettmann)

require warning labels on tobacco products and has not sponsored laws creating smoke-free zones. Cigarette smoking became fashionable in Canada about the same time as it did in the United States—during and after World War I—and government statistics record a steady increase in lung cancer and other tobacco-related diseases since that time.

Industry Response. Tobacco companies set up the Council for Tobacco Research in 1954. Over the next twenty-five years, the council spent more than $64 million to finance more than eighteen hundred reports on the effects of tobacco use. The industry also created the Tobacco Institute in 1958 to fight legislative action that might reduce sales. The main argument used by the institute is that Americans should have freedom of choice when it comes to smoking. The institute suggests that a broad range of lifestyle choices account for health differences between smokers and nonsmokers. Perhaps, institute representatives argue, smokers are simply more reckless in the way they live their lives, while nonsmokers are more concerned with good health. Industry representatives also assert that scientific studies have never determined which of the thousands of chemicals found in smoke actually cause dis-

ease. Defenders of tobacco say that without such direct evidence, there is nothing but statistics to show the relationship between smoking and health. Few outside the industry accept the logic of such arguments, however; as the U.S. surgeon general announced in 1964, and every subsequent surgeon general has reiterated, "Cigarette smoking is hazardous. . . . This is no longer a matter of opinion nor a slogan. . . . This is a flat scientific fact."

Nonsmokers who live with smokers can also suffer from tobacco-related diseases. A fourteen-year study of nonsmoking Japanese wives whose husbands smoked showed that the women had much higher rates of lung cancer than did nonsmoking wives of nonsmokers. Such reports of the effects of "second-hand" smoke have prompted many states and cities to ban smoking in most public places, including restaurants, office buildings, and airplanes. Other studies have shown that chewing tobacco and other "smokeless" tobacco cause high rates of jaw and mouth cancer.

Trends in Smoking. The campaign against smoking has sharply reduced the number of adult smokers. In 1984, 32 percent of the adult U.S. population smoked; in 1994, only 26 percent did. Only a few segments of the population have reported increases in tobacco use. According to a 1992 survey, 35 percent of white high-school seniors smoked, a level several points higher than the one found ten years earlier; however, the rate for African American high-school seniors declined sharply in the same period, from 35 percent to only 10 percent. The rate for teenage girls of both races increased dramatically, however, and they became as likely to smoke as males. Ten percent of all high-school students smoked at least one-half pack a day. More than four out of five smokers took up the practice before they were twenty years old, and the average beginning age for smokers was fourteen and a half. Industry representatives have argued that teenagers tend to smoke as a result of the influence of parents and friends; several antismoking studies issued in 1995 pointed to different causes.

Cigarettes and Advertising. Part of the reason for increases in smoking among young Americans is the intense ADVERTISING campaign the industry launched in the aftermath of the surgeon general's 1964 report. In 1968, the FEDERAL TRADE COMMISSION (FTC) banned advertisements on television and radio, claiming that the industry was "encouraging death and disease" in its efforts to sell tobacco products. Yet, fifteen years later, companies spent more than $2.6 billion on advertisements in magazines and on billboards. Much of the advertising, moreover, seemed aimed at the young.

In 1993, tobacco companies faced a major threat when the FOOD AND DRUG ADMINISTRATION (FDA) threatened to declare nicotine an addictive drug, a decision that could have led to a ban on the sale of most tobacco products. Such a prohibition seemed a real possibility after an FDA advisory panel ruled in 1994 that there was enough nicotine in most cigarettes to cause addiction. The Tobacco Institute responded that nicotine could be "habit forming" but was not addictive; the institute also argued that tobacco was not a drug because injecting it into one's body did not lead to intoxication. The Republican victory in the 1994 congressional elections ended talk of prohibi-

tion, because the new head of the committee overseeing tobacco issues was from a tobacco-growing district and a staunch defender of the right to smoke.

Lawsuits. The tobacco industry has had little to fear from courts. In 1987, the U.S. Supreme Court upheld a lower-court decision in *Cipallone v. Liggett Group*, confirming that warning labels gave companies a degree of immunity from liability in smokers' deaths. U.S. tobacco companies have had consistent success in such cases and have never been held liable for damages to a victim of smoking.   —*Leslie V. Tischauser*

SUGGESTED READINGS: A. Lee Fritschler and James M. Hoefler present a complete history of tobacco in *Smoking and Politics: Policy Making and the Federal Bureaucracy*, 5th ed. (Upper Saddle River, N.J.: Prentice Hall, 1996). Medical reports on smoking are summarized in Ronald J. Troyer and Gerald E. Markle's *Cigarettes: The Battle over Smoking* (New Brunswick, N.J.: Rutgers University Press, 1983). Essays on smoking in various cultures are found in *Smoking Policy: Law, Politics, and Culture* (New York: Oxford University Press, 1993), edited by Robert Rabin and Stephen D. Sugarman.

Snake handling: Religious practice of handling serpents as a sign of supernatural power. During a highly

The leader of a snake-handling sect displays his faith. (UPI/Corbis-Bettmann)

emotional church service, a box containing one or more poisonous snakes is placed at the front of the church on the platform. Normally, the serpent box is opened by the religious leaders, who then encourage the snake to crawl over their bodies as a testimony to their faith in God. Subsequently, several members of the congregation volunteer to "handle" the snakes. Snake handling is generally accompanied by glosso-lalia (speaking in tongues), dancing, and religious shouting.

Social contract: Theoretical construct that represents society as the product of an agreement between individual persons. Social contract theories explain why some constraints on individual freedom are permissible by specifying when and why people must cooperate. Modern Western political culture, particularly in the United States, owes its conceptions of individual rights and limitations on governmental power to the idea of the social contract.

History. One may find a sort of social contract in the book of Genesis in the Bible as well as in the dialogues of the ancient Greek philosopher Plato. These early expressions of the idea of the social contract emphasize how people's identities are formed by their connection to their God or their government rather than how their rights are preserved by it.

Three major political thinkers developed the modern idea of the social contract: Thomas Hobbes (1588-1679), John Locke (1632-1704), and Jean-Jacques Rousseau (1712-1778). These thinkers maintained that one could imagine people living in a condition they called "the state of nature," in which there was in some cases no society and in all no government. For various reasons, however, Hobbes, Locke, and Rousseau all believed that people could not live in a state of nature forever; some governmental order eventually would have to be established. Each then imagined what sort of a governmental order people in the state of nature would agree to form: Would it be a monarchy with nearly unlimited powers, a monarchy in which the ruler's powers were limited by a parliament, or a popular government? Hobbes thought the first; Locke, the second; Rousseau, the third. The agreement to establish a particular order was called the social contract.

From a contemporary perspective, it is difficult to imagine what it would be like for a group of people to live without any governmental order at all or to agree on what kind of government to form. But if the state of nature does not make sense as a description of a phase in human history, it may still be used hypothetically. As Hobbes, Locke, and Rousseau maintained, the only legitimate authority one person can have over another is authority to which the latter agrees. We are free by nature; our obligations to others arise only through the voluntary agreements we make. From the idea of the state of nature comes the idea that we are naturally free—or, as Thomas Jefferson wrote in the Declaration of Independence, that "all men are endowed by their Creator with certain unalienable Rights, that among these are Life, Liberty, and the pursuit of Happiness."

If we are naturally free, then why do we need societies or governments? Why would free people draw up a social contract for the purpose of restricting their freedoms? Hobbes believed that without a governmental order, people's desires, coupled with the scarcity of basic resources, would inevitably lead people to fight what he called a "war of all against all." We need, Hobbes maintained, to restrict our freedoms in order to live in peace and security. Locke believed that most of us have an intuitive sense of how to treat others without having to have laws, courts, and police to force us to behave as we should. Nevertheless, Locke argued, there are always a few people who will not give others their due. When there is no government (and no court system or police force), controlling and punishing such people is difficult. Therefore, Locke concluded, we must agree to curtail our freedoms for the sake of protecting ourselves and our possessions from the few who threaten them. Rousseau believed that life under a social contract was better than life in the state of nature because only under a social contract were people free to fulfill their potential. In a state of nature, Rousseau argued, people were merely independent, but also limited and brutish.

As these thinkers conceived it, the social contract was the foundation for any legitimate system of authority. It was also a vehicle for thinking about whether a particular government was doing its job in fulfilling its obligations to the people who had formed it. If societies and governments are things people make by conscious agreements, then they can also be dissolved if they stray from their original purpose. The social contract, because it is made, can also be broken. From the social contract's idea of legitimate authority, we also understand when and why authority is not legitimate and can therefore be justifiably opposed.

In the nineteenth century, the idea of the social contract was severely criticized, primarily for being ahistorical. The study of the development of social institutions, particularly among the peoples colonized by Europeans, led many to reject the idea that societies could be the conscious creations of their members or that individuals could live outside a social order.

Contemporary Context. The idea of the social contract was revived in the late twentieth century primarily by the philosopher John Rawls. Rawls argued that the idea could be used as a critical tool to allow people to imagine what a just society would be like. In Rawls's view, the state of nature was entirely hypothetical—one merely imagined oneself in it in order to think about the just society. To do so, Rawls maintained, one had to place oneself behind what he called "the veil of ignorance," meaning one had to imagine having no knowledge of one's race, ethnicity, talents, income, handicaps, and other qualities. From that "original position," Rawls believed, one could best imagine the just society and could therefore see the kinds of restrictions to one's freedom to which one would agree most clearly. The social contract, in Rawls's view, should be the basic structure of a just society imagined by anyone who places him/herself in the original position.

Political leaders in the late twentieth century have used the idea of the social contract to emphasize their desire to refashion the political community and be accountable to the electorate. In the 1992 presidential campaign in the United States, Bill CLINTON promised to establish a "new covenant" between his administration and the citizenry. Like a social contract, the new covenant was intended as a rethinking of the reasons for social cooperation, primarily in the area of aid to the poor. In 1994, Representative Newt GINGRICH of Georgia, along with many other Republicans in the U.S. Congress, published and signed a proposal known as the "CONTRACT WITH AMERICA." This "contract" consisted of a series of pledges made by these representatives to the electorate, the most significant of which were the promises to pass constitutional amendments limiting the terms of members of Congress and mandating the balancing of the federal budget. The Contract with America depended on the idea that government is created by an agreement of the people to accomplish particular ends. The more those ends can be specified, the better citizens will be able to tell whether their representatives are fulfilling the tasks they promised to undertake.

Arguments Against the Social Contract. Opponents of the idea of the social contract argue that it commits those who use it to excessively individualistic values at the expense of communal or egalitarian ones. Some critics, known as the communitarians, argue that the idea of the social contract assumes that societies are merely groups of people who cooperate only when it is advantageous to do so rather than communities of people who share basic ideas about what is valuable in life. Feminists have also criticized the idea of the social contract for its inherent sexism. The individual who makes the social contract, feminists argue, could not be just anyone but, as Hobbes, Locke, and Rousseau made clear, must be an adult man; women and children, by contrast, are not naturally free and therefore cannot make a social contract. As feminists point out, the "natural freedom" adult men are assumed to possess is the result of the care and education given to boys by women. Individuals are not born, but made. The idea of the social contract assumes that individuals are free first and constrained only later, when they agree to be. Feminists maintain that people are constrained first and can only become free later.

Summary. The idea of the social contract provides the basis for the more familiar ideals of individualism and limited government. Although it has been severely criticized during the three hundred years since its first modern statement, the social contract remains a powerful metaphor for the ideal relation between people, their societies, and their governments.

—Emily Hauptmann

SUGGESTED READINGS: Thomas Hobbes used the social contract to justify absolute monarchy in *Leviathan*, edited by Michael Oakeshott (New York: Collier, 1962). John Locke's *Second Treatise of Government*, edited by C. B. Macpherson (Indianapolis: Hackett, 1980) influenced the founders of the United States. Jean-Jacques Rousseau's *The Social Contract*, translated by Maurice Cranston (New York: Penguin, 1968) used the idea to criticize nearly all existing forms of government.

The most extensive contemporary social contract theory can be found in John Rawls's *A Theory of Justice* (Cambridge, Mass.: Belknap Press of Harvard University Press, 1971). The best example of the appearance of the idea in late twentieth century politics is *The Contract with America: The Bold Plan by Rep. Newt Gingrich, Rep. Dick Armey, and the House Republicans to Change the Nation*, edited by Ed Gillespie and Bob Schellhas (New York: Times Books, 1994). For a communitarian critique of the idea of the social contract, see Michael J. Sandel's *Liberalism and* the *Limits of Justice* (Cambridge, England: Cambridge University Press, 1982). For a feminist critique, see Carole Pateman's *The Sexual Contract* (Stanford, Calif.: Stanford University Press, 1988).

Social Security Act (1935): Federal legislation establishing national programs of unemployment compensation and social-welfare payments to individual citizens. The elimination of jobs, the foreclosure of mortgages, and the loss of savings during the GREAT DEPRESSION destroyed the confidence of many U.S. citizens in a secure economic future and intensified calls for government assistance. The Franklin D. Roosevelt Administration was also pressured to action by the popularity of income redistribution plans, such

President Franklin D. Roosevelt signs the Social Security Act into law in 1935. (AP/Wide World Photos)

as those put forth by Dr. Francis Townsend and Louisiana senator Huey Long. Responding to public pressure, in June, 1934, Roosevelt created the Committee on Economic Security, headed by Secretary of Labor Frances Perkins, for the purpose of developing comprehensive systems of unemployment compensation, old-age pensions, national health insurance, and specialized welfare programs for disabled and needy U.S. citizens.

The committee debated the merits of national or state-run systems of unemployment compensation. Supporters of a national system pointed to the need for fairness and consistency across a nation in which workers had become increasingly mobile. Proponents of a state-run system pointed to Wisconsin as a model. The so-called "Wisconsin Plan," devised by Governor Phillip F. La Follette in 1932, required employers in the state to establish unemployment reserves for their employees. By December, 1934, the committee had agreed on an unemployment compensation program that would be administered by the states and funded by a payroll tax on employers. Where state unemployment compensation laws existed, employer contributions could be deducted from the tax, creating unemployment reserves without additional expense to individual companies. The committee also set minimum standards of coverage. Within a year of passage of the act, all forty-eight states had passed unemployment compensation legislation.

Regarding old-age pensions, the committee recognized the need for a national system. Its recommendations called for the creation of a central fund through equal contributions by workers and employers. From this fund, retirees received monthly allotments based on presumed need. The program also called for federal grants to the states for public assistance for families with dependent children, the needy, and the blind. The Committee on Economic Security transmitted its proposals to the president in early January, 1935.

President Roosevelt sent his social security legislation to Congress on January 17, 1935. Opponents claimed that the system would be too expensive and would fundamentally change U.S. society, replacing individual responsibility with dependence on government funding. Fearing voter reprisals, however, opposition collapsed. The House of Representatives overwhelmingly passed the Social Security Act in April, and the Senate concurred two months later. President Roosevelt signed the bill into law on August 14, 1935.

Since then, the Social Security Act has been amended a number of times, either to extend Social Security coverage to new groups within U.S. society or to increase benefits to reflect changing national economic conditions. In 1965, health insurance for the elderly was added to the program. The nature and viability of the SOCIAL SECURITY SYSTEM became major questions with the conservative political resurgence of the 1980's and 1990's, but few politicians have been willing to consider abandoning these "ENTITLEMENT" PROGRAMS that have become integral parts of American life.

Social Security Disability Insurance (SSDI): Program established in 1956 to provide monthly benefits to people with disabilities that prevent them from working. In its early form, the SSDI program was intended for persons above the age of fifty and was to be administered cooperatively between the federal Social Security Administration and state-level agencies. Reforms and amendments in 1958, 1960, 1965, 1980, and 1984 revised the program significantly. Through the 1970's, a larger than expected number of persons were receiving benefits, and many lawmakers were concerned that the program was out of control. As a result, reforms in 1980 placed a cap on family benefits, and incentives to return to work were developed.

Social Security system: Program of pensions and medical-expense subsidies for families of elderly, disabled, unemployed, and certain other low-income persons, created in the United States in 1935. The original Social Security program had three main subdivisions: old-age pensions, paid as a matter of right to persons qualifying by working in "covered" employment and paying a special earmarked wage tax; a system of UNEMPLOYMENT compensation, to be managed by individual states; and a system of grants to states to help finance means-tested benefits for low-income persons who were elderly, with dependent children, or blind. The first of the three is what most people think of in referring to Social Security.

Old-age Pensions. The 1935 SOCIAL SECURITY ACT imposed a payroll tax, initially of 2 percent, half paid by the worker and half by the employer. Persons paying the tax could become eligible to receive a pension upon retirement at age sixty-five, regardless of whether or not they were poor. Initially the program did not cover agriculture, domestic service, govern-

Ida Fuller, the recipient of the first OASDI payment in 1940, displays a 1950 Social Security "raise." (AP/Wide World Photos)

ment or nonprofit workers, and some small firms. Since then, coverage has expanded to virtually all types of employment and to self-employed persons.

Tax collections began in 1937, while benefit payments did not begin until 1940. This was strongly deflationary and contributed to the economic RECESSION of 1937. As a result, in 1939, the law was revised to speed up the payment of pension benefits. The benefit system was extended to pay additional benefits to a retired pensioner with a dependent spouse or dependent children under sixteen. Should a pensioner die, benefits could also be paid to the surviving spouse and minor children.

The tax and benefit levels were designed to make the system financially self-supporting and, in the early years, to take in more money than was paid out. The inflowing surplus was to be collected in a trust fund, which was invested in treasury securities, with the interest from these being added to the trust fund to cover future payouts. Although the system imitated private insurance in many respects, not all workers paying tax would receive benefits. Most were required to put in ten years of covered employment. Benefits were not proportional to contributions. Low-wage workers received pensions that were a higher proportion of their former wage. Persons continuing to earn wages past age sixty-five would have their pension benefits reduced.

In response to the INFLATION of the 1940's, benefit levels were repeatedly increased. To finance these, there were periodic increases in the payroll tax and also in the maximum amount of wages subject to tax. By 1995, the tax was 7.65 percent on the worker and an equal amount on the employer. Initially, about 60 percent of employed persons were covered, but extensions in 1950 increased coverage to about 90 percent. Persons were permitted to retire as early as age sixty-two with reduced benefits.

As of early 1995, the average Social Security retirement benefit paid to individuals was about seven hundred dollars per month, and to couples, about twelve hundred dollars per month. Retirees aged sixty-five to sixty-nine were permitted to earn about eleven thousand dollars per year from employment without penalty. Beyond that level, each additional three dollars of earnings would reduce pension benefits by one dollar. This offset applied only to wage and salary income, not to income from other pensions and investments. Beyond age seventy, there was no earnings offset. Pension benefits, long exempt from federal INCOME TAX,

became partially taxable beginning in 1983.

In 1956, Congress extended the pension program to cover persons unable to work for reason of disability. The program encountered problems determining whether a person is really unable to work or simply would prefer not to. The pension program is known as Old Age, Survivors, DISABILITY INSURANCE (OASDI).

For many years, politicians were tempted to compete for votes by offering increases in Social Security benefits, a practice that threatened the solvency of the system. To reduce such political pressure and protect retired persons against inflation, legislation in 1972 began the policy of "indexing" benefits. Since 1974, pension benefits have automatically been increased each year in proportion to the increase in the CONSUMER PRICE INDEX.

Medicare. In 1965, Social Security was greatly extended with the creation of the MEDICARE program to subsidize medical expenses of persons receiving Social Security pensions. Medicare benefits were similar to those under private medical insurance: Each beneficiary was free to go to a physician of choice for treatment, with a portion of the resulting bill paid by Social Security. The wage tax was increased to cover some hospital expenses. To cover physicians' fees, an insurance premium was levied on the prospective beneficiaries, who were also required to absorb some costs through deductibles and co-payments. A parallel program called Medicaid made grants to states to subsidize medical care for eligible low-income persons.

These programs greatly increased the consumption of medical services by the elderly, driving up medical costs much more than the cost of living. The government's expenditures increased far more than had been predicted. By the early 1990's, three-fourths of physicians' expenses were paid from general Treasury revenues, while only one-fourth were covered by user charges. By the 1990's, the proportion of elderly persons in the population was rising, as was the life expectancy of elderly persons. Rapidly rising Medicare costs came in for scrutiny as a cause of federal BUDGET DEFICITS. President Bill CLINTON's controversial medical reform proposal of 1994, which was not adopted, claimed to hold costs down and still extend medical insurance coverage to persons who did not have it.

Public Assistance. The SOCIAL SECURITY ACT of 1935 also created a program to provide grants-in-aid to state governments to subsidize their programs of public assistance—that is, "WELFARE" programs paid only to low-income persons. Benefits were limited to the

Senior citizens in Washington, D.C., rally to protect the Social Security system in 1981. (UPI/Corbis-Bettmann)

blind, the elderly, and families with dependent children. The AID TO FAMILIES WITH DEPENDENT CHILDREN (AFDC) program over time became the most controversial part of the "welfare" system. Critics charged that the program discouraged marriage and encouraged child-bearing by unmarried women. By the 1990's, the number of children in POVERTY was rising rapidly, many of them born to young women without the financial, educational, or psychological resources to care for them. AFDC was a major target of proposals for welfare "reform." In 1994, about 4.6 million adults received AFDC payments representing about 9 million children.

The public-assistance elements of Social Security underwent a major change in 1972 with the creation of Supplementary Security Income (SSI). Benefits were contingent on financial need, and the program ab-

sorbed the former programs that covered the blind and elderly. Persons with disabilities were also eligible. As of early 1995, an individual was eligible for SSI only if assets were worth two thousand dollars or less (three thousand dollars for a couple), excluding home, automobile, or other personal property. Maximum monthly benefits were $458 for an individual and $687 for a couple.

Evaluations. As of 1994, more than 47 million Americans were receiving benefits under OASDI and SSI, totaling more than $300 billion per year. Whereas elderly persons had been a disproportionately large part of the poverty-level population in the 1950's, by the 1990's the proportion of elderly in poverty was less than that for other age groups. However, OASDI was criticized as unfair. In the early years, beneficiaries received benefits far exceeding the value of their contributions. This was still true in the 1990's for older beneficiaries (who paid much lower tax rates in earlier years). As long as the number of retired persons was small compared to the number of taxpaying workers, this was not a major problem. By the 1990's, however, the proportion of retirees was growing rapidly. Young working families were under a heavy tax burden to enable the fund to pay its promised benefits, often going to persons enjoying a very comfortable RETIREMENT. Opinion polls revealed that many young adults felt they would not personally benefit from Social Security in their later years. There were pessimistic forecasts that the pension system would no longer be self-supporting early in the twenty-first century.

The wage tax was criticized as bearing heavily on low-income wage earners. Unlike the personal income tax, Social Security TAXES provide no deductions for dependent children. The tax decreases business incentives to hire more workers.

In 1994, federal tax liability was extended to 85 percent of a taxpayer's OASDI benefits. Legislation was on the books to raise the basic retirement age in the future, reflecting the increasing vigor and life expectancy of persons in their sixties. There was also discussion of reducing the annual upward cost-of-living adjustment of benefits.
—*Paul B. Trescott*

SUGGESTED READINGS: Information on current tax and benefit conditions is available in numerous publi-

AVERAGE MONTHLY SOCIAL SECURITY BENEFITS, 1990

Type of Beneficiary	Amount
Retired worker and wife	$1,027
Retired worker	603
Disabled worker	587
Widow or widower, nondisabled	557
Parent	482
Widowed mother	409
Child of deceased worker	406
Wife or husband	298
Child of retired worker	259
Special benefits	167
Child of disabled worker	164

Source: U.S. Bureau of the Census, *Statistical Abstract of the United States: 1992.* Washington, D.C.: U.S. Government Printing Office, 1992.

cations of the Social Security Administration. A comprehensive study is Robert J. Myers' *Social Security,* 4th ed. (Philadelphia: University of Pennsylvania Press, 1993), which deals extensively with Medicare and public assistance as well as OASDI. Economic issues are stressed in editors Zvi Bodie and Alicia H. Munnell's *Pensions and the Economy* (Philadelphia: University of Pennsylvania Press, 1992), and editor Jack L. VanDerhei's *Search for a National Retirement Income Policy* (Homewood, Ill.: Irwin, 1987).

Socialism: Economic philosophy. Socialism is the opposite of INDIVIDUALISM. The basic question of social theory is who should control and make decisions about the important things: ECONOMICS, reproduction, ART and intellectual issues, and politics. The central thrust of socialism is that control and decision making should be collective and public, while the central thrust of individualism is that control and decision making should be individual and private.

For example, economic policy is a matter of deciding how many and what kinds of goods should be produced and traded at what price. Individualists argue that individual producers and consumers should control and decide what to do with their private resources and that, accordingly, the free-market mechanism of SUPPLY AND DEMAND will allocate resources and set prices. Socialists argue that resources should be controlled publicly and that public institutions should make production and consumption decisions for society as a whole.

Arguments for socialism range from the economic to the moral. Some socialists argue that a complex economy requires central direction; without such central direction, they say, the economy would suffer dislocations as a result of uncoordinated individual decisions. Other socialists argue that if all property is private, there will not be enough to go around, and this will unfairly limit the opportunities of those without property. Some socialists argue that private property leads to inequalities, since some people end up with much more than others, inevitably causing social conflicts between the haves and the have-nots. Other socialists argue that society as a whole has an obligation to provide the essentials of life to those unable to acquire them by their own efforts; since there is no guarantee that in a free market there will be enough charity, they conclude, the government must control society's economic resources to ensure that this is done. Other socialists argue that the free market institutionalizes self-interest and the profit motive and that these are immoral; accordingly, the government should eliminate private property, private property being the institution that encourages self-interested and profit-seeking decision making.

By contrast, individualists argue that only a free market's price mechanism is capable of coordinating the knowledge of individuals' needs and wants efficiently. They argue further that free-market economies are always innovating and creating new opportunities, so there are always opportunities for those seeking them. Individualists agree that free markets lead to inequalities but hold that inequalities are just if they are earned by voluntary production and trade. Some individualists also argue that without the profit motive, individuals will lack the incentive to produce goods of sufficient quality and quantity to maintain a healthy economy. Others argue that self-interest is a moral motive: They argue that individuals are ends in themselves and should be left free rather than be expected to subordinate themselves to the interests of others. Accordingly, the central issues of debate between socialists and individualists are whether governments or free markets are better able to satisfy human economic needs and wants and whether the collective interests of society or the interests of individuals are morally primary.

Society for the Prevention of Cruelty to Children

(SPCC): Organization formed in 1865 to fight child abuse. After two sensational cases of neglect in the nineteenth century, a New York social worker approached the Society for the Prevention of Cruelty to Animals and asked the organization to prosecute the parents of a neglected girl on the grounds that she was a cruelly treated human animal. The prosecution was successful; afterward, the SPCC was formed to be an advocate for laws to protect children from several forms of abuse, including parental abuse.

Software:

Generic term for computer programs, as opposed to tangible computer equipment or hardware. Programs written for general users, often those without extensive training in computers, are called "end-user" applications; programs that control computers themselves are termed "operating systems." Programming languages are a class of software that enables users to write their own programs for specific applications. Because computers must be able to read and copy information easily, the greatest problem facing software developers is piracy, the unauthorized copying of programs. Licensing and auditing agreements are often employed in an attempt to counteract piracy.

Somali civil war:

In 1992, civil war between several clan-based political factions in Somalia on the Horn of Africa led to widespread famine and the impending deaths of several hundred thousand people. The administration of President George BUSH persuaded the UNITED NATIONS to authorize an intervention led by the United States to restore order in the country and allow the delivery of famine-relief food.

Modern Somalia became an independent nation in 1960, unifying the former colonies of Italian Somaliland in the South and British Somaliland in the North. Somali-speaking peoples also live in the former French colony of Djibouti, in the Ogaden region of Ethiopia, and in the former British colony of Kenya. From the first, the nation of Somalia sought to reunite all Somalis in a greater Somalia. While the United States supported the regime of Haile Selassie in Ethiopia, Somalia, under the leadership of Siyaad Barre, received large amounts of arms from the Soviet Union. After the Ethiopian revolution in 1975, Somalia received aid from the United States and invaded Ethiopia, only to be defeated.

Somalis, although linguistically and ethnically one people, are divided into many clans. Barre stayed in power by playing clans against one another. By 1992, several factions had arisen, each based on a different clan alliance, and Barre was driven from the country. As fighting continued, disrupting agriculture in a generally arid country, famine loomed.

Bush arranged for the United Nations to intervene to ensure delivery of relief supplies in January, 1993. The U.N. forces included troops from the United States, Canada, and several other countries. The force, in theory neutral in the struggles among the factions, quickly chose sides, especially after Muhammad Farah Aydid's Somali National Army attacked a U.N. position and killed twenty-four Pakistani soldiers in June, 1993. Failed efforts to capture Aydid eventually resulted in ten thousand Somali casualties and the deaths of eighteen Americans in a gun battle on October 3, 1993. Shortly thereafter, President Bill CLINTON announced that the United States would withdraw its forces from

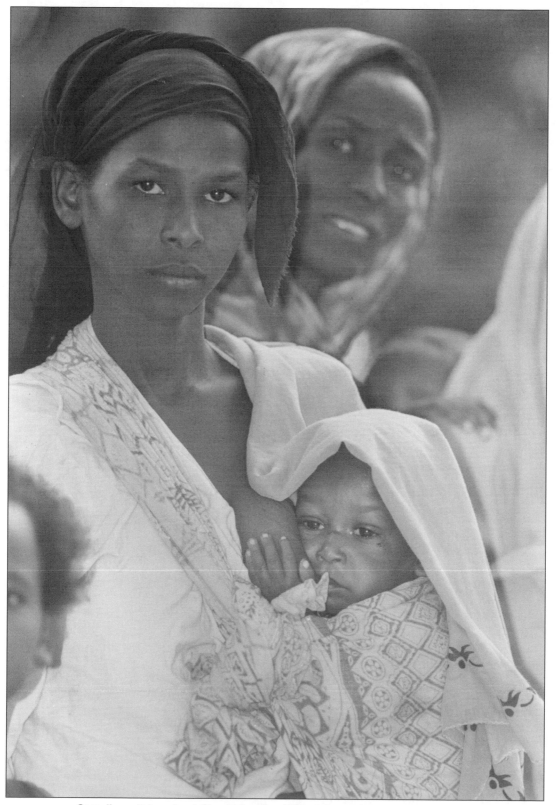

Somalis wait in a food line during the 1992 civil war. (UPI/Corbis-Bettmann)

David Souter addresses reporters following President George Bush's announcement of Souter's nomination to the Supreme Court. (AP/Wide World Photos)

U.N. operation in Somalia in March, 1994, and by the spring of 1995, all U.N. forces had withdrawn.

The failure to promote a peaceful settlement in Somalia raised several grave points about PEACEKEEPING operations. First, peacemaking, the suppression of conflict, is much more difficult and costly, as the crisis in Bosnia also showed, than peacekeeping, where the combatants want peace but need a buffer for security. Second, cases such as the beating death of a sixteen-year-old Somali by Canadian troops in March, 1993, along with several others, showed that outside intervention in a civil conflict could easily lead to an "us against them" mentality that sees all members of the local population as potential enemies to the intervening forces. Third, although Somalia has been more peaceful and famine has not returned since the intervention, building a nation might be an impossible task for an outside force. The Northern region of Somalia, where there were few U.N. forces, remained peaceful and began to construct a civil society from the grass roots during the crisis. The contrast with the South led Northern leaders to attempt to form an independent country.

Sororities. *See* **Fraternities and sororities**

Souter, David (b. September 17, 1939, Melrose, Mass.): U.S. SUPREME COURT justice. Souter was graduated from Harvard University in 1961 and attended Magdalen College in Oxford, England, the following year as a Rhodes Scholar. He was graduated from Harvard Law School in 1966. After graduation, Souter served as deputy attorney general in the state of New Hampshire and later as a justice on the New Hampshire Supreme Court. In 1990, he was named a justice on the U.S. Court of Appeals for the First Circuit. In July, 1990, President George BUSH nominated Souter to the Supreme Court, and he was confirmed by the Senate; he subsequently aligned himself with the Court's conservative block.

Southern Christian Leadership Conference (SCLC): Organization founded in Atlanta, Georgia, in 1957 to promote racial equality through NONVIOLENT RESISTANCE to segregation.

The formation of the SCLC grew out of the boycott of Montgomery, Alabama, city buses, which had been organized by the black community between December 1955 and February 1957. The Reverend Martin Luther KING, Jr., a young minister, led the boycott movement. He felt that efforts to fight SEGREGATION throughout the American South must be unified and organized. Preliminary organizing began in January of 1957, when he called a meeting of civil rights leaders in Atlanta, Georgia.

The organization called itself the Southern Christian Leadership Conference, reflecting its composition of primarily black ministers and its commitment to principles of Christian nonviolence. King based his philosophy of nonviolent resistance on the teachings of Mahatma Gandhi, who had used those principles in the fight for India's independence from Great Britain after World War II. The philosophy advocated refusal to cooperate with unjust laws, but maintained a strict refusal to be drawn into any violent confrontation.

The SCLC's first major campaigns involved voter registration efforts throughout the south. Its leaders met with President Dwight D. Eisenhower in 1958 to urge the passage of federal CIVIL RIGHTS LEGISLATION. The organization also sponsored SIT-INS to desegregate restaurants and lunch counters in 1960, and FREEDOM RIDES to desegregate bus stations in 1961.

In August of 1963, the SCLC was one of the organizers of the MARCH ON WASHINGTON in support of federal civil rights legislation. A crowd of 250,000 people gathered to hear King deliver his now-famous "I Have a Dream" speech. In 1964, King was awarded the NOBEL PEACE PRIZE for his efforts; the SCLC was one of the recipients of the prize money. Largely as a result of the efforts of the SCLC, Congress passed the CIVIL RIGHTS ACT OF 1964 and the VOTING RIGHTS ACT in 1965.

In 1965, the organization expanded its areas of concern with a call for negotiations to end the war in Vietnam. In 1966, the SCLC began organizing branches in northern cities and putting greater efforts into voter registration in such cities as Chicago, Illinois, and Cleveland, Ohio. Partly as a result of their efforts, Carl Stokes became the first black mayor of a major U.S. city when he was elected mayor of Cleveland in 1967. In 1968, the SCLC was involved in organizing the Poor People's March on Washington, in which three thousand people camped out on the Mall in Washington, D.C., from May 12 to June 24. At its peak in the mid-1960's, the SCLC had a full-time staff of 150 and an annual budget of more than $1 million.

When King was assassinated in April of 1968, the

Southern Christian Leadership Conference members march in a 1987 Virginia demonstration. (UPI/Corbis-Bettmann)

SCLC lost its most dynamic leader and had a resulting decline in membership and effectiveness. In addition, many militant young blacks left the organization because they were disillusioned with the concept of nonviolence in the wake of the assassinations and riots of the late 1960's. The Reverend Ralph Abernathy, a close King associate, led the organization from 1968 to 1977. Since then, its influence has continued to decline, and it has been overshadowed by other civil rights organizations.

Soviet Union, dissolution of: 1991 breakup of one of the world's two superpowers as a result of internal pressures and independence movements in its constituent republics.

Background. In 1917, the Russian Empire was overthrown as a result of two revolutions. The Bolshevik (Communist) government led by Vladimir Ilich Lenin controlled Russia first, then spread control to neigh-

boring states such as Ukraine, Belorussia, Georgia, and Armenia, which had been part of the Russian Empire; the process led to creation of the Soviet Union in 1922. By the end of World War II, the Soviet Union had gradually expanded its borders, reconstituting the area of the former Russian Empire through revolution and war.

Despite propaganda about the unity of the Soviet people, the multinational Soviet Union was anything but one people. Through the resettlement of populations, Russians, for example, the largest national group in the Soviet Union, could be found in every republic. Some peoples were forcibly resettled to other regions. Russian was the official language of the Soviet Union, but each national group could, within limits, maintain its own language and culture. During the rule of Joseph Stalin (1924-1953), the state maintained firm control over all the republics. According to the Soviet constitution, a republic could secede from the union, but this right existed only on paper. In the post-Stalin era, grad-

Moscow demonstrators pull down a statue of KGB founder Felix Dzerzhinsky in the wake of the failed hardliner coup of August, 1991. (Reuters/Corbis-Bettmann)

ual liberalization gave rise to more local and regional autonomy and a revival of some national cultures.

During the administration of Mikhail GORBACHEV (1985-1991), greater political liberty fueled latent nationalist sentiments, and various republics organized independence movements, especially the Baltic states and Moldavia. National conflicts had not been erased, as evidenced by the war that began in 1988 between Armenia and Azerbaidjan over possession of an Armenian enclave within Azerbaidjan. Gorbachev tried to quiet nationalist sentiments, initially by promising a looser union and later by offering to develop a constitutional procedure for withdrawal.

Talk had little effect, however, and nationalist uprisings were forcibly put down in Georgia in 1989 and in the Baltic in 1991. As pressures mounted, a new republic treaty was negotiated in 1991 to give greater autonomy to the fifteen republics. It was scheduled to be signed in August, 1991, but a few days before the republics convened, a coup against Gorbachev was engineered by a group of top leaders who wanted to curtail reform. Gorbachev was forcibly held captive at his vacation home.

Boris YELTSIN, the president of the Russian Republic, led the opposition to the coup, assisted by countless citizens and by support from Western countries via telephone and fax. Gorbachev was rescued, but his power was significantly diminished. A number of Communist Party and governmental leaders were implicated in the coup. The Supreme Soviet (the parliament), which had elected Gorbachev president, was dissolved. Gorbachev resigned as general secretary of the Communist Party of the Soviet Union, and the Party itself, at Yeltsin's initiative, was abolished in Russia, effectively ending its hegemony at the center of power.

Gorbachev remained the titular president, but as the fall progressed, the republics refused to acknowledge the authority of the central government. Russia, in particular, began to absorb some of the functions of the Soviet state. In early December, the presidents of Belarus, Russia, and Ukraine formed the COMMONWEALTH OF INDEPENDENT STATES (CIS), which eight other republics joined shortly afterward. CIS leaders indicated they would no longer recognize the Soviet Union as of January 1, 1992. On December 25, Gorbachev resigned as president, and on January 1, 1992, there was no more Soviet Union.

The dissolution was rapid and relatively peaceful. The ramifications of the breakup of the Soviet Union were not fully comprehended in the hectic fall of 1991. The newly independent republics had to cope with complexities of the rapid severance from the highly centralized Soviet Union. Years of interdependence and commingled economies made a separate existence difficult, and strife continued within and between the former Soviet republics.

On the world scene, the breakup of the Soviet empire precipitated the end of the COLD WAR and led to a radical change in East-West relations. Although the fall of the repressive Soviet regime was broadly applauded around the world, the civil strife and economic woes that beset the former republics in the wake of the collapse concerned many Western observers, who worried that the vast military and scientific resources of the Soviet empire might fall into the hands of terrorists or military adventurers. Debate thus raged in Western circles over how best to deal with the former adversary, with most Western nations, including the United States, opting for a policy of constructive engagement meant to encourage the development of democratic regimes and capitalist freedoms in the former Soviet states.   —*Norma Corigliano Noonan*

SUGGESTED READINGS: The last years of the Soviet Union are addressed in John B. Dunlop's *The Rise of Russia and the Fall of the Soviet Empire* (Princeton, N.J.: Princeton University Press, 1993) and Philip G. Roeder's *Red Sunset: The Failure of Soviet Politics* (Princeton, N.J.: Princeton University Press, 1993).

Space debris: Material abandoned in Earth orbit as a result of human space activity. Space debris includes SATELLITES that are no longer operational, discarded fuel tanks and protective panels, and tools lost during spacewalks. At any given time, several thousand such objects larger than a few centimeters can be tracked orbiting the Earth. Microscopic objects, including paint chips and particles given off by rocket exhaust may number in the trillions. Most large orbiting objects vaporize on re-entry and pose little hazard to the Earth's surface. Small debris particles have caused damage to spacecraft, but the worst effect of space debris is contamination of the near-Earth environment, compromising observations made in space.

Space exploration: The investigation of the universe beyond Earth's atmosphere by means of manned and unmanned spacecraft. The observation of Earth from orbiting SATELLITES and the exploration of the solar system by robotic and human explorers has furthered scientific understanding of the earth, increased international communications and understanding, provided the foundations for possible settlement of the Moon and Mars in the twenty-first century, and given a better insight into the origins of the solar system.

The "space age" began with the launching of the world's first Earth-orbiting satellite, Sputnik I, by the Soviet Union on October 4, 1957. The launching of the United States' first satellite, Explorer I, by the U.S. Army's Redstone Arsenal followed on January 31, 1958. Explorer I, in the first significant scientific discovery of the space age, detected the Van Allen radiation belts, two huge, doughnut-shaped rings of charged particles circling Earth. These regions of intense radiation can cause harm to unshielded electronics in satellites circling at their altitudes and could harm astronauts orbiting at those heights.

The military in both the United States and the Soviet Union quickly recognized the importance of earth-orbiting satellites as spy platforms. Satellites designed for photographic surveillance and communications monitoring were quickly designed and launched. They replaced high-flying aircraft, such as the U-2, which flew near or over the territory of potential enemies at the risk of being shot down and provoking an international incident. The spy satellites provided a measure of security for both countries, contributing to a decrease in COLD WAR tension, since each country could observe the military preparations of the other and be assured that a sneak attack was not coming.

The role of military surveillance satellites expanded with the development of many special purpose satellites. The Soviets launched a series of Radar Ocean Reconnaissance Satellites that used high-power radar to track ships at sea. The United States launched the Vela satellites, which detected the bright flash of light from an above-ground nuclear detonation. Vela satellites, and their equivalents launched by the Soviets, provided the verification needed to allow the United States and the Soviet Union to enter into agreements banning atmospheric nuclear tests and have the assurance that the other side would not cheat.

Civilian applications for Earth-orbiting satellites, taking advantage of their regional and global surveillance capabilities, followed from these military developments. In the United States, the NATIONAL AERONAUTICS AND SPACE ADMINISTRATION (NASA) was established in 1958 to direct the civilian space program. NASA initiated projects to develop satellites for weather monitoring, global resource mapping, and communications relay.

Weather satellites continuously monitor weather patterns around the world, providing such advantages as the advance warning required for evacuation of populated areas threatened by hurricanes. Earth resources satellites have mapped geological formations indicative of underground oil deposits; located tin, nickel, and copper mines; monitored farmland to predict annual crop yields; detected illegal diversions of irrigation water; and assisted archaeologists in their search for remnants of ancient civilizations. Other satellites continuously monitor the planet for the radio signals of Emergency Locator Transmitters, carried by civilian aircraft and activated automatically in a crash, to determine the location of the downed aircraft and alert search and rescue forces. Satellites of the Global Positioning System transmit radio signals to hand-held receivers allowing the positions of boats, airplanes, land survey markers, and explorers to be determined to an accuracy of a few feet.

Communications satellites have produced the most direct impact on the daily lives of the people of Earth. These satellites provide instantaneous communication around the world by radio, television, and telephone. Live news transmissions from the scenes of demonstrations are credited by some observers with inhibiting repressive governments from taking military action against their citizens. People in remote areas now have access to medical advice, government broadcasts, and entertainment transmitted to their homes or villages by communications satellites.

Astronomical satellites, including NASA's HUBBLE SPACE TELESCOPE, have surveyed the solar system, the galaxy, and the universe, providing astronomers with new insights about the hazards to Earth of comets and asteroids, the origin of our solar system, and the age of the universe.

The Moon and the planets have been examined by robot explorers. U.S. Surveyor spacecraft and the Soviet Luna spacecraft landed on the Moon and returned with scientific data. Two U.S. Viking spacecraft landed on Mars in 1976, and the Soviet Venera spacecraft landed on Venus. Mercury, Jupiter, Saturn, Uranus, and Neptune have been explored by Mariner, Pioneer, and Voyager spacecrafts, which obtained scientific data and photographs during flybys of these planets. These missions have produced scientific results allowing preliminary assessment of the resources available on these planets. The study of cratering on the Moon, Mercury, and Mars indicated to scientists that objects that could pose hazards to Earth still strike solar system objects, and this was demonstrated graphically in the summer of 1994 when Comet Shoemaker-Levy 9, estimated to have been several kilometers in size, was photographed impacting Jupiter.

The era of human exploration of space began on April 12, 1961, when the Soviet Union launched the first cosmonaut, Yuri Gagarin, on a ninety-minute flight making one orbit around Earth. The United States followed with the launching of astronaut Alan Shepard on a fifteen-minute rocket flight over the Atlantic Ocean on May 5, 1961. With the successful landing of two Apollo 11 astronauts, Neil Armstrong and Edwin Aldrin, on the Moon on July 20, 1969, the exploration of other objects of the solar system by humans began.

The Apollo landing on the Moon was a first step in meeting twenty-first century goals established by the National Commission on Space, established by President Ronald REAGAN, of initiating "the settlement of worlds beyond our planet of birth [freeing] humankind to move outward from earth as a species destined to expand to other worlds." On July 20, 1989, the twentieth anniversary of the Apollo 11 landing on the Moon, President George BUSH announced as two goals of the U.S. space program a return of humans to the Moon, this time to stay, and the human exploration of Mars. Such settlements were expected to provide the same opportunities for economic expansion in the twenty-first century as the development of North America did over the past five centuries.

During the Cold War era, space exploration served an important political objective, demonstrating a nation's technological capability to the rest of the world. Historians generally agree that the major objective of the Apollo project was to enhance the international prestige of the United States.

In the 1990's, the political objective of space exploration changed, with the United States undertaking cooperative missions with the Soviets principally to provide employment for Russian space engineers. This was expected to minimize the possibility that those engineers would be hired to develop weapons systems by nations regarded as potential adversaries.

The exploration of space evolved into two distinct programs, one focused on human exploration and the second using unmanned, robotic spacecraft. Each has produced significant results. The ingenuity of humans provides flexibility on space missions threatened by unanticipated events. For example, the Apollo 13 astronauts, flying a spacecraft crippled by an explosion, were able to return safely to Earth by improvising substitutes for various spacecraft systems. In addition, humans have demonstrated the capability of repairing malfunctioning spacecraft, including the HUBBLE SPACE TELESCOPE, at a lesser cost than the launching of a replacement. Robotic spacecraft serve as pathfinders, returning preliminary information about the Moon and other planets prior to human exploration missions. These robots can be sent on one-way trips, returning information by radio, and on high-risk missions, since human life is not at risk. In an era of budget pressure, however, human and robotic spacecraft competed for the same pool of available resources, provoking discussion of which program provides the most return for the dollar.

Critics of the space program have charged that the money spent on space exploration could be better spent on problems "here at home." Officials of the space program are quick to point out, however, that the money is spent at home—employing engineers, scientists, factory workers, and office staff. In addition, they point out that space exploration has fostered the development of new technologies that result in consumer products, biomedical monitoring devices, and smaller, faster computer systems providing for growth in the domestic economy. The National Commission on Space observed that "historically, wealth has been created when the power of the human intellect combined abundant energy and rich material resources. Now America can create new wealth on the space frontier to benefit the entire human community by combining the energy of the Sun with materials left in space during the formation of the Solar System." The Commission sees a vigorous program of space exploration as a key to economic prosperity in the twenty-first century.

—George J. Flynn

SUGGESTED READINGS: Bruce Murray's *Journey into Space: The First Three Decades of Space Exploration* (New York: W. W. Norton, 1989) provides an account, by the director of NASA's Jet Propulsion Laboratory, of the accomplishments of unmanned planetary probes. Thomas R. McDonough's *Space: The Next Twenty-Five Years* (New York: John Wiley & Sons, 1989) describes U.S. space exploration from the formation of NASA through the space shuttle. Richard Lewis' *Space in the Twenty-first Century* (New York: Columbia University Press, 1990) and the National

The space shuttle *Discovery* is carried aloft atop a NASA 747. (Archive Photos, Reuters, NASA)

Commission on Space's *Pioneering the Space Frontier* (New York: Bantam Books, 1986) put space exploration in a historical context and set forth goals for the twenty-first century.

Space shuttle program: NATIONAL AERONAUTICS AND SPACE ADMINISTRATION (NASA) project that developed the first reusable manned orbital spacecraft. Hopes that the program would make space travel cheaper and easier were dashed by high development costs, long development time, high operating costs, and slow launch rate. Reliance on the space shuttle caused the United States to cease building conventional launchers for a time; as a result, when the space shuttle CHALLENGER exploded in 1986, causing a two-year hiatus in the program, the U.S. space program lost almost all of its launch capability. Critics of the program argue that manned space tasks can usually be performed by robotic spacecraft with greater safety and at less expense.

Special Olympics: Athletic tournaments for disabled persons who are excluded from other such competitions because of their physical or mental limitations. Founded in 1963 by Eunice Kennedy Shriver, the competitions were originally aimed primarily at the mentally disabled. The events, held year-round in the United States, Canada, and several other nations, have an annual operating cost of approximately $40 million. Events are held for participants age eight and above, ranging throughout almost all levels of athletic skills.

Sperm and egg donation: The need for donated sperm and eggs (gametes) was recognized when an increasing number of infertile people sought ways to become parents and advances in reproductive technology made the use of donated gametes feasible.

The use of donated gametes to achieve conception has been controversial. Unanticipated social and medical consequences have raised several perplexing questions related to the legal and moral status of human reproductive products and the rights and responsibilities of donors, recipients, and resulting children.

The proliferation of new procedures and the issues they raise are widely debated among ethicists, attorneys, medical personnel, and theologians. Such procedures include ARTIFICIAL INSEMINATION by donor sperm (AID), *IN VITRO* FERTILIZATION (IVF), in which gametes are fertilized outside of women's bodies, and SURROGATE motherhood, the gestation of a child by a woman for someone else after being inseminated *in vivo* (in the body) or through IVF. These procedures

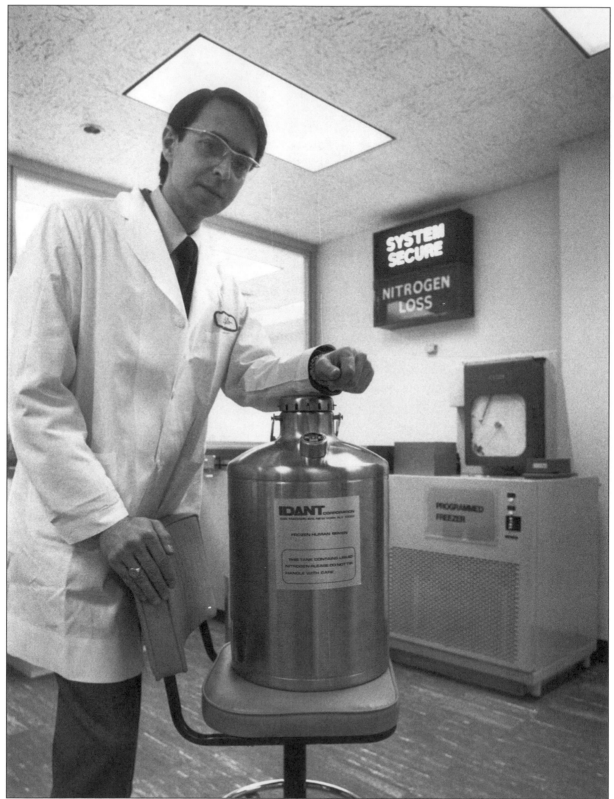

The president of a chain of sperm banks poses with a container of frozen sperm. (UPI/Corbis-Bettmann)

have greatly increased the number of procreative options available to infertile couples.

Cryopreservation, the ability to freeze and store sperm and embryos, has created additional choices for achieving parenthood, with great flexibility regarding the timing of planned pregnancies, the age of the mother, and the use of gametes from deceased donors.

Egg donation is less common than is sperm donation because the current methods of egg retrieval carry physical risks, there is a continuing shortage, and there is a need to undergo repeated attempts because of low success rates. In addition, eggs alone cannot survive freezing.

People who have attempted to use donated gametes and frozen embryos have been involved in cases that focused on issues such as whether frozen embryos are property and, if so, who has the right to claim ownership, how to dispose of excess embryos, how to regulate sperm banks, and whether anonymous donors should have legal obligations to their resultant offspring.

Transracial sperm and egg donation has raised socio-cultural questions about motivation and outcome, and commercialization is a troubling social issue as the practice of selling donor eggs, sperm, and embryos is contemplated.

"Embryo kidnapping" has been charged in cases in which a couple's frozen embryos were allegedly given to another couple without the knowledge or consent of the first couple. The artificial inseminations of fifty-nine and sixty-one-year-old women have raised questions about whether age limits should be set for motherhood. In another case, a doctor was convicted of inseminating more than seventy women with his sperm when they believed that they were receiving the sperm of anonymous donors.

The retrieval of sperm from dead men and eggs from dead women has created the possibility of a child being born having parents who were both dead at the time of his or her conception. The ability of persons sentenced to death to donate gametes has been debated from legal, civil rights, and ethical perspectives.

Spielberg, Steven (b. Dec. 18, 1947, Cincinnati, Ohio): Film director and producer. Spielberg has directed many of the highest-grossing motion pictures in

Steven Spielberg in 1987. (UPI/Bettmann)

history. His versatility as a director is apparent in the variety of projects he has undertaken, including the 1982 science fiction drama *E.T.*, the Indiana Jones adventure trilogy, and the acclaimed historical drama *Schindler's List* (1993), for which he received an Academy Award as best director. Other Spielberg films include *Jaws* (1975), *Close Encounters of the Third Kind* (1977) (which he also produced), and *The Color Purple* (1985) (based on the Alice Walker novel of the same name).

Spiritual health: Dimension of well-being composed of inner experiences related to God, self, community, and the environment. Efforts to attain spiritual health can include both traditional actions such as prayer and meditation and less traditional processes such as reading and listening to music. Though many researchers have not given it serious attention, believers claim that a high level of spiritual health transcends the individual, enabling one to have a greater concern for others while seeing oneself as part of a greater experience.

Sports, amateur: Defining an "amateur" athlete has always been a difficult task. At first glance, the person who plays for fun is an amateur, and the one who plays for pay is a professional; however, the line between these two concepts is not always a clear one. The university football player whose tuition is waived is considered an amateur, while many professional athletes have fun at what they do. Therefore, in order to understand amateurism, one must look at the concept's original meaning and evolution.

The term "amateur" was originally intended as a means of separating the social classes. Amateurs were "gentlemen"; professionals came from the lower socioeconomic classes. Because they could receive no payment for their skills, amateurs needed to be wealthy in order to pursue a sport extensively. Sometimes a competitor's motivation was used as a means of distinguishing the amateur from the professional. The word "amateur," derived from the Latin word for love, *amor*, referred to competitors who played for the good feeling derived from participation. Amateurs were expected to play for the pleasure derived from sport. Winning was important, but not as important as the intrinsic rewards. The professional, on the other hand, took competition and winning seriously, as participa-

tion was considered to be the professional's work.

Amateurism no longer carries the connotations of class distinction, but modern interpretations of the concept differ. Nowhere is this more apparent than in the Olympic Games, long the foremost bastion of amateurism. Most Olympic athletes train at least as diligently as most professionals. In addition, many countries provide monetary support for their Olympic aspirants, although these athletes are still classified as amateurs.

The Olympics were revived by Baron Pierre de Coubertin in 1896. Coubertin's intent was to increase athletic interest among French youth and to provide a substitute for war between nations. The International Olympic Committee (IOC), formed to govern the games, decided that the games should be free from governmental influence as a means of guaranteeing exclusively amateur participation. As those belonging to the IOC were all upper-class sportsmen, "amateur" was defined based on their standards. Ultimately, however, the realities of world politics changed the definition.

Intercollegiate sport has also stretched the original definition of amateurism. Winning and moneymaking are primary objectives of most collegiate athletic programs, and such goals are largely incompatible with the principles of amateurism. So that colleges can meet these goals, many athletes are given tuition waivers and other financial assistance to play for their schools. While many consider such indirect payments to constitute professionalism, the National Collegiate Athletic Association (NCAA) considers athletes to be amateurs so long as they and their schools abide by NCAA rules. Critics charge that these rules exploit student-athletes, enabling the schools and their coaches to make substantial amounts of money that the athletes are forbidden to share.

Sports, college: Organized athletic activities sponsored by colleges and universities. Intercollegiate sports teams compete as independents or as part of a conference organization. Recruiting violations, the exploitation of athletes, admissions standards, and gender equity represent a few major concerns facing college sports.

History. In 1852, the first college sports competition in the United States was a rowing event between Harvard and Yale. Rutgers and Princeton played the first college football game in 1869. The first college athletic conference was formed in 1895. The need for an organization to establish rules and regulations and to

Legendary athlete Jim Thorpe was stripped of his 1912 Olympic medals because of questions regarding his amateur status. (AP/Wide World Photos)

address problems in college athletics was evident by 1905; the Intercollegiate Athletic Association began operation in that year. The name of this regulatory group was changed to the National Collegiate Athletic Association (NCAA) in 1910.

Structure of College Sports. Intercollegiate athletic programs, sponsored by four-year colleges and universities, are largely regulated by the NCAA, the largest and most powerful organization in college sports. Small-college athletic programs are overseen by the National Association of Intercollegiate Athletics (NAIA). The College Football Association (CFA) is a voluntary association promoting the interests of "big-time" football programs.

The NCAA has more than eight hundred members and more than two hundred affiliated conferences. Four major categories, each reflecting a different level of competition, are available within the NCAA. Division I, which represents the highest level of athletic competition, is subdivided into Division I-A and Division I-AA for football. Division I-A is the highest level of football competition, and offers the largest number of scholarships of any division; approximately 280 institutions are classified in the Division I category. Each school is required to field teams in seven sports to qualify for membership in this classification level.

Football, men's basketball, women's basketball, and baseball are the most visible college sports and receive the most media coverage. College football and college basketball (both men's and women's) are most likely to serve as revenue-producing sports. In 1994, more than 36 million fans attended college football games; revenue from bowl games exceeded 60 million dollars. In the mid-1990's, one television network paid the NCAA $143 million for the television rights to the men's basketball tournament.

Problems, Dilemmas, and Controversies. According to many observers, the growth of college sports has lead to an overemphasis on winning, both on the field and financially. Critics argue that these aspects of intercollegiate athletics have corrupted the goals and ideals of higher education. Proponents counter that college sports promote school unity, generate financial support from alumni and boosters, and serve an important public-relations function. Abuses are infrequent, defenders claim, and the benefits of sports to higher education institutions far outweigh occasional problems.

The potential exploitation of college athletes has emerged as a new problem in higher education. Universities often earn large sums of money from their athletic programs. Businesses may also earn considerable sums of money from selling university-authorized products such as sweatshirts and hats. Athletic administrators, coaches, and support personnel earn their living from college sports. Yet the principal laborers—college athletes—receive no direct compensation and are considered amateurs. College athletes can receive full scholarships for room, board, and tuition, but according to NCAA rules, athletes may not receive additional compensation or work during the season. Many observers argue that an athletic scholarship is nothing more than a work contract and that such scholarships represent a unique form of economic exploitation. Athletes represent their institutions in competitions with some risk of injury, producing public recognition and monetary gain for their schools. The athletic scholarship for this level of activity and risk could be considered the equivalent of a wage below the poverty level. According to this argument, college sports programs operate like a corporation, keeping overhead low (in the form of scholarships) in order to make money for the school. In contrast, proponents of the continued amateur status of athletes argue that the current system encourages academic success among athletes by encouraging them to finish college.

The relationship of college sports to professional sports is an additional area of controversy. Professional sports teams, especially in football, basketball, and baseball, rely on college programs to develop young players, who in turn may have the opportunity to earn substantial incomes in professional athletics. To the extent that colleges serve as "farm clubs" for professional teams, critics say, schools should receive compensation from professional teams. Other scholars of college athletics argue that treating college teams as professional farm teams would erode fan support and cause athletes to be seen as employees of colleges. In turn, scholarships might be considered taxable income, and contributions by athletic boosters could be reduced.

The recruiting process represents an additional controversial issue in college sports. Representatives of athletic programs have utilized numerous illegal recruiting practices (such as providing gifts or money to athletes), altered school transcripts, arranged credit for classes never attended, and helped recruits cheat on admissions tests. The NCAA has addressed problems in the recruitment process, but abuses have continued.

Gender equity has emerged as the most controversial social issue surrounding college sports in the 1990's. Title IX, a key provision of the federal Educational

College sports have become big business, leading some observers to call for payment of student athletes. (Impact Visuals/Robert Fox)

Amendments Act of 1972, required schools that receive federal funds to provide equal opportunities for males and females in all educational programs. Athletic programs at the college level were greatly affected by this legislation, and the number of women's sports programs has grown substantially since 1972. Enforcement of Title IX, which mandated gender equity in high-school and college sports, was delayed for several years. In February, 1984, the U.S. Supreme Court ruled in the case of *Grove City College v. Bell* that Title IX was applicable only to a specific educational program that receives federal funds. The outcome of this case was that gender equity in athletics was no longer enforced under Title IX; federal agencies suspended more than thirty investigations involving gender equity in college sports as a result of the ruling.

In the next four years after the decision, a number of women's groups successfully lobbied for passage of the Civil Rights Restoration Act, which was passed in March, 1988. This law again mandated equality of opportunity in all educational programs receiving federal funds. The net effect of the law on athletics was to restore the concern for gender equity originally contained in Title IV. The emphasis on gender equity, with its focus on equal facilities, equal opportunities, and equal-valued scholarships in athletic programs, has reduced gender discrimination in college sports. Many major universities, however, continue to express concern about achieving full gender equity, largely because of the large size and high cost of college football programs. Some observers thus predict a move by major college sports programs to lobby for the exclusion of college football from gender-equity guidelines.

—*J. B. Watson, Jr.*

SUGGESTED READINGS: Problems in college football and recommendations for reform are explored in Rick

Sports, professional

Telander's *The Hundred Yard Lie: The Corruption of College Football and What We Can Do to Stop It* (New York: Simon & Schuster, 1989). Murray Sperber focuses on economic problems and the potential for exploitation in "big-time" college sports programs in *College Sports Inc.: The Athletic Department vs. the University* (New York: Henry Holt, 1990). An overview of problems in college sports and the social forces contributing to these problems is provided by Stanley Eitzen and George Sage in *Sociology of North American Sport* (Dubuque: Iowa: William C. Brown, 1993).

Sports, professional: The distinction between an amateur and a professional athlete was fashioned in the nineteenth century. The professional received money or other compensation for playing a sport; the amateur did not. By the late twentieth century, professional sports had become a major industry replete with its own bureaucracies and its own press; its participants, including players, team owners, labor negotiators, and officials, were at the center of many highly public controversies.

History. Professionalism came at various times to various sports. Boxing, or "prizefighting," had professional participants at least as far back as the eighteenth century; the concept of professionalism is also native to certain other individual sports such horse and dog racing, in which competition for monetary awards is a principal objective. Yet the growth of the professional sports industry is most closely tied to the rise of organized team sports and their necessary adjuncts, leagues; this process began in the latter nineteenth century with the rise of professional baseball and continued throughout the twentieth century, as new sports came to attain the broad acceptance and generate the financial interest necessary to sustain professional structures.

In 1869, baseball became the first sport to introduce a professional team, the Cincinnati Red Stockings; seven years later, the National League, the first professional league to achieve lasting success, was formed. The establishment of the American League in 1901 was followed by an alliance between the two "major" leagues, which were distinguished from numerous "minor" leagues by their generally higher levels of play and by the location of their franchises in generally larger cities. Although the two leagues remained largely independent entities, they cooperated not merely on such matters as playing rules and the organi-zation of the annual World Series but also on numerous business and labor issues. By the middle of the twentieth century, virtually all of the minor leagues—which had once been independent, though smaller, rivals of the majors—had been incorporated into the structure of "organized" professional baseball, making the minor-league teams mere subsidiaries of the major-league franchises.

Professional baseball's relation to the fabric of American life has been unrivalled by that of any other sport, and many of baseball's most notable controversies have become familiar pieces of social history. Most notable, perhaps, were the "Black Sox" scandal, in which members of the Chicago White Sox conspired with gamblers to fix the outcome of the 1919 World Series, and the breaking of baseball's color line by Jackie Robinson in 1947. The first episode shook public confidence in the professional game and threatened its economic foundation, leading to the appointment of an independent commissioner with broad powers to regulate the sport. The second made baseball a focal point for many of the issues of race that were simmering in postwar America and that would reach the boiling point by the early 1960's. By the century's end, however, the principal social issues capturing the baseball public's attention involved labor disputes and franchise movements; in these as in most other respects, baseball long set a pattern that would be followed in the other major professional sports.

Professional football grew steadily throughout much of the century, coming to rival baseball in popularity by the mid-1960's. The National Football League (NFL), founded in the 1920's, came of age in the 1950's after absorbing the most successful franchises of a defunct rival, the All-America Football Conference. In 1966, the NFL ended half a decade of rivalry with the American Football League (AFL) by merging with the upstart league. Formation of the Canadian Football League (CFL) in the 1950's brought professionalism to the Canadian version of the sport, which is played under slightly different rules than the American game.

Professional basketball was the slowest to organize of the major American team sports. In the 1920's, the best-known professional teams were mostly barnstorming squads. The National Basketball League, sponsored by the General Electric, Firestone, and Goodyear corporations, began play in 1937; its 1949 merger with the newer Basketball Association of America created the National Basketball Association

(NBA). A rival league, the American Basketball Association (ABA), came into existence in 1967; the ABA failed after nine seasons, but the NBA absorbed four of its most successful teams. Professional basketball boomed in the 1980's and 1990's; by 1996, the NBA had expanded to twenty-nine teams, including the first Canadian franchises in Toronto and Vancouver.

America's fourth major team sport, ice hockey, became professionalized in the early 1900's, a development that was formalized by the 1917 creation of the National Hockey League (NHL). Although hockey quickly gained broad popularity in Canada and many northern U.S. cities, it was slow to be accepted in more temperate parts of the continent, where weather conditions ill-suited for recreational play made it difficult for many sports fans to develop a personal association with the game. The NHL enjoyed a substantial rise in popularity in the 1990's, however, and successful franchises spread to such warm-weather cities as Miami, Houston, Anaheim, and San Jose.

Soccer, long the world's most popular team sport, has had difficulty making professional inroads in North America. A series of professional leagues foundered from the late 1960's into the 1990's, and skeptics argued that the sport would never find a large American audience. The 1994 staging of soccer's most prestigious international competition, the World Cup, in the United States generated substantial momentum, however, and the strong 1996 debut of the Major Soccer League (MSL) gave hope to fans that professional soccer might at last have established a secure American foundation.

Strikes and Labor Disputes. The mid-1970's attainment of the right to free agency by major-league baseball players led to a rapid escalation in player salaries and an adjustment of the balance of power in the sport's labor issues, a balance that had long favored team owners. Tensions between the factions led to short player strikes in 1972 and 1985 and to lengthy strikes that interrupted the 1981 and 1994 seasons; the 1994 strike, precipitated by management efforts to reduce player salaries via the imposition of a salary cap, led to the cancellation of the World Series for the first time in ninety years and delayed the start of the 1995

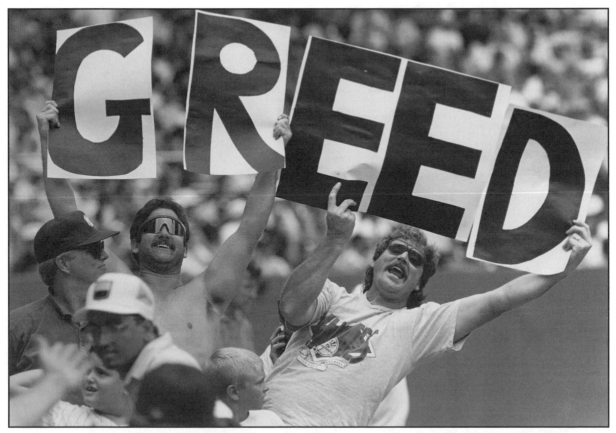

Two New York fans express the sentiments of many critics of professional sports. (AP/Wide World Photos)

season. In the face of a broad public backlash, both owner and player representatives publicly resolved to consider the interests of fans and of the sport as a whole in future negotiations, but most observers reacted to such statements with cynicism.

In labor issues, as in many others, baseball led the way for the other major team sports. Football players also attained free-agency rights in the mid-1970's, although player representatives unwisely gave away such rights in subsequent negotiations. Football too was shaken by mid-season players' strikes in 1982 and 1987; the owners' crushing victory in the 1987 strike led players to abandon collective bargaining in favor of court action to win back free agency, a tactic that did bring effectual free agency to the NFL in the 1990's.

Hockey also experienced labor strife in the 1990's,

as owners engaged in a lockout—a preemptive move to avert a player strike—before the 1994-1995 season. The sides reached agreement on free agency and salary-cap issues in time to prevent the NHL from becoming the first major league to lose an entire season to a labor dispute.

Alone among the major American team sports, professional basketball remained relatively free of labor strife into the mid-1990's. The NBA's early 1980's adoption of a league-wide salary-cap agreement that split revenue between owners and players set the stage for the league's subsequent resurgence, but efforts to ape the NBA's policies in other sports proved contentious.

Franchise Movements, Expansion, and Antitrust Issues. The age of player free agency arrived in team

Striking professional football players in 1987. (UPI/Corbis-Bettmann)

sports in the 1970's; team owners had produced their own version of free agency even earlier, moving established franchises to new cities that offered better business prospects. Other franchises used the leverage provided by the threat of moving to negotiate lucrative deals with their host cities. The landmark move was the transfer of the baseball Brooklyn Dodgers and New York Giants franchises to Los Angeles and San Francisco, respectively, in 1958. By the 1990's, many teams with storied traditions had moved or threatened to move, often to the dismay of their fans; the NFL, in particular, became the object of much negative publicity in the mid-1990's when four of its franchises announced moves within a one-year period. Although leagues sometimes attempted to expand to meet the demand for teams, most established leagues were butting up against practical size limits by the 1990's, leading to occasional calls for federal antitrust action.

Drug Use. Innumerable professional athletes have been arrested for or otherwise implicated in the use of illegal drugs. Stung by the negative publicity that attended revelations of widespread drug abuse in baseball and other sports in the early 1980's, the major professional leagues instituted drug policies that called for random testing of athletes and mandated treatment, suspension, or outright banning for players found to be in violation. Although the exposure of individual cases of drug abuse by professional athletes remained almost daily fodder for the sports pages, there was little doubt that the policies had had some effect in curbing illegal drug use; after the early 1980's exposures of the Pittsburgh Pirates and Kansas City Royals as teams riddled with drug problems, for example, baseball experienced no similar widespread incidents through the mid-1990's. Civil libertarians decried such policies as infringements on players' rights, but such policies were incorporated into most collective-bargaining agreements with little resistance.

Yet the professional sports world's actions against illegal recreational drug use did not extend to effective efforts to control the use of performance-enhancing drugs such as anabolic steroids and prescription painkillers. The widespread use of muscle-developing steroids, which have been linked to a variety of serious health problems, has been an open secret of professional football for decades, and by the 1980's it was widely suspected that steroid use had become common in other sports. Although amateur track and field, swimming, and weightlifting bodies instituted testing programs to detect steroid use, the major American team sports generally ignored the issue. Moreover, the issue of the abuse of prescription drugs to combat pain has never been effectively addressed by American professional leagues, a fact highlighted by the admission of Green Bay Packers football star Brett Favre to a substance-abuse clinic in 1996. Favre became only the latest in a long line of professional sports stars to admit to long-term abuse of painkillers as a means of continuing in their profession.   —*John D. Windhausen*

SUGGESTED READINGS: Benjamin G. Rader's *American Sports: From the Age of Folk Games to the Age of Televised Sports* (Englewood Cliffs: Prentice Hall, 1990) is a fine survey of professional baseball, basketball, football, and associated issues. Canadian professional sports are surveyed in Don Morrow and Mary Keyes' *A Concise History of Sport in Canada* (Toronto: Oxford University Press, 1989). George H. Sage's *Power and Ideology in American Sport: A Critical Perspective* (Champaign, Ill.: Human Kinetics Books, 1990) includes a useful essay on "The Professional Sport Team Industry." Relevant pieces on government and sports can be found in the *Sports Encyclopedia North America*, edited by John D. Windhausen (Gulf Breeze, Fla.: Academic International Press, 1987-1994).

Sports, professional, free agency in: Process by which athletes in professional team sports can negotiate contracts with teams of their choosing. Debates over free agency are at the heart of many of sports' most contentious labor issues.

Teams and their players have been at war over control of the enormous revenues generated by team sports since the rise of the first professional leagues in the late nineteenth century. As the oldest, biggest, and most lucrative American team sport, baseball long set the pattern followed by leagues in other sports. When the stability of the first professional leagues was threatened by players who changed teams in midseason—and when the profit margins of team owners were reduced, as players used the leverage of competing offers to compel more lucrative contract terms—owners banded together to introduce the "reserve clause" as part of every player contract. The reserve clause deprived players of most of their negotiating power; according to its terms, a team could unilaterally renew, or "reserve," the contract of any player upon the contract's expiration. In effect, once a player signed a contract, he was bound to a team for

Curt Flood (left) and Marvin Miller discuss their efforts to win free agency for professional baseball players. (AP/Wide World Photos)

his entire playing career; a player could change teams only if his contract was traded or sold with the team's approval. If a player was not satisfied with his salary, his only real alternative was to refuse to play.

The adoption of the reserve clause had the desired effect, deflating salaries and halting most player movement. The legality of the owners' practices was upheld in a 1922 Supreme Court decision in which Justice Oliver Wendell Holmes opined that baseball was a sport, not a business, and therefore not subject to labor ANTITRUST laws. As a consequence, baseball team owners long enjoyed nearly unrestricted freedom in labor negotiations, and player salaries remained rela-

tively low despite the often large revenues taken in by teams.

The reserve clause was not seriously challenged again until 1970, when Curt Flood, a star outfielder for the St. Louis Cardinals, sued to have the clause invalidated. Flood had been traded to Philadelphia without his consent, and he went to court in an attempt to win the right to negotiate his own contract. The case eventually reached the Supreme Court, which ruled against Flood on the basis of the 1922 decision.

In 1976, however, a neutral arbitrator ruled that the reserve clause bound players to their teams only for a one-year period; after the expiration of a player's con-

An arbitrator's ruling in the case of baseball player Andy Messersmith ushered in the era of free agency in professional sports. (AP/Wide World Photos)

tract, he could, after a year, sign a new contract with any other team. Players could thus become "free agents." The effect of the new freedom on labor negotiations was drastic and almost immediate: In 1976, just prior to the arbitrator's decision, the average major-league salary was $51,500; by 1979, it had more than doubled to $113,558. By 1993, it had climbed to $1.3 million.

Labor relations in North America's other major professional leagues followed similar patterns. Although basketball, football, and hockey did not enjoy baseball's antitrust exemption, neither did they for the most part generate such large revenues, and player bargaining strength was limited by the financial frailty of many leagues; moreover, labor leadership in those sports tended to be less effective. For example, player representatives in the National Football League (NFL) also won free agency for all players in a 1976 court decision—and then immediately negotiated it away. As a consequence, football salaries lagged far behind baseball salaries, even though football overtook baseball in popularity at about the same time. Predictably, when free agency did arrive in the NFL in the late 1980's—as the result of two major STRIKES and the decertification of the players' union—the average player salary skyrocketed.

The across-the-board escalation in player salaries has led to bitter labor disputes in virtually every professional team sport, and free-agency rights have often been the central issue. Fans often deplore free agency for its effects on their favorite games, claiming that rapid player movement from team to team retards the development of fan loyalty; fans also often decry the high player salaries fueled by free agency. Owners and league officials use many of the same arguments in assailing free agency, often adding that free-agency-fueled salary escalation threatens the very existence of many teams and even some leagues. Players and their representatives typically endorse free agency as a simple application of market principles to the business of sports, dismissing owner complaints of poverty as mere bargaining propaganda. Moreover, they argue that the issue is not one of economics but one of personal freedom; free agency, they say, is nothing more than the extension into the world of sports of rights unthinkingly enjoyed by workers in other fields.

Sports, professional, salary caps in: Financial restrictions imposed by professional sports leagues on team spending for player salaries. The use of salary caps in sports was pioneered by the National Basketball Association (NBA). In the late 1970's, the NBA, struggling to attract fans and with several franchises on the verge of bankruptcy, implemented a league-wide salary cap to control labor costs; labor representatives agreed to the cap, which guaranteed that 53 percent of the league's total revenues would be used for salaries, as a necessary measure to stave off disaster for the league. The cap and revenue-sharing provision stabilized the league's financial fortunes and helped set the stage for the NBA's resurgence in the 1980's and 1990's. As a result, management representatives in other professional sports attempted to sell various forms of salary caps to player representatives; in 1993, the National Football League adopted a cap system allocating 64 percent of revenues to salaries. Cap proposals were central to the bitter major-league baseball strike of 1994-1995; player representatives rejected management proposals as artificial and unnecessary restrictions on player earnings and freedom of movement. At the same time, NBA labor representatives negotiating a new agreement with the league attempted to remove the original cap, arguing that in light of the NBA's great financial success, the rationale for the cap no longer existed.

Sports, professional, strikes in: Labor disputes are among the most controversial aspects of professional team sports. Although both team owners and player representatives generally express reluctance to provoke or to call for work stoppages, strikes have been a recurring part of the sports world since the early 1970's.

The first modern sports strike occurred at the beginning of the 1972 baseball season, when the major-league players' union announced its growing strength by boycotting the first weeks of the season until a compromise could be reached in a dispute over baseball's pension fund. Although the 1972 strike was, by later standards, a minor work stoppage over a relatively small issue, it represented a significant advance for players in their dealings with management; hitherto, players' unions had been largely ineffective, and management had generally dictated its terms. The players were led in the 1972 strike by Marvin Miller, a former United Steelworkers of America lawyer who helped transform the baseball union into an effective, unified negotiating entity.

Fans vent their anger on the eve of the 1994 baseball strike. (AP/Wide World Photos)

In 1981, baseball was shaken by a second, far longer strike that wiped out nearly a third of the season. The players again demonstrated the union's strength by holding their ground and giving up little in settlement negotiations. The 1981 strike was precipitated by a dispute over compensation to be received by teams for the loss of free-agent players; management representatives claimed that compensation was necessary to repay teams for their often large investments in player development, while player representatives claimed that such compensation represented an artificial and unjustifiable restriction on players' freedom of movement—and, hence, on player salaries. Disputes over various aspects of FREE AGENCY would loom large in most of the major player strikes of the 1980's and 1990's.

Emboldened by the success of their baseball brethren, players in the National Football League (NFL) engaged in work stoppages in 1982 and 1987. The NFL players, however, were much less well organized, and their strikes achieved little. The 1987 strike ended in disaster for the players' union, as strikebreakers and replacement players quickly eroded the union's strength. In the wake of the debacle, players voted to decertify the union as their negotiating arm in order to pursue independent legal challenges to NFL labor practices, a tactic that did indeed prove more effective than the union's efforts had.

Strikes obtruded on the sports scene even more glaringly in 1994 and 1995. In August, 1994, baseball players again went on strike to protest management intransigence in negotiating a new collective bargaining agreement; according to player representatives, owners were stalling negotiations until the current agreement expired, at which point the owners would be free to impose their own terms on the players. Fans were horrified when the owners announced the resultant cancellation of the playoffs and World Series; the strike continued into the beginning of the 1995 season, when the players returned to work after receiving a federal judge's concurrence that the owners had bargained in bad faith. Although a new bargaining agreement was not quickly reached, players and owners agreed to conduct business according to the expired agreement until a settlement took place. Central to the 1995 strike was management's insistence on a salary cap on team payrolls and on restrictions on players' rights to arbitration in salary disputes, proposals players again resisted as unnecessary and unfair.

In October, 1994, moreover, National Hockey League (NHL) owners, fearful of a player strike over negotiations regarding the NHL's collective bargaining agreement, undertook a player lockout, the management equivalent of a strike. Again at issue were free-agency rules, salary caps, and arbitration rights, terms that had become all too familiar to American sports fans. The lockout threatened to make the NHL the first major league to lose a full season to a labor dispute, but an agreement was finally reached in time for the season to begin in January, 1995.

Of America's principal professional leagues, only the National Basketball Association (NBA) managed to reach the late 1990's without enduring a major work stoppage. Although players and owners alike called for recognition of their mutual responsibilities to their sports and to their fans, few of those fans expected news of labor strife to disappear from the sports pages any time soon.

Sports, women and: In Canada and the United States as elsewhere, institutionalized sporting events have traditionally been viewed as settings for the development, display, and perpetuation of masculine traits and identity. The emphasis on men's sports and comparative neglect of women's sports continue to be sources of conflict as women fight for greater recognition and greater equality of opportunity.

Just as the informal games children play teach them lessons about expectations and roles in society, organized sports, from grade school to professional athletics, perpetuate cultural expectations about traditionally acceptable behavior (for example, aggression, teamwork, and competitiveness) and values (for example, hierarchical achievement and loyalty).

Perhaps the greatest cultural lesson learned from sports relates to what is taught about gender. The gender bias that exists in society is reflected in and reinforced by an institutionalized athletic hierarchy that differentiates between male and female sports. Assumptions about proper roles have caused men and women to participate in different kinds of sports. Historically, women were expected to be spectators and cheerleaders rather than participants. This idea is still predominant for certain kinds of masculinized sports like football, boxing, wrestling, and ice hockey—sports that involve bodily contact and the use of physical force to overpower opponents. Sexist attitudes have caused women to participate mainly in "feminine" sports such as swimming, tennis, gymnastics, aerobic dancing, and figure skating—all of which emphasize movement, beauty, and grace.

Athletic sex segregation tends to limit the aspirations of girls and boys. Boys who enter predominantly female sports risk being labeled "sissies," and girls who enter predominantly male sports are often viewed as less feminine than other girls. As youths, girls and boys are also taught through sports that men are expected to be dominant and aggressive "doers," while women are expected to remain passive and on the sideline. Another lesson is that the activities of boys and men are more valued in society. In high schools and colleges, sports facilities, financial resources, and general community support has nearly always favored men's athletic activities over women's.

In the United States, one way the issue of gender bias is being addressed is through legislative changes. Since the passage of Title IX of the Educational Amendments Act in 1972, the money spent on women's sports has increased, and female athletic participation has expanded. The Act requires that schools receiving federal funds must provide equal opportunities for females and males. The 1994 Equity in Athletics Disclosure Act requires that colleges report publicly on male and female participation rates, financial support, and other information on women's and men's intercollegiate athletic programs. This requirement makes it easier to validate charges of sexual discrimination and inequity.

Between 1971 and 1987, the number of high-school girls participating in U.S. interscholastic sports increased from 294,015 to 1,836,356. Participation in college athletics also grew. Despite gains, female coaches and athletic administrators continue to achieve only marginalized status. As female athletics gain recognition, many of the positions formerly held by women are being filled by men. Thus, women who

A female boxer trains in a New York gym in 1995. (Impact Visuals, Andi Faryl Schreiber)

Boston marathon officials attempt to stop a woman from entering the 1967 race, which was then open to men only. (UPI/Corbis-Bettmann)

aspire to coaching and athletic administration are confronting greater barriers to entry and advancement as men continue to control positions of power.

Sports and health: Sports and health used to be virtually synonymous. By the late twentieth century, however, competition to reach the highest levels of many sports had created pressures on many athletes to excel at all costs. Thus, the unhealthy aspects of sport have increased.

Sports that put stress on specific joints or muscle groups are especially ripe for overuse injuries. Swimmers and baseball players often have shoulder problems; golfers often develop bad backs; football players frequently injure their knees; and runners commonly experience stress fractures. Improved equipment and better sports medicine now often allow athletes to compete following what before were career-ending injuries; however, such developments can also be used to keep athletes competing beyond the point at which they should stop to avoid further damage.

Ergogenic aids, or efforts to try to improve performance, are used by most athletes. Some are legal, such as carbohydrate "loading" or simple use of the best available equipment. Others, such as anabolic steroids and blood "doping," are illegal, generally because such practices can cause health problems. Anabolic steroids have received the most publicity of such illegal aids and have probably had the widest use. According to some studies, more than 60 percent of high-school athletes surveyed in the 1980's had experimented with steroids, which work to increase muscle mass (if accompanied with a heavy strength workout) but which can cause side effects ranging from mood swings to cancer. Stopping the use of steroids causes muscle mass to decrease, so there is often a psychological need to continue use; the worst side effects occur with prolonged use.

Other athletes, mostly females, develop disordered eating habits such as anorexia or bulimia to lose weight or to maintain an ideal weight; such athletes are

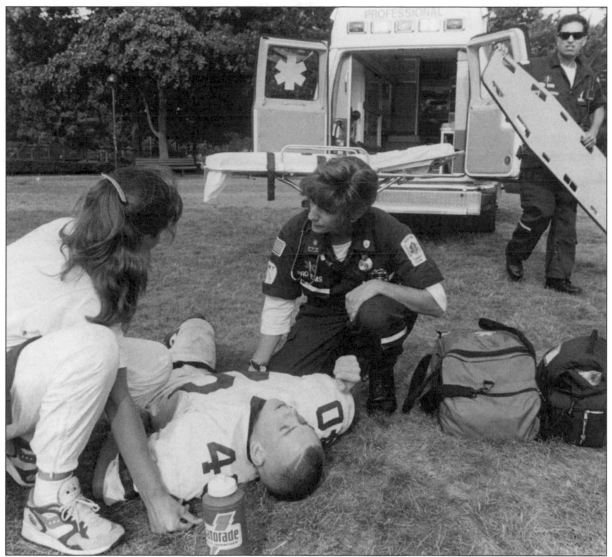

A Massachusetts high-school football player is treated for head and neck injuries. (Impact Visuals, Kenneth Martin)

at high risk of health problems. Eating disorders in athletes can cause amenorrhea, or the absence of menstrual cycles and loss of estrogen in females, and decreased testosterone production in males. Eating disorders can also lead to osteoporosis, or loss of bone density, and resultant fractures. Although osteoporosis is normally a problem of old age, athletes with eating disorders can experience related bone fracture in their twenties, and the damage is irreversible.

Health specialists note that virtually all of the health problems associated with sports can be either eliminated or reduced. Prevention, largely through education, is essential, such experts say; such a process, they state, needs to be a joint effort between coaches, athletes, parents, sports-medicine personnel, educators, and the media.

Sports franchises, movement of: Since the rise of the first professional leagues in the late nineteenth century, teams in the major American sports have shifted their bases of operations in the search for improved financial opportunity. Until the late twentieth century, most such movements involved struggling teams in newly formed or financially shaky leagues; traditionally, once a team in a stable league had found a profitable home, it stayed there. For example, after baseball's major leagues attained relative stability in

Fans of the National Football League's Cleveland Browns, including Cleveland mayor Michael White, protest the team's 1995 move to Baltimore. (AP/Wide World Photos)

the first decade of the twentieth century—following a developmental era in which franchises and leagues moved and folded with regularity—no major-league team changed cities for fifty years.

By the latter part of the century, however, professional franchises in the major American sports had become such hot properties that cities began to compete for existing teams. In this new environment, a number of teams left their traditional homes for greener financial pastures, and many more took advantage of the leverage provided by competing offers to negotiate lucrative new deals with their host cities. In effect, teams

and their owners had discovered the principles of FREE AGENCY that had dramatically escalated individual player salaries in many sports. The public reaction was similar in each case: Fans and media analysts complained that loyalty was being subordinated to mercenary impulses and that unchecked greed was "ruining" sports.

The factors that created the new context were fairly obvious. As professional basketball, hockey, and—especially—football grew in popularity, team owners became the beneficiaries of a rising tide of demand for their products. At the same time, dramatic population increases in the American South and West created huge cities that lacked both top-level teams and the "major-league" status they conferred. Expansion of the major existing leagues helped to alleviate some of the pent-up demand, but by the 1980's, those leagues were approaching practical size limits. Moreover, many owners of established franchises were unenthusiastic about expansions, which generally created struggling teams that did not draw fans to road games.

Baseball's Boston Braves inaugurated the era of major franchise shifts by moving to Milwaukee in 1953. Other teams soon followed suit; the St. Louis Browns became the Baltimore Orioles in 1954, and the Philadelphia Athletics moved to Kansas City in 1955. Those moves, however, involved financially troubled franchises that had traditionally produced weak teams. The landmark 1950's moves, therefore, were the transfers of the Brooklyn Dodgers and New York Giants, two highly successful and much-beloved teams, to Los Angeles and San Francisco, respectively, in 1958. Although the Giants experienced indifferent financial and on-field fortunes in their new home, the tremendous success of the Dodgers, who broke attendance records year after year, served as a clear example to other owners. Moreover, the fact that baseball officials could ignore the complaints of the bereft Brooklyn fans—arguably the most loyal and most celebrated in all of sports—showed that sentiment need impose few limits on such opportunism.

Nevertheless, leagues were generally cognizant of the image problems that could result from widespread franchise moves, and most did try to regulate such shifts. In 1982, however, football's Oakland Raiders moved to Los Angeles in defiance of National Football League (NFL) regulations, and Raiders owner Al Davis prevailed over NFL officials in ensuing litigation. The legal precedent was set; soon thereafter, Baltimore and St. Louis also lost NFL franchises to other cities that offered more lucrative terms. In the mid-1990's, the NFL became the object of much criticism—and a fair amount of derision—as a "carpetbaggers' league," as the Los Angeles Raiders, Los Angeles Rams, Cleveland Browns, and Houston Oilers all announced moves within a one-year period. In the face of intense negative publicity, the NFL subsequently called a moratorium on franchise shifts, blocking the efforts of the Seattle Seahawks and several other teams to move into the vacant Los Angeles market; the legality of the league's actions, however, remained in doubt.

Teams that have not moved have also benefited widely from the demand for franchises. Numerous teams have used the threat of moving to force their host cities to construct publicly financed playing facilities, often with such perquisites as "luxury boxes" and "personal seat licenses" that guarantee substantial income to owners. Politicians have proven largely unwilling to face the voter hostility that can accompany the loss of a team, and officials often justify the public construction of new stadiums and arenas by pointing to the community-wide economic benefits produced by professional teams. Critics counter that studies consistently fail to confirm the existence of such benefits and that the use of tax money to subsidize the wealthy owners of professional teams represents a reprehensible misuse of public funds.

Stagflation: Term in economics. In a period of stagflation, prices are increasing (inflation) but national output is not increasing (stagnation). Stagflation occurred in response to the international petroleum price increases of the 1970's. Other episodes reflected delayed responses to periods of demand-driven inflation, when wages and prices continued to increase while total demand increased only slightly. Stagflation tends to be self-correcting as time passes, and many economists believe that it can be avoided if government demand-management policies do not generate substantial inflation. Only temporary shocks to the economy would then result in stagflation.

Standardized tests: Means of measuring an attribute and yielding a score that remains stable across time and examiners. Scores are statistically derived and are based on the bell curve, which demonstrates that most scores occur in the midrange, while fewer scores fall at either of the extremes.

Originally designed to assess school instruction, standardized tests have been developed for a variety of purposes. Each year, most students participate in national standardized-achievement testing, which measures one's knowledge compared to others in the same grade. The Stanford Achievement Test and the California Achievement Test are examples of such tests. Students approaching high-school graduation may avail themselves of vocational testing to help select an occupation for which the individual may hold both an interest and aptitude. Test results may suggest previously

Standardized tests

unconsidered alternatives or may serve to confirm choices. Suggested vocations can be investigated to determine entry requirements and occupational outlook. The Armed Services Vocational Aptitude Battery is designed to sort military personnel to best utilize human resources. Because of its breadth, it is sometimes used by schools and industry. The Strong-Campbell Interest Inventory and the Kuder Occupational Interest Survey are additional examples of widely used vocational tests.

College-bound students take entrance exams such as the Scholastic Aptitude Test (SAT) and American College Test (ACT). Such exams purport to measure current academic achievement and to predict the probability of completing a college degree. College students who wish to pursue a graduate degree often take the Graduate Record Exam (GRE) and possibly one of several GRE subtests specific to their chosen field. Alternatively, a discipline-specific test, such as the Law School Admissions Test (LSAT), may be selected.

Even after completing the necessary training, a further demand may remain to earn a qualifying score on a standardized test before being permitted to practice one's chosen occupation. Cosmetologists, electricians, contractors, teachers, doctors, and lawyers, for example, must all obtain an adequate score on a stand-

Education Secretary William Bennett addresses changes in standardized test scores. (UPI/Corbis-Bettmann)

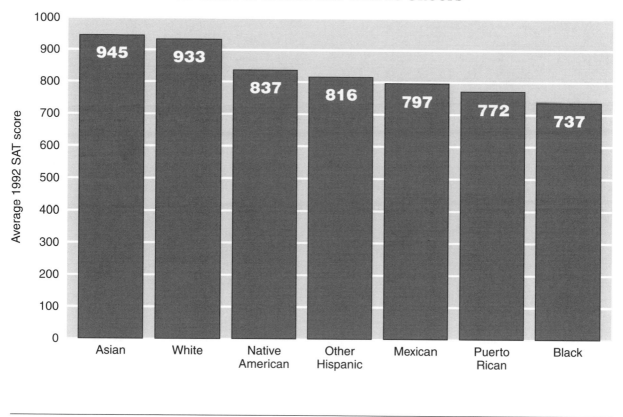

AVERAGE 1992 COMPOSITE SAT SCORES
FOR VARIOUS RACIAL AND ETHNIC GROUPS

Source: Marlita A. Reddy, ed., *Statistical Record of Native North Americans*. Detroit: Gale Research, 1993.

ardized test before receiving the licensing necessary for employment.

Like achievement tests, psychological tests are standardized and have been widely used for decades. INTELLIGENCE TESTS measure cognitive abilities and yield an intelligence quotient (IQ). The Stanford-Binet and the Wechsler tests are of prime import. Personality tests, such as the Minnesota Multiphase Personality Inventory, measure psychological functioning for diagnostic purposes. For example, antisocial personality traits might be detected in a criminal, and psychotic thought processes might be revealed in a schizophrenic person.

Objective standardized testing represents a significant improvement over the subjective oral and essay examinations. Nevertheless, the impartiality of standardized testing has been questioned and challenged in the courts. Opponents argue that these tests are culturally biased, favoring middle-class whites over other racial and socioeconomic groups. Indeed, there are established differences in the scores obtained by different groups. Because standardized test scores are used for eligibility and placement decisions, safeguards against abuse have been implemented. Test users are required to use tests in accordance with ethical codes and legal standards. Interpretation of scores must include consideration of the subject's race, culture, and socioeconomic background. Academic institutions should base admission decisions on more than one criteria (such as grade-point average and recommendations), and employers should only use tests clearly related to the demands of a particular job.

Stanton v. Stanton (1975): U.S. Supreme Court case. Following the precedent of *REED v. REED* (1971), the Court struck down a Utah law that required divorced fathers to support their sons until the age of twenty-one but their daughters only until the age of eighteen. Avoiding the question of whether gender classifications are inherently suspect, the Court ruled that the law was irrational because it could no longer be assumed that males should be assumed to need more education than females. The decision suggested that the Fourteenth Amendment prohibited laws that perpetuate traditional gender stereotypes.

Statelessness: Condition of being without citizenship in any country. Statelessness can be the consequence of renouncing one's citizenship without gaining acceptance by any other country. Children born in a country that recognizes only descendants of its own nationals as citizens are stateless if their parents are nationals of another country that extends citizenship only to those born within its boundaries. In the wake of World War II, many refugees, especially those who fled communist-dominated countries of Eastern Europe, were unable to claim passports or protection from their native countries and were, in effect, stateless.

States' rights: Idea that state governments share political power with, and are not simply subjects of, the federal government. This has resulted in an ongoing struggle between the two over authority, complicating issues such as national growth, unity, race relations, and ABORTION.

Overview. Thomas Jefferson first advanced the idea of states' rights in the 1798 Kentucky Resolution. In that Resolution, the United States was defined as a compact among the member states. Thus, as the originators of the Union, the member states have the authority to override the laws of the Union.

Quickly taken to heart by the political leaders of the southern section of the United States, the concept of states' rights became central to, and interwoven with, the issue of SLAVERY. Claiming to be the champions of historic state political powers, Southern congressmen and senators complicated the growth of the United States by demanding on every occasion that new states be admitted as slave states.

Thus, the subtle link between the status of African Americans and the power struggle between state governments and the federal government was forged early in the nineteenth century. Predominantly Southern in

nature, the connection between states' rights and African American culture would resurface on several occasions throughout U.S. history, severely complicating and poisoning race relations. Beginning in the 1970's, the federal government began to overturn state abortion legislation, extending the states' rights debate into Northern and Western states.

Constitutional Origin. One major faction at the Constitutional Convention of 1787 argued that since the state governments were the inheritors of the colonial tradition, they were older than, and should retain more power than, the new federal government. The opposing faction argued that to form the United States, the member states turned over their political power in total, leaving the federal government more powerful than the states.

In the process of approving the new CONSTITUTION, some state legislatures worried that they were signing away their political powers. For this and other reasons, the BILL OF RIGHTS was added to the Constitution prior to its ratification. Most of these rights affected individual citizens; however, the Tenth Amendment specifically addressed the powers retained by the states. Because no agreement could be reached at the convention concerning the exact amount of political power each state government would retain, the issue was deliberately glossed over.

The Tenth Amendment reads: "The powers not delegated to the United States by the Constitution, nor prohibited by it to the states, are reserved to the states respectively, or to the people." This admittedly vague statement concerning state powers is the seed of the concept of states' rights. The complex nature and the intensity of the states' rights struggle is probably due to the vagueness of the Constitution on the issue.

Notable Conflicts over Federal Powers. The first notable conflict between federal and state powers occurred in the Missouri Crisis of 1820. Missouri was the first part of the Louisiana Territory to request statehood. Federal power supporters, many from Northern states, claimed that Congress had the right to prevent Missouri from becoming a slave state. State theorists claimed that Congress had no such power. The government was paralyzed over the issue for several months until it was solved by compromise. Even though no firm statement was made in the compromise concerning the relation between federal and state powers, it is seen as a victory for states' rights because it prevented the federal government from outlawing slavery in a state.

The next important conflict between federal power and state power was the Nullification Crisis of 1832. Fearing a precedent that could enable the federal government to interfere with slavery, the South Carolina legislature invoked the Tenth Amendment and the Kentucky Resolution and overruled a federal tariff law. The president of the United States, Andrew Jackson, threatened military force to ensure South Carolina's compliance. Although the Nullification Crisis was defused by compromise, it stood as a precursor for later Southern state resistance to federal power.

The third major conflict occurred in the 1860's. Unable to resolve the relationship between federal and state political power by further compromise, the Northern and Southern sections of the United States broke down into Civil War. The unexpected length and severity of the war called for drastic measures. In one of those measures, President Abraham Lincoln issued the Emancipation Proclamation, which committed the federal government to eliminating slavery in the Southern states.

After the defeat of the Southern states by the federal Union and for several years thereafter, the theory of federal supremacy ruled unchallenged. During this period, the federal government forced the Southern state governments to free their slaves as a condition for readmission to the United States. The free slaves were also given CITIZENSHIP and VOTING RIGHTS, which were protected by the power of the federal government.

After their readmission in the late 1870's, the Southern states began to regain most of the power they had lost in the Civil War. During the following eighty years, African Americans paid the social cost of this major fight between state and federal power. In this struggle, the Southern state governments were able to dismantle federal protection of black voting and citizenship rights and resubject blacks to a condition of second-class citizenship. A states' rights victory was ultimately recognized in the Supreme Court decision *PLESSY V. FERGUSON* (1896).

Another conflict between the competing governmental theories occurred during World War II. The expansion of the federal government required to defeat Japan and Germany, combined with the "common cause" felt by Americans at all levels of government, resulted in a period of federal supremacy.

The participation of African Americans in the war effort resulted in the eventual DESEGREGATION of the U.S. armed forces. In 1954, the Supreme Court ruled in *BROWN V. BOARD OF EDUCATION OF TOPEKA, KANSAS*, that school SEGREGATION was against federal law. *Brown*, which effectively overthrew *Plessy*, is recognized as the stamp of federal supremacy on the era. In the most memorable episode of that era, in the spring of 1963, Governor George Wallace of Alabama was literally forced to step aside as federal marshals enforced desegregation of the University of Alabama.

In the mid-1960's, the federal government enacted civil rights and voting rights legislation. Under President Lyndon B. Johnson, an avalanche of social and economic legislation was directed at the condition of the African American. Because the federal government was able to enforce these federal laws inside the states, the second half of the twentieth century can be interpreted as a period when federal power rose above that of the states.

In what might be regarded as an attempt to further expand its powers at the expense of the states, in the early 1970's the federal government turned its attention to the ABORTION issue. The Supreme Court decision *ROE V. WADE* (1973) stated that state laws making abortion a crime were unconstitutional. In the decision, the Court claimed that state governments had no power to exercise control in matters of maternal health.

In 1976, Representative Henry Hyde of Illinois was successful in his campaign to have Medicaid benefits cut for abortions. In this context, the resulting Supreme Court decision *HARRIS V. MCRAE* (1980), which declared that the government has no legal responsibility to provide abortions to the poor, is seen as an example of state power attempting to reassert its rights over the federal government.

The overall trend, however, seems to be one of federal ascendancy over state power. The concept of states' rights may be a passing phenomenon in American constitutional law, as evidenced by the eventual federal victories in all of the areas in which the struggle has been fought.

Other areas in which the federal government is expressing its power at the state level are federally guaranteed student education loans, federal highway funding rules requiring state passage of seat belt laws, and the federal speed limit. Although several states acted to repeal the federal speed limit in the mid-1990's, such state actions were undertaken with the forbearance of the federal government and were not examples of state power expressing itself in the historical sense.

—Tim Palmer

SUGGESTED READINGS: A well-rounded explanation of both sides of the issue can be found in M. J. C.

Vile's *The Structure of American Federalism* (London: Oxford University Press, 1965). An in-depth description of the constitutional origins of the states' rights debate is offered in Edward S. Corwin's *The Commerce Power Versus States' Rights: "Back to the Constitution"* (Gloucester, Mass.: Peter Smith, 1962). There is an excellent discussion of the contribution of the states' rights issue to the American Civil War in James McPherson's *Battle Cry of Freedom: The Civil War Era* (New York: Ballantine Books, 1988). The original text of the *South Carolina Exposition and Protest* (1828) offers an excellent presentation of the states' rights position. This document can be located in editors Raymond M. Hyser and J. Chris Arndt's *Voices of the American Past: Documents in U.S. History*, Volume 1 (Fort Worth, Tex.: Harcourt Brace College Publishers, 1995).

Status offenses: Acts that are illegal for children and adolescents but not for adults. These include failure to obey parents, school TRUANCY, running away from home, and consumption of alcohol or tobacco.

In the JUVENILE JUSTICE SYSTEM, status offenses are the largest category of offenses referred to the courts. There is controversy about the proper management of status offenders. The offenses often stem from family discord or lack of family resources. Some experts want the juvenile court system to continue handling both status offenses and more serious delinquency cases, while others want most status offenses removed from juvenile court jurisdiction.

Statutory rape: Consensual sexual intercourse between a man and a female who is below the age of consent. The age at which a female may have consensual sex varies across jurisdictions but is generally set at sixteen or seventeen. The crime is unlike most offenses in that a man can be convicted of statutory rape even if he did not intend to violate the law. This practice of strict liability in the absence of criminal intent has been questioned in many jurisdictions. In addition, many critics argue that the law should be gender neutral, thereby also making it illegal for a woman to have sex with an underaged male.

Stealth bombers: Aircraft designed to be undetectable by radar. The first stealth aircraft were built and tested by the United States in strict secrecy and flown at night over sparsely populated areas to minimize the likelihood of chance observation. Their use during the Persian GULF WAR in 1991 caused basic information about the aircraft to become public. Stealth aircraft have an angular appearance caused by the use of flat surfaces to reflect radar signals at angles that prevent their being received. The aircraft make extensive use

A U.S. Air Force stealth bomber. (Corbis-Bettmann)

of nonreflective materials and surfaces that absorb or dissipate incoming radar signals.

Steinem, Gloria (b. Mar. 25, 1934, Toledo, Ohio): Writer, editor, and feminist organizer. As a reporter and writer in the 1960's, Steinem became frustrated by her inability to obtain assignments on important topics, and she became involved in the recently revived feminist movement, joining the newly formed National Women's Political Caucus and helping to found the Women's Action Alliance. In 1972, with the support of this group, she founded the first completely woman-

operated national magazine for women, *Ms.*. Steinem has since been an outspoken advocate of the feminist movement.

Stereotyping, racial: Oversimplified generalization that emphasizes only selected traits of a racial group. A stereotype tends to evoke a generalized reaction to any member of that racial group. In most instances, stereotypes enhance PREJUDICE, an attitude unfavorable to the entire racial group.

Racial stereotypes are often related to characteristics that are deemed virtuous in the larger society.

Feminist advocate Gloria Steinem addresses the 1972 Democratic National Convention held in Miami Beach, Florida. (UPI/Corbis-Bettmann)

Stereotyping, sexual

The stereotyped group is seen as having too much or too little of a trait that in moderation is prized by the dominant group. For example, in the dominant white, Anglo-Saxon, Protestant culture of the United States, hard work is valued. In typical stereotypes, this group sees some minority groups as "lazy" and "shiftless."

An assumption with stereotypes is that the traits are inborn and hereditary and that no change in the treatment of the stereotyped group is necessary. If a person comes in contact with someone who does not fit a preconceived stereotype, the first person tends to view the second as an exception. If a prejudiced white meets a member of a racial group who is an ambitious worker, the white sees that individual as unusual in order to leave the stereotype unaffected.

The media can reinforce stereotypes. Since newspapers, magazines, television, and other forms of mass communication depend on popular approval for their sales, they may present racial groups in stereotypical ways.

Racial labels have special power over people. The emotional content of such words can be overpowering, blocking out other kinds of realities about people. By clumping racial group members together and generalizing about all of them based on the observations of one or two individuals, each person's individual characteristics are unappreciated.

Stereotypes used to characterize racial groups can also become self-fulfilling prophecy. Defining all members of a group as "lazy" legitimizes keeping members of that group from jobs that require a high degree of dedication, industry, and energy output. If other jobs are not available, the stereotyped individuals are kept from employment and are liable to be seen idle while others are at work. Seeing them idle reinforces the original stereotype of laziness, while the basic discrimination that created the "laziness" passes unnoticed.

Prejudice and stereotyping cannot be outlawed. However, DISCRIMINATION based on such values and beliefs is against the law. Racial stereotyping restricts and damages the human potential of some members of society. Many sociologists believe that unless the United States can come to terms with such discriminatory treatment, a viable democracy is not possible.

Stereotyping, sexual: Folk beliefs about the differences between men and women that limit their rights, roles, and responsibilities. Gender is socially con-

structed; being male or female implies a great deal more than simple biological differences. Whether a newborn is a boy or girl determines to a large extent the nature of the child's experiences, attitudes, behaviors, and feelings and also affects the reactions of others. This differential treatment is not an accident. Sociologist Esther Greenglass argues that sex is employed as a salient cue for dichotomizing the experiences of boys and girls within the Western world. Consider the books children are read, the style and color of their clothing, the toys and marketing techniques that are sex-specific, and the range of activities considered appropriate for mainly boys (contact sports, modeling Power Rangers) or only girls (kitchen sets, mothering dolls).

As a social construct, experts note, gender involves three interrelated dimensions: differentiation, traits, and hierarchy. As differentiation, gender implies a biological distinction upon which an elaborate set of meanings have been built. Gender as traits refers to societal norms identifying what women and men should be, feel, and do in order to exhibit masculinity or femininity. A third aspect to gender content, hierarchy, involves the ranking of males and females in such a way that there is a cultural devaluation of female characteristics and activities.

The content of gender socialization includes shared meaning and values related to maleness and femaleness, and, by extension, men and women, boys and girls. The scripts for gender socialization are learned during childhood, first and foremost from parents, and then through the influence of teachers, peers, the media, and other institutions, including the church. While not all families teach the same gender-role curriculum, psychologist Jean Lipman-Blumen contends that the family is the site of the original context for learning and enacting gender and SEX ROLES.

Gender role attitudes comprise one part of the gender script learned in childhood. These attitudes include consensual beliefs about the differing characteristics of men and women, coupled with a tendency to ascribe greater social value to masculine, rather than feminine, behaviors. For example, the adjectives "aggressive," "assertive," and "strong" are typically associated with men, while "nurturing," "sensitive," and "caring" are attributes associated with women. At present, modern society generally values assertiveness more than it values sensitivity.

Gender role attitudes are undergoing modest revision, and a noticeable shift has been observed in attitudes toward the rights and responsibilities of women in modern society. Notwithstanding these alterations, large differences in gender role attitudes can still be observed.

Sterilization: Medical procedure undertaken for the purpose of ending fertility. It does not interfere with sexual activity or feelings.

Surgical sterilization is the most effective means of birth control and, for that reason, is the method chosen by most individuals who wish permanently to end their fertility. For men, the procedure is simple and inexpensive and requires only a brief appointment: A local anesthetic is applied to the groin area, and the physician makes a small cut through the skin of the scrotum, cutting the vas deferens, the tube that carries sperm to the urethra. After just a few days, the man's semen will no longer contain sperm, so he can engage in sexual intercourse, complete with ejaculation, without using any form of birth control or worrying about a possible pregnancy. For women, the procedure requires a general anesthesia and a more intrusive surgery: The surgeon makes an incision into the abdomen to cut (or tie) the fallopian tubes, which carry the eggs to the uterus. Although the woman will continue to ovulate, sperm and egg will not be able to meet one another, thus preventing fertilization. Although surgical sterilization is safe and effective, it is generally irreversible and is not a recommended option for those who are unsure whether they will want to have children in the future.

Generally speaking, surgical sterilization is not a controversial issue. There are, however, two settings in which the ethics of sterilization are debated. The first is when the person considering sterilization is mentally retarded or mentally ill. In such circumstances, it is not always clear whether the patient is knowingly and voluntarily choosing to forgo having children, or whether the decision is being forced or otherwise suggested by a family member or health-care professional. For a good part of the twentieth century, physicians would routinely sterilize patients in mental institutions without consulting them; while this practice is not as common as it once was, it still can be done with the permission of the patient's legal guardian, and it remains a difficult ethical decision.

The second controversial situation is when a judge offers a convicted criminal the option of sterilization instead of prison—an offer that is sometimes made to sex offenders and sometimes to mothers who have been convicted of abusing or murdering their children. When the convict in question is a sex offender, sterilization is not accomplished with a simple vasectomy, as is used for birth control, but with either a surgical or a chemical "castration"—so that the result is not just infertility, but a complete lack of sexual desire and sexual function. Although chemical castration is reversible, it is often associated with feminizing side effects. Controversy revolves about whether such a decision can be truly "voluntary," and whether forcing someone to make such a choice constitutes humane punishment.

Stern, Howard (b. January 12, 1954, New York, N.Y.): Radio TALK SHOW host. Stern rose to prominence in the late 1980's as the host of a morning talk

In the 1990's, radio "shock jock" Howard Stern gained notoriety for his outrageous and often offensive remarks on racial and gender issues. (AP/Wide World Photos)

show on New York's WNBC; he and rival "shock jock" Don Imus became notorious for their often outrageous (and often tasteless) commentary. By the mid-1990's, Stern's radio program was nationally syndicated, and he had briefly hosted a television show, starred in a movie, and written several best-selling books, including *Private Parts* (1993) and *Miss America* (1995). Critics derided Stern as racist, misogynistic, and crude, but his many fans defended him as candid and amusing.

Steroids and steroid abuse: Hormone-like DRUGS that have been associated with the ability of the human body to increase muscle mass. Anabolic steroids are commonly taken by mouth or intramuscular injection and are available by prescription, though they are also sold illegally. The appropriate dosage and purity of such drugs, however, are often not known, and the safety and effects of such drugs should be regarded with caution. Because steroids can affect physical maturation in ways that are irreversible, particularly in teenagers, they should not be used without medical prescription and thorough supervision.

Steroids can be abused when they are taken for nonmedical purposes and without medical guidance. It is not uncommon for both male and female teenagers, young adults, and professional athletes to abuse steroids in an effort to enhance physical appearance or athletic abilities. Among high-school students, estimates suggest that between 1 and 5 percent of students have used anabolic steroids at some time. Among athletes, use is even higher, with upwards of a third or more reporting steroid use at some point in their training. Some users report increased feelings of wellness associated with the use of steroids; however, it is not clear whether these effects are from the drugs. Instead, the experience of wellness may result from feelings related to enhanced physical appearance and expectations of achieving these effects with the steroids. Additionally, while steroids are linked to increased muscle mass, there is no guarantee that performance or competitive abilities will improve proportionally. In reality, the side effects of steroid use actually may present obstacles for individuals seeking to achieve improved athletic performance. Regular use of steroids has been linked to severe physical problems and mental states, leading to self-harm or harm to others. Although improved physical condition can lead to better performance or competitive abilities, impaired concentra-

tion, judgment, and emotional control can lead to problems. Thus, steroids must be used with caution.

In terms of mental problems, steroid use and cessation of use have been linked to severe states of anxiety, DEPRESSION, paranoia, and aggression. Significant changes in appetite and sleep patterns may also accompany heavy use. Violent outbursts and other irrational behavior may result from steroid use during periods when moods are exaggerated or thinking is disturbed. The liver, heart, and reproductive system may also be harmed by steroid use. Increased levels of cholesterol, diminished liver functioning, abnormalities in blood-sugar regulation, and increased risk for developing arterial problems and heart attacks have been noted. Further, in males, testicular atrophy, decreased sperm production, increased baldness, and breast development can occur if natural testosterone production is disrupted. Similarly, in females, sexual organs can be affected to the point where menstrual cycles become irregular and the reproductive organs shrink or, alternatively, become exaggerated. Further, in both males and females, severe acne and problems with water retention may develop. Taken together, these physical and mental risks suggest a need for caution in decisions to use these drugs and emphasize the importance of medical supervision if these drugs are to be used for any reason.

Stimulants: Substances that activate the nervous system and increase activity. As commonplace as nicotine, antidepressants, Ritalin, and the caffeine in coffee and chocolate, they are also as controversial as crack or powder COCAINE, amphetamines, and anabolic STEROIDS. The general effects of ingesting, injecting, or inhaling these substances include alertness, enhanced mood, and increases in behavioral activity in users. Because of their sympathetic nervous system effects, some stimulants can also cause excitement, nervousness, chills, stomach upset, and laxative effects. Further, the abusive use of stimulants may lead to agitation, paranoia, and profound psychological disturbances such as psychosis and mania.

Sting operations: Undercover investigations of varying duration and complexity in which law-enforcement officials pose as participants in illegal activities. Sting operations are designed to gain the confidence of criminal participants; officers then record, manually or electronically, details of criminal acts and perpetrators. The evidence gathered is presented to a grand jury to obtain secret indictments, followed by coordinated mass arrests of criminal participants. A variation of the sting is the "reverse sting," in which law-enforcement officers pose as consumers of illegal goods and services.

Stock markets: Financial institutions that bring together investors who wish to purchase and sell shares, or units of ownership in a company.

In buying and selling, individuals act on their judgments of the value of the company whose shares they are trading. Companies that are doing well find that more individuals want to buy their shares than want to sell; the prices of those companies' shares rises. Such companies find it easier to raise new capital for new enterprises or expansion. Companies that are not doing well find that more individuals want to sell their shares than want to buy; the price of these companies' shares falls. Such companies find it more difficult to raise capital. In this way, the market price of a share tallies the judgments of many individuals about how well a company is doing and thus reflects the flow of capital: Capital flows to companies that are performing productively and away from those that are not.

Over time, these cumulative judgments represent the best indication of a company's value. In the short run, however, prices can diverge greatly from a company's actual value. Panics can cause prices to underrepresent a company's value, while gullibility or

The New York Stock Exchange is the most active U.S. stock market. (AP/Wide World Photos)

Traders in action at a Chicago stock market. (AP/Wide World Photos)

FRAUD can cause prices to overrepresent a company's value. Over time, however, accurate information and accurate judgments of such information emerge. Accordingly, stock markets depend crucially upon information about how well companies are doing. Two organic metaphors summarize the value of stock markets: Stock markets are the circulatory system of the economy, because they provide capital to productive enterprises, and they are the nervous system of the economy, because they process information.

To perform their functions, stock markets bring together the services of many individuals. Some provide capital (investors), some make allocation decisions (analysts and fund managers), and some bring together the investors and the users of capital (brokers and exchange managers). Arbitrageurs improve the efficiency of markets by increasing liquidity (the ease with which shares can be traded) and by keeping different markets in sync with one another by making trades in different markets. Other speculators increase liquidity and the total of information available to the market. The success of all such individuals participating in the market is a function of the quality of their information and their ability to analyze and act on it.

Attitudes toward stock markets vary, in part because attitudes toward money vary, from views of it as a valuable tool to views of it as the root of all evil. Stock markets are most developed in free markets, so opponents of free markets tend to carry over their opposition to stock markets. Understanding most market operations (such as arbitrage and trading in futures, or options) requires specialized knowledge, and this can create a gulf between those with greater and lesser abilities to act in the market; those with lesser abilities may be more likely to believe that they can be manipulated. Moreover, because information is crucial to market success and some individuals have more access to key information, questions arise about whether those with such information have unfair advantages; the ethicality of "INSIDER TRADING" has thus been one of the most hotly debated issues related to the stock markets.

Stonewall Inn riots (June 27-July 2, 1969): Civil disturbances in New York City. During the 1960's, the Stonewall Inn, in the heart of Manhattan's Greenwich Village, catered to young, mostly African American and Hispanic homosexuals, including many drag queens and runaways. Its flamboyant and ragged clientele was not particularly welcome even in other gay establishments. The Stonewall had no liquor license but was rumored to have ties with ORGANIZED CRIME.

The rights of homosexuals to congregate and express their HOMOSEXUALITY in public was at best tentative, and the police periodically conducted crackdowns on gay bars. On June 27, 1969, two plainclothes detectives entered the Stonewall just before midnight. They presented a search warrant, confiscated cases of liquor, announced the closure of the club, called for reinforcements, and expelled the approximately two hundred customers. Paddy wagons arrived to haul away the bartender, doorman, and others, including "queens" in full drag.

The last customer led out, a lesbian, put up a struggle. As police subdued her, the crowd grew unruly and then virtually exploded into rebellion. A rain of coins, beer bottles, and cobblestones was released on the police, who sought refuge in the empty club. They locked the doors, but protestors uprooted a parking meter and battered their way back in. Tactical patrol units arrived; the rioters dispersed but continued the protest, and soon the Stonewall erupted in flames. The riot itself began shortly after 3:00 A.M. and lasted about forty-five minutes.

The following evening, throngs of young men congregated at the burnt-out building to condemn police behavior. Tensions mounted, and by midnight several hundred gatherers resumed the protest, throwing bottles and setting small fires. Tactical patrol force units again arrived and combed Christopher Street to control and disperse the protestors. Twice the police line broke, and helmeted officers charged the crowd. An estimated four hundred policemen and two thousand rioters were involved. Eventually, the crowd dispersed, and the police withdrew at approximately 4:00 A.M. Into the week, tensions were high on Christopher Street, and sporadic protesting, vandalism, and trash fires persisted.

The riots died down, but a movement had been born: For the first time, homosexuals had rebelled in numbers and with force against systematic social and legal oppression. Within a week, the GAY LIBERATION FRONT was organized. On June 28, 1970, the first anniversary of the riots, an estimated 5,000 to 10,000 people marched down Christopher Street to commemorate Gay Liberation Day.

American society did not wholeheartedly embrace homosexuality, nor even acknowledge the equal rights of those whose sexual orientation deviates from the norm. But the Stonewall Inn riots permanently changed the way that homosexuals confront societal attitudes, and the way that society understands and accepts homosexuality.

SUGGESTED READINGS: *Before Stonewall: The Making of a Gay and Lesbian Community*, by Andrea Weiss and Greta Schiller (New York: Naiad Press, 1988), is a companion volume to the authors' acclaimed documentary film about gay life before 1969. Donn Teal's *The Gay Militants* (New York: Stein & Day, 1971) is a definitive report on the riots and the emergence of gay liberation in the year that followed.

Strategic Defense Initiative (SDI): Missile-defense system. In a major televised address on March 23, 1983, President Ronald REAGAN announced that the United States was going to develop a defensive "umbrella," which would protect the country by destroying incoming missiles during a nuclear attack.

When Reagan took office, the international community depended on a doctrine called MUTUALLY ASSURED DESTRUCTION (MAD) to deter the United States and the Soviet Union from launching nuclear strikes against each other. Political and military leaders believed that if one superpower attacked the other, the nation under attack could still launch its nuclear weapons, engulfing both countries in nuclear destruction so horrible that neither side would risk setting off such a holocaust.

Reagan was horrified at the thought that hundreds of millions of people would die if either superpower launched an attack. Military experts told him that even if the United States won a nuclear war, 150 million Americans would die and the survivors would be left with a poisoned environment and a dying civilization. Reagan was disturbed to realize that such deterrence depended on the good sense and morality of Soviet communists for its effectiveness.

Reagan found support for the idea of building a strategic defensive system. Some individuals (led by physicist Edward Teller) were enamored of the scientific and technological breakthroughs SDI research would bring. Some defense experts (including the JOINT CHIEFS OF STAFF) feared that the United States was becoming vulnerable to Soviet attack. Other advisers (for example, National Security Adviser Robert C. McFarlane) regarded SDI as a "bargaining chip" that the president could trade away for Soviet concessions in matters like arms control.

Reagan thus proposed building such a defense system. He deplored the fact that the United States and the Soviet Union had to rely on "mutual threat" to deter attack. "Wouldn't it be better to save lives than to avenge them?" he asked. He announced that the United States would begin research and development of a system to intercept and destroy enemy ballistic missiles before they struck the United States.

Some opponents dismissed SDI as a "star wars" science-fiction fantasy. Allied leaders feared that if the United States protected itself with SDI, it would weaken its commitment to its friends. Arms experts feared that SDI would destabilize the system of deterrence that had kept nuclear peace since 1945.

Opponents in Congress blocked the high-priority program that Reagan wanted, but the United States began to invest billions of dollars in SDI research. Although some in Congress derided SDI as fantasy, the Soviets took it very seriously. Soviet premier Mikhail GORBACHEV, trying to pump life back into his nation's failing economy, realized that SDI raised Soviet-American competition to a level Moscow could not match. SDI helped convince Gorbachev that he had to bring the COLD WAR to an end, and in that way it promoted change that created a less dangerous world than when the superpowers depended on MAD to prevent a nuclear holocaust.

Stress: Physical, environmental, or psychological strain. The effects of stress show how the mind and body are connected. Stress can worsen difficulties in daily functioning, slow recovery from mental and physical problems, and impede immunological processes. Ongoing stress, such as overcrowding, noise, and interpersonal or financial difficulties, can have a measurable effect on one's body and mind. As a result, stress-reduction techniques have been developed in disciplines such as psychiatry, psychology, ALTERNATIVE MEDICINE, and immunology.

Strikes: Labor-incited work stoppages. Strikes result from stalemates in the collective bargaining process, either in negotiation of a new contract or interpretation of an existing agreement. Collective bargaining agreements, or contracts, are primarily economic in nature, specifying wages, provision of health care, retirement income, and other fringe benefits. The bargaining process to reach these contracts is largely political. If

Air-traffic controllers who went on strike in 1981 were fired by President Ronald Reagan. (AP/Wide World Photos)

union leadership and management fail to reach a mutually beneficial settlement, the union may go on strike. The purpose of strikes is to bring economic pressure on management to return to the bargaining table or settle the dispute.

The terms of negotiated contracts depend in large part on the relative strength and the bargaining abilities of the union leadership and management. Strikes are extremely risky for both union members and management. For union members, they mean going without pay for an extended period of time and possibly losing their jobs permanently. For management, they mean losing production time and having facilities sit idle while some unavoidable costs, such as rent and payments on debt, continue to accrue.

Labor unions resort to strikes relatively rarely. In 1991, for example, only 0.02 percent of estimated working time was lost because of strikes.

In a simple economic model of the labor market, wages are determined by the interaction of SUPPLY AND DEMAND for labor. With unions and collective bargaining, the process of wage determination becomes more complicated because unions become the suppliers of labor and control large segments of it, rather than individual workers negotiating their own contracts. The classical assumption of impersonal market forces is no longer valid. Large unions can mount public relations campaigns and bring public opinion and politics into the negotiating process.

Permanent Replacement. There are debates whether firms should be able to replace striking union workers permanently with nonunion workers. Those who support the right of management to replace striking union workers contend that this will force union leadership to bargain in good faith and think carefully before ordering members to strike. Those opposed to permanent replacement argue that management will refuse to bargain in good faith, having little to lose in the event of a strike. The economic issues surrounding worker permanent replacement are complicated. Short-run savings from replacing highly paid union workers with nonunion workers may not be enough to overcome productivity losses resulting from use of less experienced workers, days lost in the processes of hiring and training new workers, and negative publicity emanating from strikes. Management may hold out against striking union workers by having management personnel assume tasks performed by union workers, selling from accumulated inventories, or offsetting the loss of revenues by the reduction in labor cost.

The effectiveness of strikes as means of accomplishing the goals of labor depends on several factors, some of which are clearly beyond the control of union leadership. Such factors as public attitudes, congressional support, existing legislation or threat of legislative changes, global competition, and technological innovations affect the relative bargaining positions of union leadership and management.

Decline in Union Membership. The overall influence of unions decreased during the second half of the twentieth century, consistent with the decline in union membership. In 1975, about 29 percent of all wage and salary workers in nonagricultural businesses were unionized. Membership dropped dramatically in the 1980's, and by 1992 only 11.5 percent of the same group of workers belonged to unions. The erosion of union membership and power is attributable to many sources: loss of public support resulting from negative public images of unions and labor leaders; an antiunion political climate; the growth in the relative importance of service jobs, where unionism has not had a strong presence; and the decline in blue-collar manufacturing jobs, where unions have had more success.

Change in attitudes toward strikes among businesses and the public are noteworthy. Probusiness interpretations of labor laws by courts and success in surviving or breaking strikes led more firms to decide to resist unions' strike threats. This change in attitude perhaps was best demonstrated by President Ronald REAGAN in 1981, when he refused to concede to demands of striking air-traffic controllers. He fired 11,400 AIR-TRAFFIC CONTROLLERS and replaced them with nonstrikers and new workers. Such an action would not have been feasible without a significant shift in public support from workers to management, which in this case was the federal government.

History of Unions. Unionization began in the United States and elsewhere in direct response to the low wages and brutal working conditions in nineteenth century factories. Although wages and working conditions have improved significantly, supporters of unions contend that unions are still needed to keep firms from exploiting their workers.

The main development in the nature of unionization in the United States since the 1950's, besides the steady decline in union membership, has been the stabilization of union-management relations. In most instances, union leadership and management choose cooperation over confrontation.

LABOR UNIONS are classified into two groups, craft and industrial. Craft unions, the more common type among early unions, restrict their membership to workers who have specific skills, such as electricians or plumbers. Industrial unions, rather than restricting membership to workers with a specific skill, represent all workers in a specific industry, regardless of their skills. For example, workers performing different tasks in the automobile industry are represented by the UNITED AUTO WORKERS.

Craft unions may require that members complete an apprenticeship program or meet some other entrance requirement. Industrial unions are broader in focus. By restricting the supply of workers, a union may be able to keep members' wages and fringe benefits above what they would have been in a more competitive labor market. As a matter of policy, many unions limit employment in order to obtain higher wages and better fringe benefits for members. Training, educational, and licensing requirements can be seen as means to restrict membership and the supply of workers as well as of controlling the quality of work provided by union members.

Although each union faces unique problems in bargaining for wages, benefits, and working conditions, there are several interests that unions share in common. These include developing educational programs and public relations campaigns to promote unionism and establish public support as well as lobbying legislators regarding employment law. To further their common interests, unions have formed national organizations such as the AMERICAN FEDERATION OF LABOR (AFL) and the Congress of Industrial Organizations (CIO), which in 1955 merged to form the AFL-CIO.

Threats to Unions. Increasing global competition, corporate DOWNSIZING, and technological innovations have made firms in unionized industries less willing to be burdened with high labor costs, inefficient work rules, and job guarantees that limit their ability to compete and adapt. The large-scale relocation of firms in the United States from the Northeast, which was heavily unionized, to the South, which had right-to-work laws limiting unions' power, provides strong evidence that firms believe that costs of unionization outweigh benefits such as standardization of contracts. Some firms have moved out of the United States to avoid unions altogether.

The greatest threat to unions comes from nonunion workers who supply the same product. In this respect, unions face a triple threat: relocation of unionized firms to right-to-work states, DEREGULATION of domestic industries, and foreign competition. The deregulation of many industries, such as air travel and trucking, opened them to the entry of nonunionized firms. When these industries were regulated and unionized, the unions had a virtual monopoly of labor supply. After deregulation, nonunionized firms entered and undercut established firms with lower-cost labor, thereby eroding the power of unions.

Although strikes have become less prevalent since World War II, the threat of strikes remains the most potent bargaining chip for unions. Less drastic measures such as "work to rules," whereby workers follow all precautions and other rules exactly, can slow production but avoid breaking the labor contract.

Sometimes labor leaders seem to fail to realize that negotiating a pay raise for jobs that will no longer exist is an empty victory; a "better" contract may mean that an employer relocates, taking away all jobs. Unions have been forced to recognize that they operate in a national or even international context.

—*James Gaius Ibe*

SUGGESTED READINGS: For an economic analysis of strikes and unions, see Paul Samuelson and William D. Nordhaus' *Economics*, 14th ed. (New York: McGraw-Hill, 1992). For analyses of changing approaches by unions to recruit and organize workers and bargain collectively, see Peter F. Drucker's "Reinventing Unions" (*Across the Board*, September, 1989) and Peter Kilborn's "Labor, Seeking to Reverse Decline, Turns to Hungry Young Organizers" (*The New York Times*, June 3, 1993). For a discussion of issues important to unionized workers, the changing strength of unions, and the changing economic environment that makes bargaining more difficult, with emphasis on the stakes and problems faced by striking United Mine Workers, see Robin Toner's "Striking Coal Miners Fight to Protect Shrinking Power" (*The New York Times*, June 8, 1993).

Stroke: Non-technical term for damage to the brain resulting from bleeding or blocked blood flow in the arteries. Stroke is the third-leading cause of death in Western countries, following HEART DISEASE and CANCER.

Stroke is a type of cerebrovascular disease—that is, problems with the blood flow in the brain. It typically refers to ischemia, or inhibited blood flow. Strokes most often occur when a clot formed elsewhere in the body travels up a blood vessel into the brain; the clot becomes stuck when the vessel narrows and blood backs up behind it. The brain tissue beyond the clot, normally fed oxygen and nutrients by the vessel, starves and dies. Stroke sometimes refers to cerebral hemorrhage: when a vessel oozes blood or bursts, blood pools around the vessel, and the pressure distorts the brain's structure and damages its cells.

A variety of factors increase the chance of stroke. The first is age. Strokes most commonly occur between the ages of sixty and sixty-nine, and men have them slightly more often than do women. A prior history of cerebrovascular disease, high blood pressure, heart disease, atherosclerosis (vessels clogged from high cholesterol), and diabetes are major risk factors. Cigarette SMOKING, OBESITY, some oral CONTRACEPTIVES, and ALCOHOLISM also raise the risk.

As the term implies, strokes usually strike quickly and devastatingly. Symptoms often develop in minutes and drastically alter bodily control, thinking and speaking, and personality. Varying with the type of stroke, the symptoms include dizziness and loss of balance, double vision, partial blindness, slurred speech, difficulty swallowing, weakness or paralysis, nausea, vomiting, sleepiness or unconsciousness, severe headache and stiff neck, and irritation from light. Because

Blood pressure tests are recommended for people at risk of stroke. (James L. Shaffer)

The effects on society are also great and raise several social issues. The diet and habits of American adults often predispose them to strokes, a fact that helps make nutrition a national health-care issue. Long-term care of stroke victims burdens insurance and MEDICARE resources. Finally, many stroke patients eventually fall into a coma or develop a life-threatening disease, often pneumonia. Whether to keep them alive with medical technology or to let them die naturally is a difficult ethical and emotional problem for doctors and family members.

Student Nonviolent Coordinating Committee (SNCC): Civil rights organization formed 1960. Arising out of student groups formed after a successful SIT-IN in Greensboro, North Carolina, in 1960, the SNCC was organized to help college students coordinate nonviolent protests against SEGREGATION in the South. Based in Atlanta, the organization participated in demonstrations and other direct-action protests in the early 1960's, achieving particular success with its voter-registration drives. Disillusionment with nonviolent tactics led the organization to a more confrontational philosophy, beginning with chairman Stokely Carmichael's call for black power in 1966. More radical groups soon appeared, however, leaving the SNCC to fade from national attention.

Students for a Democratic Society (SDS): Radical student organization of the 1960's. Organized in 1960, the group in 1962 issued a statement, drafted primarily by future California politician Tom Hayden, attacking Cold War hysteria, poverty, and racism. The SDS evolved into the major campus peace organization of the decade and also engaged in community-

the brain comprises two hemispheres, each of which controls half of the body, a stroke may impair one side of a person's body and leave the other unaffected. Major strokes produce permanent symptoms, although they may improve slowly; the symptoms of minor strokes may disappear with therapy.

A stroke can also affect a patient's family. The patient becomes an invalid and depends upon family care. The parent, spouse, child, or sibling who provides the care is likely to find it exhausting and frustrating. Patients may have personality changes and behave childishly or inconsiderately, further straining the caregiver's stamina. The care is also sure to be expensive, especially if the patient requires placement in a NURSING HOME.

An SDS member holds a balloon calling for draft resistance at a 1967 rally. (UPI/Corbis-Bettmann)

organizing projects. In 1968, the SDS led the Columbia University uprising in New York City. By the end of the decade, however, SDS was fatally splintered by various factions, including the tiny group of violent militants known as the WEATHERMEN.

Substance abuse: Definitions of substance abuse vary concerning the types and frequency of substance use that qualify as "abuse." All types of substance abuse involve the use of mood altering chemicals such as alcohol or other DRUGS, use that is not warranted by medical need. The term "substance abuse" sometimes is used interchangeably with other terms such as "drug dependency," "substance dependency," and "chemical dependency." Most definitions include as abuse the drinking of alcohol or usage of other drugs in excess of accepted social standards.

Background. Throughout history, people have sought and found ways to alter the normal state of consciousness, using naturally occurring hallucinogenics, alcohol, food, and even oxygen deprivation. Various societies have found some drugs, such as alcohol, to be socially acceptable and have developed rules and norms for their use.

Substance abuse affects all facets of the abuser's life, perhaps also affecting the lives of those with whom the abuser interacts. In its broadest sense, it refers to a pathological relationship that a person experiences with a mood altering chemical. Maladaptive use of a chemical agent can lead to significant impairment in a person's social, psychological, volitional, physical, and occupational functioning.

Substance abuse is progressive, chronic, and potentially fatal if left untreated. The condition manifests itself as a compulsion or extreme urgency to ingest alcohol or drugs despite problems caused by use. The substance abuser becomes preoccupied with the drug, and his or her lifestyle revolves around the drug.

Denial is paramount as a defense mechanism employed by users to maintain their chemical usage. They deny that their substance use is causing problems in their lives. During the course of treatment, this denial is confronted directly through the use of constructive confrontation and group therapy. Loss of control is another hallmark of substance abuse. A person may want to quit using a drug and, after many unsuccessful attempts, be unable to do so.

Prolonged use of any drug may lead to addiction. In a broad sense, "addiction" refers to dependence on a drug. Part of this dependence is physiological, in that withdrawal symptoms occur when the drug is discontinued. Withdrawal symptoms include headaches, nausea, tremors, and irritability. It is common for the abuser to have cravings for the drug upon cessation of use. In alcohol use, this occurs because chronic alcohol use can significantly reduce the brain's production of a group of chemical messengers found in the brain's pleasure center, endorphins and enkephalins. Increased tolerance for the drug also occurs. Some drugs have been found to be more addictive than others. A drug can be said to be psychologically addicting if its use is reinforced by pleasant or rewarding feelings.

It has been postulated that all disorders of behavior, including substance abuse, might be the result of biochemical interactions in the brain. It is thought that some people may have predispositions toward becoming substance abusers because of a deficiency of certain brain neurotransmitters.

Alcohol Abuse. Because alcohol is legal for use by adults in the United States, some people do not think that it is a drug. Alcohol long has been termed a "social lubricant," in that it is used frequently in celebrations, weddings, and other occasions and helps people feel more at ease in social situations. At least two-thirds of the adult population of the United States consumes alcohol.

Chronic abuse of alcohol interferes with the body's sleep cycle. Although alcohol may induce sleep, it also interferes with the cycle of sleep that has to do with dreaming, the rapid eye movement (REM) stage. Upon cessation of drinking, an REM rebound effect occurs, characterized by vivid, intense dreams. These dreams can be so frightening that they drive people back to drinking. This interference with the sleep cycle may last for up to a year in some individuals who stop using alcohol.

Alcohol is a central nervous system depressant. The use of alcohol interferes with or lowers the activity of the brain. It releases inhibitions, so that persons consuming alcohol may engage in behaviors unusual for them. Alcohol is considered to be one of the most dangerous and widely used drugs throughout the world, and it has great potential for causing adverse effects on all parts of the human body.

The liver is the organ most affected by alcohol use. After being exposed to large amounts of alcohol or other drugs for a period of time, the liver becomes more efficient in breaking down or metabolizing the chemical substance, which it considers to be a foreign

Teenagers in Massachusetts enjoy a last drink before the legal drinking age rises to twenty in 1979.
(UPI/Corbis-Bettmann)

A heroin user gives herself a fix. (UPI/Corbis-Bettmann)

body. If the liver is continuously exposed to the chemical, the cells that are responsible for metabolizing chemicals will increase so that elimination of the chemical occurs more rapidly.

Fatty liver is usually the first sign of liver damage. This condition is caused by alcohol, in that the liver becomes enlarged from prolonged drinking and does not function normally. If abusive drinking continues, alcoholic hepatitis may develop. Individuals with this condition may have a low grade fever, an enlarged liver, jaundice, dark urine, and general malaise.

Another condition, cirrhosis of the liver, may develop as a result of continued alcohol use. In this condition, fat deposits form in the liver, the liver becomes scarred, and large areas of the liver are permanently damaged. This condition can result in other complications, such as liver cancer and sodium and water retention. It can allow poisons to build up in the blood. This swelling of the liver puts pressure on blood vessels, which then may burst, causing massive bleeding.

Alcohol has also been implicated in pancreatitis, or inflammation of the pancreas. About one-third of all pancreatitis cases have been linked to chronic alcohol abuse. Chronic use of alcohol also contributes to gastritis, or inflammation of the lining of the stomach. Gastritis may result in bleeding, contributing to the development of ulcers.

In the chronic alcoholic, red blood cell formation is suppressed. This causes clotting problems and anemia. The chronic use of alcohol has been found to lower resistance to disease by affecting the immune system. Prolonged drinking also can damage the muscle tissue of the heart, resulting in high blood pressure and inflammation of the heart muscle.

Chronic drinking also contributes to vitamin deficiencies. This malnutrition leads to a condition called Wernicke's encephalopathy. This condition develops when the body is deprived of thiamine. Chronic thiamine deficiency results in brain damage. The person diagnosed with Wernicke's disease appears confused and disoriented and exhibits nystagmus, a pattern of abnormal eye movement. Up to 80 percent of those diagnosed with Wernicke's encephalopathy develop a condition known as Korsakoff's syndrome. This is a chronic organic brain syndrome in which a person's memory is affected. Individuals with Korsakoff's syndrome are unable to remember the past and have difficulty learning new information.

Cocaine Abuse. Another popular drug of abuse is COCAINE. The most common way of ingesting cocaine in the United States is through smoking "crack," a form of solidified cocaine that has been treated with baking soda. Cocaine also can be inhaled. Overdoses may be fatal because cardiac arrest or ventricular fibrillation can occur. Other problems that heavy users experience are hypertension, cerebrovascular bleeding, and strokes. Heart failure appears to be a risk even for young, heathy users. Chronic users often experience a sensation of flashing bright lights, double vision, or fuzzy vision.

The behavioral effects of cocaine are much like those of amphetamines, but the duration of effects is much shorter. The high lasts about two to five minutes, after which the user will become depressed, irritable, and anxious, with a strong craving to use the drug again. The intensity of the cocaine high varies from one individual to another depending on expectations of users, their personal moods, and the circumstances surrounding drug use. Users generally describe a positive state of increased energy and euphoria after using the drug. The more a person uses, the more difficult it is to achieve the previous "high" or even a satisfactory state of feeling good. When the user is not high, he or she often feels agitated and paranoid. Persons who smoke crack regularly experience lung irritation, sore chest and neck, and swollen glands, and they may develop a raspy voice.

If cocaine is inhaled, or "snorted," it enters the bloodstream relatively quickly through the mucous membranes in the nose. The effects of cocaine reach the brain approximately three minutes after snorting. Results are quicker when cocaine is "freebased" or smoked; the effects reach the brain in about six seconds. In chronic inhalers, the nasal septum perforates, resulting in a runny or stuffy nose. Eventually, the wall dividing the halves of the nose disintegrates, and the user is unable to breath through his or her nose.

If cocaine is injected into the body in a water solution, it takes about fourteen seconds to deliver feelings of well-being and euphoria. Some users prefer a combination of cocaine and HEROIN known as a "speedball." The heroin is thought to lessen the anxiety and unpleasantness in coming down from the drug. Injecting speedballs poses a great risk of overdose. There also are other risks associated with intravenous drug use, such as contracting hepatitis or HIV (HUMAN IMMUNODEFICIENCY VIRUS, the precursor of AIDS).

Amphetamine Abuse. Millions of people have used amphetamines legally as a treatment for anxiety or DEPRESSION and to achieve weight loss. Amphetamines also are one of the most commonly abused types of drugs. Low dosages of amphetamines usually produce heightened mental acuity, feelings of increased energy, increased motor activity, feelings of euphoria, increased heart rate, lessening of appetite, constriction of blood vessels, dryness of the mouth, and feelings of confidence. Low doses slightly enhance sexual performance, whereas higher doses cause sexual dysfunction.

New users generally ingest these drugs orally. Highs are obtained faster by snorting or injecting these drugs. After coming down from the drug, the user usually experiences depression and apathy, has a variety of aches and pains, and has an increased appetite. The user may sleep for hours because of exhaustion. Chronic use may lead to tachycardia, hypertension, cardiac arrhythmias, liver damage, and cerebral hemorrhages. Users are at a high risk for heart failure if they combine amphetamines with alcohol. Chronic users also usually experience malnutrition because of their high energy level and low intake of calories.

Repeated use leads to addiction, tolerance, and the need for increasingly larger doses to achieve the same effects. Chronic users develop toxicity that is manifested in mental, physical, and behavioral symptoms. The most extreme form is called amphetamine psychosis. The individual becomes increasingly paranoid and suspicious of others, is physically tired, and appears confused. Perceptual disturbances such as hallucinations and delusions may occur, along with violent aggressive behavior. Tactile hallucinations are common. An individual, for example, may feel bugs crawling on his or her body.

Marijuana Abuse. MARIJUANA is another drug that is commonly abused. The majority of marijuana users experiment with the drug briefly and discontinue its use, but many people become habitual users. The active ingredient in marijuana is the chemical delta-9-tetrhydrocannabinol, commonly called THC. The liver detoxifies THC that is inhaled or ingested. Because the liver is slow in breaking down THC, THC has a tendency to bind to the fat cells in the liver. This enables THC to be released slowly into the bloodstream once the person stops using the drug. This is one reason why heavy marijuana users may test positive for THC weeks after they have discontinued use of the drug.

Tolerance usually develops rapidly, so that in order to maintain the initial effects, the chronic user must use more potent cannabis, inhale more deeply, or use larger amounts of the drug. Marijuana usually is smoked; less commonly, it is ingested. Effects from smoking occur almost immediately and reach a peak in about thirty minutes. After an hour, the effects begin to diminish. The user initially will feel mild anxiety, followed by feelings of euphoria and relaxation.

As with other drugs, users' expectations have an influence on how they perceive the drug. Persons intoxicated on marijuana will have an altered perception of time as well as fluctuations in mood. During the first phase of marijuana use, individuals sometimes report feeling as if they are on the edge of a great personal insight but are unable to explain what this is. Following acute intoxication, the user becomes sleepy.

Physical problems exacerbated by marijuana use include obstructive pulmonary diseases, memory problems, and damage to the immune system. Marijuana is thought to bring about a condition called amotivational syndrome, characterized by apathy and lack of motivation.

Other Drugs. Caffeine, a stimulant, can be found in coffee, tea, cocoa, and many soft drinks. Many over-the-counter drugs such as analgesics and stimulants contain caffeine. Caffeine stimulates the cortex, causing increased mental awareness, alertness, and quickening of the thought processes. Restlessness, agitation, tremors, and cardiac dysrhythmias can occur at higher doses. At extremely high doses, convulsions and death can occur.

Many other drugs are abused. These include prescription drugs that offer users pleasant feelings, such as painkillers. Some people sniff airplane glue to get high; this is a relatively inexpensive drug with many potential adverse effects, including brain damage.

Cultural Factors in Abuse. Cultural factors must be explored in understanding why people use and abuse drugs. Decisions to use or not use drugs are made within the boundaries of a particular culture. All cultures have attitudes and belief systems that govern the use of mood altering drugs. These cultural beliefs influence individuals' decisions about drug use and provide standards by which drug use is perceived.

In some social groups, drug use is seen as a sign of maturity or a right of passage in growing up. In the United States, young people look at use of alcohol, or perhaps use of drugs, as a way of entering adulthood.

Individuals who try drugs and find them psychologically and physically rewarding will continue to use them. If there are sanctions against use, the individual must try to find a way to justify the drug use within his or her social group, stop usage of the drug, hide usage, or find a social group that supports drug use.

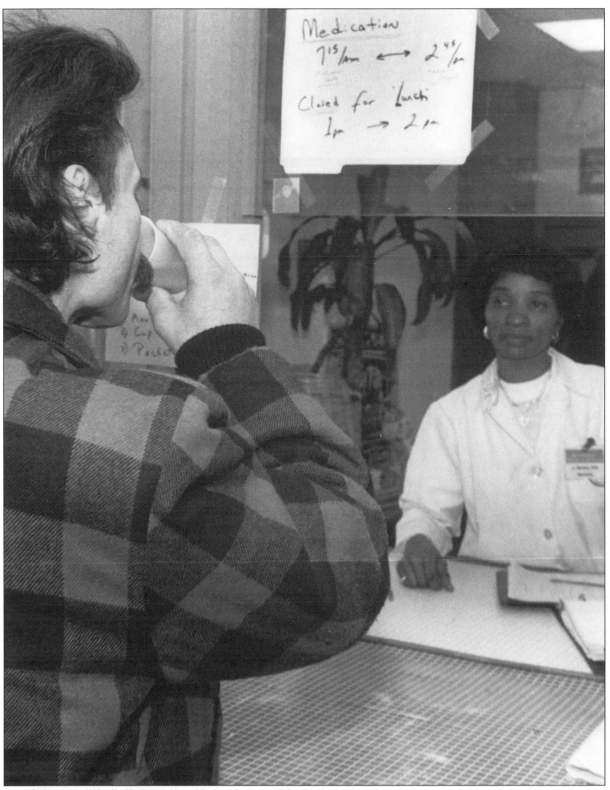

A patient at a clinic in Harlem, New York, takes a methadone treatment as a means of withdrawing from drug use. (Reuters/Corbis-Bettmann)

A father and son talk at a facility that helps teens escape their dependence on drugs. (UPI/Corbis-Bettmann)

Societies have tried to deal with abuse problems in a number of ways. One of these is to regard substance abuse as a sin and users as morally weak. Some people believe that substance abuse is a legislative issue and that laws can help solve the problem. In the United States, for example, use of alcohol was outlawed during the PROHIBITION period (1919-1933).

Some of the most forceful sanctions against drug use arose out of the temperance movement. The temperance movement coincided with a belief in the efficacy of law to resolve human problems. Originally, it condemned only excessive drinking and the drinking of distilled liquor. The aims of the temperance movement were moral, uplifting, and rehabilitative.

Problems Caused by Abuse. A major definitional issue of substance abuse is whether it is a bad habit, a disease, or a moral weakness. The main motivator behind substance abuse is a desire to feel better; therefore, it often is said that people who abuse chemical agents are affected by low self-esteem. They are motivated to feel better but, because of low frustration tolerance, decide to take a "quick fix" and feel better as a result of chemical use rather than making improvements in themselves and in their lives.

Alcohol abuse can prove to be very damaging. Because it releases inhibitions and impairs judgment, it may lead some people to violent behavior. Because alcohol and others drugs impair judgment and psychomotor performance, they may make users dangerous to themselves and others. Driving while drunk or under the influence of other drugs is a major contributor to traffic accidents and fatalities.

Drugs can cause users to become paranoid and to misread reality and exhibit delusional thinking. These delusions of suspicion or persecution may bring forth assaultive acts against imagined tormentors. The intense craving to use the drug can result in a number of different criminal behaviors that can be violent. A large proportion of petty crime is blamed on drug addicts trying to get money to pay for drugs. Persons who are high or intoxicated often become combative and may become hyperactive and violent. Drug-induced feelings of bravado may obstruct one's sense of caution and lead to harm to oneself or others.

Social Responses. One response to problems of drug abuse is to limit supplies of drugs through law enforcement. Arrests of drug dealers and seizures of large quantities of drugs may limit the availability of drugs and reduce the number of first time users. As a form of primary prevention, such enforcement is necessary, but it has proven to be expensive and inefficient. Law enforcement generally is viewed as either a secondary or tertiary prevention measure when it involves early detection of use, arrest, and referral of drug users to treatment.

Drug testing has become prevalent as technology has developed relatively inexpensive ways to detect drug use. Although testing itself does not prevent use, when combined with punishment it can deter people from using drugs. Many employers have instituted drug testing and imposed policies of not hiring anyone who tests positive or firing current employees who test positive. Drug testing has proven to be helpful in preventing initial drug use as well as deterring relapse and promoting sobriety.

Legal Issues. Decriminalization and legalization have been suggested as solutions to various drug problems. A policy of decriminalization, or removal of sanctions against possessing certain drugs, was in place in 1996 in nine states for small quantities of marijuana. Possessing an amount above the stated limit could result in arrest and prosecution.

Drug legalization is not precisely the same as decriminalization, although they overlap and advocates of one usually advocate the other. Decriminalization refers to the removal of criminal penalties against engaging in a certain action. The state no longer has a legal role in the control of the behavior in question. In legalization, the state plays a central role in developing a set of rules. Legalization allows the state to have control over specific aspects of behavior, for example, who may purchase alcoholic beverages and where these beverages may be purchased.

Beginning in the 1960's, calls increased for legalization or decriminalization of currently illegal drugs. Advocates assert that abuse would not rise much under legalization and that authorities could assert more control over use. Abusers would be more likely to seek treatment because their behavior would not carry the same stigma and they would not have to fear punishment. Supporters also believe that drug use would not increase much after legalization; they believe that those who want to find drugs do so regardless of legality. They also argue that crime associated with drug use would decrease because if drugs were legal, their price would fall. Those favoring criminal sanctions against drug use argue that legalizing use would increase both the harms associated with use and the scope of use. Experiments with legalization and decriminalization, particularly in Europe, have provided evidence on both sides of the debate.

Alcoholism and other drug addictions are now considered addictive disorders rather than failings of personal character. Addiction to a single substance, such as alcohol, is becoming comparatively rare. About half of all people seeking treatment for substance abuse use more than one drug.   —*Linda L. Marshall*

SUGGESTED READINGS: An in-depth look at the topic of substance abuse can be found in C. Aaron McNeece and Diana M. DiNitto's *Chemical Dependency: A Systems Approach* (Englewood Cliffs, N.J.: Prentice-Hall, 1994), Thomas Byrd's *Addictive Awareness* (Dubuque, Iowa: Kendall-Hunt, 1990), James A. Inciardi and Karen McElrath's *The American Drug Scene* (Los Angeles: Roxbury, 1995), Robert R. Pinger and Wayne A. Payne's *Drugs: Issues for Today*, 2d ed. (St. Louis, Mo.: Mosby-Year Book, 1995), and Robert McAuliffe and Mary B. McAuliffe's *The Essentials of Chemical Dependency: Alcoholism and Other Drug Dependencies* (Chanhassen, Minn.: American Chemical Dependency Center, 1975).

Information pertaining to alcohol abuse, and theory and research pertaining to it, can be found in P. Clayton Rivers' *Alcohol and Human Behavior* (Englewood

The inventor of an infant-monitoring system displays his device, which he developed after he lost his son to sudden infant death syndrome. (UPI/Corbis-Bettmann)

Cliffs, N.J.: Prentice-Hall, 1994) and Jean Kinney and Gwen Leaton's *Loosening the Grip: A Handbook of Alcohol Information* (St. Louis, Mo.: Mosby, 1993). For information on statistics and legal issues of drugs, refer to Erich Goode's *Drugs in American Society*, 4th ed. (New York: McGraw-Hill, 1993).

Sudden infant death syndrome (SIDS): Leading cause of death among Western children between one month and one year of age. For reasons that are not well understood, SIDS causes apparently healthy infants to stop breathing, usually during the night, and suddenly die. Biological risk factors such as prematurity, low birthweight, and respiratory problems have been linked with SIDS. Infants who sleep on their abdomens or who live in homes of cigarette smokers are much more likely than other infants to die of SIDS. Parents of young children are thus often advised to keep infants away from cigarette smoke and off their stomachs when sleeping.

Suffrage movement: Nineteenth and early twentieth century efforts to win the right to vote for American women. The suffrage movement reached its triumphant conclusion in 1920 with the ratification of the Nineteenth Amendment to the U.S. Constitution.

Origins. In the mid-nineteenth century, increasing numbers of American women began questioning their disadvantaged status. The Seneca Falls, New York, convention of 1848 provided a forum in which both women and men presented a call for greater equality between the sexes. The primary focus at the convention was upon obtaining legal reform, equal educational opportunities, and equal opportunities in the workforce. Women during this time were virtually enslaved by the men in their lives. Married women had

A 1913 suffrage march. (UPI/Corbis-Bettmann)

no rights to own property, no access to their children in cases of divorce, and were not allowed to keep their earnings; they were also not allowed to enter into contracts or to sit on juries. Their educational opportunities were limited; admission to institutions of higher learning was rarely granted to women. Likewise, women in the workforce were paid substantially less than their male counterparts. Awareness of these issues continued to grow throughout the century, as women began to organize and identify with one another through their involvement at conventions and other meetings.

Growth and Dissent. After the Seneca Falls convention, feminists held conventions in other areas of the country on a regular basis. These conventions served to introduce like-minded individuals and laid the foundations for a social movement. New leaders emerged, and the number of followers of the nascent movement increased. The publication of the journal *The Revolution* provided yet more people with discussion of the vote as central to women's quest for equality.

The women's movement split in 1869, forming two rival organizations: The NATIONAL WOMAN SUFFRAGE ASSOCIATION (NWSA) and the American Woman Suffrage Association (AWSA). The NWSA association, the more radical of the organizations, worked toward passage of a constitutional amendment giving women the right to vote. The AWSA was more conservative, working primarily to advance the cause for women's suffrage on the state level.

The women's movement became more conservative as the years passed. During the last twenty years of the nineteenth century, the movement mirrored society, and the leadership became more conservative and middle-class oriented.

The two organizations reunited in 1890, overshadowing the radical branch and focusing primarily on suffrage as a mechanism for obtaining greater access to mainstream society. As the years passed, a number of other suffrage organizations were formed to work toward passage of the Nineteenth Amendment, also known as the Anthony Amendment after the movement's most celebrated leader, Susan B. Anthony, who was arrested and fined for illegally attempting to vote in the state of New York.

By 1917, an estimated two million women had joined in the struggle for women's suffrage, and they were supported by increasing numbers of men. The Nineteenth Amendment was enacted August 26, 1921, bringing the suffrage movement to a successful close.

Its leaders, including Anthony and Elizabeth Cady Stanton, and its strategies later served as models and inspirations for the many feminist organizations that sprang up in the 1960's and 1970's in renewed pursuit of equal rights for women.

Suicide: Self-inflicted, intentional death. While the morality of suicide has been debated for generations, in the 1980's the RIGHT-TO-DIE MOVEMENT gained momentum, intensifying debate among physicians, ethicists, politicians, and the general public.

Motives for Suicide. The phenomenon of suicide has, over the years, generated many theories attempting to understand, predict, and control it. However, most researchers conclude that while some common tendencies may exist in those who contemplate or commit suicide, the reasons why any particular individual chooses to end his or her own life are always complex, enigmatic, and a product of unique personal experiences and impulses. The act is most often—in Freudian terms—overdetermined, meaning that it arises from multiple causative factors.

Generally speaking, motivational factors can be divided into two basic categories: interpersonal and intrapersonal. Interpersonal motivations occur when the suicidal individual attempts, by his or her behavior, either to bring about an action on the part of another person or persons or to effect a change in attitude or feeling within another person or persons, or both. The suicidal behavior can thus be seen as a means to influence, persuade, force, manipulate, stimulate, change, dominate, or reinstate feelings or behavior in someone else. The other person is most often someone who has been in a close relationship with the suicidal individual, such as a spouse, partner, or family member. While interpersonal motivations can be found in all age groups, they are usually predominant in the younger and middle-aged population.

Intrapersonal motivations appear most often in older persons and thus in situations in which ties with others have dissipated or dissolved. The typical person to attempt suicide is a male aged sixty or older who has recently suffered the death of a loved one, whose physical condition has deteriorated so that there is illness or pain, or whose children are married or living independently. This individual is often depressed, withdrawn, and physically and emotionally exhausted. An important dynamic is the need to maintain "psychological integrity" or self-esteem although accomplished through

A 1982 suicide in New York City. (AP/Wide World Photos)

the seemingly paradoxical act of self-destruction. If this individual embarks upon a suicidal course, he or she usually does so with a full intent to die.

Rates. In 1992, suicide ranked as the eighth leading cause of death in the United States (heart disease was number one). While most media reports focused on teenagers, there were almost fifteen hundred more suicides in the twenty-three to thirty-four age range than among those fifteen to twenty-four. Men commit suicide up to three-and-a-half times more often than women, but about three times more women attempt suicide. Among African Americans, the ratio of men to women who commit suicide is even higher, underscoring the fact that the suicide rate among African American males has increased sharply. Native Americans have a high rate of suicide, given their relatively small numbers, although media attention has sometimes distorted the supposed increase.

In terms of professions, dentists and doctors have long ranked at the top among those who choose death, proving that wealth, education, and social standing are no guarantees against suicide.

The highest rate of suicide for any group in the United States, however, has continued to be white males over the age of sixty-five. In 1990, this rate was 24.1 per 100,000. Especially vulnerable are those who are in poor health and separated, divorced, or widowed. Loss of familiar surroundings often contributes to the depression that precedes many suicides in this age group.

Teenage Suicide. From 1950 to 1990, the rate of reported suicides among young people nearly tripled. After accidents, suicide is the leading cause of death among fifteen-to-nineteen-year olds. National surveys report that about 40 percent of high-school students in the United States have contemplated suicide.

While every suicide concludes a unique and complex life, statistics about suicidal young people lead to several generalizations: It is five times as common among young men as women; the rate for whites is more than double that for blacks; youth rates are highest in the Western states; and Ivy Leaguers are more likely to take their lives than are other university students.

Although there are many theories to explain the so-called youth suicide epidemic, no consensus has been reached. Some experts view it as a symptom of the nation's moral and religious decay or the breakdown of the family. Others blame the ease with which young people gain access to alcohol, drugs, and firearms. Another theory is that suicide rates are higher in more "crowded" generations when young people are under more pressure because of increased competition to succeed.

Researchers have identified circumstances that appear to put young people under increased risk of suicide. It is estimated that three out of four youth suicide victims have abused drugs or alcohol. They are also more likely than other youths to have been sexually abused or learning disabled, homosexual, or close to someone who committed suicide. When the adolescent pressure to conform takes a deadly turn, the rare but intensely publicized "copycat" suicides also occur.

Assisted Suicide. At the other end of the age spectrum, adults who are terminally ill and the elderly have in some cases chosen to end their lives rather than to

continue in intolerable pain or to be a burden to others. The right-to-die issue was first debated publicly in America in the landmark case of Karen Ann Quinlan in 1975. For the first time in history, Americans were asked to decide the crucial question of whether it is morally permissible for a human being to end his or her own life or to assist another in doing so.

By far the most publicized and controversial figure in the debate over suicide in the 1990's was Dr. Jack KEVORKIAN, also known as "Dr. Death," who assisted numerous terminally ill persons in taking their lives. His assisted suicides, using a machine called a "mercitron," which patients themselves activated, resulted in his repeated arrest.

Arguments for the Right to Die. Proponents argue that planned or assisted suicide can provide a dignified affirmation of liberty in the face of brutal circumstances. Patients who choose to assert control over their final suffering or death infuse an often formless reality with uniquely human meaning and compassion. Planned suicide can be a justified response to the intolerable burden that life represents for some terminally ill patients, but safeguards against interference by doctors and the state, they maintain, must be established to prevent abuses of assisted suicide. Public policy should prevent state authority from blocking an individual's right to die because this power would lead to state decisions on who is fit to live. Moreover, they argue that physicians, though necessary in an advisory capacity, should not be involved directly in ending life.

Arguments Against the Right to Die. Opponents of the right-to-die movement appeal to a wide range of orthodox Jewish and Christian dogma. They draw also upon the organizational strength of the right-to-life movement, which portrays EUTHANASIA as one more step toward justifying the elimination of the helpless and the unfit. For them, the biblical command "Thou shalt not kill" applies to oneself as well as to others, thus precluding suicide as well as assisted suicide. The absolute sanctity of life takes precedence over all other considerations; life must be prolonged at any cost.

Even within the religious community, however, there is a vast gray area. Though suffering and death underlie Judeo-Christian theology, basic compassion seems to dictate that a patient in terrible pain should be allowed to die. This is a proposition that the Roman Catholic Church appears to endorse. While both suicide and euthanasia are strictly forbidden, in 1980 the Vatican declared that refusing treatment is not equivalent to suicide. They maintained that it should be considered as an acceptance of the human condition or a desire not to impose excessive expenses on the family or community.

Other opponents of the right to die believe that society must maintain the taboo against suicide because the right to choose one's own death can become confused with the right to "choose" someone else's. If suicide were legal, these people foresee a quick descent into other forms of euthanasia, an unreasonable expansion of the powers of physicians, and an increase in state control over life.

Suicide and the Law. Suicide is no longer a crime in the United States, but assisting in one is illegal in more than twenty states. No one knows how often doctors write the prescription or whisper the recipe for a deadly overdose, but one informal survey of internists in 1990 found that one in five say they have helped cause the death of a patient. Poll after poll shows that as many as half of Americans favor doctors doing so.

By 1991, twenty-eight states had ruled that patients had the right to refuse life-sustaining treatment. In some locales, the courts indicated that competent, mentally alert people could make this judgement; in other states, doctors and relatives were allowed to initiate death when patients were unable to request it themselves. Nine states specifically allow the withdrawal of artificial feeding tubes from patients in a vegetative state, allowing them to starve to death.

On November 8, 1994, voters in the state of Oregon narrowly approved the first physician-assisted suicide measure in U.S. history. Oregon thus became the first jurisdiction in the world to legalize such a measure.

—Genevieve Slomski

SUGGESTED READINGS: In *Voluntary Euthanasia* (London: Peter Owen, 1986), edited by A. B. Downing and Barbara Smoker, experts debate the right to die. George Howe Colt's *The Enigma of Suicide* (New York: Summit Books, 1991) analyzes suicide from a historical perspective, while *Suicide in America*, by Herbert Hendin (New York: W. W. Norton, 1995), gives a psychosocial perspective. Teen suicide and medically assisted suicide are discussed in *Suicide*, ed-

A Georgia policeman talks a suicidal man from a fourth-story ledge. (UPI/Corbis-Bettmann)

ited by Robert Emmet Long (New York: H. W. Wilson, 1995).

Summit meetings: Encounters between the highest officials of major powers; the term has often been used to refer to meetings between the top political leaders of the United States and the Soviet Union (and, later, Russia). Summit meetings were important during the COLD WAR as instruments for direct dialogue between the top leaders in an effort to reach major breakthroughs in key areas, especially arms control. Summit conferences became more routine as international tension declined after the Cold War. Among the major summit meetings were the Geneva Conferences of 1955 and 1985.

Sunshine laws: Legislation designed to ensure above-board conduct by government agencies. U.S. federal sunshine laws require federal agencies headed by two or more persons to open their meetings to the public; closed meetings are allowed only for specific reasons, such as national defense or invasion of pri-

A 1994 summit meeting of world leaders in Naples. (Reuters/Corbis-Bettmann)

vacy concerns, and even in such cases, verbatim transcripts, with deletions of material exempted by the law, must be kept. Federal law also requires a seven-day advance public notice of the date, place, and subject matter of such meetings. Many states also have sunshine laws.

Superconductivity: The disappearance of electrical resistance at low temperature. In 1911, it was discovered that some common metals completely lose their electrical resistance at a temperature close to absolute zero. For example, an electric current circling in a superconducting ring made of lead showed no detectable decrease after two years. Initially, however, there was little practical use for this phenomenon because the technology of creating very low temperatures is expensive. In the 1980's, a new class of high-temperature ceramic superconductors was discovered. In the medical profession, superconducting magnets are widely used for magnetic resonance imaging (MRI) to obtain excellent pictures of internal organs or tumors.

Superfund (1980): Officially known as the Comprehensive Environmental Response, Compensation, and Liability Act (CERCLA), Superfund is a U.S. federal law providing for cleanup of hazardous waste sites. Taxes on crude oil and designated commercial chemicals maintain a fund that can be used to clean up, or remediate, designated hazardous waste sites.

The Superfund program was a response to public concern voiced when poisonous chemicals in Hooker Chemical Company's Love Canal dump near Niagara Falls, New York, began leaking into nearby homes. That incident ultimately led to the abandonment of 600 houses, the

relocation of 2,500 residents, and the identification of innumerable health-related problems.

The largest program administered by the Environmental Protection Agency (EPA), Superfund targets the nation's most hazardous dumping grounds. The indiscriminate disposal of by-products of the mining industry, municipalities, chemical manufacturers, and others are blamed for poisoning streams, coastal harbors, and both urban and suburban areas. Lead, arsenic, mercury, vinyl chloride, benzene, and cadmium are some of the wastes that have polluted the groundwater and/or air, thereby posing a risk to human health and natural resources.

Although only a small percentage of the sites earmarked for Superfund cleanup are said to present an imminent public-health hazard, contaminants in af-

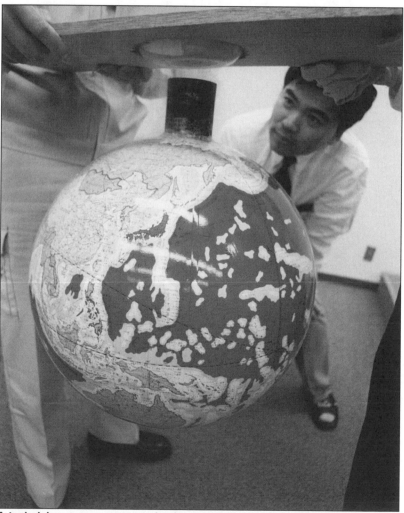

A technician uses a superconductive magnet to suspend a twenty-two-pound globe. (Archive Photos/Eriko Sugita/Reuters)

This New Jersey toxic waste dump was designated for cleanup under the federal Superfund program. (UPI/Corbis-Bettmann)

fected neighborhoods have been blamed for an increase in cancer, reproductive defects, lung and respiratory disease, neurotoxic disorders, and liver and kidney dysfunction.

The Superfund program has undergone criticism, however, by those who helped draft the law, as well as by its administrators. Despite expenditure of $11 billion in public funds and untold billions in private sector money, less than 10 percent of the 1,300 sites on Superfund's National Priority List (NPL) have undergone actual cleanup.

The first Superfund cleanups were, out of necessity, pioneer projects, calling for the development of safety standards as well as the actual technology. The technology for cleaning a site, rather than sealing it, is often inadequate and expensive. There is disagreement even about what constitutes waste and what should count as hazardous.

With an estimated 35,000 sites waiting to be evaluated for placement on the NPL, and each cleanup taking a dozen or more years to complete at an average cost of twenty-five to thirty-five million dollars, total cleanup could take decades to accomplish and cost more than one trillion dollars.

Cited as a major factor in Superfund's problems is its fund-rasing mechanism, which is based on a retroactive joint and several liability provision. This means any one Potentially Responsible Party (PRP)—anyone contributing to a Superfund contamination—can be held accountable for the total cost of a cleanup, even if others contributed to the contamination of the site.

Faced with massive liability issues, the PRPs seek others to share the cost. This has led to a proliferation of lawsuits as the EPA sues PRPs, and PRPs sue the EPA, one another, and their insurers. Often, the actual cleanups must wait while these lengthy and complicated PRP searches and ensuing litigations take their circuitous course.

Although Superfund was reauthorized by Congress in September of 1994, additional amendments to the law have been proposed in an effort to make the Superfund program faster, fairer, and more efficient.

Superpowers: Term used extensively to describe the United States and Soviet Union (later Russia). The term connotes superior military and economic strength that cannot be matched by other great powers. After World War II, the title was first applied to the United States, which had emerged as the world's strongest power and which was the only country that possessed the atomic bomb. When the Soviet Union acquired comparable nuclear power, both countries were recognized as superpowers. Although rivals in the COLD WAR, they cooperated in regulating the spread of nuclear weapons and in other scientific and cultural areas.

Supplemental Food Program for Women, Infants, and Children: Federal program established in 1972. The WIC is designed to help low-income pregnant women and children who are at nutritional risk. Poor nutrient intake during pregnancy or early childhood can have significant detrimental effects on a child's growth and development; the program thus provides nutrition education, vouchers to redeem for specific foods, and access to health-care providers. Supporters of the program claim that the WIC has led to a decrease in the percentage of low-weight infant births and in the number of infant deaths in the United States.

Supply and demand: Mechanism by which a free market determines what will be produced and consumed, in what quantities, and at what price. In a free market, suppliers are free to provide what they wish and to ask whatever price they wish, and consumers are free to purchase or not purchase and to offer whatever prices they wish. Since suppliers prefer to receive more than less money while consumers prefer to pay less than more, a compromise price must be found, or no transaction is made.

Cumulatively, the actions of suppliers and consumers, as indicated by the prices and quantities sold of goods and services, determine the flow of resources in an economy. Suppose a producer of a good believes there is a desire for a given good and so decides to supply the good at a given price. Many consumers then make independent choices about whether that good is worth that price to them. The consumers' choices, collectively, determine how much money goes to the supplier. If many consumers purchase the good, the supplier receives much money and is thereby signaled to continue supplying the good. If few consumers buy the good, the supplier receives little money and is thereby signaled to lower the price or stop supplying the good. In this way, the supplier is pressured by consumers to supply goods at the price consumers judge is appropriate. Successful suppliers receive enough money both to make a profit and to purchase the raw materials needed to continue supplying the good. Unsuccessful suppliers receive less money, which means they are less able to take profits and less able to continue to purchase the raw materials needed to continue supplying the good. Overall, the combined signals of suppliers and consumers determine how resources are used: Resources flow to the successful suppliers, who are those who deliver goods that consumers want at prices that consumers are willing to pay.

The opposite policy is for a government to override the signals suppliers and consumers send each other in the free market. In such cases, the government's goal is to favor a group of suppliers or consumers. An example of a policy that benefits suppliers is a minimum-wage law: By setting a minimum wage, the government hopes to increase the amount of money that suppliers of labor receive for their services. An example of a policy that benefits consumers is rent control: By lowering the cost of rent, the government hopes to decrease the amount of money consumers of rental units pay.

Such policies are controversial. Advocates of government interference argue that some suppliers and consumers need special help or protection in the marketplace. Advocates of free markets argue that government interference has perverse, unintended consequences. For example, by raising the minimum wage, the government decreases the demand for labor, thereby causing unemployment; by lowering rents, the government decreases the supply of housing, thereby causing shortages.

Supply-side economics: Theory that provided the basis for President Ronald REAGAN's 1980's economic program. Supply-side advocates believed that cutting taxes and reducing governmental economic regulations would give business and labor incentive to work harder and save more, spurring increased investment and higher productivity.

Supply-side theory found favor during the economic doldrums of the late 1970's, a time of declining productivity rates, double-digit inflation, 20 percent interest rates, nearly eight million people unemployed, and falling wage rates. People lost confidence in attempts by the government to "fine tune" the economy, since established techniques for fighting inflation increased unemployment, while attempts to increase employment fueled inflation.

Journalist Jude Wanniski, economist Arthur Laffer, and Congressman Jack Kemp were among those who brought supply-side theory into the Reagan camp. They argued that the solution to economic decline was to trust in the dynamism of the American capitalistic system, in its inherent propensity to expand unless it was held back by excessive taxation and costly, market-distorting government regulations. Supply-side ideas fit Reagan's belief that the solution to American economic problems was, in his phrase, to get government off the backs of the people.

On February 18, 1981, Reagan presented his economic plan to a joint session of Congress. He proposed cutting government spending, reducing taxes, and eliminating unnecessary and unproductive economic regulations. He promised that his program would return government to its proper limited province, while restoring to the people the right to decide how to dispose of their earnings. He asked Congress to cut $41.4 billion from eighty-three programs, and he proposed 10 percent reductions in individual income taxes in each of the following three years.

Reagan fought hard for his budget and tax proposals, and on August 13, 1981, he signed the Economic Recovery Act of 1981 and the Omnibus Budget Reconciliation Act of 1981. The budget act cut nearly $35.2 billion from the 1982 budget. Supply-side advocates were more interested in Reagan's tax legislation, and again Congress gave him most of what he wanted. The final bill reduced all individual income tax rates by 5 percent on October 1, 1981, 10 percent on July 1, 1982, followed by an additional 10 percent on July 1, 1983. The bill liberalized depreciation allowances for business, reduced the top rate on investment income from 70 percent to 50 percent, and indexed individual tax brackets to inflation, preventing inflation from pushing people into higher brackets. Reagan told reporters that over a three year period, the tax bill would represent $750 billion in tax cuts.

Although the economy plunged into a severe recession, that downturn was followed by the longest period of sustained economic growth in American history. While Reaganomics led to unprecedented budget deficits, supply-side proponents believed that if the nation released the inherent power of capitalism, economic growth would steadily shrink the national debt in relation to the size of the gross national product. After Reagan left office, supply-side supporters looked to such conservative leaders as Newt GINGRICH to carry on their fight.